MW00414371

DOCUMENTS ON THE HISTORY OF THE GREEK JEWS
*Records from the Historical Archives
of the Ministry of Foreign Affairs.*

MINISTRY OF FOREIGN AFFAIRS OF GREECE
UNIVERSITY OF ATHENS
DEPARTMENT OF POLITICAL SCIENCE AND PUBLIC ADMINISTRATION

DOCUMENTS ON THE HISTORY OF THE GREEK JEWS

*Records from the Historical Archives
of the Ministry of Foreign Affairs*

SECOND EDITION

RESEARCHED & EDITED BY
PHOTINI CONSTANTOPOULOU & Prof. THANOS VEREMIS

INTRODUCED BY
THEODOROS PANGALOS
MINISTER OF FOREIGN AFFAIRS
Prof. STEVEN BOWMAN
Department of Judaic Studies
UNIVERSITY OF CINCINNATI

KASTANIOTIS EDITIONS
ATHENS 1999

PROLOGUE: *Photini Constantopoulou.*

INTRODUCTION: *Photini Constantopoulou & Thanos Veremis.*

LIST OF DOCUMENTS, TIME CHART, BIOGRAPHIES, NOTES, SUGGESTED BIBLIOGRAPHY,
INDEX, EDITING: *Photini Constantopoulou, Eleftherios Stavropoulos & Stelios Zachariou*

ENGLISH TRANSLATION: *Geoffrey Cox, John Solman.*

© Copyright Ministry of Foreign Affairs Athens 1998

All rights reserved. No part of this work covered by the copyright hereon may be reproduced or used in any form
or by any means - graphic, electronic, or mechanical, including photocopying, recording, taping, or information
storage and retrieval systems - without the written permission of the publisher.

KASTANIOTIS EDITIONS S.A.
11, Zalongou St., GR-106 78 Athens
☎ 330.12.08 - 330.13.27 FAX: 384.24.31

ISBN 960-03-2330-5

CONTENTS

FOREWORD

The purpose of the present publication is to illuminate certain aspects of the history of Greek citizens of the Jewish faith which have long remained obscure. The Greek State has a longstanding debt to throw light on the history of the Jews who first settled in Greece during the time of Alexander the Great, used the Greek language in their everyday life and their religious texts, came into contact with the beauty of ancient Greek civilisation, and established firm ties with a country for which they developed a deep affinity.

The mass arrival in Thessaloniki –in 1492– of Sephardic Jews from the Iberian peninsula meant a demographic revival for the city. Thessaloniki was at once transformed into a major commercial and economic hub of the Eastern Mediterranean. Letters and the arts flourished; and the setting up of the community's schools, libraries and printing presses made the city the largest centre of Sephardic Jewry in Europe, a situation which lasted for four centuries – from the 16th to the Holocaust. In the meantime, there were fresh arrivals of Ashkenazim Jews from Europe, who, like the Sephardim, were often the victims of the fanaticism and religious intolerance which festered in most societies of Central Europe at that time. During the liberation of Thessaloniki in 1912, King George I recognised the Jews as Greek citizens with equal rights.

The support given by the government of Eleftherios Venizelos for the setting up of a Jewish state in 1917, four months before the Balfour Declaration, further strengthened the bonds between the Jewish element and their new homeland.

Greek Jews played their part in Greece's social and military history and were present in the struggle against the Fascist and Nazi invaders.

The Second World War was a time of severe trial for Greece, but of all the Greeks the Jews suffered the harshest blow, in spite of the efforts by the people, the clergy and even those officials who collaborated with the occupation forces to shelter them. The letter of Archbishop Damaskinos to German Ambassador Altenburg is rightly considered a monument of courage and humanity. It is due to the efforts of the Church that the entire Jewish community of Zakynthos (Zante) was preserved, a phenomenon unique in Europe.

The Greeks have always resisted the debasement represented by racism. All the Constitutions of Greece, from the very first Provisional Constitution of Epidaurus in 1822, enshrined the principle of freedom in the choice of religion and the performance of religious duties.

In 1945, Greece's Central Board of Jewish Communities was set up. In the meantime, by a 1944 decision of George Papandreou's government, the Greek State became the first in Europe to return Jewish properties which had been confiscated in the course of the War. Furthermore, it waived its lawful right of inheritance to those properties whose owners had not left descendants to the fourth degree, and the property of the deceased was transferred to a common fund to aid Jews impoverished by war.

It is a stroke of good fortune that this publication sees the light at a point in time when an effort to reinstate historical fact and justice is underway. It coincides with the task of allotting responsibility for crimes committed in the troubled time when the Nazis brought death, terror and ruin to unsuspecting and innocent victims whose only crime had been their faith.

This volume is dedicated to the memory of the victims of the Holocaust and to the unsung heroes who sacrificed themselves in the attempt to save them.

Athens, 11 November 1998
THEODOROS PANGALOS
Minister of Foreign Affairs

PREFATORY NOTE

Greek-Jewish relations, now over three millennia in duration, present the oldest continuous inter-ethnic relationship in history and constitute, as it were, the double helix of Western civilisation. As with every relationship it is double-edged, with elements of competition and fusion. Towards the end of the first millennium B.C.E., invading Aegean warriors and their families, now settled in the land of the Philistines, clashed with the Israelites returning to their ancestral homeland after centuries of slavery. The Israelite champion David eventually became ruler over a vast empire stretching from the Brook of Egypt (Wadi el Arish) to the Euphrates. Philistine and Cretan mercenaries constituted the core of David's fighting force, and after his conquest of the Philistine cities the two peoples merged under the banner of the God of Abraham and Moses and David. In the course of time Aegean legends even found their way into the biblical record. Some seven centuries later the conquests of Alexander and his successors gave new incentive to the Philistines to resurrect their Hellenic connections and a new age entered the land of Israel during which the heirs of Moses and David adopted Hellenised speech, thought, and institutions. Hellenism penetrated slowly under the Ptolemies of Egypt, but clashes with the Seleucids of Syria led to a renewal of Jewish independence under the Hasmoneans. Throughout the Greek-speaking world a rich Judeo-Greek culture and literature flourished, and through the extensive works of Philo, Paul and Josephus a new fusion of Greeks and Jews set the pattern for the next two millennia, while expanding commentaries on their respective oeuvres continue to guide new immigrant peoples to the West into the logical and moral heritage of these two traditions.

From Alexander's time, if not before, Hellenophone Jews have been living and creating in Hellas and among the Hellenes in all the lands surrounding the Aegean. Throughout the medieval period in the territories subject to Constantinople these Jews were engaged in a series of competitions with the Greek Orthodox tradition, although the Jews were at a distinct political disadvantage as an increasingly second-class minority. Nonetheless their very existence, as well as their literary heritage, provided opportunities for heretics and converts to challenge the control of state and church. The 19th century resurrection of the Greeks to national independence reverberated first among Balkan and later East European Jews in their Zionist awakening and still influences contemporary Jewish nationalism.

From its inception, Jews have been an integral part of the new and expanding Greek state, including its fighting forces, despite the animosity of a minority of aggressive nationalists who were unable to separate Greek from Orthodox. The tragic and criminal deportation of Greek Jews from their homeland by Nazi Germany during World War II left less than one fifth of pre-war Greek Jewry to cope with the ensuing civil war. The establishment of the State of Israel in 1948 and the vicissitudes of post-war Greece stimulated the emigration of two-thirds of the survivors such that there are scarcely more than 5,000 Jews in today's Greece.

The documents released by the Ministry of Foreign Affairs in this volume are an important contribution to our understanding of the nation-building process that preoccupied Greeks during the inter-war period, indeed since the acquisition of Thrace and Macedonia just prior to World War I. Until 1922 Greece was concerned for nearly a century with the acquisition of territory, an irredentism of two millennia to incorporate the Greek Diaspora surrounding the Aegean into a vibrant new Hellenism. After the Asia Minor disaster, the *Megale Idea* was transformed into a process to Hellenise the citizens and immigrants to the Greek kingdom. With the transfer of most of the Turkish-speaking Muslims, the largest body of non-Orthodox non-Grecophones was the Sephardic Jewish population which had been resident in the towns along the ancient Roman Via Egnatia since the beginning of the sixteenth century. The question was how to assimilate them to the new Greece and how to adjust their economic predominance in Thessaloniki (Salonica). Since the 19th century modern Greek nationalism fought to expand its frontiers; beyond the frontiers consuls and educators fought to expand a Greek literate community, since that definition of Greek was the basis for the claim that a given territory should be included within the new state. Hence much of the inter-war documentation included in this volume deals with the Hellenisation of Jewish education, primarily in Thessaloniki but also in Corfu and elsewhere, and the challenges between the growing nationalism of the immigrants for Greece and the growing nationalism of the Jews for Israel. These documents, then, not only delineate the state-building process but also chronicle the internal tensions within the Jewish community where modernising French and Greek and Hebrew options posed unavoidable challenges to the traditional Spanish-Ottoman masses. This linkage intensifies for the reader the range of internal problems dividing the Jews rather than fragmenting these facets of the modern challenge according to the bent of the particular investigator. The post-war documentation illustrates the honour of Greek governments to return to its [Jewish] citizens their property confiscated by the Nazis. At the same time it illuminates the internal and external problems that the scent of money engenders.

While these documents do not add new chapters to our framework of Greek-Jewish relations in the 20th century – most of the documents discuss contemporary problems already discussed in Jewish sources and can be paralleled by reports in other national archives – the Greek Government is to be praised for making this material available to scholars as well as the general public. We shall now have available to us the official and bureaucratic policies that motivated Greek-Jewish relations during the turbulent inter-war period and an official record for the immediate post-war period. These documents will counterbalance the heretofore historical record told from the perspective of outside observers and a beleaguered minority in the new territories of Macedonia and Thrace. These documents also show the legal and moral framework within which the Greek Government operated in its approach to the problems of Thessaloniki. We can only hope that the positive reception of this material will encourage the MFA and other Greek ministries to release all the documentation from the restoration of Greek national freedom in Autumn 1944 – including foreign pressures on Greece's humanitarian treatment of Jewish refugees both before and after the Nazi Holocaust and negotiations with Israel.

PROF. STEVEN BOWMAN
University of Cincinnati

PROLOGUE

The idea of carrying out this study was born of the imperative need for research into the period which relates to the events of the Second World War, and it was made possible by the organisation on a new footing and ultimate computerisation of the files of the Historical Archives of the Ministry of Foreign Affairs.

Today, after eight months of systematic research into a host of files between the years from the begining of the century until the late 1950s, it has proved possible to amass an exceptionally full body of material which researchers will be able to consult as an independent archival unit, entitled *Archive of the History of the Greek Jews*. This specific unit is made up of seven large files with 50 sub-files and a total of 1,500 documents, of which a selection of 150 has been published in the present volume. These documents are divided into two basic categories: before and after the declaration of war. All the documents are, regardless of whether or not they have been published, available to researchers who wish to study them. The Archive of the History of the Greek Jews is enriched almost every day with new documents which have been found in various sets of material, such as, for example, the archive of the Cairo Embassy, which contains a number of documents bearing on the part played by the Greek Jews of Egypt in the War. Each document bears a note of the file from which it has been taken.

There are two reasons why files concerning the history and activities of the Jewish communities in Greece are kept in the archives of the Ministry of Foreign Affairs: first, because Thessaloniki, the home of the largest Sephardic community in Europe, remained until 1912 under the Ottoman state. Up to that point there were Greek consulates in the city, just as there were in other cities of Northern Greece. The reports of the Greek consuls during the long period which elapsed between the year of the declaration of the War of Independence (1821) and the setting up of the modern Greek state give a detailed and eloquent description of events in their areas of responsibility. The second reason applies to documents of the period after 1912 until the end of the War and has to do with the fact that many members of the Jewish communities held dual –Greek and foreign– citizenship. Thus, as the reader will see, there is a correspondence in this connection between the Ministry of Foreign Affairs and the Greek prefectures of Thessaloniki, Kavala, and Didymoteicho, and the General Governance of Macedonia. During the course of the War, and immediately after it, the correspondence between Jewish organisations abroad, concerned about the fate of their co-religionists, and the national governments of the countries which had suffered in the War was handled through the embassy and consular authorities of the countries in question. For this reason, the reader will notice frequent correspondence of this kind, chiefly via Greece's representatives in America, and particularly the Greek Embassy in Washington and the Consulate General in New York. However, the same was true of the correspondence with Jewish organisations in Europe, which properly addressed themselves to the local diplomatic authorities of Greece.

In the course of our many months of research into the files of the Ministry of Foreign Affairs, we sought and received the help of historians of the Jewish communities, with a view to checking and cross-referencing data about events and persons with a decisive role in the history of the communities, and thus of the country.

During the many hours spent in such discussions, we learnt that among the scores of Jews who were saved thanks to the humane feelings of the Greek people was Yitzhak Persky, father of Shimon Peres, the former Prime Minister of Israel and winner of the Nobel Peace Prize.[1] However, since accounts of this event differed to varying degrees, we asked to have a private conversation with the Israeli leader.

The meeting took place in 1998 in Tel Aviv, and, in spite of the fact that it started out as a matter of work, it has remained in my memory more because of the warmth and cordiality of my distinguished interlocutor – a historic leader who by his policies has had a decisive influence on the peace process in one of the most explosive regions of the planet.

For Shimon Peres, finding time has remained a problem; his programme and his meetings continue to be very much the same as when he was serving as Prime Minister. This meeting was for that reason doubly precious; it lasted a considerable time, during which the Israeli leader allowed his memories to unfold. Sometimes this was easy, as his gaze seemed to drift away from the actual place and time of the discussion, and sometimes it was difficult, as when he tried to remember the name of the monastery in Attica which sheltered his much-loved father for a whole year. The events unfolded before us until the moment came and the story was at an end, and the toiling of the heart which had striven to match its pace in harmony with these events themselves had left all round us a gentle

---

1. Many Israelis changed their names after 1945, following the example of David Ben Gurion (from Gruen or Green). Thus Moshe Sharett became Shertock, Levi Eshkul, Shkoluik, Goldie Myerson, Golda Meir, etc. (Paul Johnson, *A History of the Jews*, N.Y. 1998).

Photini Constantopoulou and Shimon Peres in Tel Aviv, February 1998.
During the warm and genial conversation in his office, Shimon Peres narrated to the
Director of the Historical Archives his memories of the story told by his father of how he
was rescued by Greek rebels and protected by the Orthodox monks at a monastery
in Attica.

To Photini Tomai
Constantopoulou –

With many thanks
for the unabated task
she took upon herself –
for the sake of history,
and Greek – Jewish friendship

Shimon Peres

26.2.98

Handwritten dedication from Shimon Peres which was a motivation and a stimulus for the editor in the completion of the valuable and timely research which led to the publication of this volume.

The family of Yitzhak Persky in 1945. Seated on the right is Yitzhak; on his immediate right is his wife; followed by their son Shimon. In the top row, from the left, Shimon's wife Sonia Peres, his brother Gershon and his wife Carmela.

elation. Swiftly, Shimon Peres left behind the ocean of his unerring memories and with a rare generosity gave his permission for us to write an account of his father's tumultuous acquaintance with Greece.

Yitzhak Persky was from Vishneva, which, though belonging administratively to Byelorussia, was controlled after the First World War by Poland. He volunteered for the British Army, and was parachuted in 1942 into the mountainous region of Attica-Boeotia, but was unlucky enough to be captured by the Germans almost immediately. However, he soon managed to escape from prison and spent months wandering in the wooded parts of Attica, living on weeds and lizards. In the course of his wanderings he met some Greek monks,[2] who cared for him for around a year at their monastery,[3] at great risk to their own lives, since their area was frequently the object of German visits prompted by intense suspicion. The monks helped him for months to recover, supplying him with fresh clothes and food; they also put him in contact with resistance organisations. From that point on, everything was carefully planned: the undercover journey to Olympus and from there, after a brief stay with another 18 British, Australian and New Zealand officers and men, they crossed the Aegean by caique, making for Turkey via Samos. There were five of them in the caique, headed by Charles Coward, who was later to earn the sobriquet of the 'Angel of Auschwitz'.[4] Their voyage by caique ended a little off Samos, where they ran into a German patrol. In the meantime, in the course of the voyage, a New Zealander had died of cold and hardships. Charlie, making his companions swear never to reveal the identity of Yitzhak Persky, threw the body into the sea and supplied Persky with all the documents of the unfortunate New Zealander, which meant that when they were arrested by the Germans, they all received the same treatment. It was precisely

---

2. Also ref. to Shimon Peres, *Battling for Peace*, Random House, N.Y. 1995.

3. Shimon Peres had great difficulty in remembering the name of the monastery. However, we concluded, from conversations after my return to Athens, that it must have been that of Hassia, near Mt Parnes. This was because a detail which remained vivid in the memory of Persky, and which he never failed to mention in his accounts of the story to his grandchildren, was that then the skies were so clear that you could see on the horizon the rock of the Acropolis.

4. For organising dispatches of food and clothing to the notorious concentration camp when he was himself a prisoner nearby. Together with Yitzhak Persky they had been taken there after their fourth escape attempt. It was ironic that Charlie Coward should bear the surname that he did; after the War he was awarded the Victoria Cross for his courage. But he returned to his humble occupation as a guard at a timber company, and soon afterwards found himself unemployed and reduced to poverty, having failed even to secure the royalties from his book about so exciting a life *The Password is Courage*, which became a best-seller and was made into a film.

for this reason that Persky was able to survive after their, unsuccessful, fourth attempt to escape. Coward demanded that the German officer should bring a priest to hear the confessions of Persky and himself, since they had both been condemned to death, as international law required.[5] Otherwise, the German officer, as Coward reminded him, was in danger of being tried as a war criminal after the end of hostilities. By the time the priest reached the camp, Coward and Persky had made their fifth heroic escape attempt, successfully this time, on horseback. But they came close to being killed by Allied fire at the lines of General Patton, where the troops did not know who they were until they heard their desperate cries of "We're British, we're British"!

A review of the history of the Greek Jews, as it emerges from the diplomatic archive of the Ministry of Foreign Affairs, has been a debt which the Greek State owed to its citizens of the Jewish faith, who contributed so much to the country's progress before their martyrdom at the hands of the Nazis of the Third Reich.

Today, the historian who wishes to study that period, and the country's recovery after the war, has at his disposal a wealth of archival material which the Service of Historical Archives deposited with the London Conference. A special place among the archives is occupied by material which deals with the persecution of Greeks of the Jewish faith. There were many Greek families who have their own story to tell about hiding Jews and helping them to safety and this volume is a tribute to the memory of those who sacrificed themselves in this endeavour. Alongside these unknown citizens there are many whose names are well-known and who have been honoured by the Yad Vashem Foundation for their valour with the title of 'Righteous among the Nations'.[6] Among them are Princess Alice (mother of Prince Philip and grandmother of Charles, Prince of Wales), Arch-bishop Damaskinos, the Metropolitan Bishops of Zakynthos (Zante) (Chryso-stomos), Thessaly (Gennadios), and Chalkis (Gregorios), and many others.

Justice cannot be done without the establishment of historical truth, and, therefore, without the opening of the national archives of all states involved in this war, whether as belligerents or evasive neutrals. The Special Research Bureau of the State Department has devoted a long report to the dealings of Nazi Germany with countries which remained neutral in the Second World War. These dealings had their starting-point with the gold taken from the victims of the Holocaust, national gold and other sources of wealth in the occupied countries, amounting to 300 million dollars (present-day value 2.6 billion dollars). With this wealth the

---

5. Convention signed at Geneva on 27 July 1929 (supplemented in 1949) on the treatment of the wounded and sick and the fate of prisoners of war.

6. Scroll of honour and planting of a tree with the name of the person honoured.

Nazis purchased raw materials from such 'neutral' countries as Turkey,[7] Argentina, and Portugal, which allowed them to continue the war.

Oppressive measures against the Jews in the mid-thirties became a pattern in
many places.[8] In 1934 the large Jewish community of Edirne[9] and the region
around the western side of the Turkish straits, was summarily moved and relo-
cated within two months in Istanbul.[10] The incident attracted considerable
international attention and was criticised in diplomatic quarters[11] but this did not
prevent further anti-Jewish activities from breaking out.[12]

The implementation of the law on the collection of the capital tax, the notorious 'Varlık Vergisi', served a heavy blow to the Jewish and Christian communities, since their members were forced, literally, to 'donate' their property to the
state. This law [13] imposed a tax on the basis of an arbitrary assessment of the
fortunes in question carried out by tax officials, without any means of appeal for
the taxpayers. In this way, many who were not in a position to pay the huge sums

---

7. William Slany, Department of State, *U.S. and Allied Wartime and Postwar Relations and Negotiations with Argentina, Portugal, Spain, Sweden and Turkey on Looted Gold and German External Assets and U.S. Concerns About the Fate of the Wartime Ustasha Treasury*, June 1998. On the disappearance of Jewish property during the War and the detention of Jews in labour camps in Turkey see: Bernard Lewis, *The Emergence of Modern Turkey*, Oxford 1968, pp. 298-9, A. Levi, *A History of the Jews of the Turkish Republic*, 1992 (in Hebrew), A. Levi, *The Jews of Turkey on the Eve and in the Course of the Second World War*, 1984 Peanim, 34, 1984.

8. A. Levi, *The Anti-Jewish Disturbances in Thrace*, 1934, 1987, Peanim 29 (in Hebrew). See also Documents 64, 82, 83, 84 and 85 in the present volume. *The Times*, London, 4, 5, 7, 16 July 1934.

9 The population of Jews was about 14,500 (1920 census). They made up 12 quarters (*havras*) and received considerable aid from the Alliance Universelle. Distinguished members of the local community, traders, members of the learned professions and businessmen, the Jews had contributed to the city's economic prosperity.

10. A. Levi, *The Anti-Jewish Disturbances in Thrace, 1934*, 1987, Peanim (in Hebrew). On the hardships, food shortages, and the efforts of the Chief Rabbi of Instanbul to care for the homeless, see *The Times* (London), 5 July 1934. Also, advice to Jews in the neswpaper *Zaman*, 9 July 1934.

11. FO 371/23301/E1214. Annual Report of the British Ambassador, Sir George Clark.

12. William Slany, Department of State, *U.S. and Allied Wartime and Postwar Relations and Negotiations with Argentina, Portugal, Spain, Sweden and Turkey on Looted Gold and German External Assets and U.S. Concerns About the Fate of the Wartime Ustasha Treasury*, June 1998.

13. Faik Ökte, *The Tragedy of the Turkish Capital Tax*, London 1987. Faik Ökte was director of the State Accounting Office, charged with the application of the law in the Istanbul vilayet. Ökte calls the law "catastrophic", and this study was drawn up as a kind of report to the then Turkish Prime Minister, Sükrü Saraçoglu.

demanded by them, were immediately displaced to forced labour camps.[14] The atmosphere of this period is rendered in the confidential reports of the American (Steinhardt)[15] and of the British (Sir George Clark)[16] Ambassadors in Ankara, and in reports of the famous journalist Cyrus L. Sulzberger[17] in the *New York Times*.

The efforts to save Jews from countries occupied by the Nazis concerned the fate of those with Turkish citizenship (mainly in Greece, France and Italian-occupied Rhodes). By a law passed in 1936, those citizens who left Turkey before 1923 and had not returned by 1927 were deprived of their Turkish citizenship. To such people the Turkish consuls did not give, nor were they able to give, any assistance. As the French Prof. Benbassa informs us,[18] all such Turkish Jews were sent to extermination camps. Even in the case of Greek Jews who escaped with the aid of the Resistance to Turkey, the mediation of the British was necessary to ensure that they could stay there temporarily without being handed over to the Nazis, until they could be taken to the Allied camp at Aleppo in Syria. A little before this time, the vessel *Struma*, which was carrying hundreds of Jewish refugees from Romania to Palestine, did not obtain permission to pass through the Straits; instead, it was taken by the Turkish authorities out into the Black Sea and sunk. All the refugees on board lost their lives.

Today, more than 50 years since the end of the War, humanity seeks the vindication of historical truth. If this, as well as the material compensation of the victims of the Holocaust, proves possible, then the present publication will have made, in its own way, a contribution to this process. Greece is in principle in agreement with the American proposal on the compilation of educational programmes to intensify research into this particular field of knowledge. This is the purpose which this publication in part serves – a publication which would not have taken the shape it has today without the assistance of the representatives of the Jewish community of Greece: the President of the Central Board of Jewish Communities of Greece, Mr M. Konstantinis, the President of the Jewish Community of Thessaloniki, Mr Andreas Sefiha, and the writer Albertos Nar, of the Jewish Museum of Thessaloniki, whose help has been constant and unstinting.

---

14. Of these, the Aşkale camp, at Erzurum in Eastern Turkey, had the worst repution for inhuman conditions. Ahmet Emin Yalman, *Yakin Tarihte Gördüklerim ve Geçirdiklerim* (What I have seen and experienced during recent history), Istanbul, p. 375, see also Faik Ökte, *op. cit.*, pp. 65,68,87

15. Foreign Relations, 1943, iv, pp. 1079 - 81, Steinhardt to Secretary of State, Ankara, 18 January 1943.

16. FO 371/30031/R5813, Ankara Chancery to Southern Department, 4 June 1941.

17. *New York Times*, 9 - 12 September 1943.

18. E. Benbassa, *Les Juifs des Balkans*, 1992.

December 1940.
Harry Nahmia during his tour
of duty. Donated by the Sabi
Kamhi family.

Jacob Nahmia, brother of
Harry. Cairo 1942, donated by
the Sabi Kamhi family.

ΑΠΟΘΗΚΗ ΥΦΑΣΜΑΤΩΝ

ΧΑΪΜ ΝΑΧΜΙΑ

ΑΘΗΝΑΙ
ΟΔΟΣ ΝΤΕΚΑ ΑΡ. 11
ΤΗΛΕΦ. 31-144
ΤΗΛΕΓΡ. ΔΙΕΥΘ. "ΧΑΝΑΧΜΙΑ,,

Ἐν Ἀθήναις τῇ ___ Νοεμβρίου 1940
ΟΔΟΣ ΝΤΕΚΑ 11

[Handwritten letter in Greek]

Extract of the letter from Jacob Nahmia to his brother Harry, serving in the front lines of the Greek Army. The Nahmia family and the Kamhi family are directly related to the current President of the Jewish Community of Thessaloniki, Mr A Sefiha.
The Palestinian Jews referred to here were among the 2,000 volunteers who enlisted in the British Army and fought in the Greek campaign. Twelve soldiers were killed in the line of duty, and 1,500 captured as prisoners. On 8 September 1998, a memorial service for the fallen was held at the British cemetery in Alimos, Athens.

The investigation, classification and computerisation of the Archive of the History of the Greek Jews are the result of many. months of toil on the part of two outstanding scholars, Messrs Eleftherios Stavropoulos and Stelios Zachariou. Finally, we would like to express our warmest thanks to Prof. Maria Efthymiou for her valuable advice, and to Mrs Maria-Roza Goulimi, who checked on details of the translation of the texts into English.

Greece, which in the War had –proportionally– greater human and material losses than any of the Allies or of the vanquished, makes by means of this book an offering of its own gold to the memory of the victims of the Holocaust.

PHOTINI CONSTANTOPOULOU
Director,
Service of Historical Archives

INTRODUCTION

The adventures and vicissitudes of the Jewish people are known to us from time immemorial, thanks to a multitude of Greek sources on the history of this people and its contacts with the ancient Greek world. The interaction between Greek and Jewish mercenaries is widely recorded in the Hellenistic East, but its antecedents go back in history. Greeks and Jews had ample opportunity to meet in Mesopotamia and Egypt, both as traders and as soldiers.[1] The relationship, however, began in earnest in the times of Alexander the Great and the collapse of the Persian Empire. Soon the command of the Greek *lingua franca* was such that it overtook all other languages of communication. According to Judaic tradition, Alexander visited Jerusalem and bowed before the High Priest and acknowledged the God of the Jews who prophesied his victories. During the reign of Ptolemy II it became a necessity to translate the Torah (Pentateuch) into Greek because (according to the prevailing view) it needed to become accessible to the Jews of Egypt. In the second century BC the rest of the Old Testament was also translated by seventy Hellenised Jewish scholars and during the first century AD, three out of the four Evangelists wrote their gospels in Greek (Matthew wrote his in Aramaic, translated later into Greek).

References to the Jews by Greek writers abound: Clearchus[2] and Theophrastus[3], both students of Aristotle, write about the Jews extensively. The Diaspora had already begun before Alexander, but increased in Hellenistic times. Tradition has it that Ptolemy I brought 12,000 Jewish prisoners to Alexandria; these were set free by his son, Ptolemy II, and became permanent residents of the great city. The Egyptian Kingdom of the Ptolemies as well as the Mesopotamian realm of the Seleucids were poles of attraction for Jewish immigrants, who acquired their own political entities there. According to the rules of those Greek kingdoms, upward social mobility was not impeded by origin or creed, and many Jews occupied

---

1. In Egypt, native and Persian Kings employed Greek as well as Jewish mercenaries. "The graffiti left by these soldiers (589 BC) at Abu Simbel in Lower Nubia are famous. If the information of Aristeas is correct, Jewish and Greek soldiers must have rubbed shoulders in the same campaign." Arnaldo Momigliano, *Alien Wisdom,* Cambridge 1993, p.76

2. In his work 'Βίοι' or 'Περί βίων'. All Greek authors are edited and translated in Menahem Stern, *Greek and Latin Authors on Jews and Judaism*, Vol. I, Jerusalem 1974

3. 'Περί Ευσεβείας'. Preserved in the work of the neo-Platonic philosopher, Porphyrius, 'Περί αποχής'.

posts of prominence. In Egypt, courts of law designated for Egyptians and Greeks operated simultaneously and the Jews were referred to the Greek courts.[4]

Jewish scholars such as Aristobulus, Jason from Kyrenia, Josephus (who wrote the history of the Jews in Greek) and Philo from Alexandria represented the Jewish spirit in Greek garb. There was, however, a strong resistance to Hellenising influences from conservative quarters. A break in the interaction of the two cultures occurred in 168 BC when Hellenised and conservative Jews clashed in Jerusalem. The Seleucids entered the conflict against the conservatives because the latter challenged the authority of the state .

Salo Wittmayer Baron describes the rift within Jewish society: "Conflict developed between the two principal sects, the Sadducees and the Pharisees. The Sadducees were as patriotic as the Pharisees, but their patriotism was permeated with Hellenism. Belonging for the most part to the upper classes of priests and landowners, the Sadducees had undergone a degree of assimilation before the antihellenistic reaction set in. In the Hellenistic empire, as later in Rome, the state was the paramount life principle; religion and nationality were recognised only in so far as they were instruments of the state. The new vast empires, embracing so many dissimilar ethnic components, emphasised even more strongly the supremacy of the state over nationality."[5]

The independent Jewish state came to an end in 63 BC when Romans established their rule in Judaea. The revolts of 66-73 AD and 132-135 AD were crushed with ferocity by the Romans, who banished all Jews from the holy city of Jerusalem. Part of the ensuing Diaspora came to Greece and joined the Romaniots who were already established there. They settled in Crete, Rhodes, Cos, Delos, Corinth, Athens, Sparta, Ioannina and Chalkis.[6]

.As a distinguished theologian has put it: "the New Testament is from beginning to end, a Greek book".[7] He refers to the Alexandrian *Koine* (common)

---

4. See M. Hengel, *Judaism and Hellenism*, London: SCM Press, 1974, E.J. Biekermann, *The Jews in the Greek Age*, Cambridge, Mass: Harvard University Press, 1988.

5. Salo Wittmayer Baron, 'Ethnic Pharisaism versus Nationalist Sadduceeism', *The Encyclopedia Americana*, Vol.XVI, New York, 1962, p.73.

6. Evidence concerning the Jewish community of Crete can be found both in Roman and Jewish sources. Traces of the community of Delos and a synagogue were unearthed in 1909 by French archaeologists (A. Filadelfeus, *Delos*, Athens 1909). The Ioannina Jews, according to tradition, were captives in a Roman fleet which ran aground at Parga on its way to Rome. From the testimony of Flavius Josephus there is evidence that in 66-70 AD Vespasian sent 6,000 Jews to work on the isthmus of Corinth.

7. Frederick C. Grant, 'Languages of the New Testament', *The Encyclopedia Americana*, Vol.III, New York, 1962, p.654.

Greek, spoken from the Roman camps of the Danube to the markets of Gaul and the entire Near East up to the borders of India. This was an ideal instrument of communication for transmitting the word of the Gospels East and West. Such fundamental terms and concepts of the new faith as 'Christ' (the anointed), 'angel' and 'devil' were already circulating in the Greek-speaking synagogues of the western Diaspora and, of course, the 'logos' (Word) meaning not 'speech' or 'reason', but the divine mediator between God and creation (John 1:1-18). [8]

In a brief introduction such as this it is impossible to deal with the medieval centuries of Greek-Jewish relations.[9] It will be sufficient to say that in the summer of 1453, R.Michael B. Shabbethai Cohen Balbo, from Crete, wrote a lament over the fall of Constantinople in which he associated the fate of the Jews with that of the Greeks.[10]

From the 14th century, the Greek-speaking Romaniot Jews were joined by Ashkenazi refugees from Central Europe. The first groups came to Thessaloniki in 1378 from Hungary. In 1492 Sephardi Jews expelled from Catholic Spain appeared in Thessaloniki.

Throughout the Greek War of Independence, Jews from the Western European Diaspora such as the famous Parisian journalist Georges Laffitte, the Chief Rabbi of Westphalia and Moses Gaster from the Netherlands aided the Greek cause. In the 1897 Greek-Turkish war, two hundred Jews fought in the Greek army, and many (given the small number of Romaniots) fought in all the Greek campaigns between 1911 and 1922.[11]

The annexation of Thessaloniki in 1912 was the beginning of a new era in the life of the local Jewish community. Unlike the Romaniot Jews, who asserted their Greekness and merged into the Athenian environment, the Sephardic Jews formed a separate constellation within the decentralised Ottoman system.[12] The highly centralised nation state of Greece and its cultural homogeneity posed a significant challenge to the most populous Jewish community of Greece living in the great Byzantine city. The 75,000 Jews of Thessaloniki not only constituted the majority of the population but included members of the entire social spectrum. Naturally, the division of the European lands of the Ottoman Empire between Serbia, Greece

---

8. *Ibid.* Especially Genesis 1,3.

9. For a most useful summary see Nicholas Stavroulakis, *The Jews of Greece*, Athens: Talos Press, 1990, pp.22-28. Also Joshua Starr, *The Jews in the Byzantine Empire 641-1204.* Athens 1939, and Steven Bowman *Jews and Byzantium 1204-1453.* University of Alabama Press, 1985.

10. *Ibid,* p.32.

11. The well-known hero of the Second World War Mordechai Frizis distinguished himself in the Asia Minor campaigns, Daniel Besso and Azaria Atoun, among others, were decorated by King Constantine for valour.

12. Nicholas Stavroulakis, *The Jews of Greece*, Athens: Talos Press, 1990, p.52.

and Bulgaria diminished the former role of the city as a commercial hub and deprived it of its hinterland. The Jews therefore suffered their first loss as a consequence of this development. The fears of the community that it would become a marginalised minority on the periphery of a Hellenised state were fanned by Serbian, Bulgarian and Austrian propaganda which sought to persuade the population to ask for the formation of an international city.[13] The idea was that of Baron Josef von Schwegel, who had participated in the Berlin Conference of 1878 and later suggested to the Austrian Ministry a free trade zone for Austria based on a free and neutral city. Although the local Zionists proposed that the community support the Austrian proposition, the Central Zionist Organisation overruled them, mainly because they realised that the alleged independence of the city would soon be undermined and that it would revert to the sovereignty of one or the other state.

It was therefore to the advantage of the Greek authorities to allay such fears as Austrian propaganda encouraged and reassure the leaders of the community that the Greek administration would not undermine their privileges. Furthermore, economist M. Kofinas informed the Jews that the Greek state planned to transform the port into the centre of a tariff-free zone among Balkan states and a focal point of international transportation.[14]

The Thessaloniki Jews resisted Bulgaria's attempts to convince them of the advantages of Bulgarian rule mainly because of the violence committed against the Jewish populations of Stromnitsa, Serres and Kavala, which brought terrified refugees to Thessaloniki. There were no reactions to similar attempts by the Serbs, who argued that the port was more valuable to them than either the Greeks or the Bulgarians.

In this beginning of Greek administration in Macedonia, one can trace the subsequent strained relationship between Eleftherios Venizelos and his Liberal Party with the Thessaloniki Jews. Although Venizelos made early advances to the community, the Jewish votes in the elections of 1915 favoured his opponent Dimitrios Gounaris. The community on the whole opposed Greece's participation in the First World War and favoured the neutrality professed by the royalists which benefited Austrian and German policy in the region. Despite the French influence in Thessaloniki, the pro-Zionism of Vienna and Berlin determined the preferences of a significant sector of the Jewish population of northern Greece.[15]

---

13. Rena Molho, 'Η αβεβαιότητα της ελληνικής κυριαρχίας στη Θεσσαλονίκη το 1912' (The uncertainty of Greek sovereignty in Thessaloniki after 1912), Σύγχρονα Θέματα, Nos 52-53, July-Dec. 1994, p.25.

14. Molho, op. cit. pp.27-29.

15. Isaiah Friedman, Germany, Turkey and Zionism, 1897-1918, Oxford University Press 1977, pp. 268-280.

By 1917 the Entente policy towards the Jews had reversed the position of the Zionists vis-à-vis the Great War, and Foreign Minister Nikolaos Politis declared himself in favour of an independent Jewish state in Palestine five months before the Balfour Declaration. The following year, the Thessaloniki community celebrated the first anniversary of the Balfour Declaration with "a grandeur unprecedented for most Jewish communities in Europe."[16]

The fire of 1917 devastated almost all of the city, including its historical nucleus, its business centre, the offices and buildings of local administration and public services and splendid monuments such as the fifth-century Church of St Demetrius, probably the most treasured shrine of Christendom in South-Eastern Europe. The 120 hectares of scorched land included 9,500 houses. As a consequence, 70,000 people out of a population of close to 170,000 were left homeless. The Thessaloniki Jews suffered the hardest blow from the disaster.[17]

As if this were not enough, 100,000 refugees began to descend upon the city following the 1922 evacuation of Asia Minor by the Greek troops and the flight of its native Greeks. In 1924, the Jewish community of Thessaloniki delivered a report on their condition to Henry Morgenthau, Chairman of the Refugee Settlement Commission, describing their plight and needs.[18] Morgenthau, a Reform Jew from New York and a personal friend of Woodrow Wilson, committed two years of his life to the Herculean task of coping with the settlement of Greece's refugee population. His dedication to the war-stricken and the homeless made his term an extraordinary beginning for the Refugee Settlement Commission.

By 1924, 2,500 Jewish families had been provided with shelter in six quarters, while another 7,000 still remained homeless.[19] In the meantime, the camps of the destitute Christian refugees became hotbeds of resentment and anti-Semitism and the source of constant irritation for the Jews of the city throughout the inter-War

---

16. Molho, *op. cit.* p.32.

17. For a detailed account of the fire's toll and the subsequent effort to provide relief to those stricken, see Papastathis 'Ένα Υπόμνημα για την Πυρκαγιά της Θεσσαλονίκης στα 1918...' (A Report on the Fire of Thessaloniki in 1918...), *Μακεδονικά*, III, 1979.

18. Albertos Nar, 'Μία Ανέκδοτη Έκθεση για την Δομή της Εβραϊκής Κοινότητας Θεσσαλονίκης στην Περίοδο 1912-40' (An Unpublished Report on the Structure of the Israelite Community of Thessaloniki, 1912-40), *Θεσσαλονίκη μετά το 1912* (Thessaloniki After 1912), City of Thessaloniki 1986.

19. Vilma Hastaoglou, 'Για την Κατάσταση της Εβραϊκής Κοινότητας Θεσσαλονίκης Μετά την Πυρκαγιά του 1917. Ανέκδοτο Υπόμνημα και Άλλα Στοιχεία από το Αρχείο του H. Morgenthau' (On the Condition of the Jewish Community of Thessaloniki after the Fire of 1917. Unpublished Report and other Evidence from the Papers of Henry Morgenthau), *Σύγχρονα Θέματα*, Nos 52-53, July-December 1994, pp.33-44.

period, while the peripheral settlements of the low-income Jews were the natural habitat of the Left.

The *Ethniki Enosis Ellas* (National Union Hellas), known to its followers as the Triple Epsilon (EEE), was founded in 1927 and allegedly attained a membership of 3,000 in Thessaloniki during its heyday, mostly consisting of refugees. Its anti-Semitic provocations culminated in the burning of a large part of the Jewish suburb of Campbell in June 1931. It was the worst anti-Semitic incident in the history of the Greek state and forced the authorities to take measures to preclude a repetition.

On the far left of the Jewish political spectrum was the *Federacion Socialista Laboradeva* which was formed in 1909 and appealed to all willing ethnic groups. The *Federacion* supported the anti-Venizelist coalition in the elections of May 1915 and elected two deputies with the conservative forces. It became, however, one of the founding groups of the Greek Communist Party in 1918 and contributed the most consistent communist vote in Thessaloniki throughout the inter-War period.[20] The Communist Party in turn manifested a particular interest in the Jewish community and condemned any form of discrimination against it.

George Mavrogordatos rightly points out the complexity of internal politics in the developed and differentiated community of the Thessaloniki Jews: "The profound class cleavage between the Jewish bourgeoisie and the Jewish proletariat was reflected in the extreme polarisation between a conservative, bourgeois, religious and Zionist Right and a distinctly working-class socialist and communist Left, which had its strongholds in the Jewish suburbs. Between the two, a smaller party of Moderates was also distinctly bourgeois."[21] The distribution of votes was stable. The Zionists of all varieties held the majority and usually maintained control with 52% of the 'seats', the Left commanded around 28% and the Moderates 20%. Zionists opposing assimilation were the most critical of the Venizelist state between 1918 and 1932 and therefore voted for the anti-Venizelist conservative forces. The Left initially supported the conservatives as a form of protest against Venizelist bourgeois nationalism, but later turned to the Communists. The Moderates cast their vote for Venizelos and backed his assimilationist policy. It is therefore not strange that Ioannis Metaxas, a traditional political foe of Venizelos, took the Jewish community under his dictatorship's wing in 1936-40.[22]

---

20. George Mavrogordatos, *Stillborn Republic. Social Coalitions and Party Strategies in Greece 1922-1936*, Berkeley: University of California Press, 1983, pp. 253-56.

21. Mavrogordatos, *op. cit*, pp.255. Even though the Zionists were split between a conservative party – Mizrahis – and a nationalist revolutionary group – Revisionists.

22. Mavrogordatos, *op. cit*, pp.255-257.

Jews in the Greek Army, photographed on 24 March 1940. Standing on the left is Nissim Tarabulus from the Didymoteicho area. Seated on the left is Jacob Modiano from Orestiada. Archive of the Jewish Community of Thessaloniki, donated by Theodorou Zani, Komotini.

On 28 October 1940, Prime Minister Metaxas rejected Mussolini's ultimatum to surrender the country to the Fascist forces gathered on the Albanian borders and Greece entered the War on the side of the same states with which it had aligned itself during the First World War. In the general mobilisation that followed, 12,898 Jews from all parts of Greece were conscripted. The 50th regiment of Thessaloniki, consisting mostly of local Jews, took an active part in the campaigns.[23] Of the Jewish conscripts, 343 were officers and non-commissioned officers, and Colonel Mordechai Frizis, who had made his name during the First World War, was the first Greek high-ranking officer to fall in action. He was not the last Jew to give his life for Greece. The toll of the War for the Jews was 513 dead and 3,743 wounded, of whom 1,412 were disabled. The list of heroes of the Albanian campaigns included Colonel Errikos Levis from Ioannina, Doctor Jean Allalouf from Thessaloniki, Major Salvator Sarfaty[24] and officers Joseph Varouh and Leon Dosti from Ioannina. Following the German occupation of Greece, most wounded and disabled Jews were rounded up from hospitals and shipped to the notorious Birkenau camp. Very few survived.[25]

The saga of the Jews who went underground and fled to the mountains[26] to fight with the Greek resistance has yet to be written, but testimonies abound. Many joined such resistance organisations as EDES and ELAS and escaped the fate of their Thessaloniki brethren. South of Mt Olympus more than 80% of the Jews alerted to the impending Holocaust survived. North of that line, however, disaster struck like a thunderbolt. One of those who were able to escape was Yitzhak Persky, a Polish volunteer in the British army, who escaped the Germans and was assisted by the Greek resistance to leave the country.[27]

On the eve of Second World War, over 70% of Greek Jews lived in Thessaloniki, while the remainder were in Athens (3,500), Kavala (2,000), Corfu (2,000), Ioannina (1,950), Drama (1,200), Larissa (1,175), Kastoria (900), Volos (882) and a few smaller communities elsewhere.

Arrests and deportations began in Thessaloniki in March 1943. The task of rounding up the Jewish population was facilitated when the Chief Rabbi of the city, Cevi Koretz (whose name appears in the documents of this volume when he was

---

23. The regiment was nicknamed the 'Cohen Regiment' because most of the recruits were from the Jewish district.

24. Sarfaty was captured by the Germans and died in Auschwitz.

25. The 'General Association of Wounded and Disabled during the War' appealed to the German authorities for their Jewish members to be excluded from this measure, but to no avail.

26. Especially Vermio, Pelion, Olympus, Hassia and Pindos.

27. Persky was the father of Shimon Peres.

first appointed to his high office) surrendered to the Germans the archives of the community. The role of Koretz has remained a contentious issue but the prevailing view is that he was guilty of naiveté rather than collaboration.[28]

Perhaps more tragic was the fate of the Jews in Greek territories held by the Bulgarian allies of Germany. Although the government of King Boris did not surrender the Jews of Bulgaria, it did deport nearly all the members of the communities in Greek Eastern Macedonia and Thrace, which it was occupying. These deportees were later exterminated in Treblinka.[29]

After the Italian armistice in September 1943, the Germans tried to locate the Jews of Athens. A universal refusal to hand them over to the occupation authorities and organised concealment saved most of the Athenian Jews. The EAM-ELAS movement, the Archbishop of Athens, Damaskinos, and the Chief of the Athens Police, Angelos Evert, in contact with the British, all conspired to save the Jews from the Nazi liquidation programme. On Evert's orders, the police issued about 18,500 false identity papers to protect all those hiding from the Germans.

One of the first acts of defiance against the occupation forces in Athens deserves notice. In the autumn of 1942, a clandestine resistance organisation with the initials PEAN succeeded in blowing up the offices of a Fascist organisation set up by the Italians in Athens. Panayotis Kanellopoulos was the titular leader of PEAN, but among those who carried out the operation, several were caught and executed: Thanos Skouras, the heroic air-force officer, Costas Perrikos, Yannis Katevatis and Julia Biba became martyrs of the resistance.[30]

The major question of anti-Semitism in modern Europe and the gradation of the phenomenon from the most acute forms (Hungary, Austria, Poland, Germany, Croatia, Russia, Romania) to the cases of minimal anti-Semitism (Serbia, Bul-

---

28. Michael Molho and Joseph Nehama, *In Memoriam. The Destruction of the Jews in Salonika*, Vols 6 and 7, Thessaloniki 1978, is the standard work on the Thessaloniki Holocaust.

29. Nadejda Slavi Vassileva, 'On the Catastrophe of the Thracian Jews', and Aleksander Matkovski, 'The Destruction of Macedonian Jewry', in *Yad Vashem Studies on the European Catastrophe and Resistance*, 3 (1959). For a recent account of the Thessaloniki Jews see Errika Kounio-Amarilio, Albertos Nar, *Προφορικές Μαρτυρίες Εβραίων της Θεσσαλονίκης για το Ολοκαύτωμα* (Oral Testimonies of Thessaloniki Jews on the Holocaust) Thessaloniki: Παρατηρητής, 1998.

30. One item of the little data about occupied Athens included in the computer of the Holocaust Museum in Washington DC is about a Fascist organisation with the initials ESPO in 1941. What is not included is the fact that ESPO was sabotaged (22/9/1942) by the resistance organisation of PEAN (Panhellenic Union of Youth Fighters). Many were arrested and paid with their lives for this act of defiance. C. Christides, *Χρόνια Κατοχής 1941-44* (Years of Occupation), Athens 1971, pp. 505, 555.

garia, Greece) still begs for a documented answer. A first glance at the cases might produce a working hypothesis that the ideological basis of organised state and para-state anti-Semitism rests on prototypes provided by societies with strongly entrenched *anciens régimes*.

Although the Nazi extermination programme required the efficiency of a modern totalitarian state, the antecedents from which such movements as the Iron Guard, the Ustasha, the Arrow Cross, and Fascism drew their inspiration were the principles of predestination and ascription which inspired medieval aristocracies. Societies without aristocratic but with middle-class commercial élites such as that of Greece partake of values which have on the whole preserved them from that deadly contagion that devastated Europe in the twentieth century. It is therefore not surprising that the Greek state founded on bourgeois values was free of any implication of anti-Semitism.

After the repatriation in 1945 and 1946 of those who survived the death camps of Poland in 1949 and the 8,000 who emerged from the underground and hiding, the count was gruesome. Out of 70,000 only 10,000 remained. On Zakynthos (Zante) the Mayor and Archbishop saved the entire community (a unique case in the chronicles of Europe), but Epirus and Crete lost their ancient Jewish communities.

Immediately after liberation the Greek State passed legislation for the restitution of Jewish properties to their legal owners. According to documents from the Foreign Ministry Archives, the Greek authorities set a laudable precedent by appointing the Jewish communities as administrators of all property whose legal owners had perished or were lost without trace. Besides the automatic return of property to its rightful owners, the Cabinet of George Papandreou, during its meeting of 24 August 1944, resolved that all Jewish property which remained in abeyance due to the absence of heirs up to and including the fourth degree was not to revert to the state, as laid down by law, but was to be ceded to a common fund for the rehabilitation of indigent Jews (Law 846/1946).

In an article (31.1.1948) under the title "Unlimited property is sought for Jews", the *New York Times* printed a statement by attorney Milton Winn, who, as representative from the American Jewish Council, suggested the Greek legislation on Jewish property as a model to be followed by the other European countries. Even in March 1945, the then Prime Minister, General Nikolaos Plastiras, declared that Greece was a poor but honest country and that it would be unthinkable for it to take advantage of the fact that a number of its citizens had been exterminated in order to fill its till.

On 8 May 1947, the Cabinet resolved to grant the sum of 8,000,000 drachmas as a first instalment to meet urgent educational and religious needs of the Jewish

communities. In a communication dated 26.1.1948, the Military Command of the
Dodecanese reported the surprise expressed by the representative of the US
Embassy Miner at the country's decision to proceed to the enforcement of the
relevant legislation at a time when it was itself in such dire circumstances.

Greek Jews shared common historical experiences and fought on the same
fronts as the majority of their Christian fellow citizens. However, they devoutly
kept up their traditions, and if in Greece they were never confined in ghettos, they
did follow a certain way of life which extended beyond their religion to their
language and particular mores. In the post-War period, Greek literature, more
than any other in Europe, dealt with the life and fate of the Greek Jews, mainly
the victims of the Holocaust, thus providing the general public with a unique
description of their lives.[31]

This post-War phenomenon, however, should not lead us to ignore the fact
that characters and subjects pertaining to the Jewish nation had inspired writers
and poets since the Middle Ages. Among others, one could mention Vincenzo
Cornaro ('The Sacrifice of Abraham', a drama in political verse), Dionysios
Romas ('Circumnavigation'), Kosmas Politis ('Chez Hadjifrangou'), Nikos
Kazantzakis ('Travelling to Jerusalem', 'Dedication to El Greco'), I. Venezis,
Michalis Karaghatsis, Alexandros Papadiamantis ('The Repercussion of the
Mind'), George Theotokas, Stratis Tsirkas, Nikos Bakolas ('The Big Square'),
Iakovos Kambanellis ('Mauthausen'), Vassilis Vassilikos, George Vafopoulos
('Esther', a biblical tragedy in verse), Kostoula Mitropoulou ('Rachel'), Demetris
Hadjis ('Sambethai Kabili'), and Demetris Psathas, among others. Poets such as
Anghelos Sikelianos, Kostis Palamas, C. P. Cavafy, Manolis Anagnostakis, Takis
Varvitsiotis, Nikos Engonopoulos, Zoe Carelli, have dealt in their poems with
events and persons from the ancient as well as current lore of the Jewish people.

Customs, traditions and other characteristics of a distinct way of life can be also
found in the Jewish Press with several magazines and newspapers issued by the
Jewish communities in Ladino,[32] French and Greek. The first newspaper issued
in Thessaloniki in 1865 was Jewish, as was the first printing press in the city.

---

31. The word 'ghetto' means the confinement of Jews to a special quarter of the city. The
term originates from the foundry of a small island outside Venice where all Jews in Venice
had been forced to settle for a time. With the exception of Greece, there were ghettos all over
Europe. Only in cases where the Jews themselves wanted it, did they concentrate in certain
neighbourhoods, e.g., in Ioannina or Thessaloniki. In Athens, the Jews were scattered among
various quarters of the city and this was one of the reasons which saved them from Nazi
persecution.

32. The term 'Ladino', which has prevailed in historiography, means the idiom spoken by

In pursuing the history of the two peoples, it is easy to observe their common characteristics: their inclination to trade, their love for art and literature, their long subjection to conquerors and their Diaspora, have been dealt with in many treatises. Their love of freedom, respect for the individual, and their cosmo-politanism, which, however, never broke the bonds with their country of origin, are a few other characteristics which linked the two nations. As Winston Churchill wrote: "The Greeks rival the Jews in being the most politically minded race in the world...No other two races have set such a mark upon the world. Both have shown a capacity for survival inspite of unending perils and suffering from external oppressors, matched only by their own ceaseless feuds, quarrels and convulsions. The passage of several thousand years sees no change in their characteristics and no diminution of their trials or their vitality. They have survived in spite of all that the world could do against them, . . . No two cities have counted more with mankind than Athens and Jerusalem."[33]

PHOTINI CONSTANTOPOULOU
& PROF. THANOS VEREMIS

the Sephardi descendants of the exiled Jews of Spain who settled in their majority in the Balkans, Asia Minor and Africa. It originates from the dialect spoken in Castile in the 15th century and has retained certain archaisms and acquired Portuguese, Italian, French and Turkish elements. See also Robert Attal, *Les Juifs de Grèce de l' Expulsion d' Espagne à nos Jours.* Bibliographie Jerusalem 1984; Additifs à la première édition Jerusalem, 1996

33. Winston Churchill, *Triumph and Tragedy,* Houghton, Mifflin Company Boston, 1951 (Volume V, Book II, pp. 532-533).

DETAILS OF DOCUMENTS

NOTE: Most of the documents in this volume have been translated from the original Greek. A few, however, marked (*), are printed, without alteration, in the original French or English.

1	[without specific date] 1918	Aide-mémoire	Treatment of Jewish claims regarding compensation for property following the fire of 1917.	71
2	28 February 1918	Proceedings of the Hellenic Parliament (XX Session, 3rd Sitting)	Speech by MP M. Kofinas, regarding the friendly stance of the Greek Government with respect to the creation of the Jewish State in Palestine.	72
3	18 April 1918	E.Venizelos, Prime Minister, to the Greek Embassy in London	Assurances to the Anglo-Jewish Association that the compensation measures for the victims of the fire of Thessaloniki are fair and immediately applicable.	75
4*	London, 19 April 1918	Lucien Wolf, Joint Foreign Committee of the Jewish Board of Deputies and the Anglo-Jewish Association, to I. Gennadios, Ambassador in London	Request presented by the Anglo-Jewish Association addressed coincidentally (with a day's difference) by E. Venizelos, (see doc. 3).	76
5*	London, 22 April 1918	I. Gennadios, Ambassador in London, to Lucien Wolf, the Anglo-Jewish Association.	The Greek Ambassador reassures the Anglo-Jewish Association that their request will be relayed to the Greek Government.	77
6*	London, 23 April 1918	Minutes of discussion between E. Venizelos, Greek Prime Minister, and	A deputation of the Anglo-Jewish Association meets with Prime Minister E. Venizelos, in Paris, in	77

Attach. = Attachment

		representatives of Jewish associations in London	order to receive a personal reassurance that the Greek State will proceed with all the protection measures for the victims of the Thessaloniki fire. Venizelos reassures them that all victims have already been cared for, and that the reconstruction of the city is continuing.	
7	London, 12/25 April 1918	I. Gennadios, Ambassador in London, to the Greek Ministry of Foreign Affairs	The Greek Ambassador in London relays to the Greek Government a follow-up letter from the Anglo-Jewish Association which reiterates the requests presented by the deputation during their Paris visit to E. Venizelos. The Ambassador suggests that the letter is politically motivated since actions are already being taken for the reconstruction of the city.	79
8	16 May 1918	Ministry of Transport	State aid given by the Ministry of Transport following the fire of 1917 in Thessaloniki. Law No. 1027/1917 does not discriminate concerning the protection of the victims of the Thessaloniki fire, regardless of whether they are Christians, Jews, or Muslims.	80
Attch. to 8	16 May 1918	Ministry of Transport	Note on the State aid to fire victims of Thessaloniki. Special attention is given to the needs of the Jewish community. Following the Chief Rabbi's request, separate accommodation has been built for the Jewish families while priority is given to the reconstruction of the Jewish schools.	81
9	Thessaloniki, 1 June 1918	P. Argyropoulos, General Governor of Macedonia, to the Ministry of Foreign Affairs	Argyropoulos confirms that 65% of the total aid provided has been allocated to the needs of the Jewish community, and states,	82

		with satisfaction, that he awaits the arrival of an American delegate who will personally examine the situation.	
10	Athens, 21 September 1918	The Greek Minister of Foreign Affairs to all Greek Embassies	Greek embassies abroad are notified of the "agitation" that the "supposed" tardiness of the Greek Government in enforcing protection measures for the Jews has created. The statement of the Chief Rabbi of Thessaloniki, which also invokes the report of the American Consul, states that at no time did he complain or blame the Government over the issues.	83
11	Athens, 25 September 1918	The Cabinet	Permission to join the British Army is granted to Greeks of the Jewish faith living in Egypt. The same applies to the Jews who live in Greece, provided that they have not been called up to serve in the Greek Armed Forces.	85
12	Kavala, [illegible] February, 1919	The Jewish Community of Kavala to the Sub-Governance of Eastern Macedonia	Mandate of the Jewish Community of Kavala to congratulate the Greek Government for its stance regarding the resolution of the territorial issue of an independent Jewish State.	86
13	Athens, 11 February 1919	L. Paraskevopoulos, Chief of the Army General Staff, to the Ministry of Foreign Affairs	The Greek Army has never forced compulsory labour upon the Jews. This fact is confirmed by the Rabbi of Kavala, as well as the Rabbi of the town of Drama.	87
14*	Paris, 12 February 1919	E. Venizelos, Prime Minister, to the General Governor of Macedonia	Greek Prime Minister E. Venizelos gives instructions, from Paris, for the proportional and fair representation of the Jews of Thessaloniki on the Municipal Council.	87

Attch. a to 14	19 February 1919	A. Pallis, Deputy General Governor of Macedonia, to the Ministry of Foreign Affairs	The General Governance of Macedonia reports that the Chief Rabbi of Thessaloniki has visited the Mayor, and thanked him for the proportional representation of the Jewish community on the Municipal Council of the city.	88
Attch. b to 14*	Paris, 19 February 1919	E. Venizelos, Prime Minister, to the General Governor of Macedonia	The Greek Prime Minister expresses his satisfaction with the progress of the matter concerning proportional representation in the structure of the Municipal Council of Thessaloniki.	88
Attch. c to 14*	Paris, 2 March 1919	E. Venizelos, Prime Minister, to the General Governor of Macedonia	The Greek Prime Minister requests the replacement of three municipal councillors of Thessaloniki with three Jews, in order to reduce the disturbance created by the non-proportional representation on the Council of the city.	89
15	21 February 1919	Frangistas, Thessaloniki Press Bureau, to the Ministry of Foreign Affairs	The Chief Rabbi of Thessaloniki refutes unsubstantiated articles presented in the Jewish-Swiss Press regarding the "alleged" persecution of Jews in Greece.	89
Attch. a to 15	Paris, 22 February 1919	E. Venizelos, Prime Minister to E. Repoulis, Deputy Prime Minister	The Greek Prime Minister, writing from Paris, requests the support of the Jewish community in Greece in dealing with the unsubstantiated allegations submitted to the Jewish Association in France, regarding the "alleged" persecution of Jews in Greece.	90
Attch. b to 15*	Paris, 22 February 1919	N. Politis, Minister of Foreign Affairs, to E. Venizelos, Prime Minister	Politis informs the Prime Minister about the reception of the Greek Jewish delegation by the British Prime Minister Lloyd George	91
Attch. c to 15*	[without specific date] 1919	Alliance Israélite Universelle	The Jewish Union of Greece reassures Paris and London that the Jews of Greece share the same	91

			benefits with other Greek citizens, and states that it comes as a surprise that their co-religionists can state otherwise.	
16	17 March 1919	J. Cazes to the General Governor of Macedonia.	Interpretation of the voting results of the Zionist Convention in Thessaloniki. The writer comments on the way the Jews of the city view their position in Greek society, as citizens of a different religion, with special privileges.	92
17	Thessaloniki, 25 April 1919	S. Protonotarios, Director, the Thessaloniki Press Bureau, to the Ministry of Foreign Affairs	Information regarding an Italian campaign of propaganda in Thessaloniki which does not hesitate to use, as a tool, certain extreme elements of the city's Jewish Community.	93
18	Thessaloniki, 30 April 1919	A. Adossidis, General Governor of Macedonia, to the Ministries of Foreign Affairs, Transport and the Army	The General Governor of Macedonia introduces specific proposals to co-responsible ministries with regard to the housing of the unfortunate Jewish victims of the fire who are still in temporary shelter. Such a situation inevitably re-ignites the Italian propaganda campaign against the Greek State, and eventually against the Jews themselves.	94
Attch. to 18*	10 March 1919	A. Adossidis, General Governor of Macedonia, to N. Politis, Minister of Foreign Affairs, Greek Legation in Paris	Proposals of the General Governor of Macedonia with regard to housing destitute Jews, victims of the fire.	96
19	Thessaloniki, 29 May 1919	S. Protonotarios, Director, the Thessaloniki Press Bureau, to the Ministry of Foreign Affairs	Concern of the Greek Government regarding the actions of foreign interest groups, which wish Thessaloniki (and its harbour) to be a 'free' zone, and do not hesitate to use, for the promotion of their goals, certain	97

26	Athens, 4 September 1924	G. Roussos, Minister of Foreign Affairs, to all Greek Embassies and Consulates	Following a circular of the Ministry of Foreign Affairs, Jews and Armenians who live in Thrace and possess a Greek passport are recognised as *ipso jure* Greek citizens.	111
27	Thessaloniki, 21 August 1926	I. Minardos, Director, the Thessaloniki Press Bureau, to the Thessaloniki General Governance	Attempts by Zionist organisations in Thessaloniki to change the character of high school education for the Jewish children of Thessaloniki.	112
28	Thessaloniki, 24 September 1926	The Director of the Thessaloniki Press Bureau to the Ministry of Foreign Affairs	Information that Zionists insist on maintaining complete control of any education for the duration of the Greek-Jewish programme.	113
Attch. a to 28	Thessaloniki, 22 September 1926	The Thessaloniki Press Bureau to the Ministry of Foreign Affairs	Newspaper article from *Renacencia Giudia*, entitled: 'Let's Found the Jewish Secondary School This Year'. The articles defends the idea of the foundation of a Jewish-Zionist secondary school.	114
Attch. b to 28	Thessaloniki, 5 September 1926	Z. Kon, Inspector of the Jewish Community Schools of Thessaloniki, to Frances, editor of the *Renacencia Giudia* newspaper	Letter from the inspector of Jewish Community Schools, concerning the work of community education and its scholarships.	116
29	Thessaloniki, 29 September 1926	The Director of the Thessaloniki Press Bureau to the Press Department of the Ministry of Foreign Affairs	Information about the conduct of the Béne-Bérith Union, and the attack made by Zionistic circles on this union's work.	117
Attch. to 29	Thessaloniki, 27 September 1926	Z. Kon, Inspector of the Jewish Community Schools of Thessaloniki, to the *Pueblo* newspaper.	The inspector of the Jewish Community Schools of Thessaloniki submits a letter explaining how the education of Jewish children is organised throughout the world, and states that a Zionist secondary school should not be set up.	118

30	Thessaloniki, 23 December 1926	The Thessaloniki Press Bureau to the Ministry of Foreign Affairs	Financial support from the Greek State for the education of Jews of Thessaloniki.	120
31 The original document is partly damaged	Thessaloniki, 16 December 1926	The Director of the Thessaloniki Press Bureau to the General Governance of Macedonia	The issue of education for the Jews of Thessaloniki.	121
32	Thessaloniki, 4 February 1927	D. Kalapothakis, Director, the Thessaloniki Press Bureau, to the Ministry of Foreign Affairs	The impact of governmental promises, reported in the Jewish Press of Thessaloniki, on the Jewish Member of Parliament M. Bessantchi regarding the Government's support for the Jewish schools.	124
Attch. a to 32*	Thessaloniki, 2 February 1927	The Thessaloniki Press Bureau to the Ministry of Foreign Affairs.	Newspaper article from *Indépendant* entitled "Une Subvention sera accordée aux écoles israélites".	125
Attch. b to 32*	Thessaloniki, 4 February 1927	The Thessaloniki Press Bureau to the Ministry of Foreign Affairs.	Neewspaper article from *Indépendant* entitled "Le Gouvernement Accordera Une Subvention Aux Ecoles Israélites. M. Michalacopoulos Appuiera les Demandes de la Communauté".	125
33	Thessaloniki, 8 April 1927	D. Kalapothakis, Director, the Thessaloniki Press Bureau, to the Ministry of Foreign Affairs	Diverging views of Zionist and non-Zionist groups of the Jewish community of Thessaloniki regarding the type of education in the city. The majority supports Greek-Jewish schools.	126
34	Corfu, 24 June 1928	The Inspector of Primary Education in Corfu to the Ministry of Education	Report on the operation of School No. 3 in the Jewish quarter of Corfu.	131
35	Thessaloniki, 29 October 1928	D. Kalapothakis, Director, the Thessaloniki Press Bureau, to the Ministry of Foreign Affairs	Report on article of the Thessaloniki newspaper *Progrès* regarding the lack of Jewish members on parliamentary committees.	134

Attch. to 35*	Thessaloniki, 26 October, 1928 & 27 October 1928	The Thessaloniki Press Bureau to the Ministry of Foreign Affairs.	Newspaper articles from *Progrès* regarding the lack of Jewish members on parliamentary committees.	135
36	Thessaloniki, 6 November 1928	D. Kalapothakis, Director, the Thessaloniki Press Bureau, to the Ministry of Foreign Affairs	Summary of the minutes of the assembly of the Jewish Community printed in the Zionist newspaper *Flambeau*.	136
37	Thessaloniki, 21 August 1929	The Director of the Thessaloniki Press Bureau to the Ministry of Foreign Affairs	Report in the local Press of Thessaloniki regarding the results of the recent elections.	137
38	Thessaloniki, 3 October 1929	The Director of the Thessaloniki Press Bureau to the Ministry of Foreign Affairs	Report on the recent publications which address the issues of the allocation of special funding by the Government for the teachers of the French language in Jewish schools.	139
Attch. to 38	Thessaloniki, 29 September 1929	The Director of the Thessaloniki Press Bureau to the Ministry of Foreign Affairs	Newspaper article from *Action* reports on Education Law 1374 which lays down the teachers of the Jewish community schools are regarded as civil servants and will be paid accordingly by the State.	139
39	Thessaloniki, 26 October 1929	I. Minardos, Director, the Thessaloniki Press Bureau, to the Ministry of Foreign Affairs	The Jewish Press of Thessaloniki responds to the statements of the Prime Minister of Greece and the General Governor of Macedonia with regard to an anti-Semitic article in the Press.	142
40	Thessaloniki, 24 December 1929	Haim R. Habib, *locum tenens* of the Chief Rabbi, and J. Cazes, President of the Jewish Community of Thessaloniki, to the Prime Minister	Request of the Jewish Community of Thessaloniki to the Cabinet to retract their decision on the expropriation of land which is within the boundaries of the city's Jewish cemetery.	144
41	Thessaloniki, 26 December 1929	The President and the Secretary of the Zionist and religious	Jewish organisations intervene regarding the establishment of Sunday as a day of rest. The	146

		organisation Misrachi to the Minister of Foreign Affairs	Jewish organisations request that freedom of choice between Saturday and Sunday be applied.	
42	Athens, 14 February 1930	D. Kalapothakis, Director, the Thessaloniki Press Bureau, to the Ministry of Foreign Affairs	The Thessaloniki Branch of the Peace League.	147
Attch. to 42*	Thessaloniki, 2 February 1930	The Thessaloniki Press Bureau to the Ministry of Foreign Affairs.	Newspaper article from *Progrès* entitled "La question du cimetière Israélite."	148
43	Thessaloniki, 16 March 1930	D. Kalapothakis, Director, the Thessaloniki Press Bureau, to the Ministry of Foreign Affairs	Article in *La Verdad* addressing the issue of Sunday as a day of rest.	149
44	Thessaloniki, 7 April 1930	S. Gonatas, General Governor of Macedonia, to the Ministry of Foreign Affairs.	Structure and operation of the Jewish Community of Thessaloniki.	149
45*	Thessaloniki, 10 May 1930	The Thessaloniki Press Bureau to the Ministry of Foreign Affairs.	Newspaper article from *Avanti* entitled "La Vie des Travailleurs Israélites dans l' Armée Bourgeoise".	154
46*	Thessaloniki, 19 Mai 1930	The Thessaloniki Press Bureau to the Ministry of Foreign Affairs.	Newspaper article from *Tiempo* entitled "La Situation des Juifs de Turquie. Demie Heure Avec Un Ancien Salonicien Installé à Stamboul".	158
47	Thessaloniki, 29 May 1930	D. Kalapothakis, Director, the Thessaloniki Press Bureau, to the Ministry of Foreign Affairs	Newspaper article from *Ephedrikos Agon* against the Jews.	159
Attch. a to 47	Thessaloniki, 27 April 1930	The Thessaloniki Press Bureau to the Ministry of Foreign Affairs	Newspaper article from *Ephedrikos Agon* entitled "Let them Think Carefully".	161
Attch. b to 47	Thessaloniki, 20 April 1930	The Thessaloniki Press Bureau to the Ministry of Foreign Affairs.	Newspaper article from *Ephedrikos Agon* entitled "The Jewish Communists"	161

48	Athens, 16 June 1930	G. Papandreou, Minister of Education and Member of Parliament for Lesvos	Explanatory report on the draft law concerning the amendment and supplementation of Law 2456 referring to the Jewish communities.	162
49	Thessaloniki, 12 July 1930	D. Kalapothakis, Director, the Thessaloniki Press Bureau, to the Ministry of Foreign Affairs	Report on the rights of Jews of foreign citizenship to vote in the election procedure of the Community Assembly.	164
50	Athens, 25 July 1930	Law 4837	Concerning the amendment and supplementation of Law 2456 concerning Jewish Communities.	165
51	Athens, 13 August 1930	G. Papandreou, Minister of Education, to the Ministry of Foreign Affairs	Concerning Law 4837, which requires the acquisition of Greek nationality by the rabbis and the Chief Rabbi of Greece.	167
52	Thessaloniki, 21 September 1930	D. Kalapothakis, Director, the Thessaloniki Press Bureau, to the Ministry of Foreign Affairs	Decision of the Greek Government to set up five new elementary schools for the Jews of Thessaloniki.	167
Atch. to 52	Thessaloniki, 22 September 1930	D. Kalapothakis, Director, the Thessaloniki Press Bureau, to the Ministry of Foreign Affairs	Reactions from the Council of the Jewish Community regarding the setting up of the previously reported five new elementary schools.	168
53	Thessaloniki, 14 October 1930	D. Kalapothakis, Director, the Thessaloniki Press Bureau, to the Ministry of Foreign Affairs	Election results of the Jewish Community of Thessaloniki.	169
54*	Thessaloniki, 8 January 1931	The Thessaloniki Press Bureau to the Ministry of Foreign Affairs	Newspaper article from *L' Action* entitled: "Le Grand Rabbin Ouziel et notre communauté. Son opinion sur le nouveau conseil. Ce qu' il pense des écoles étrangères - Il viendra nous visiter à la première occasion".	172
55*	Thessaloniki, 9 January 1931	The Thessaloniki Press Bureau to the Ministry of Foreign Affairs	Newspaper article from *L' Action* entitled: "Le Judaisme de Salonique sans direction".	174

63	Thessaloniki, 23 March 1932	I. Minardos, Director of the Thessaloniki Press Bureau, to the Inspector of Primary Schools of Thessaloniki	Newspaper article from *Tiempo* regarding the compulsory participation of Jewish pupils in Christian ceremonies.	211
Attch. to 63	Thessaloniki, 4 April 1932	The Inspector of Primary Education of Thessaloniki to the Editor of the *Tiempo* newspaper	The reports of *Tiempo*, regarding the compulsory participation of Jewish pupils in Christian ceremonies, are denied.	212
64	Athens, 18 July 1932	C. Diamantopoulos, Director, Directorate of the Press, Ministry of Foreign Affairs, to B. Directorate for Political Affairs of the same Ministry.	A report from Paris indicating the possible migration of 'Oriental Jews' to Palestine, supported by a brief analysis of the state of the Jewish population in Turkey, printed in the *Tiempo* newspaper of Thessaloniki.	213
65	Corfu, 8 July 1932	The Prefect of Corfu to the Ministry of Foreign Affairs	The Prefect suggests that the proposal submitted by the Prefecture, regarding the financial assistance of the local Jewish Community, be accepted.	214
66	Thessaloniki, 9 October 1932	The Thessaloniki Press Bureau to the Ministry of Foreign Affairs	Report with commentary added, on a Zionist newspaper article, translated into Greek, regarding the education of Jewish children. The article is entitled: "The education of Jews and the Zionists".	215
67	Athens, 20 October 1932	V. Dendramis, Director, Press Directorate of the Ministry of Foreign Affairs, to the Ministry of the Interior	Commentary on a pamphlet of the 'Greek Anti-Communist and Humanitarian Social Union'.	216
68	Thessaloniki, 20 December 1932	The Director of the Thessaloniki Press Bureau to the Ministry of Foreign Affairs	Articles of local Jewish newspapers regarding the visit to Thessaloniki of the envoy representing the Executive Committee of the Jewish Agency, Dr Senator.	217
Attch. to 68	Thessaloniki, 14 December 1932	The Thessaloniki Press Bureau to the Ministry of Foreign Affairs	Newspaper article from *Pueblo*. Report and extracts referring to the speech of Dr Senator in Thessaloniki (11.12.1932).	219

69	Thessaloniki, 31 December 1932	The Director of the Thessaloniki Press Bureau to the Ministry of Foreign Affairs	Zionist interest groups of Thessaloniki express their satisfaction at the conclusions reached at the 9th Annual Conference of the Zionists in Greece, relating to the education being provided for Jewish children.	220
Attch. to 69	Thessaloniki, 30 December 1932	The Thessaloniki Press Bureau to the Ministry of Foreign Affairs	Newspaper article from *Renacencia Giudia* regarding an address delivered by a spokesman of the Zionist Federation during the 9th Conference.	221
70	5 January 1933	The Director of the Thessaloniki Press Bureau to the Ministry of Foreign Affairs	Newspaper article from *Pueblo*, regarding the migration of the Thessaloniki Jews.	222
71	Thessaloniki, 14 February 1933	The General Governor of Macedonia to the Ministry of Foreign Affairs	Notification of the visit of the President of the Jewish Community, accompanied by the Polish Rabbi Koretz, in order to support the candidacy of the latter as Chief Rabbi of Thessaloniki.	223
72	Thessaloniki, 10 April 1933	P. Dragoumis, General Governor of Macedonia, to the Ministry of Foreign Affairs	Dispatch of memorandum by the Jewish Community of Thessaloniki in which the candidacy of Dr Koretz for Chief Rabbi of Thessaloniki is announced.	225
Attch. a to 72	Thessaloniki, 20 March 1933	The Jewish Community of Thessaloniki to the General Governor of Macedonia	Memorandum regarding the candidacy of Dr Koretz for the position of Chief Rabbi of Thessaloniki.	225
Attch. b to 72	Berlin, 11 March 1933	I. Politis, Ambassador in Berlin, to the Greek Ministry of Foreign Affairs	German authorities transmit information regarding Dr Koretz.	227
Attch. c to 72	Thessaloniki, 2 May 1933	I. Minardos, Director, the Thessaloniki Press Bureau, to the Ministry of Foreign Affairs	Commentary on articles printed in the newspapers *Indépendant* (02.05.1933) and *Progrès* (15 and 28.04.1933) regarding the arrival	227

		(11.05.1933) of the Chief Rabbi of Thessaloniki and the issue of his nationality.	
73	Berlin, 3 May 1933	I. Politis, Ambassador in Berlin, to the Greek Ministry of Foreign Affairs	The move of Dr Koretz and his family from Berlin to Thessaloniki to undertake his duties as Chief Rabbi is announced.	228
74	Thessaloniki, 5 August 1933	The Director of the Thessaloniki Press Bureau to the Ministry of Foreign Affairs	Management issues of the Jewish Community of Thessaloniki.	229
75	26 September 1933	The Minister of Foreign Affairs to the General Governance of Macedonia	The Greek Government cannot provide financial assistance to Greek Jews wishing to emigrate to Palestine.	231
76	Thessaloniki, 3 October 1933	P. Dragoumis, General Governor of Macedonia, to the Ministry of Foreign Affairs	The financial position of the Jews of Thessaloniki compared with the rest of the citizens, and restricted, yet unproblematic, migration to Palestine.	232
77	Thessaloniki, 22 November 1933	The representatives of the Union of Jewish Communities of Greece, of the Council of the Jewish Community of Thessaloniki, of the Chief Rabbinate and of all the Jewish organisations	Mandate of protest against the policy of the British Government regarding the migration of Jews to Palestine.	232
78	Thessaloniki, 8 December 1933	The Directorate of Police in Thessaloniki to the Gendarmerie Headquarters	Assembly of the Jewish Association *Zionism* in Thessaloniki (03.12.1933).	234
79	London, 14 February 1934	D. Kaklamanos, Ambassador in London, to the Greek Ministry of Foreign Affairs	Dispatch of a letter of the Agudas Israel World Organisation, concerning the observance of the Sabbath.	235
Attch. to 79*	London, 7 February 1934	H. A. Goodman, Agudas Israel World Organisation,	The full text of the above letter.	235

Attch. b to 93*	[without specific date] 1944	A. Mallah, President of the Assembly, 'United Committee in Favour of Greek Jewry'	Excerpt from the Union's resolution, which expresses gratitude for the stance of the Greek people and Government on the issue of Greek Jews.	262
94	[without specific date] 1944	Directorate of Special War Services (Bureau II A)	Information concerning German atrocities against Greek Jews in Greece.	262
95*	[illegible] February 1944	World Jewish Congress	Reports entitled: "Notes on the present situation of Greek Jewry".	279
96	Jerusalem, 1 March 1944	M. Sakellariadis, Consul General for Palestine and Trans-Jordan, to the Greek Ministry of Foreign Affairs in Cairo	Dispatch of a translation of a letter of the 'General Federation of Jewish Labour in Palestine'.	289
Attch. to 96*	Tel Aviv, 23 February 1944	D. Ramez, General Secretary of the General Federation of Jewish Labour in Palestine, to M. Sakellariadis, Consul General for Palestine and Trans-Jordan	Feelings of gratitude are expressed by the General Federation of Jewish Labour in Palestine to the Greek people for their noble stance and support towards the Greeks of the Jewish faith.	289
97	Jerusalem, 1 June 1944	G. Christodoulou, Consul in charge for Palestine and Trans-Jordan, to the Greek Ministry of Foreign Affairs in Cairo	Regarding an article published in the Palestinian Press describing the stance of the occupied Greek population towards the Jews. Call for action, primarily by the Press, to report on the true situation.	290
98*	London, 6 June 1944	News Bulletin, issued by the Information Office of the Greek Embassy in London	Conditions of transport of Jews of Greek and foreign nationality by Germans to concentration camps in Poland. The valuable assistance of Greek citizens in rescue efforts is noted.	292
99	Jerusalem, 13 June 1944	G. Christodoulou, Consul in charge for Palestine and Trans-Jordan, to the Greek Ministry of Foreign Affairs in Cairo	Information regarding the anti-Semitic conduct of Greek employees of the Aleppo camp, and actions for the avoidance of leakage of such information to the Palestinian Press.	293

Attch. a to 99	Cairo, 17 June 1944	P. Dragoumis, Deputy Minister of Foreign Affairs, to the Greek Ministry of Welfare in Cairo	It is requested that the employees of the Aleppo camp who have shown anti-Semitic feelings against Jewish Greek refugees be removed and punished in an exemplary manner.	293
Attch. b to 99	Aleppo, 9 July 1944	A. Demertzis, Infantry Lieutenant, to the Greek Ministry of Welfare in Cairo	Concerning the allegations against Warrant Officer Emmanouil Apostolatos and the civilian Vassilios Papazian.	294
Attch. c to 99	Cairo, 8 August 1944	P. Skeferis, Ambassador, Greek Ministry of Foreign Affairs in Cairo, to the Greek Consulate General in Jerusalem	The accusations regarding the alleged anti-Semitic conduct of the Warrant Officer of the Aleppo camp, Apostolatos, are unsubstantiated.	295
100	Jerusalem, 15 July 1944	G. Christodoulou, Consul in charge for Palestine and Trans-Jordan, to the Greek Ministry of Foreign Affairs in Cairo	Circulation of letter sent by the Chief Rabbi of Palestine expressing his gratitude for the stance of the Greek people and of the Orthodox Church towards the persecuted Jews of occupied Greece.	295
Attch. a to 100*	Jerusalem, 10 July 1944	Benzien Meir Hay Ouziel, Chief Rabbi of the Holy Land, to G. Christodoulou, Consul in charge for Palestine and Trans-Jordan	Above-mentioned letter in its entirety.	296
Attch. b to 100*	Jerusalem, 15 July 1944	G. Christodoulou, Consul in charge for Palestine and Trans-Jordan, to Benzien Meir Hay Ouziel, Chief Rabbi of the Holy Land	Gratitude is expressed for the letter of 10.07.1944 by the Chief Rabbi. In this letter there is also reconfirmation that, despite existing difficulties, the Greek people will continue to help their Jewish compatriots.	298
101	Jerusalem, 20 July 1944	G. Christodoulou, Consul in charge for Palestine and Trans-Jordan, to the Greek Ministry of Foreign Affairs in Cairo	Actions for the refutation of an article printed in the *Palestinian Post* (19.07.1944) which contains an unfavourable but also inaccurate description of the suspension of	299

			negotiations between the Greek Government and the EAM.	
102	Cairo, 18 September 1944	D. Pappas, Ambassador in Cairo, to the Greek Ministry of Foreign Affairs	Extract from the minutes of the session of 16 August 1944 of the Managing Committee of the Greek Jewish Community of Egypt.	299
103	Cairo, 20 September 1944	D. Pappas, Ambassador in Cairo to P. Dragoumis, Under-Secretary of Foreign Affairs	Forwarding of a letter written by the President of the Greek-Jewish Community of Egypt.	301
Attch. a to 103	Cairo, 8 July 1944	I. Bessos, President of the Community of Greek Jews in Egypt, to D. Pappas, Ambassador in Cairo	Transmission of a copy of the letter addressed to the Greek Prime Minister, G. Papandreou.	301
Attch. b to 103	Cairo, 8 July 1944	I. Bessos, President of the Community of Greek Jews in Egypt, to G. Papandreou, Prime Minister	Intense lobbying of important Jewish organisations in the USA, resulting in two resolutions by the Jewish American Committee and the World Jewish Congress, respectively. Dispatch of the two enactments.	302
Attch. c to 103*	New York, 11 May 1944	Dr M. Porlzweig, Political Department of the World Jewish Congress, to I. Bessos, President of the Community of Greek Jews in Egypt	Resolution of the Executive Committee of the World Jewish Congress expressing their admiration for the heroic stance and sacrifice of the Greek people with regard to the Jewish citizens of Greece.	303
Attch. d to 103*	New York, 9 May 1944	J. Proskauer, President of the American Jewish Committee, to I. Bessos, President of the Community of Greek Jews in Egypt	Admiration for the firm stance and solidarity of the Greek people towards their Jewish brothers.	304
104*	Jerusalem, 19 October 1944	Benzien Meir Hay Ouziel, Chief Rabbi of the Holy Land, to the Jewish Community in Athens.	Letter of support to the Jewish Community, followed by an invitation to emigrate to Palestine.	305

105	27 October 1944	Z. Benzonnanas, Jewish Community of Athens, and A. Molho, Jewish Community of Thessaloniki, to the Prime Minister	Good wishes on the occasion of the first post-War celebrations of 28 October.	306
106*	London, 10 November 1944	J. Romanos, Counsellor, Greek Embassy in London, to the Secretary of the World Jewish Congress	The Greek Government announces the implementation of Law 2/10.11.1944 (regarding the restitution of Jewish property), rescinding Laws 1977/44 and 1180/44.	307
107	Athens, 10 November 1944	Government Gazette *(Ephimeris tis Kyverniseos)*, Volume 1, issue No. 11, 10 November 1944.	Law 2/10.11.1944 rescinding Laws 1977/44 and 1180/44 and restituting Jewish property.	307
108	Jerusalem, 21 November 1944	G. Christodoulou, Consul in charge for Palestine and Trans-Jordan, to the Greek Ministry of Foreign Affairs	Reactions of the Greek Jews residing in Palestine to the appointment (by the Greek Government) of the Board of Management of the Jewish Communities of Athens and Thessaloniki.	309
109	Cairo, 17 November 1944	D. Pappas, Ambassador in Cairo, to P. Dragoumis, Minister of Foreign Affairs	Discontent of Jewish interest groups of Palestine and Egypt regarding the *ex officio* appointment, by the Greek Government, of the Board of Management of the Jewish Communities of Athens and Thessaloniki.	310
110	[without specific date] 1945	Directorate of Special War Services to the Greek Legation in Egypt	Letter of the Directorate regarding the action taken by the Greek Government in favour of the Jews and the gratitude expressed by Jewish authorities and organisations.	311
111	[without specific date] 1945	Greek Cabinet	Note on matters pending in need of immediate attention which are related to the Jewish Community.	315

112	Athens, 26 March1945	C. Amantos, Minister of Religious Affairs and National Education, to the Ministry of Foreign Affairs	Regarding the submission to the Council of Ministers of the law concerning the reconstitution of the Jewish Communities.	317
113	Athens, 19 April 1945	G. Lambrinopoulos, Under-Secretary to the Prime Minister, to the Ministries of Foreign Affairs, Supply, Agriculture, and the National Economy	Note regarding the issues discussed during the meeting of the Prime Minister with the Chargé d' Affaires of Foreign Relations of the Jewish Agency, Mr M. Shertock. The ministries responsible are requested to look into the demands submitted which fall within their competence and to report their actions to the Cabinet.	318
Attch. to 113	15 April 1945.	The Political Office of the Prime Minister	Matters regarding the Greek Jews discussed between the Prime Minister and the Chargé d' Affaires of the Jewish Agency, Mr Shertock, during their meeting on 15 April 1945.	318
114	Athens, 31 May 1945	M. Pesmazoglou, Minister of Finance	Ministerial Decision 788/31.05.1945 deals with the issue of restitution of Jewish property to its rightful owners.	319
115	Jerusalem, 27 June 1945	G. Christodoulou, Consul in charge for Palestine and Trans-Jordan, to the Greek Ministry of Foreign Affairs	Reports on articles in the Jewish Press of Palestine regarding the Jews of Greece.	325
116*	Lausanne, 3 July 1945	Dr Leon Cuenca, reservist health officer of the Hellenic Army, to the Greek Legation in Berne	Report on the condition and fate of the Jews who were deported to concentration camps.	327
117	Washington, 28 August 1945	K. Diamantopoulos, Ambassador in Washington, to the Greek Ministry of Foreign Affairs	Letter of gratitude of the Central Congress of American Rabbis.	328
Atch. to 117*	St Louis, 8 August 1945	F. Isserman, Chairman, Commission of Justice and Peace, Central Conference	Gratitude is expressed for the help of the Greek people given to their persecuted Jewish	328

of American Rabbis, to K. Diamantopoulos, Greek Ambassador in Washington

compatriots during the German occupation of Greece.

118	London, 3 September 1945	J. Romanos, Counsellor, Embassy in London, to the Greek Ministry of Foreign Affairs	Special European Conference of the World Jewish Congress in London, held on 22 August 1945. The Greek Government announces the new measures it intends to implement regarding heirless Jewish property.	329
Attch. a to 118*	30 August 1945	Dr S. Wise and Dr W. Goldman, Chairmen of the World Jewish Congress, to Admiral Voulgaris, Prime Minister	Gratitude is expressed for the legislative solution given to the matter of the issue of heirless Jewish property.	330
Attch. b to 118*	London, 29 August 1945	Report from *Palcor Agency*	Title: "Important decision by the Greek Government" regarding the legislative solution of the heirless Jewish property issue.	331
Attch. c to 118*	London, 29 August 1945	Report from *Jewish Telegraphic Agency*	The heirless property of deceased Greek Jews will be made available first for the rehabilitation of Jewish survivors.	331
Attch. d to 118*	London, 22 August 1945	R. Raphael, Greek delegate to the Special European Conference of the World Jewish Congress.	Extract of address delivered by the Greek Delegate. Review of the history of the Jewish Community in Greece since 1944.	332
Attch. e to 118*	Athens, 16 August 1945	Report from *Palcor Agency*	Report regarding the special decree authorising the passage of 380 Greek Jews to Palestine.	333
119	Jerusalem, 6 September 1945	G. Christodoulou, Consul in Charge for Palestine and Trans-Jordan, to the Greek Ministry of Foreign Affairs	Reactions of Jewish interest groups in Jerusalem regarding the intention of Greek Jews to return to Greece. The United Nations Relief Rehabilitation Agency (UNRRA) policy regarding the Palestinian refugee issue. Actions of Zionist organisations and policy of the Greek State on the issue.	334

120	Jerusalem, 12 September 1945	G. Christodoulou, Consul in charge for Palestine and Trans-Jordan, to the Greek Ministry of Foreign Affairs	Report on the statement made by Mr Czernowitz, representative of the Red Shield of David, regarding the living conditions of the Jews in Greece.	339
121	Jerusalem, 12 September 1945	G. Christodoulou, Consul in charge for Palestine and Trans-Jordan, to the Greek Ministry of Foreign Affairs	Excerpts from an article of the weekly Jewish magazine *Heni Hamisrah* (12.09.1945), regarding the clearly superior position of Jews in Greece in comparison with their co-religionists in other Balkan nations.	340
122	[illegible] January 1946	Newspaper article from *Atlantis*	Entitled: "An anti-Semitic proclamation and an anouncement of the Diocese of Thessaloniki".	341
Attch. to 122	[without specific date] 1946	The President, M. Molho, and the Secretary, I. Tiano, of the Jewish Community of Thessaloniki to the Holy Diocese of Thessaloniki	Letter of gratitude for the Diocese's repudiation of the defamation of the Jews.	342
123	Athens, 15 January 1946	A. Kyrou, Director, Ministry of Foreign Affairs, to the Greek Consulate in Boston	Report regarding the Jews of Greece.	343
124	Athens, 3 March 1946	C. Bitsidis, Minister of Finance, to the Prime Minister	Report of the Reuters agency regarding the property of Greeks of the Jewish faith which was compulsorily abandoned during the German occupation.	346
125	Jerusalem, 12 June 1946	G. Kapsambelis, Consul General in Jerusalem, to the Greek Ministry of Foreign Affairs	Article printed in the Cairo newspaper *Phos*, regarding Jewish property in Greece.	347
126*	Buenos Aires, 2 July 1946	C. Chervin, President, and H. Triwaks, General Secretary, Central Committee for the Assistance of Jewish War	Letter of gratitude for the assistance of the Greeks to Jewish war victims.	348

		Victims and Refugees, to the Greek Chargé d' Affaires in Buenos Aires		
127	Pretoria, 3 September 1946	I. Tomazos, Press Attaché, Greek Legation to the Union of South Africa, to the Greek Ministry of Press and Information	Tomazos reports on the lecture and observations of the Oxford University professor Dr Roth, who visited Greece.	348
Attch. to 127*	[without specific date] 1946	Professor Roth, Oxford University	Speech, on Greece delivered on Johannesburg Radio.	349
128*	New York, 10 December 1946	M. Gottschalk, American Jewish Committee, to the Greek Minister of Foreign Affairs	Letter of gratitude following the rescue, by the Greek Navy, of Jews emigrating to Palestine whose ship sank en route.	352
129	Jerusalem, 17 December 1946	G. Kapsambelis, Consul General, for Palestine and Trans-Jordan, to the Greek Ministry of Foreign Affairs	Positive reactions of Jews regarding the above-mentioned actions of the Greek Government.	353
130*	[illegible] March 1947	Newspaper article from the *Palestine Economic Review*	Title: "The Settlement of the Problem of Jewish Property in Greece".	354
131*	London, 13 March 1947	A. Easterman, Political Secretary, World Jewish Congress, to the Greek Ambassador in London	The issue of Jewish property in Greece.	355
132*	London, 13 June 1947	Newspaper article from the *Jewish Chronicle*	Title: "Greek Jews' Grievances Reviewed".	357
133	28 June 1947	The Cabinet Office	Legislative measures regarding Jewish property in Greece after the War (Act 525).	358
134	Athens, 21 July 1947	I. Koutsalexis, General Director, Ministry of Foreign Affairs, to the Permanent Greek Delegation, New York	Measures of the Greek State in favour of Greeks of the Jewish faith.	360

135	Ankara, 25 July 1947	P. Skeferis, Ambassador in Ankara, to the Greek Ministry of Foreign Affairs	Newspaper article from the *Journal d' Orient* entitled "Ce que les Juifs de Grèce doivent à leur pays".	362
136	Rhodes, 18 October 1947	M. Stassinopoulos, Political Counsellor, Military Command of the Dodecanese, to the Ministry of Foreign Affairs	Population data and status of the Jewish communities of the Dodecanese.	362
137	Rhodes, 18 October 1947	Rear-Admiral P. Ioannidis, Military Commander of the Dodecanese, to the Ministry of Foreign Affairs	Jewish property in the Dodecanese.	363
Attch. a to 137*	Rhodes, 15 July 1947	J. Adam, British Custodian of Property, British Consul in Rhodes, to the Deputy Controller of Finance and Accounts of the Greek Military Command of the Dodecanese	Jewish property in the Dodecanese.	364
Attch. b to 137	Athens, 6 December 1947	I. Stephanou, Director, Ministry of Foreign Affairs to the Ministry of Finance	Confiscation of Jewish property by the presidents of the Jewish Communities of the Dodecanese.	365
Attch. c to 137*	Rhodes, 15 March 1947	Proclamation of the British Brigadier Parker.	Management of Jewish property in Rhodes.	366
Attch. d to 137	Rhodes, 15 March 1947	E. Soriano, President of the Jewish Community of Rhodes	Authorisation for the management of abandoned Jewish property in Rhodes.	366
Attch. e to 137	Rhodes, [illegible] March 1947	E. Soriano, President of the Jewish Community of Rhodes, to the Directorate of the Tax Office of the Military Command of the Dodecanese	Application for permission to take delivery of four safe-deposit boxes.	367
Attch. f to 137*	Rhodes, 15 October 1947	A. Hasson to T. Chryssanthopoulos, Greek Military Command of the Dodecanese	A. Hasson expresses his wish not to participate in the management of the Jewish Community of Rhodes.	367

138	Athens, 15 October 1947	Government Gazette	Ministerial Decision by D. Chelmis, appointing the Jewish Community Council as the manager of abandoned Jewish property in Greece.	368
139	Athens, 24 January 1948	I. Karmiris, General Director of Religious Affairs, Ministry of Education, to the Ministry of Foreign Affairs	The issue of recognition of the Jewish Communities of the Dodecanese.	370
140	Rhodes, 26 January 1948	The Military Command of the Dodecanese to the Ministry of Foreign Affairs	American reaction to the decision of the Greek Government to help impoverished Jews.	371
141*	31 January 1948	Newspaper article from the *New York Times*	Title: "Unclaimed Property is Sought for Jews".	371
142*	[illegible] March 1948	Central Jewish Documentation in Paris	Extract from the minutes of the International Conference of the 'Centrale de Documentation Juive', held in Paris.	372
143	Athens, 9 April 1948	Information Bulletin	Bulletin regarding the memorial service for the Jewish victims of Nazism in Athens.	377
144	Washington, 12 April 1948	V. Dendramis, Ambassador in Washington, to the Greek Ministry of Foreign Affairs	Remarks by R. Canetti based on her personal experience of the state of the post-War Greek Jewish population in Greece.	378
145	Athens, 17 April 1948	K. Konstantinis, President, Central Board of Jewish Communities, to the Prime Minister and Deputy Prime Minister	Foundation, by the Greek State, of the 'Organisation for the Care and Rehabilitation of Survivors' of the persecution of the Jews of Greece.	379
146	Athens, 26 April 1948	K. Konstantinis, President, Central Board of Jewish Communities to the Ministry of Foreign Affairs	List of looted Greek Jewish gold.	380
Atch. to 146	1 [partly illegible] April 1948	K. Konstantinis, President, Central Board of Jewish	Evidence regarding the property which the Germans confiscated	381

	Communities, to the Ministry of Foreign Affairs	from Greek Jews. Monetary claims and reimbursement.	
147	Athens, 7 May 1948	K. Konstantinis, President, Central Board of Jewish Communities, to the Ministry of Foreign Affairs	Additional evidence regarding the Jewish gold Nazis looted.	382
148*	Athens, 12 May 1948	K. Konstandinis, President, Central Board of the Jewish Communities of Greece, to the Ministry of Foreign Affairs	Solemn statement regarding the gold looted by the German forces from Greek Jews.	383
149*	28 May 1948	Rabbi Abraham Schreiber, Chief Rabbi of Greece, to V. Dendramis, Greek Ambassador in Washington.	Rabbi Schreiber forwards a personal interview, published as a newspaper article in the *Morning Journal*, regarding the Jewish Community in Greece.	384
150	Thessaloniki, 24 December 1948	K. Korozos, Minister of Northern Greece, to the Sub-Ministry of Press and Information	Information about the history of the Greek Jews from their establishment in pre-Christian times up to the genocide of the Second World War.	386
151	Athens, 24 February 1949	The Ministry of Foreign Affairs to the Greek Embassy in Berne	Briefing regarding Greek legislation in favour of the Jews and their property.	388
152	Volos, 10 June 1949	M. Pessach, Chief Rabbi of Volos, to His Beatitude Spyridon, Archbishop of Athens and All Greece.	Letter published in the newspaper *Atlantis* regarding the bonds of friendship between Christians and Jews.	389
153	Athens, 7 July 1949	Spyridon, Archbishop of Athens and All Greece, to His Reverence the Chief Rabbi of Volos, M. Pessach	Letter published in the newspaper *Atlantis* regarding the bonds of friendship between Christians and Jews.	391
154	16 July 1949	Newspaper article from *Ethnikos Kiryx*	Title: "The Rehabilitation of the Greek Jews".	392
155	6 September 1949	Newspaper article from *Atlantis*	Congratulations of Greek Jews to His Beatitude the Archbishop of Athens.	392

156	Athens, 12 October 1949	The Ministry of Finance to the Ministry of Foreign Affairs	Article in the *Jewish Chronicle* regarding the return of Jewish property.	393
157	[without specific date] 1950	Aide-mémoire of the Ministry of Foreign Affairs	Matters of interest to the Jews dealt with by the Directorate of Economic Affairs. • Transfer of the archives and library of the Community of Thessaloniki. • Return, from Bulgaria, of valuable objects stolen from the Jews. • Removal of the library of the Chief Rabbinate of Volos by the Germans, and efforts for its recovery. • Return of the gold stolen from the Greek Jews by the Germans.	393
158	Washington, 20 February 1950	V. Dendramis, Ambassador in Washington, to the Information Service of the Embassy	Note regarding the participation of Jews in the Greek electoral process.	395
159	23 September 1957	G. Papadakis, Director, Ministry of Foreign Affairs, to the Union for the Care and Rehabilitation of Jews of Thessaloniki	Compensation of the victims of the war by member nations of the Axis alliance.	395
Attch. a to 159	Thessaloniki, 20 July 1957	The President and the General Secretary of the Board of Management of the Union for the Care and Rehabilitation of the Jews of Thessaloniki	Proceedings regarding the compensation of Jewish War victims of in Greece.	396
Attch. b to 159	Bonn, April 8, 1957	The Greek Ministry of Foreign Affairs to the Union for the Care and Rehabilitation of the Jews of Thessaloniki	Claim for reparations on the part of the League of Jewish Hostages (deported persons) of Thessaloniki.	397

DOCUMENTS
BEFORE THE SECOND WORLD WAR

Members of the 'La Bohème' Jewish amateur association of Thessaloniki. This association appeared in 1903 with the presentation of the drama 'Until Death'. The earnings from the ticket sales went towards the Allatini orphanage. On 15 April 1904, the same association presented the drama 'Faith, Hope and Compassion'. The earnings from the ticket sales were donated to the Bikour Holim Foundation for the medical care of homeless Jews. According to the press reports of the period, the performance received disapproving comments from the more conservative groups of the Jewish community. Archive of the Jewish Community of Thessaloniki, donated by Armando Modiano.

I

Treatment of Jewish claims regarding compensation for property following the fire of 1917.

aide-mémoire   [without specific date] 1918

All the Jewish allegations reported in Ambassador Koromilas' telegram are false.

It is not true that the lower part of Thessaloniki – or any other area – is to be expropriated by the Government at an arbitrary price and then resold to a Greek company.

Under the recent law concerning the new town plan, the property lying within the burnt-out area shall constitute an entity as follows:

The value of each separate property will be estimated by a committee which will include representatives of both the City of Thessaloniki and the owners and be subject to the approval of the President of the Court of First Instance. Should an owner consider such valuation unsatisfactory, he can apply to the courts for a new one. The owners are granted interest-bearing property bonds redeemable not after a period of twenty years but by 31 December 1919 at the latest and capable of being pledged against credit up to 3/4 of their value.

On the completion of the new town plan, the new plots will be auctioned. Former owners will enjoy a preferential position by being chosen over third parties offering the same terms and being able to pay the value with their bonds, which are inalienable, instead of cash. In addition, in order to reduce competition by the new buyers, which would create an abnormal financial climate, bidding will not be allowed to exceed certain reasonable levels, with the exception of the most commercially attractive sections which it is only right to allocate to the best businessmen with the highest bids. Furthermore, the same person may not acquire more than two plots, with the exception of former owners already owning more. The proceeds of the auction shall be used in the first place to redeem the property bonds, then to meet the costs of the new town plan and 1/3 of the estimated cost of the infrastructure (streets and drains) in the burnt-out area. The remaining surplus shall be distributed in two equal parts among former owners, depending on the value of their property bonds, and the City of Thessaloniki on condition that it builds the above infrastructure. In addition, the increase in the value of all property located outside the burnt-out area obtained through the implementation of the new plan shall be estimated and one half of such increase shall be used for the construction of municipal buildings in the burnt-out area of the city.

This system was selected in view of the fact that property in Thessaloniki was so fragmented and the new plan entails such sweeping changes that preservation of the old plots was impossible and they had either to be redeveloped or altogether eliminated. Besides, any other system would have rendered impossible the quick implementation of the new plan, the exploitation of the area and, most importantly, the equitable distribution among old owners of the economic changes of the properties. Old owners, as a rule, will acquire a disproportionate increase of their value although, perhaps, there will be some plots which will be undervalued. Thus it is only fair that the general overvaluation of property in the burnt-out area should prove to the benefit of the former owners, depending on the current value of their property and, also, of the whole community which contributed to its rise.

Besides, even that part of the surplus profit which is to be allocated to the city will indirectly prove to the benefit of former owners since, considering that it will be spent on the burnt-out area, it will increase the value of their property.

The allegations that the Jews have been advised to buy plots outside the burnt-out areas are equally not true. There is no question that owing to the fragmentation of property in the centre of Thessaloniki not all former owners, whether Jews or not (there is no discrimination in the law), will be able to buy plots in the burnt-out area. Presumably, however, not all of them wish to do so. Those left out will have the opportunity to buy plots in all other sections of the city.

Finally, it should be added that property owners are allowed by the said law to form companies of their own and carry out the expropriation themselves under certain conditions and state supervision.

2

Proceedings of the Hellenic Parliament (XX Session, 3rd Sitting)

28 February 1918

Mr M. Kofinas, Member for Thessaloniki, addressed the House as follows: The gracious statement made recently by the Right Honourable Minister of Foreign

*(18-19 August 1917): Thessaloniki in flames. According to the report of the General
Secretary of the Macedonian General Command, A. Pallis, "The Jewish community has
probably been tried more than any other in terms of the number of its members affected
by the fire, and the damages inflicted on their properties." 53,737 Jews were left homeless,
while all the synagogues, schools and humanitarian institutions were destroyed. Archive of
the Jewish Community of Thessaloniki, donated by Armando Modiano.*

Affairs in connection with the reconstitution of the Jewish State in Palestine imposes upon me, as a Greek Member of Parliament, a Jew and a Zionist, the duty – conveying also the opinion of my co-religionist colleagues and all Greek Jews – of thanking the Government, from this rostrum, for the kind statement it has made. I count myself fortunate in that I have been given the opportunity to demonstrate, by my own presence and that of my co-religionist colleagues, that in Free Greece, the cradle of liberty, all nationalities live in complete equality, enjoying all the benefits of freedom and at liberty to express their feelings. The reconstitution of the Jewish State in Palestine is not only the burning, lasting and eternal yearning of the Jews but also the profound wish and interest of our great Allied Powers, and above all of Britain, which, acknowledging the injustice committed for the past 20 centuries against a great and glorious race which lives far from the land of its Fathers and has rightful claims by reason of its glorious past, are zealously working to resolve this great and vital question in accordance with the wishes of the Jews. I would like to avail myself of this opportunity to express the profound obligation I feel to thank, from this rostrum, the Allied Powers, which have stated their advocacy of a favourable solution to the question, and in particular the British Government, which, as soon as the brave Allied forces had marched into Palestine, issued an official statement, through Prime Minister Lloyd George and Foreign Minister Balfour, to the effect that it will satisfy and realise the twenty centuries old longing of the Jews to reconstitute the Jewish State, and the Government of France, which issued a similar official statement through Foreign Minister Pichon. It would be most encouraging and valuable for us if the Right Honourable Prime Minister were to grant his valuable support to the realisation, in due time, of the rights of the Jewish people, in the conviction that in future he is determined to continue the co-operation between the two peoples, Greeks and Jews, to the advantage of humanity and of those peoples themselves (applause).

Nikolaos Politis (Minister of Foreign Affairs): In Thessaloniki, I have had an opportunity of expressing the profound sympathy of the Liberal Party and, I am sure, of all Greeks, who share the desire for liberty of all those constrained in their national rights and patriotic interests, for the Jewish race, which for the last twenty centuries has been the victim of misunderstanding and persecution. I am happy to be in a position today to renew the pledge given at that time that, in due course, the Liberal Government will make every effort to assist the Jews in their national undertaking, in full agreement with Greece's great Allies. To the reasons we already possessed for sympathy with the Jewish race – which, as the Honourable Member was good enough to acknowledge, has always lived in Greece under the reign of freedom and the rule of law and has collaborated in the fields of progress and the rule of law and order with the other sections of the population — another reason has now been added. Among the other things they share, the Jewish and Greek races have the similarity that they are both among the races which have been subjected to constant persecution and oppression. Today, at a time when the blood of the Greeks has been drained by the Barbarians of the East, it is with profound emotion that I convey all my wishes to the Jewish race for their national rehabilitation. (Applause)

⊷⊷

3

E. Venizelos, Prime Minister, to the Greek Embassy in London

letter   18 April 1918

Please inform the Anglo-Jewish Association that the complaints conveyed to it are entirely groundless and that the Law passed is in compliance with all the points which I explained to the Association when I saw them in London. The compulsory purchase and re-sale of the building sites is taking place on behalf not of the city but of those affected by the fire.

Of any profit which may be realised, one half will be spent on the construction of the streets and drains of the new plan and the other half will be made over to those affected by the fire.

However, since the implementation of the new plan will also increase the value of the surrounding buildings, which were not burned, the Law determines that one half of this surplus value will be spent on the construction of the public and municipal buildings provided for under the new plan. Lastly, it is expressly laid down that the bonds to be given to the fire victims and corresponding to the value of their property will be accepted at their nominal value for the purchase of the building sites provided for under the new plan. Please ask the members of the Anglo-Jewish Association to believe that the interests of the fire victims have been served with complete justice, and that provision has been made to ensure that the terrible disaster will lead to the construction, out of the ruins, of a new city fully corresponding to the requirements of life today.

⊷⊷

4[*]

Lucien Wolf, Joint Foreign Committee of the Jewish Board of Deputies and the Anglo-Jewish Association, to I. Gennadios, Greek Ambassador in London

letter   London, 19 April 1918

Dear Mr Gennadios,

I am sorry to have to worry you again about the Salonika Reconstruction Question. My Committee continue to receive letters from Salonika – not only from local Jews but also from British Residents and visitors – complaining that the Reconstruction Scheme threatens the whole Jewish community with certain ruin and stating that it is very doubtful whether the hopes and promises expressed to us by Mr Venizelos will be realized in the eventual plans.

On two points specific statements of a very disturbing nature are made to us. You will perhaps remember that Mr Venizelos assured us that the State Bonds given by way of compensation to the owners of property to the burned area would be easily convertible, and that they would be accepted on their face value in payment for sites in the area of reconstruction which the owners might wish to acquire. We were also assured that all the profits realized from the expropriation and the resale of property would be applied for the benefit for the town of Salonika alone. On both these points our correspondents assured us that Mr Venizelos' good intentions are being ignored or defeated, and doubt is even expressed as to whether we correctly understood Mr Venizelos.

You know how anxious my Committee are to avoid all friction or misunderstanding between the Jews of Salonica and the Hellenic Government, and they would be much obliged if you will use your best efforts to clear up the doubts which have been expressed to us. I think that if Mr Venizelos could be induced to write us a letter in the terms of the verbal assurance he gave us in London, which we could publish, all difficulties would be removed. Will you kindly let me know what you think of this suggestion.

5*

I. Gennadios, Ambassador in London, to Lucien Wolf, the Anglo-Jewish Association.

letter   London, 22 April 1918

Dear Mr Lucien Wolf,

You have accurately weighed my sentiments when you have stated that they are strongly in favor, not only of avoiding all friction or misunderstanding between my government and the Jews of Salonica, but of consolidating the most amicable understanding and cooperation in all matters relating to the commonweal.

I am inclined to think that the fresh complaints which have reached you are not substantiated by the actual facts. But I will adopt your suggestion and will request Mr Venizelos to repeat to your Committee in writing the explanations he gave you when in London, in respect to the plan of reconstructing Salonica. If I am not mistaken your Committee were ten accompanied by a short-hand writer.

Please assure your Committee of my best endeavors in this matter and believe me etc.

6*

Minutes of discussion between E. Venizelos, Greek Prime Minister, and representatives of Jewish Associations in London

London, 23 April 1918

On the invitation of Mr Venizelos the Greek Prime Minister, a deputy from the Foreign Affairs Committee of the Anglo-Jewish Association waited upon H.E. at the Ritz Hotel on Friday the 23rd instant. The deputation consisted of Mr C. G. Montefiore, Mr B. Kisch and Lord Swaythling, and was accompanied by Mr M. Duparc, Secretary of the Anglo-Jewish Association, and Mr Lucien Wolf.

Mr Montefiore, in introducing the deputation, said it has not been the intention of the Committee to trouble H.E. as they were satisfied with the assurances given to them by Mr Gennadios on October 17th. Some doubt however seemed to exist as to the exact intentions of the Hellenic Government, and it would be a great satisfaction to the Jewish Community to receive from M. Venizelos a further assurance that these doubts were unfounded. The points which seemed to require elucidation had already been set forth in the documents communicated by the Committee to Mr Gennadios.

Mr Venizelos said he had asked the Committee to come to see him, as he was anxious to convince all the parties interested that there was no ground for doubting the good intentions of the Hellenic Government. The explanation he proposed to give them would, he thought, convince them that, not only had his Government no evil intentions with regard to the Jews of Salonica but that all the measures they proposed taking for the reconstruction of that city were conceived in their interest and for their benefit. It was only natural that, after the great catastrophe which had come to Salonica, the Greek Government should wish to reconstruct the city on a modern plan. Salonica had hitherto been a Turkish city, and consequently lacked many of the attractions and conveniences which a modern city ought to possess. To effect the necessary transformation, the Government was bound to take the work into its own hand. The plans proposed made expropriation inevitable, but this would not in any way bear hardly on the local population. On the contrary, it would be to their advantage. The result of the improvement that would be affected would be a largely enhanced value of the building sites. In ordinary circumstances this plus value would accrue to the Municipality, but the Government had resolved that it should be distributed among the owners of the site *pro rata*, according to the value of their properties. The expropriated properties would be sold by auction, and thus their full marketable value would be obtained and their owners would receive, in addition to the original value of their properties, the plus value thus obtained. These sums would be paid in the form of Treasury Bonds, which would be easily negotiable. They would be legal tender for the payment of sites purchased by the original owners, and they would also be legal tender for other payments to be made to the treasury. This being briefly the scheme of the Government, he was at a loss to see what the Jewish Community had to complain of. It had been said that it was a deep laid plan for the elimination of the Jews from Salonica – that, in short, the Greeks wanted to supplant the Jews. Unfortunately, in commercial transactions, this instinct for supplanting other people often manifested itself, and he had heard that there were even poor Jews who desired to supplant their richer brethren, but, whatever truth there might be in this, he could assure the deputation that the Greek Government had no such intention, and that they energetically disapproved of any desire to supplant the Jews of Salonica. In this matter they knew no difference between Greek and Jew, and regarded them all equally as Hellenic Subjects. For himself he could say that he knew how valuable an element the Jews were in Salonica, and how much they contributed to make the city the important centre that it was, and he would regard it as a real misfortune if any section of the Jewish population were forced to immigrate [*sic*]. He hoped they would more and more identify themselves with their Greek Nationality, and he thought perhaps that their foreign co-religionists might be of use to them in impressing upon them, and in pointing out that all citizens of Greece were equal, and that none could enjoy at the same time privileges and the *droit commun*.

A conversation ensued, on the invitation of Mr Venizelos who said that he desired nothing better than to deal with any criticisms of his scheme which might be raised. In answer to a question he said that the economic outlook for Salonica was very good. All the victims of the fire were now under shelter and well looked after, and owing to the presence of the Allied Armies in the city, there was ample work for all. Of course, a good deal of inconvenience was felt owing to the ravages of the fire, but the work of reconstruction would be pushed on as rapidly as possible and he thought that something like a normal situation might be reached in the course of the next six months.

Mr Montefiore thanked Mr Venizelos on behalf of the deputation and said he thought the explanations he had given would prove completely satisfactory to the Jews of Salonica and their friends.

—▸✦◂—

7

I. Gennadios, Ambassador in London, to the Greek Ministry of Foreign Affairs

letter   London, 12/25 April 1918

As I informed you by telegram some days ago, Mr Lucien Wolf, Secretary of the Anglo-Jewish Association, a powerful body in London, addressed to me a letter, of which I attach a copy, conveying the news received from Thessaloniki, according to which the Jews of that city, believing themselves to be facing disaster as a result of the way in which the re-sale of the building sites is taking place, are invoking the promises given by His Excellency Mr Venizelos during his stay here.

Those consultations were dealt with in my communications Nos 3159 (and 3506) of 4/17 November 1917.

I replied (as briefly as possible) that I was convinced of the groundlessness of the complaints of the Jews of Thessaloniki, but that I would duly report to the Government and would recommend that the promises given should be reiterated.

Today I have received a second letter from Mr Wolf forwarding to me a copy (as requested) of the notes taken during the meeting between the Prime Minister and the Anglo-Jewish Association.

I am unaware of what is exactly happening in Thessaloniki in connection with these matters. It seems very likely that the less respectable members of the Jewish community are seeking to benefit from other political difficulties. However, it is clear that it is in our interests to forestall any such move.

8

Ministry of Transport

aide- mémoire   16 May 1918

The State has granted a sum of 1,150,000 drachmas from the special budget of the Ministry of the Interior in aid to the victims of the Thessaloniki fire. This sum was delivered to the Central Aid Committee of Thessaloniki, which disposed of it together with the money and goods assembled by collection. No discrimination was ordered, and none occurred, between Greek, Jewish or Muslim fire victims. According to the report on the amounts collected and disbursed of between 2 August 1917 and 31 August 1918, a total of 1,388,880 drachmas was spent on the purchase of bread, foodstuffs, quilts, coal, medicines, doctors' fees and the cleaning of the camps – that is, for feeding, heating, public hygiene and medical care of the fire victims. A further 263,000 drachmas was spent on administrative costs, makeshift engineering works, and the procurement of tools and machinery, etc. There remains a balance of 166,845.98 drachmas still available.

In order to support the work of the Thessaloniki Central Aid Committee, three special sub-committees were set up in the city to collect money and goods for the fire victims, there being one sub-committee for each of the religious communities - that is, the Greek, the Jewish and the Muslim communities. The items collected by these sub-committees were disposed of by them among the members of their own community. According to the report on their activities down to 31 December 1917, the sub-committees had collected the following sums and goods:

1) The Greek sub-committee

30,680 drachmas
and 24 rolls of cloth
15 crates of soap
2 crates of tea
200 *okas*[#] of coffee
and 1,030 units of shirts, underwear
and pairs of men's socks

2) The Jewish sub-committee
and goods to a value of

677,614 drachmas
<u>126,395 drachmas</u>
804,009

3) The Muslim sub-committee

6,008 drachmas

It was laid down by Article 1 of Law 1027 of 1917 (240) approving a credit of 5,200,000 drachmas from the budget of the Ministry of Transport that this sum was to be used for "the housing of refugees and fire victims" without discrimination, for "the construction and repair of the market, the schools and in general the public and communal buildings of the Greek and Jewish communities alike", for "the cleaning and clearing of streets", for "the cleaning of ruined buildings", building the necessary infrastructure for settlement, for "the construction of new houses for fire victims", and for "the construction of huts to house Greek schools or those of the Jewish Community".

ATTACHMENT TO 8

Ministry of Transport

note   16 May 1918

Credits of 5,000,000 drachmas have been granted by the State for the construction of huts for the fire victims, regardless of religion, which on their

---

One *oka* is the equivalent of 1,280 grams.

---

completion are distributed among the fire victims on a completely impartial basis. At the demand of the Chief Rabbi, separate huts were constructed for the Rabbis.

As for the ban on the reconstruction of the buildings destroyed by the fire, this is temporary and was imposed by law on all buildings in the burnt-out area so as to ensure that the implementation of the new city plan was not blocked, as happened in San Francisco after the most recent great fire there.

However, permission was granted by Royal Decree for makeshift repairs to be carried out and temporary huts to be erected in some parts of the burnt-out area to house commercial establishments. The permits for these temporary repairs are granted entirely impartially, and, indeed, up to now the Jews have benefited more from the measure.

By way of exception from the general prohibition, permission was granted for all the buildings used as schools by the Jewish Community to be repaired, and these repairs have been carried out.

The law on the new city plan of Thessaloniki was drawn up in such a way as to provide complete protection for the interests of the people, and the Jews are treated on an equal basis with all the other ethnic groups in the city.

9

P. Argyropoulos, General Governor of Macedonia, to the Ministry of Foreign Affairs

telegram   Thessaloniki, 1 June 1918

In reply to your telegram 4491, inform you of impossibility of determining exact amount spent on Jews because expenditure made from general cash fund for fire victims of all religions. However, following numbers can be extracted by proportion: In September 1917, number of persons receiving free bread from Aid Committee was 8374 Christians, 24950 Jews, 8446 Muslims. Same proportion applies to other items of expenditure because number of persons receiving free bread taken as basis for welfare. Hence it can be concluded that at least sixty per cent of the aid committee's funds was spent on Jews. 15 Greek families and 172 Jewish families still living in huts erected by the City, 70 Greek and 113 Jewish families in requisitioned Greek schools, 243 Greek and 325 Jewish families in huts erected by the state. 530 Jewish families still living in tents. It is hoped that 200 of these will be housed within two months and the remainder within five, depending on the progress of buildings in new tenements.

No objection on our part to the visit of American representative, who will certainly observe impartially the rehabilitation process. For that matter, he can address himself to the representative of the American Red Cross here, who is aware of the situation and fully appreciates the work done. We suppose report to the contrary stems from Chief Rabbi, who is constantly complaining and suspecting racial prejudice.

━━◆━━

IO

The Greek Minister of Foreign Affairs to all Greek Embassies

explanatory report   Athens, 21 September 1918

Since it is possible that complaints may be submitted to you from Jewish or foreign circles in connection with the conduct of the Government towards the Jewish community of Thessaloniki, as has already occurred, we have the honour to communicate to you here all the particulars which are essential to your rebutting all such accusations as well as, in brief, the correspondence exchanged with other Embassies on this subject.

Last April, the Anglo-Jewish Association in London addressed to Mr Gennadios a letter in which it stated certain complaints on the part of the Jews of Thessaloniki. They alleged, that is to say, that, despite the promises made by the Prime Minister, the Jews of Thessaloniki were threatened with disaster because the government bonds issued to them in compensation for their plots of land were not easy to redeem nor were they acceptable at their nominal value as payment for land in the reconstruction zone, and because the compulsory purchases and the re-selling of the plots were taking place to the benefit of the city only, while half of the profits ought to have been returned to the former· owners. The complaints contained in the above letter were, of course, entirely groundless. The Prime Minister hastened to reply by telegram, via the Embassy in London, to the Anglo-Jewish Association, assuring them that all the promises given by him to the Association during his stay in London had been honoured in the Law passed on the reconstruction of Thessaloniki. He noted, in particular, that the compulsory purchases of the sites were taking place on behalf not of the city but of the fire victims, that one half of any profit which may be realised will be paid to them (the remainder being used for the construction of streets and drains), and that the bonds given to the fire victims for the value of their sites were accepted, at their nominal value, for the purchase of land within the new town plan.

Later, in the month of May, more complaints were made — now in Rome – by Mr Lubin, American representative at the International Institute of Agriculture in Rome, who had received a telegram from the Secretary of State of the United States instructing him to go to Thessaloniki and investigate the state of the Jews on the spot which, according to the information received by the Secretary of State, was desperate. Before carrying out his instructions, Mr Lubin addressed himself to Mr Koromilas, whom he informed that it would be most unfortunate for Greece if he were to ascertain that Greece had done nothing for the Jews of Thessaloniki, while on the other hand there would be incalculable benefits for us among public opinion in the United States if it were to be demonstrated that we had made sacrifices for them. He asked Mr Koromilas to provide him with all particulars about the state of the Jews in Thessaloniki; if these were satisfactory, they would create an exellent impression in the United States and would permit him to avoid the necessity of travelling to Thessaloniki.

We hastened, in an urgent telegram to the Embassy in Rome, to deny these new complaints made by the Jewish community in the United States. The Greek Government, according to this telegram, had done everything humanly possible as from the day immediately following the fire to help the victims without any discrimination as to their religion. It had distributed generous amounts of aid and had undertaken to construct special huts to house the victims. The Prime Minister, on the occasion of his presence in Thessaloniki, himself visited the temporary housing of the Jews and asked the persons housed there if they had any complaints to make. They thanked him warmly for the concern which the Greek Government had displayed towards them. Furthermore, we asked Mr Koromilas, in the same telegram, to inform Mr Lubin that we would look into the question of what more could be done for the Jews in Thessaloniki in order to improve their lot.

A few days later, in reply to a further telegram on the same subject from the Embassy in Rome, we asked the Ambassador to inform the American representative (Mr Lubin) that the Prime Minister would be pleased if Mr Lubin could proceed as rapidly as possible to Thessaloniki so as to see for himself what care we are taking of the Jews of Thessaloniki, often in excess of the means at our disposal, and ascertain the gratitude of the Jewish population to the Greek Government for this assistance.

In order to reinforce the points made in these telegrams, we dispatched, at the same time, the following details which we had received from the General

Governance in Thessaloniki. According to the General Governance, it is not possible to determine the exact amount spent on the Jews (text of telegram from Thessaloniki dated 1 June, No. 4664, follows). This information was passed on by the Embassy in Rome to Mr Lubin, who stated that it would make an excellent impression in the United States, where he was thinking of publishing it. He also asked for clarification of the following important point: he had been told that the lower part of Thessaloniki, inhabited largely by Jews, would be bought by compulsory purchase at a price fixed arbitrarily by the Greek Government and would be resold to a Greek company. The Jews living there were to receive bonds redeemable after twenty years and would be compelled to purchase land outside the burnt-out zone.

In order to rebut these new and completely unfounded complaints, we forward a note from the Ministry of Transport, which was also sent to the Embassy in Rome last June.

"It is not true ..." [there follows the text of a note attached to the communication from the Ministry of Transport No. 5713].

The discussions caused abroad concerning the state of the Jews in Thessaloniki being thus to date, I feel it is my duty to add that the Chief Rabbi of Thessaloniki, during his most recent visit here, expressly stated to me, citing also the American Consul in Thessaloniki as a witness, that he had simply requested aid and building materials from America and had never complained against the Greek Government, whose impartiality and concern towards the Jewish population of Thessaloniki he was happy to acknowledge.

II

The Cabinet

resolution   Athens, 25 September 1918

In connection with the enlistment of Jews of military age as volunteers in the British Army in Palestine, the Cabinet resolved as follows:

1) That it gives its permission, in general, for Jews of military age and of Greek citizenship in Egypt to enlist as volunteers in the British Army in Palestine. A list of these volunteers will be dispatched via the Greek consular authorities in Egypt to the Army Ministry so that their position can be regularised.

2) Similar permission is granted to the Jews of Greek citizenship of Thessaloniki who do not belong to the classes already called up.

3) Permission is also granted to those belonging to the classes already called up to enlist in the above volunteer units on condition that they state that on reaching Palestine they will agree to serve in the front line.

The Prime Minister   The Members
E. Venizelos   E. Repoulis
                                                    N. Politis
                                                    I. Tsirimokos
                                                    M. Negrepontis
                                                    A. Papanastassiou

12

The Jewish Community of Kavala to the Sub-Governance of Eastern Macedonia

resolution   Kavala, [illegible] February 1919.

The Jews of our city, wishing to express their good will to the Thessaloniki Conference, hereby resolve:

1) In the name of all the Jews of Kavala, to express their gratitude and congratulations to His Excellency the Prime Minister of Greece, Mr Eleftherios Venizelos, to His Excellency the Minister of Foreign Affairs, Mr Politis, and to the Greek Government for the kind statements made both by the Prime Minister and by the Minister of Foreign Affairs, and also to the Christian Press of Greece for its sincere and spontaneous support of our national cause.

2) Palestine must be returned to the Jews, who have a natural entitlement to it.

3) In those cities in which the Jewish element is evidently predominant, governments, regardless of state should recognise their national authority, i.e, recognition of religious leaders, schools, language, etc.

4) Regardless of the state in which they are settled, Jews should enjoy equality of rights; that is, they should enjoy the same rights towards the state as their other fellow-citizens residing in it.

5) The present resolution will be submitted to the Sub-Command of Kavala,

which will forward it to His Excellency the Prime Minister of Greece, Mr Eleftherios Venizelos, and the Minister of Foreign Affairs, Mr Politis. It will also be submitted to the Conference of Jews meeting in Thessaloniki.

13

L. Paraskevopoulos, Chief of the Army General Staff, to the Ministry of Foreign Affairs

telegram   Athens, 11 February 1919

In connection with the Jews of Kavala, I have the honour to report that no pressure is being exerted on them. During the first days of the occupation of Kavala, the city was in a state of such filth that general compulsory labour was ordered to clean it. The proportion of Jewish inhabitants was indeed larger during the first days of the occupation because of the general deportation of Christians by the Bulgarians, but it was wrongly thought that only Jews are used. I have ordered a reduction in the compulsory labour of Jews and proved to the Chief Rabbi that the accusation was unfair. I received the reply from the Chief Rabbi that he acknowledged the groundless nature of the charges, and also received a report from the Jewish community of Drama stating unequivocally that the Jewish community has never been subjected to different behaviour on the part of the Greek military or civil authorities. A similar report from the Prefect of Drama states that no complaints from Jews have ever been submitted to him.

14[*]

E. Venizelos, Prime Minister, to the General Governor of Macedonia

telegram   Paris, 12 February 1919

Je vous communique dépêche que je viens de communiquer à notre gouverneur Salonique et je vous prie d' en donner copie au Ministre de l' intérieur pour sa gouverne.

'Les israélites se plaignent de ne pas être suffisamment représentés au conseil municipal de Salonique. Il est nécessaire réparer cette inégalité à cause de la campagne menée en Europe et Amérique. Dans ces conditions étant donné que d' après loi municipale le nombre des conseillers municipaux d' une ville comme Salonique doit être supérieur au nombre actuel, veuillez nommer un certain nombre d' Israélites de façon à rétablir une proportion logique entre nombre conseillers juifs et ..... [sic] population israélite. Pour expliquer cette mesure vous pouvez vous appuyer dans l' arrêt que vous prendrez sur nécessité porter nombre fixé par la nouvelle loi municipale. Veuillez télégraphier d' urgence exécution'.

ATTACHMENT A TO 14

A. Pallis, Deputy General Governor of Macedonia, to the Ministry of Foreign Affairs

telegram   19 February 1919

Number of City Councillors before implementation of Law 4057 was twenty, of whom four were Jews, twelve Greeks and four Muslims. On installation of City Council, in accordance Law 4057, Council consists of thirty members, of whom sixteen Greeks, eight Jews and six Muslims. Number of Jews thus doubled, and Jewish President of Council (Assael) elected. After installation of City Council, Chief Rabbi visited Mayor and congratulated him for the proportion kept. To remove all possible complaints, however, we will fill the first places to fall vacant with Jews.

ATTACHMENT B TO 14*

E. Venizelos, Prime Minister, to the General Governor of Macedonia

telegram   Paris, 19 February 1919

Je m' empresse de vous communiquer dépêche suivante que je viens d' adresser à notre Gouverneur Général Salonique. En réponse à notre dépêche

télégraphique concernant nombre conseillers municipaux je vous prie person-
nellement vous entendre de ma part avec le maire de Salonique et nos meilleurs
amis parmi les conseillers municipaux afin que trois conseillers Grecs donnent leur
démission et nous permettent ainsi nommer trois Israélites. Ce sacrifice de leur
part me facilitera grandement ma tâche ici et mettra fin à une malveillance contre
notre administration. Du reste les élections municipales qui ne tenderont [sic] pas
mettront toute chose au point.

ATTACHMENT C TO 14*

E. Venizelos, Prime Minister, to the General Governor of Macedonia

telegram   Paris, 2 March 1919

Je vous communique dépêche que je viens de communiquer à notre gouver-
neur général Salonique.
'Votre réponse transmise par Ministère Affaires Etrangères ne me satisfait pas.
Veuillez dire au maire Salonique qu' il est urgent que deux ou trois conseillers de
nos .....[sic] pussent être amenés à démissioner pour être remplacés par Israélites.
Des raisons d' ordre plus général m' obligent à insister à cela'.

15

*Frangistas, the Thessaloniki Press Bureau, to the Ministry of Foreign
Affairs*

telegram   21 February 1919

In reply to your 3843, Chief Rabbi authorises Thessaloniki Press Bureau to
categorically deny news item published in Swiss Jewish review concerning alleged
persecution of Jews in Greece. 'On the contrary we live in complete security. We
are grateful to the Greek Government for its toleration and sympathy towards the
Jewish nation'.

ATTACHMENT A TO 15

E. Venizelos, Prime Minister, to E. Repoulis, Deputy Prime Minister

telegram   Paris, 22 February 1919

Please take note of the telegram from Mr Kaklamanos dispatched to the Ministry of Foreign Affairs concerning the action of Jews in Thessaloniki in collaboration with their co-religionists in Poland and Romania. I believe it essential that all the Jewish communities in Greece should take the action necessary to address telegrams as rapidly as possible to the Jewish Association in Paris protesting against the representations made by certain irresponsible persons portraying the Jewish element in Greece as being the victim of persecution. In appealing to the sincerity and sense of justice of the above communities, we are sure that they will hasten to declare that the Greek Jews have no complaints, that they enjoy complete equality before the law and that they have always received the most impartial support of the government. As for the manner in which this action is to be taken, please consult with Mr Konstantinis, to whose feelings I personally appeal. Please let me have copies of the telegrams sent.

ATTACHMENT b TO 15[*]

N. Politis, Minister of Foreign Affairs, to E. Venizelos, Prime Minister

telegram   Paris, 22 February 1919

Je vous communique dépêche que je viens de recevoir de M. Kaklamanos avec prière d' en porter contenu au plus vite à la connaissance Gouverneur Général Salonique.

'D' après des informations M. Saias délégués juifs ont tenu diverses réunions courant semaine dernière. Délégation Juifs Salonique y a présenté question Juifs Grèce mais congrès se considérant incompétent a décidé rapporter question à association Israélite Paris. On se serait adressé aussi communautés Israélites

Constantinople et Smyrne pour demander formuler leurs voeux dans pétition adressée à association. 60 délégués représentant Pologne Roumanie et Grèce ont été reçus par M. L. George pour lui exposer leurs doléances. Président du conseil anglais a déclaré délégués Juifs Grèce qu' il n' était pas renseigné sur situation Juifs Pologne et Roumanie mais quant à ceux habitant vieille et nouvelle Grèce il se refusait admettre ... [sic] leurs différends avec Grèce. Il a ajouté que ses renseignements lui permettaient d' être catégorique sur ce point et qu'il demandait preuves pour croire contraire. Délégués Salonique après cette entrevue ont adressé à Lloyd George requête pour exposer doléances. Pour prendre devant je prépare sur données que vous m' avez fournies un memorandum que je compte remettre Gouvernment anglais et quelques personnes pouvant avoir voix dans la question. M. Saias part pour Paris après-demain'.

—∞—

Attachment c to 15*

Alliance Israélite Universelle

telegram   [without specific date] 1919

Nous avons été péniblement supris de voir que quelques-uns de nos congénères sans avoir aucune qualité pour parler au nom des communautés Juives de Grèce se permettent de faire des déclarations et des démarches tendant à faire croire que sous l' administration hellénique les Juifs sont traités sur un pied d'infériorité vis-à-vis des autres sujets hellènes. Nous devons nous élever vivement contre ces sortes d' agissements. Egaux devant la Loi à nos concitoyens grecs, jouissant de la plénitude des droits civils et civiques et de toutes les libertés reconnues aux autres communautés, nous n' avons aucun motif de plainte contre le Gouvernement Hellénique dont l' attitude envers l' élément Juif a été jusqu' ici des plus paternelles et qui nous a toujours accordé la plus impartiale protection.

—∞—

16

J. Cazes to the General Governor of Thessaloniki

letter   17 March 1919

In reply to your communication No. 8866 of the 13th inst., I have the honour to inform you that at the conclusion of the Zionist Conference I ceased to be Chairman since further action has been assigned to an executive committee of which I am not a member.

The extract from the resolution concerning the national autonomy of Jews is identical with the relevant extracts of the resolutions passed by the conferences of Jews all over the world.

The essential points of this national autonomy, which coincides with religious freedom, were outlined in the speech delivered by Mr Matalon and can be explained as follows:

The Jews express the desire that in such places as they are gathered in numbers they should live as communities recognised by the state, that they should be able to have schools which, in parallel to the language and the learning of a curriculum, should also cultivate their own national language and endow their children with a Jewish education so as to mould them into good patriots and also good Jews who will be of use to their country and their ethnic group. They wish also that the Jews living in such a manner should have their own hospitals and their charitable institutions, for moral and religious reasons, and that these schools and foundations should receive the same assistance from the budget as the schools and foundations operated by the state. The Jews request also that, since they do not work on Saturdays, they should not be compelled to observe Sunday as a holiday, and likewise with the other non-Jewish holidays, and that they be permitted to conduct ceremonies of marriage in accordance with their religion. Ultimately, it is requested that the concept of 'national rights' should be the medium by which the Jews maintain themselves as a nation. In this there is nothing damaging to the interests of the state in which the Jews live. On the contrary, if the Jews enjoy these rights they will be happy citizens who contribute to the welfare of the state in which they live.

In view of this, I do not believe that there is any scope for incompatibility with the interests of the state.

17

S. Protonotarios, Director, the Thessaloniki Press Bureau, to the Ministry of Foreign Affairs

confidential report   Thessaloniki, 25 April 1919

Further to my telegram of the same number, I have the honour to inform the Ministry that, as I reported in my communication No. 270 of 16 April, the efforts of Italian propaganda to internationalise Thessaloniki and obtain autonomy for Macedonia are gradually becoming more obvious. For this purpose, on the one hand, it slanders the Greek administration abroad and, on the other, it collaborates with the Bulgarian *komitadjis* and certain Jews in Thessaloniki – most of them foreign nationals – in an effort to cause disturbances in order to justify and strengthen its malicious policy.

This is confirmed by the discovery on the part of the military authorities of collaboration between Italian soldiers and certain Jews employed by the Zionist Club of Thessaloniki to arrange the escape of Bulgarian and German prisoners by disguising them as Italian soldiers and by the arrests made here and on the border, almost every day, of Bulgarians wearing Italian uniforms.

Subsequent to this discovery, the Secretary of the Zionist Union, Mr Ouziel, editor of the official Zionist mouthpiece *Esperanza*, and Mr Hassid, a member of the Union, were arrested. In a discussion with some members of the Board of Management of the Union, who visited me, I emphasised the strict integrity of the Greek judiciary and expressed the opinion that it would be in the interests of the Zionists to seize the opportunity of taking some deliberate action – such as issuing an official announcement – to proclaim once more that they are law-abiding citizens of the Greek state and that they deplore groundless publications such as those of the Italian periodical *Israel* of Rome. The Zionist Union hastened to send to the periodical, and to communicate to me, in copy, the announcement which I dispatched to the Ministry by my telegram of the same number and sent a summary abroad, on the basis of which I issued the semi-official announcement published in all the Greek and foreign-language news-papers of Thessaloniki, which I enclose as an extract from the newspaper *Opinion*.

18

A. Adossidis, General Governor of Macedonia, to the Ministries of Foreign Affairs, Transport and the Army

report   Thessaloniki, 30 April 1919

The Jewish community in Thessaloniki, understandably distressed by the absolutely miserable state of thousands of families who were victims of the fire and who have been living for two years in the most dreadful conditions in caves, ruins, barns and dilapidated huts, asked me as early as January to mediate with the Government so as to obtain housing for the fire victims who are most exposed to danger – the number of which has increased by several hundreds as a result of the storms and flooding that broke out here three days ago.

At the same time, however, since the new Vardari settlement is incapable of dealing with even one quarter of the urgent needs of the fire victims, the Jewish Community addressed itself to the Allies in the hope of purchasing the facilities necessary to house the destitute and homeless Jews. For this purpose, the Community was offered, at an extremely low price, the Italian huts erected around and among the Greek Engineer Corps barracks and in which Italian troops had been living since they first landed here more than two years ago.

However, the use of these huts, which in themselves are inadequate to contain all those in urgent need of housing, would be impractical unless the Engineer Corps barracks were also made over to the Community.

On this question, there were two main points of view: on the one hand, there was the purely charitable view, which saw the Government as being under an inescapable obligation to house the numerous victims of the fire.

On the other, there were the purely political considerations, which can be summed up as follows:

For some time, propaganda being circulated around the Peace Conference has attempted to depict the Greek administration as creating a position of disadvantage for the Jewish population of Thessaloniki. It has repeatedly been said and written, *inter alia*, that our purpose is allegedly to remove the Jews from Thessaloniki, and that we have deliberately multiplied the hardships caused them by the fire.

Some of the Italian newspapers have been systematically campaigning on these points, and I have no doubt that it was in connection with these malicious activities that the Italian Government ordered the Army huts here to be turned over to the Jews almost free of charge, so as to create, by contrast, an unfavourable impression of us – who, we must admit, were slow to take action for the care of the fire victims.

It should be noted that Americans have also become involved in this question on an unofficial level, that the issue has resulted in reports on the part of members of the American Red Cross who belong to the Jewish element, and, in general, that the matter has become extremely delicate.

For all these reasons, I saw it as expedient to agree to mediate in favour of the granting of the Engineer Corps barracks to the Jewish Community, particularly in view of the fact that the barracks were built, without a prior expropriation order, on a site belonging to the Jewish Community. Even today the site has not been expropriated.

The Prime Minister, to whom, after briefing the General Staff in Thessaloniki, I addressed myself for a solution to the question, telegraphed instructions to the Commander-in-Chief that the above barracks were to be placed at the disposal of the Jewish Community.

Now, as soon as the Italians vacate the barracks, I will take delivery of them from the military authorities and hand them over to the Chief Rabbi's office.

However, in order to settle the families of the fire victims there, the Community will have to convert the interiors of the barracks and the adjacent (Italian) huts and it calculates that the cost of this will be approximately 150,000 drachmas. Before this money can be spent, it will be necessary: 1) For the land belonging to private citizens on which the barracks were constructed – also without previous compulsory purchase – to be acquired on behalf of the Community by expropriation. This land is marked in yellow on the diagram dispatched to the Ministry of Transport. 2) A document will have to be issued by the Ministries competent in the present instance – that is, the Ministries of the Army and Transport – showing that the barracks have been ceded and thus safeguarding the Community's possession of them.

As for the ceding of the barracks, we have secured the consent of the Prime Minister, who has approved that the barracks should be ceded without payment of their value in accordance with the proposal that we submitted to him. However, we believe that when, at some later date, the manner in which the State will be compensated for the settlements of Aghia Paraskevi and Kara-Hussein which it has constructed for the fire victims is settled, the same method ought to be applied to the settlement of compensation for the barracks.

We have therefore, the honour to ask you to propose the issue of the appropriate Royal Decree concerning the expropriation of the land on which the Italian huts stand, informing us, as soon as possible, of the action taken in this case.

ATTACHMENT TO 18*

A. Adossidis, General Governor of Macedonia, to N. Politis, Minister of Foreign Affairs, Greek Legation in Paris

telegram   10 March 1919

Il résulte enquête circonstanciée à laquelle me suis livré que deux questions principales sont source effervescence israélites Salonique. D' abord loi reconstruction ville spécialement articles 13 et 37 stop. Intéressés redoutent avec raison que délai indemnisation fixé à 31 Decembre 1919 ne soit reculé à infini par lois subséquentes stop. Réprouvent aussi, comme je l' ai longuement exposé au Président septembre disposition article 37 suivant laquelle au cas où il résulterait du chef expropriation et application loi déficit, ce déficit soit réparti entre propriétaires expropriés, au lieu d' incomber à propriétaires à venir.

Ai tout lieu de croire que même en ce moment si gouvernrment s' engage à donner sans retard satisfaction sur ces deux points parti mécontent se désagrégera.

Seconde cause mécontentement c'est grands retards déjà constatés et prévus pour avenir dans application loi reconstruction Salonique stop. Dans ces retards propriétaires sont pour quelque chose, en raison obstruction qu' ils ont faite au travail cadastrage avec espoir faire échouer application loi obstruction qui n' a été neutralisée que par récentes lois imposant fortes amendes à obstructionnistes. Mais retards incombent surtout à services d'abord à commission plan dont travaux risquent de traîner si Ministre n' intervient pas énergiquement stop. Ensuite service cadastrage dirigé par Lambadarios qui s' applique à établir cadastre exagérément parfait et minutieux, qui ne saurait être achevé avant plusieurs mois alors que de l' avis de toutes personnes compétentes, un cadastre sommaire susceptible être achevé quatre mois serait tout a fait suffisant, stop. Je ne saurais trop insister sur nécessite urgente que Président intervienne auprès Ministre Communication afin activer cadastrage stop. Ce qui rend plus brûlante encore question reconstruction c'est état misérable sinistrés israélites logeant dans décombres, sous – sols humides et caves stop. Fais mon possible pour activer achèvement quartier Vardar destiné à loger environ six mille sinistrés stop. Mais prie Président télégraphier à Ministre communication activer de son côté. Prière aussi télégraphier Quartier Général Grec donner avis favorable à demande communauté Salonique appuyée par délégués israélites américains pour cession petites casernes génie Grec actuellement voisines hôpital Hirch, actuellement occupées par Italiens et que nos autorités militaires avaient construites sur terrain appartenant communauté israélite Salonique stop. A proximité susdites casernes se trouvent baraques italiennes que quartier général italien offre à communauté intention propagande stop. Ces baraques avec casernes grecques pourraient loger vingt mille sinistrés stop. Ai fait démarches réitérées persuader quartier général donner avis favorable, mais n' ai rien obtenir jusqu' ici stop. Mon avis est que ces petites casernes baties sur terrain communauté israélite doivent être cédées gratuitement et non comme juifs proposent contre indemnité stop.

Envoie par courrier texte ici reconstruction stop. Crois savoir que Président sera saisi question par délégués américains conférence agissant sous pression israélites influents Amérique. Insiste aussi sur nécessité modification loi expropriation susceptible amener contrecoup favorable sur attitude juifs Salonique.

❦

19

S. Protonotarios, Director, the Thessaloniki Press Bureau, to the Ministry of Foreign Affairs

very confidential report   Thessaloniki, 29 May 1919

I have the honour to inform the Ministry that in some circles of Jews and foreign residents here the view is being circulated, though not in specific terms, that despite the liberal intentions of the Government where other racial groups are concerned, it will be very difficult, if not impossible, for Thessaloniki to prosper after peace under the current system of complete economic and customs equality with the other ports of Greece. The reduction in the rate of reconstruction of the city caused by war conditions, the absence of a sufficient expanse of hinterland, and the preference discerned by the above circles for Piraeus rather than Thessaloniki will have the effect – once more according to these circles – of demoting Thessaloniki to the status of a secondary port in Greek Macedonia which will be incapable of safeguarding the prosperity of the current commercial population which, in such circumstances, would see no other salvation than emigration. As a result, the wish is being expressed that Thessaloniki might enjoy the benefits of being a free city or a free port.

During a conversation yesterday with M. Grayet, the French Consul here, he told me clearly that Thessaloniki is a port not only for Greece but also for all of south-eastern Europe, for which reason it ought, for the time being, to be declared a free port and, perhaps later, a "free city", and that he had repeatedly reported to Paris in this vein.

The Consul added that if this view were to prevail, "the Greek state would lose the customs duties it collects today, but Greek Macedonia, on the one hand, and the entire Balkan Peninsula, on the other, would benefit a hundred-fold, as would the export trade of the great Powers which trade with Thessaloniki and the Balkan states".

Jewish circles, who are very probably aware of these thoughts among some of the foreigners in Thessaloniki, seem to have taken unofficial action in the same spirit and are about to proceed – if, indeed, they have not already done so – to submit official representations to the Paris Conference or to some of the Allied governments calling for Thessaloniki to be declared a free city or a free port.

There are those who believe that the departure of the Chief Rabbi for Palestine, reported in my telegram No. 355, was a result of his wish to be absent from the city if and when the question of Thessaloniki is raised officially.

The fact that competent Jewish circles have to date avoided denying the spurious and malicious news item published in the Bulgarian newspaper *Zora* on 20 May (of which I enclose a true translation) may, furthermore, not be unrelated to this intention on their part.

❦

20

A. Adossidis, General Governor of Macedonia, to the Ministry of Foreign Affairs

telegram   Thessaloniki, 4 February 1920

The French-language Jewish newspaper *Indépendant*, as well as a delegation of the Jewish community of Drama who visited me, suggested that government's attention should be drawn to the decision of the authorities in Drama to forcibly impose Sunday as day of rest for Jews. This decision disturbed the Jewish community of Drama.

On Prime Minister's instructions, I have undertaken to negotiate with the Jewish community some matters of their concern. Included is the issue of whether

Saturday or Sunday should be regarded, optionally, as day of rest. I believe it would be expedient, if the above mentioned news item is correct, that the measure taken by the authorities in Drama be lifted in order to prevent turmoil among Jews here and abroad.

⇢⇠

21

A. Adossidis, General Governor of Macedonia, to the Ministry of Foreign Affairs

confidential letter   12 February 1920

In reply to your telegram in connection with the issuing of voting booklets to the Jews of Thessaloniki, I have the honour to inform you of the following.

The Committee which, in accordance with the law, issues the voting booklets is chaired by Mr Nikolaou, Judge of First Instance, who has been paid for this service. From the first moment at which the Committee began its work, complaints were submitted to me by the Jewish Community against the Chairman of the Committee, who was alleged to have refused to facilitate fully the Jews presenting themselves to receive voting booklets and to have obstructed them in a large number of ways, in contrast to the facilities he extended to the Greek population.

Unfortunately, it would appear that these complaints are not groundless. They are the result not only of the narrow view taken by the Chairman of the Committee of the interpretation of the relevant provisions of the law, but primarily of his deliberate and scandalous action in trying to avoid issuing voting booklets to the Jewish population. In view of this, we summoned the above judge, to whom we pointed out that he should not only cease to put obstacles in the way of those presenting themselves to him but that it was his duty to facilitate them in every possible way so that, on the one hand, it would become possible for all those entitled to exercise their right to vote and, on the other, to avoid the justifiable complaints of the Jews, which might prove harmful in a variety of ways.

Despite these warnings, the said judge persisted in applying the same approach to the Jewish element. We summoned him once again and reprimanded him on his conduct, which is an embarrassment to the Greek Administration. I was compelled to seek the intervention of the President of the Court of Appeal and of the Deputy Public Prosecutors of the Appeal Court, Mr Tsapralis and Mr Toman, in the hope that they would bring all possible pressure to bear in this respect.

However, while it now appears that the judge in question is facilitating, in a lawful manner, the Jews, he has begun to apply his former policy to the Muslim population.

I would have taken the appropriate measures against the above person had he not been a judge. Although the task of issuing booklets is now approaching its end, and only 15 days are left, I believe it is politically expedient and necessary that this judge should be recalled forthwith and that his alternate should take over as Chairman of the Committee so as to make it possible for the remaining voters to be issued with their booklets.

⇥⇤

22

S. Protonotarios, Director, the Thessaloniki Press Bureau, to the
Minister of Foreign Affairs

confidential letter   Thessaloniki, 24 March 1920

Minister

With reference to my telegram under the same number to the Ministry (Press Department), I have the honour to inform Your Excellency that for some time now the Jewish circles here, and even the Zionist nationalist circles, have been manifesting greater satisfaction than ever before over the favour which the Government has displayed towards the Jewish element.

In a recent conversation with another Jew, the President of the Jewish Community, Mr Cazes, summed up the Jewish view as follows:

> "In view of the Government's concessions over the question of military service and of its generally favourable attitude, we have to admit that if it were not for the question of the reconstruction of Thessaloniki the city would be a true paradise for the Jews."

Even the opposition manifesting itself to date over this question has begun to fade somewhat as a result of disillusionment over the hopes that foreign intervention would be effective, as a result of the vigorous attitude adopted by the Ministry of Transport, as well as of the facilities which the Ministry has undertaken to grant property-owners.

Those in the circle of the Jewish Community, apparently imbued with a disposition of this kind, have recently declared their intention of collaborating politically with the governing Party at the forthcoming elections. Yesterday's Jewish feast of Yom Asekel ('collection day'), dealt with in the above telegram, revealed a highly favourable attitude towards the State and the Government. The speech delivered by Mr Ascher Mallah, President of the Zionist Federation of Greece, was interrupted by loud applause when he emphasised the favourable attitude towards Zionism of His Excellency the Prime Minister, of Your Excellency, of Mr Adossidis, General Governor of Thessaloniki, and of the undersigned.

Having been invited by a communication of which I attach a copy to take the floor after the above festival, I delivered a speech – composed by arrangement with the General Governance – which I also enclose, in the form of a cutting from the newspaper *Opinion*, together with a cutting from the Zionist periodical *Renacencia Giudia* concerning the overall conduct of the feast.

The large audience interrupted, with loud cheers, the points in my speech where I referred to His Excellency the Prime Minister and Your Excellency, and in particular to your statements to *Pro-Israel* of 1 July 1917.

⎯⬖⎯

23

S. Protonotarios, Director, the Thessaloniki Press Bureau, to the Minister of Foreign Affairs

confidential press report   Thessaloniki, 17 May 1920

Minister

I have the honour to submit, herewith, to Your Excellency a cutting from the French-language Jewish newspaper *Indépendant*, published in Thessaloniki, revealing the difficulties encountered by the negotiations taking place in Athens between the Government and Mr Cazes, President of the Jewish Community of Thessaloniki, in connection with the privileges of the Community. This article which, according to reliable information I have received, draws on a report by which Mr Cazes calls for the support of the Community in overcoming the difficulties encountered, did not have the anticipated effect because it does not reflect the beliefs of all the Jews of Thessaloniki but only of the leading plutocratic and theocratic section of the community. The Community Council has indeed never been elected by universal ballot among all the Jews but only among those of them who, having paid the community tax (*petcha*), are entitled to take part in the elections. These persons number no more than about 2,200 out of the Jewish population of approximately 68,000 souls. None of the non-taxpayers – that is, the majority of the Jewish population – are represented on the Community Council. These Jews include, on the one hand, the workers and socialists, who account for approximately half the population, and, on the other, numerous liberals who would welcome freedom of thought and religious conviction. These people believe that if the current demands of the Jewish Community were to be codified, the Greek State would appear to be granting its official protection to a plutocracy and a reactionary theocracy in the midst of the twentieth century, since all the Jews of Thessaloniki, regardless of their religious convictions, would be obliged to comply with certain religious formalities.

Many powerful Jews who are liberal and well-disposed towards the State, including the editor of the Jewish newspaper *Pueblo* (Mr Veissi), have told me that the existing situation which compels all Jews to observe Sunday as a day of rest is damaging for them. Additionally, the new bill should avoid establishing Saturday as a day of rest for all Jews since it would be to the detriment of the material interests of many of them. These people say that the bill to be passed, in order to protect the Jews, ought to lay down simply that "the Jews are free to observe Saturday as a day of rest". The same discretionary principle should, according to the same Jews, be applied to the question of the community tax. My interlocutors contend that if the Government were to agree to enter into negotiations with representatives of the Jewish unions, associations and socialists in addition to the representatives of the Community, who should first hold elections by universal suffrage in order to elect their true representatives, then the view which would emerge would be that expressed by my informants, based on the principle of 'toleration and liberty'. My interlocutors particularly emphasised that under no circumstances should the Jewish Community be allowed to have responsibility for drawing up the school curriculum, since it is quite considerably influenced by Zionist circles who are opponents of assimilation and standard-bearers of nationalism, as stated in my report No. 30 of 18 January of this year. I conclude with the note that the other representative in Athens of the Jewish Community is Mr Yakov Modiano, an Italian citizen and a relative of Dr Leon Modiano, who was responsible, from Thessaloniki, for creating the uproar abroad about the reconstruction of the city.

24

Law 2456
Concerning Jewish Communities

We, ALEXANDER,
KING OF THE HELLENES,
resolving unanimously with Parliament, hereby decide and pronounce the
following.

CHAPTER I
Jewish Communities. Their assets. The Community Council and its jurisdiction.

Article 1
In those towns of the Realm where more than twenty Jewish families dwell permanently and a synagogue is functioning it shall be possible to establish by Royal Decree a 'Jewish Community'. This Community will be recognised as a legal entity of public law.

Article 2
In each city, town or village there may be only one Jewish Community, to which all the movable and immovable property already in existence or to be acquired in the future shall belong.

Article 3
The Jews permanently resident in Greece shall be subject in matters of religion to the Jewish authority based in each Community.

Article 4
In order to carry on and advance their charitable, religious and educational purposes, the Jewish Communities may accept donations *mortis causa* or *inter vivos*; they shall, more particularly, be entitled to accept: a) voluntary offerings and the product of collections carried out among the members of the Community or other Jews for the general purposes of the Community or for a specific one. Such offerings and collections shall be deemed to have been accepted by the Community and as having created in its favour a legal claim. When taken up publicly within the Jewish synagogue or in the residence of the donor, it is permitted in the case of offerings and donations in the synagogue for the testimony of witnesses to stand as proof and for such offerings made in the home to be proved by oath and admission before a court; b) the fees set for the ceremonies and certificates of all

kinds of the Jews as well as for the cession of grave sites in the Jewish cemeteries; c) the contributions imposed by each Community upon its members (*petcha*); d) the special fees collected by ancient custom as *gabella* by the Communities on the foodstuffs and beverages called *kosher*, including the special sugars and unleavened bread and the flour for the unleavened bread consumed at Passover.

If so laid down by Royal Decree issued on the proposal of the Community, and on condition that the said Royal Decree has determined the manner of debiting, the rights and fees of sub-paras (b) to (d) above may be collected from those in arrears in accordance with the law on the collection of public revenue on the application of the Community.

Article 5

1. The Jewish Communities shall be entitled to found and maintain schools for Jewish children.

2. The curriculum of subjects taught in these schools, drawn up by the Communities, must not conflict with the general laws of the State, must be in accordance with accepted educational principles and must ensure that the official language of the State is taught adequately. Apart from the teaching of Greek as a language, the teaching of history, geography and science is to be conducted in Greek. The staff to teach the Greek classes will be appointed in the same manner as the staff of Greek state schools. All the other lessons on the curriculum drawn up by each Community may be taught in whatever language each Community may wish.

3. The functioning of the Jewish schools must be in accordance with the principles of school hygiene accepted for the state schools.

4. The schools of the Jewish Communities will be subject to state inspection. The duties and rights of the inspectors will be determined by Royal Decree.

5. The pupils and graduates of the Jewish schools may, after passing entrance examinations whose details will be determined by Royal Decree, register as pupils of state primary and secondary schools.

6. The graduates of the Jewish schools shall be deemed to have the same qualifications as graduates of state schools of the same level on condition that the curriculum of these schools has been approved by the Ministry of Education as equivalent to that of the corresponding state schools, and the graduation examinations in those schools shall be conducted before a committee and on terms to be determined by Royal Decree.

Article 6

The Community Council in each Community shall manage the Community's assets and, in general, all its affairs including, in particular, matters connected with the charitable and educational institutions and the foundations operated for religious, charitable and educational purposes.

*Teachers of the Jewish schools circa 1920. Prior to the Holocaust the Jewish community
supported nine public schools and two private schools. Archive of Jacob Stroumtsa, Israel.*

Article 7
The Community Council may take valid decisions to sell movable or
immovable property belonging to the Community, to purchase movable or
immovable property to belong to the Community and, in general, on all matters
in connection with the interests of the Community.

Article 8
The Community Councils shall appoint special committees to administer the
synagogues and manage the property belonging specifically to them and shall also
appoint the committees to operate the charitable and educational institutions of
the Community.

These committees will be answerable exclusively to the Community Councils.

CHAPTER II
Representation of the Communities

Article 9
Each Community shall be governed in matters of religion by a Chief Rabbi
appointed and dismissed by Royal Decree issued on the proposal of the Community.

Article 10

1. The Community shall be represented before the administrative authorities by the Chief Rabbi, or, when he is absent or incapacitated, by the President of the Community.

2. When the President, too, is absent or incapacitated, the Community shall be represented before the Courts by the Deputy President.

CHAPTER III

The Rabbinate and its jurisdiction

Article 11

1. Each Community shall have a Rabbinical Council, chaired by the Chief Rabbi.

2. The Rabbinical Council will decide on all religious matters of interest to the Community.

Article 12

1. A Religious Court under the title Beth-Din and appointed by the Rabbinical Council shall decide on the following matters:

2. On the cases of Law 147/1914, Article 4, sub-para. (a), and in particular on instances of the institution and dissolution of marriages between Jews, of the personal relationships of the spouses during the marriage, of alimony for wives and children, and of the return of dowries and bride-goods in the event of divorce, on condition that the relevant claims stem from holy Jewish law.

Article 13

The Beth-Din Religious Court shall take final decisions on the dissolution of marriages, relying on holy Jewish law.

Article 14

1. The decisions of the Beth-Din Religious Court shall be declared enforceable, on the application of the interested parties, by the President of the Court of First Instance of the district in which the Religious Court issuing the decision is sitting in accordance with Article 119, sub-para. 2 of the Code of Civil Procedure.

2. The President of the Court of First Instance shall examine only whether the decision was issued within the limits of the jurisdiction set for the said Court by the present law. In the event of the President of the Court of First Instance declining to declare the decision of the Religious Court enforceable, the case shall be brought, by application, before the competent Court of First Instance and shall be heard under the procedure for summary trials. The Court of First Instance, too, shall confine itself to examining only whether the decision was issued within the limits of the jurisdiction of the Court.

CHAPTER IV
Concerning the National Chief Rabbi

Article 15

1. On the application of the majority of the Chief Rabbis in the State, the General Assembly of Chief Rabbis appointed in accordance with the present law may elect one of their number as National Chief Rabbi.

2. The National Chief Rabbi may set up a Religious Court of the Second Instance which will judge the decisions of the Beth-Din Religious Court as a court of appeal.

3. Matters concerning the election of the National Chief Rabbi, his jurisdiction over the Jewish Communities and the other Chief Rabbis, the setting up of the Religious Court of Second Instance, the work of that Court and the general procedure for appeals shall be settled by Royal Decree.

CHAPTER V
The Community Assembly

Article 16

1. The supreme authority of each Community shall be the Community Assembly, to which the Chief Rabbi and the Community Council shall be answerable.

2. The Community Assembly of each Community shall consist of a number of delegates who shall be defined by the by-laws of each Community and elected by all male Jewish Greek citizens over the age of 21 years permanently resident in the area of the Community and not deprived of their civil rights.

3. By way of exception and for a period of ten years from the entry into force of the present law, Jews who are foreign nationals and were at the time of passing of the present law members of the Community Councils of the former Jewish Communities shall take part in the Community Assembly and may be elected as members of the Community Councils and Management Committees.

CHAPTER VI

Article 17

Each Jewish Community shall submit for approval to the Ministry of Ecclesiastical etc., Affairs its own statutes, which shall be ratified by Royal Decree and come into force as of their publication in the Government Gazette[#].

[#] Government Gazette = *Ephimeris tis Kyverniseos*

The statutes shall specify:

a) The operation of the Community organisation.

b) The rights, duties and jurisdiction of the Community Assembly, the Chief Rabbi, the Rabbis, the Community Council, the Special Committees and of the sub-division into sections of the Rabbinical Council in accordance with Articles 11, para. 2 and 12.

c) The rights and contributions of Article 4 and the manner in which they will be collected.

d) The manner in which the Chief Rabbi and the delegates to the Community Assembly will be elected, the number of members of the Community Council, the Rabbinical Council and the Beth-Din Religious Court and the manner of their election, and the terms on which the Chief Rabbi or the Rabbinical Council may appoint the other functionaries of the Jewish religion.

CHAPTER VII
Penal sanctions

Article 18
It shall be forbidden for any functionary of the Jewish religion to conduct any ceremony of marriage or circumcision or any funeral or other religious ceremony without the written permission of the Chief Rabbi of the Community.

Offenders will be subject to disciplinary and penal sanctions in accordance with Article 487 of the Penal Code.

Article 19
Any person who, without being a lawfully appointed Chief Rabbi, presents himself as holding such office or performs an act permitted only to a Chief Rabbi shall be punished in accordance with Article 227 of the Penal Code.

Article 20
Any person usurping the duties of a Rabbi of the Jewish religion, of whatever rank, without having been lawfully appointed as such or usurping such duties outside the region for which he has been appointed shall be punished in accordance with the provision of Article 227 of the Penal Code.

Article 21
On the application of the Chief Rabbi or the President of the Community, any person wilfully selling as *kosher* foodstuffs and beverages which are not *kosher* shall be subject to the penal provisions and their civil consequences as well as to the legal procedure concerning unfair competition.

Article 22
The legal provisions and exceptions protecting the non-commercial things of

divine law under the prevailing religion shall also be applied to the sacred and holy objects of the Jewish religion, on condition that the categories of these objects have been defined by Royal Decree.

CHAPTER VIII
Tariff exemption

Article 23

The items imported from abroad by the Jewish Communities in connection with the religious worship of the Jews, such as the unleavened bread for Passover or the flour for the making of such bread, the special sugar imported for Passover, and procurements of items useful for teaching in the Community schools, with the approval of the Minister of Education, shall be free of all import tariffs and all state and municipal duties.

CHAPTER IX
Grants from the State and Municipalities

Article 24

All State and Municipal annual budgets may provide for grants to the Jewish Communities to further their educational, religious and charitable purposes in accordance with similar grants to other communities.

CHAPTER X
General provisions

Article 25

Jews who are unable to keep their commercial books in the Greek language may validly use their own dialect (Ladino) or the French language for that purpose.

Article 26

1. Jews shall be entitled to treat Saturday of each week instead of Sunday as a day of rest, being subject to the legal provisions concerning Saturday as a holiday in the same manner as other Greeks are subject to the provisions concerning Sunday. However, those who prefer to have Sunday as their holiday may do so without interference, on condition that they inform the police authorities of their choice.

2. The administrative authorities will be under the obligation not to summon Jews to appear before them on Saturdays or on Jewish religious feast days, which will be determined by Royal Decree as exceptionable. The same obligation shall apply to the staff of the criminal investigation departments, apart from exceptionally urgent cases.

Concert at the 'Dancing Place' in Thessaloniki on 9 September 1920. In the first row, fourth from left, is Dr Albert Menache. Dr Menache had been a student at the Conservatory of Toulouse and played the flute. He was a member of the Auschwitz-Birkenau prisoners' orchestra. Archive of the Jewish Community of Thessaloniki, donated by Isaac Menache (Athens) and David Amir (Israel).

Article 27

The details of implementation of the present will be regulated by Royal Decree.

The present law, passed by Parliament and ratified by Us today, is to be published in the Government Gazette and enforced as a law of the State.

In Athens, 29 July 1920
ALEXANDER
The Minister of Ecclesiastical etc. Affairs, D. Dingas
Was confirmed and the Great Seal of State affixed
In Athens, 29 July 1920
The Minister of Justice I.D. Tsirimokos

25

A.Zaimis, Minister of Welfare, to the Ministry of Foreign Affairs

letter   Athens, 16 February 1921

We have the honour to inform you that Mr Dimitrios Gounaris, Acting Prime Minister and Minister of the Army, announced during his tour of Thrace – in response to an appeal from the Jewish Community of Adrianople – that fifteen thousand drachmas would be granted to the Orphanage and ten thousand drachmas to the Jewish Community Hospital. In implementation of this undertaking, we requested the General Governor of Thrace to pay the above sums from the credits allocated to the welfare of Greeks abroad.

However, as can be concluded from the attached telegram, the Committee of Management, basing itself on the letter of the law, refused to agree to the financial support of the Jewish Community referred to above, which, nonetheless, ought for reasons of expediency to be provided.

Consequently, we hereby request you, bearing the above in mind, to send the above sum as a matter of urgency via the General Governance of Thrace, drawing it from the contingencies account.

If, however, for any reason you are unable to do this, please propose to the Ministry of Finance that it supply the special fund of Law 2378, mentioned in telegram No. 9041 of the General Governor of Thrace.

26

G. Roussos, Minister of Foreign Affairs, to all Greek Embassies and Consulates

circular   Athens, 4 September 1924

With reference to the inquiries submitted by various Consular Authorities as to whether Jews and Armenians holding certificates or passports issued by the Greek Authorities of Eastern Thrace stating that the holders are citizens of one of the municipalities in what was then Greek-occupied Eastern Thrace may be regarded as Greek citizens and entered on the registers of the Consulates in that capacity, thus enjoying Greek protection, we have the honour to inform you of the following.

Thrace, Eastern and Western, was annexed to Greece by Law 2493 of 10 September 1920, Article 8 of which laid down that the inhabitants of those areas who had been subjects of the state previously occupying it acquired Greek nationality by virtue of the annexation.

Consequently, those persons resident in Thrace at that time acquired Greek nationality *ipso jure* and have continued to hold it after the Treaty of Lausanne, at least, as far as Greek law is concerned.

It follows that when such persons present certificates from municipalities in Eastern Thrace or Greek passports in which they are stated to be citizens of the municipality in question, they are to be recognised by us as Greek citizens and added to the registers of the Consular Authorities. At the same time they should submit applications to be transferred to another municipality in the State.

Please dispatch such applications, with the certificates or passports, to the Ministry of the Interior for the appropriate action.

However, the interested parties should be aware that it may not be possible for them to contend that they hold Greek nationality *vis-à-vis* Turkey.

→◆←

27

I. Minardos, Director, the Thessaloniki Press Bureau, to the Thessaloniki General Governance

confidential Press report   Thessaloniki, 21 August 1926

I have the honour to submit to you, in translation, an article from the newspaper *Indépendant*, of yesterday's date (20th inst.) concerning the work of the Committee which is dealing with the founding of a Greek-Jewish secondary school in Thessaloniki.

In connection with this committee, there is information to the effect that the Zionists who serve on it intend to give the foundation under study a purely Zionist character, turning their backs on any tendency for it to be used for the assimilation of the Jews with the rest of the population. Those who believe that this is the case point as evidence to the deliberate failure to invite Messrs. Kon, Dzachon and S. Modiano, known for their pro-assimilation views, to take part in the recent meetings of the committee. The *Indépendant* reports that these three members of the committee were incapacitated and did not take part in the meeting, but the *Progrès*, published yesterday morning (before the *Indépendant*) reports that many of the members of the committee were unable to attend because they had not been invited.

This is particularly regrettable, notes the newspaper, because the irregularity in the invitations prevented some of the most able members from taking part in the most recent meetings, which were far from unimportant. The newspaper returns to the question again today, in greater detail, and in reply to the *Indépendant* explains how the meeting of the committee was improperly convened.

The Zionist journalist David Florentin, one of the members of the committee, was heard to say that care will certainly be taken to ensure that Hebrew will be taught as widely as possible in the school.

Furthermore, a poor impression has been created by the participation on the committee of a well-known young Jew (who until recently worked as a journalist) who, indeed, has been appointed secretary of the committee: this person is completely lacking in seriousness of purpose and is known to be one of the most loyal supporters and admirers of Abraham Recanati of *Pro-Israel*, the leader of the intransigent chauvinists in Thessaloniki.

❖

28

The Director of the Thessaloniki Press Bureau to the Ministry of Foreign Affairs

confidential Press report   Thessaloniki, 24 September 1926

Further to my reports Nos. 3659 and 3701, I have the honour to submit to you enclosed herewith, in translation, an article entitled 'Let's Found the Jewish Secondary School This Year' published in yesterday's issue of the newspaper *Renacencia Giudia* as a continuation of the newspaper's campaign against the Béne-Bérith scholarships and the attendance of Jewish children at Greek schools, together with a letter from Mr Kon, inspector of the Jewish Community schools, published in the same issue. This is the letter of which the newspaper had published some extracts in an earlier issue (a translation of them was submitted with my report No. 3659). It has now been compelled to publish the entire text.

It can be seen from this new article in the Zionist newspaper that attempts are being made to set up a Jewish secondary school of a purely Zionist nature as soon as possible, regardless of the Jewish-Greek school whose foundation is being studied, out of the fear lest the foundation of the latter should prevent the establishment of the former. This is because the Greek-Jewish secondary school would not be in a position fully to satisfy the Zionists since it would not be under their complete control.

<hr>

ATTACHMENT a TO 28

The Thessaloniki Press Bureau to the Ministry of Foreign Affairs

newspaper article from Renacencia Giudia   Thessaloniki, 22 September 1926

Title: 'Let's Found the Jewish Secondary School This Year'

All those who are interested in the affairs of our community and already know the extent to which the work being done by our community schools has grown, unanimously believe and declare that the Jewish secondary school is needed – and needed urgently, at that – and that no serious efforts have yet been made to found such a school. Béne-Bérith, which two years ago formally promised us at a large public meeting that it would realise the plan seems to have abandoned the intention it had at that time, replacing it with the scholarships which, as we demonstrated in our last issue, are quite without benefit. The managers of Béne-Bérith and the successive community education committees seem to have been profoundly scared by the burden which the Jewish secondary school would place upon them. However, after detailed study involving all those who know about educational matters, we have formed the conviction that the plan for the secondary school is something which we could carry out with the resources we possess and which would be very easy for the community. Our conviction was further strengthened by the information we received to the effect that the work of community education can find the 60-70,000 drachmas required each year to sustain the scholarships without colossal efforts.

According to our information and the reliable opinion of those in a position to know, the Jewish secondary school, all of whose pupils would pay fees, could not have a deficit - as an average for the first three years after its foundation - of more than 150,000 drachmas per annum. And if all the money spent on the scholarships were to be channelled into the Jewish secondary school (which the current holders of the scholarships would attend), this deficit would be reduced by half: that is, to the sum of 75,000 drachmas.

In order to make up the other half of the deficit, the above committee (the education committee) would have to spend a sum out of its budget, which amounts to 1,500,000 drachmas per year. We know that this sum of 1,500,000 drachmas is just sufficient to maintain the community schools already in existence; yet we also know that without a secondary school, to constitute the essential supplement and crown of our educational work, the efforts made, the money spent on schools, and all the devotion and self-abnegation of our community teachers are wasted. As long as those leaving the community schools are unable to make use of the knowledge they have acquired there to make their way in life in a manner and under conditions similar to those who have graduated from private and foreign schools, we will certainly not have the right to say that we have done anything to further the education of the broad mass of our people.

It would not be excessive to spend 2-3% of the budget of our community schools to cover part of the deficit of the Jewish secondary school. If this left a deficit of 30-40,000 drachmas per year, it would not be hard to find such a sum. Of course, as the secondary school grows, so the deficit will increase proportionally. However, this should not frighten us, if we bear in mind the example of what happens with the charitable institutions, which rest on very strong foundations. A few years ago, without any resources at all and with four orphans, we opened the *Aboav Orphanage*, and thanks to the dedication of a few members of *Misrachi* and a handful of Zionists, that orphanage now supports 31 orphans at an annual cost of 200,000 drachmas. We are sure that a public which can contribute 200,000 drachmas to the *Aboav Orphanage* can also contribute a further 200,000 drachmas if there are energetic people to ask for it in the cause of maintaining the secondary school, which, if not more essential than the orphanage, is at least as necessary.

We have been talking recently about founding a Greek-Jewish secondary school. It strikes us that the founding of our Jewish secondary school ought in no way to depend upon, or be subject to, the success of Professor Louvaris' plan. Unfortunately, the foundation of the Greek-Jewish secondary school is not dependent upon the disposition of the distinguished pro-Jewish Professor Louvaris.

Past experience allows us to believe that the plan will remain for a long time at the mercy of the various forms of political instability in this country and of the favourable or unfavourable dispositions of the various rulers. There is a place in our community for a Jewish secondary school. For that matter, it would not be difficult to implement the plan once the action of Professor Louvaris bears fruit, but we should not consign ourselves to waiting for a Messiah who may never appear.

Consequently, our duty is to get down to work IMMEDIATELY [*sic*] and to begin – this year, even – the establishment of the first two classes of the secondary school so that within a very few years it will be possible for the plan we espoused so warmly years ago for an advanced Jewish school to become reality.

The Béne-Bérith lodge, which has already undertaken formal obligations in this spirit, should abandon its expensive scholarships and devote itself to the foundation of the secondary school. The assistance of all Zionists is assured in advance.

ATTACHMENT b TO 28

Z. Kon, Inspector of the Jewish Community Schools of Thessaloniki, to Frances, Editor of the Renacencia Giudia

letter   Thessaloniki, 5 September 1926

Last week we referred to a letter addressed to us by Mr Kon on Community Education work and published the main points of it, thinking that the letter was not intended for publication. It was addressed to Mr Frances in person and from a number of points of view it would have lost its importance if it had been published in full, given that it was composed in a tone quite different from that used by our newspaper. However, to prevent any confusion arising and to forestall misunderstandings, we publish the entire letter below, as it stands.

Concerning the work of Community Education and its scholarships

Dear Mr Frances,

I have been informed that you are among the editors of the *Renacencia Giudia*. If this is true, allow me to be so bold as to address these few lines to you on the subject of the campaign being waged by one of your journalists - who I believe ought to sign his articles - against Community Education.

My wish is not to reply in detail to these attacks. One does not reply to things of no significance, or to a person who engages in futile activities. Community

Education is a Jewish task *per se*, and the idiotic thought of using it for the assimilation of pupils attending Greek schools has never crossed the minds of those who administer it. Those pupils have an excellent teacher of Hebrew and Jewish studies. Everyone is familiar with, and applauds, the curriculum of the work being done.

I shall thus not dwell on that point.

However, I would like to draw your attention to the fact that your journalist returned to the question in the most recent issue, writing and stating in public that Community Education has appropriated money intended for the founding of the Jewish secondary school. This is a gross slander against which I hasten to protest in the strongest terms. However, I should like to know what money is being referred to, since I am aware only of a promise that money will be made available for the Jewish secondary school without any payment of such money, even the slightest, ever having been made.

I would thus be grateful, dear Mr Frances, if you were to categorically deny this calumny. It would be wrong of you to give credence to such ridiculous myths. Nor should we forget that this defamation did not come from the pen of any ordinary journalist, but from the mouthpiece of the Zionist Federation of Greece, whose articles have a certain influence.

29

The Director of the Thessaloniki Press Bureau to the Press Department of the Ministry of Foreign Affairs

Press report   Thessaloniki, 29 September 1926

Further to my earlier reports by which I submitted to you various articles published by Zionist newspapers here declaring their opposition to the attendance of Jewish children at our schools and in particular to the scholarships granted by the Béne-Bérith association, I have the honour to submit, attached, in translation, a letter from Mr Kon, inspector of the Jewish community schools, which appeared in *Pueblo* two days ago (on the 27th of the month).

In this letter, Mr Kon, who was among the persons primarily responsible for the Béne-Bérith scholarships and has been the target of attacks on the part of Zionist journalists for that reason, demonstrates that a Jewish secondary school such as that which the chauvinist Jews are attempting to set up would serve no purpose since it would be unable to gain state recognition. In order to achieve this, and for the pupils graduating from the school to be able to enter university, its curriculum would have to be in accordance with the legislation in force. But in this case the complete teaching of only one language is possible, and not of three as is the aim of those promoting the cause of the foundation of a Jewish secondary school.

—◈—

ATTACHMENT TO 29

Z. Kon, Inspector of the Jewish Community Schools of Thessaloniki, to the Pueblo newspaper

letter   Thessaloniki, 27 September 1926

"A Jewish Secondary School or a Greek-Jewish Secondary School?"

The question of the foundation of a Jewish secondary school, so often discussed in the past, has been raised once again in the Jewish Press, and everyone, without exception, acknowledges this to be essential for the education of future generations which will be fully developed and conscious of their duties towards their people. There is little need to go into the numerous details in order to demonstrate the urgent need for the establishment of such a foundation. Furthermore, the time for discussing such an important question seems to have gone, and all that one can do today is to concentrate all the good efforts being made to realise the project. The dispute which broke out recently over the question does not seem to have produced any results. What is of interest now is practical work, without the pompous phrasing uttered on the matter by word-coiners who have no knowledge of the subject. Only the setting up of the Jewish secondary school is entitled to find itself on the agenda. That is the only subject to concern us in our study. We shall, in addition, be happy if we are able to clear the field for the discussion, given that at the moment it seems to be strewn with obstacles.

The question immediately presents itself as one which is urgently in need of resolution. There is general confusion between two concepts: with the exception of a very few experts, the public tends to put on an even footing – if one can use that term in such a case – the Jewish Lyceum and the Greek-Jewish secondary school. They are not the same thing at all. The Jewish Lyceum can be no more than a secondary school in which the effort made in the Community primary schools to balance the teaching of three languages will be continued. There, efforts will be made to reach a compromise between three demands which are in conflict with the principles of educational theory, in its proper sense. In other words, efforts will be made to satisfy the demands of the laws of the country in connection with the Greek language, of the pro-Jews in connection with Hebrew (the ancient tongue, not Ladino), and of the parents, the majority of whom cannot conceive of education without the teaching of the European languages, and of French in particular.

If, however, this educational balance is maintained in our primary schools (with considerable sacrifices), it will not be possible to achieve it in a secondary school. In a secondary school or a lyceum it is essential to teach one language which will generally be dominant over the others. Otherwise, secondary studies will be impossible. The curriculum of a secondary school contains at least 18 to 20 periods of technical subjects. It is obvious that a similar number of periods will have to be set aside for the teaching of one language. What will be left over for the other two languages? Far too few periods to satisfy the other claims. This is so true that in all the world's secondary schools it has proved impossible to set aside more than 3-4 periods per week for foreign languages. This is in order to exclude the possibility of overburdening the pupils, as is done in some schools, where the object is to implant all of human knowledge in the brains of the pupils within a very short space of time – without any result whatsoever.

Let us assume for a moment that by cutting back and reducing and adding on we have succeeded in preparing a curriculum which appears to meet the demands we referred to above. Would this be sufficient to ensure that our secondary school stood on firm foundations? I do not think so.

There is also another very important question which we ought to look into: the question of what will happen after graduation. No secondary education is of any value unless it leads to higher studies – that is, to the university. The leaving certificates issued by such a school would not be recognised by the Ministry of Education, for the very simple reason that the school itself would not be recognised.

I have already heard numerous complaints from those who, knowing nothing of the mechanisms of secondary schools, are unwilling to accept this (i.e, non-recognition by the Ministry, etc.). That, however, is the way things are. No matter how loudly we may protest and cry out, no matter how often we may make representations and send delegations to Athens, we will be unable to cause a change in a fundamental law which governs the state schools in Greece – as well as in other countries. In France there are excellent private secondary schools where the education provided is no less comprehensive or sound than that of the state schools. Nonetheless, it is a requirement for matriculation at a university that the candidate should have a certificate equivalent to that of a secondary school, and such certificates are issued only by the state by means of public examinations conducted before a committee appointed by the state. That is what happens in all the world's schools.

Thus I cannot see how a Jewish secondary school would function in the manner wished for by some of our friends WITHOUT THE RECOGNITION OF THE STATE [sic]. People will say, that can be achieved. If it is so, we should expect that the state will impose a curriculum on us. That is something which does not tempt me to touch on the question of a Jewish secondary school.

—◆—

30

The Thessaloniki Press Bureau to the Ministry of Foreign Affairs

confidential Press report   Thessaloniki, 23 December 1926

I have the honour to report that the Jewish newspapers here have systematically published a series of articles arguing in favour of the need for a set grant to be obtained from the Greek state for their community schools in Thessaloniki. It is common knowledge that the absence of such a grant has always been the subject of appeals and protests on the part of the Jewish element in Thessaloniki, who contend that they are entitled to be put on the same footing as the Greek element since they bear the same burden of taxes and other obligations to which Greek citizens are liable.

Given that on this occasion the action being taken is more systematic and intensive, the Jews believe it to be certain that they will achieve the objective they set themselves so many years ago. Yesterday, citing exclusive information from Athens, the *Indépendant* announced that its Editor (and Member of Parliament) Mr Bessantchi had made representations to Mr Louvaris, General Secretary of the Ministry of Education, who promised that a separate item of expenditure for the Jewish schools of Thessaloniki will be included in the budget. I attach the relevant issue of the *Indépendant* (22nd inst.), adding that today's issue announces that Mr Louvaris is expected here and will settle with the Jewish Community Council the details of the financial aid to be granted.

Of course, there is no more justified claim that the Jews of Thessaloniki could make in the present instance. On the other hand, it is equally right that the money to be made available by the Greek state should be used to educate true Greek citizens and to teach them the Greek language. This, however, will not be achieved as long as the Jewish schools teach the Greek language as a by-work. No wholesale change of this situation is possible, but a step forward has to be taken. In view of this, and when the contents of the confidential report which I submitted to you on the 16 inst. (No. 4906) concerning the Greek-Jewish secondary school are taken into account, I believe that it would not be deemed inexpedient for the assistance applied for to be paid, by whatever formula, as salaries disbursed directly by the Treasury to those who already receive salaries for the teaching done by the Jewish community.

The Jewish community is not prepared under any circumstances to accept such assistance, and has even rejected it when covered by legislation (see my communication No. 4906) in Law 3215 of 1924. However, I do not believe that anyone would describe the satisfaction of such a demand as just and therefore necessary. Encouragement should not be given to the Jewish tactics in their approach to government policy. When they are claiming a right, they demand that they should not be treated on a footing inferior to that of the Greek population. However, when it comes to fulfilling their obligations, they make demands creating an environment which could cause great national damage.

In the letter published in the issue of the *Indépendant* which I attach, Mr Kon, inspector of the Jewish community schools, attributes ill will to the Ministers of the Greek state, treating them sarcastically as would-be liberals. However, he passes in silence over the fact that he was opposed to the payment of the salaries of the Jewish teachers from the Treasury, as those of the Greek teachers are paid (1924), and the Community threatened at that time that any of the teachers who took advantage of the provisions of the law would be dismissed.

---

3 I#

The Director of the Thessaloniki Press Bureau to the General Governance of Thessaloniki

very confidential Press report   Thessaloniki,16 December 1926

I have the honour to report that for some weeks now the Ladino Jewish Press here has been conducting an intensive campaign arising out of the results of the

---

The original document is partly damaged. The part missing is marked by [......]

parliamentary elections of the 7th ult. and of a series of articles published in the *Pueblo* by Mr Elie Veissi, its other editor, advocating the urgent need for assimilation of the Jewish element into the Greek population, attributing the amazing success of the Communists in the said elections to Zionist opposition to this assimilation.

Given that this extensive series of articles - confined exclusively to the Ladino Press so as to prevent the Greek-language Press from becoming aware of the campaign being conducted, something which would not be in the interests of the Zionists – has revived the entire Jewish question and revealed or confirmed the objectives on various matters of those in charge of the affairs of the Jews in Thessaloniki, I wish to submit to you a detailed report as soon as I finish assembling various particulars which are essential for this purpose. Although I shall deal in greater detail in my report, *inter alia*, with the question of education, which is the most important issue concerning the Jews, I feel the need to submit the present to you in order to inform you of the recent action taken in this respect by the Jews here.

You were informed in earlier reports submitted by me to the Ministry of Foreign Affairs, and more specifically by my report No. 2434 of 9 July 1926, of the Greek-Jewish committee set up on the initiative of Professor Louvaris of Athens University to study the manner in which a Greek-Jewish secondary school might be founded in Thessaloniki.

While everything appeared to be turning out correctly, it suddenly emerged from reports published in late August in the Francophone Jewish Press that there had been a split among the members of the committee and that the three Jews who were regarded as liberals and inclined towards assimilation had not been invited to attend the meetings of the committee.

In my report No. 3295 submitted at that time (on 21 August) I informed you that as a result of this dispute the Zionists participating in the committee were attempting to give the public foundation whose establishment was being considered a purely Zionist nature, suppressing any tendency to use the foundation for the assimilation to us of the Jewish element.

A mud-slinging match in the newspapers then followed, in which a leading role was played by Varuch Cimbi, the secretary of the committee, a person of very little seriousness of mind who is quite unsuitable for such a task; he was a correspondent at that time of the *Indépendant*, is among the extreme Zionists, and is a prominent member of the intransigent Zionists here called *Misrachi*. Since that time, there has been no further talk of the Greek-Jewish secondary school despite the fact that the report of the committee ought to have been submitted to the Jewish Community for approval and then to the Government for adoption.

Although the matter was then forgotten and nothing was ever said about it unless one of the Jewish newspapers wished to depict the Government as failing to provide for the education of the Jewish element, the violent and astonishing articles published in *Renacencia Giudia* – which, let it be borne in mind, were noticed only by ourselves and by no other Greeks – then followed. These articles in the official organ of the Greek Zionists declared war on the attendance of Jewish children at Greek schools and called for the Greek-Jewish secondary school to be set up as a purely Jewish foundation. These publications and the debate around them were covered in a series of reports submitted by me: Nos 3483/8.9.36, 3659/19.9.26, 3701/22.9.26, 3719/24.9.26, 3797/29.9.26, 4022/15.10.326, 4232/29.10.26, and 4309/4.11.26.

While the matter of the Jewish secondary school had been forgotten, there occurred the appointment of Professor N. Louvaris who, undoubtedly, is not aware of the articles on the project he had inspired and, in general, of those concerning the education of Jewish children in Greek schools. His appointment was greeted with enthusiastic comments of the Press. In a leader published yesterday, which I attach hereto, the newspaper *Progrès* extols the appointment and deals with the whole subject of Jewish education, mentioning also the matter of the Jewish secondary school. In a conversation I had with the newspaper's Editor, I told him that he ought not to have mentioned this matter as long as it is not known whether the Jewish Community has approved the Committee's project nor if it has submitted it to the Government which, in the absence of such submission, cannot be held responsible for the non-realisation of the educational project under consideration. This gave me the opportunity to discover that the local Jewish leaders, being certain of eventually achieving their object of creating a Jewish school, had postponed the whole matter. Now that Mr Louvaris has been appointed General Secretary - as confirmed by *Progrès*, in the clipping I am sending you - they hasten to examine the Committee's project and submit it to the competent authorities hoping that, given his very favourable attitude towards them, they will be able to achieve their aim.

[.....] to be managed by the community as it wishes, and which are destined for the education of Jews who, rather than Greek, will learn not Hebrew – about which they profess to be so concerned but of which they are entirely ignorant – but Ladino and French, so that foreigners who come here after 14 years of Greek sovereignty hear those languages spoken everywhere and, thanks to them, there are seven foreign-language newspapers in Thessaloniki as opposed to a small number of Greek-language papers.

They will reject any assistance offered in the near future in any form other than payments to the Community which it can manage as it pleases, and despite the persistence of the Inspector of primary schools they will prohibit the teachers in the Jewish school from benefiting from Law 3218, by which (Article 11) they are assimilated to the teachers in Greek schools and receive the same basic salary.

I reserve the right to revert in more detail to other points in connection with Jewish issues as soon as I can assemble the relevant supplementary particulars. Please bear in mind that we are facing difficulties in monitoring the Jewish Press rapidly and continuously since a Greek-speaking Jewish citizen has not been appointed as assistant to the special translator from Ladino.

32

D. Kalapothakis, Director, the Thessaloniki Press Bureau, to the Ministry of Foreign Affairs

telegram   Thessaloniki, 4 February 1927

I have the honour to submit to you, enclosed herewith, two telegrams from Athens published in the French-language Thessaloniki newspaper *Indépendant* (1st and 2nd inst.) in which its Editor, and Member of Parliament, Mr Bessantchi, reports from Athens that he has received assurances from various members of the Government – whom he mentions by name – concerning the provision of a grant for the Jewish schools here.

According to information I have gathered since the publication of these telegrams, the members of the Jewish community and Zionist circles more generally are confident that the question has been resolved in accordance with their wishes. The Jewish schools will receive support in the form of the payment of a specific sum into the funds of the Community without any control as to whether this sum is actually spent on the schools. Thus, the payment from the Public Treasury of any salaries or salary supplement to the Jewish teachers will be avoided.

ATTACHMENT a TO **32**[*]

The Thessaloniki Press Bureau to the Ministry of Foreign Affairs

neswpaper article from Indépendant   Thessaloniki, 2 February 1927

Title: "Une Subvention sera accordée aux écoles israélites".

Athènes 15 heures.-

M. Bessantchi député de Salonique s'est entretenu avec M. Kafantaris au sujet de l' allocation d' une subvention gouvernementale aux écoles israélites de Salonique. Le Ministre des Finances a promis à notre député d'approuver l'in-scription d'un crédit spécial en faveur des écoles israélites dans le budget du Mi-nistère de l'instruction publique.

M. Bessantchi s'est également entretenu sur le même sujet avec M. Papa-nastassiou qui a aussi promis d'appuyer la demande de la communauté israélite.

M. Bessantchi a été nommé membre de la commission parlementaire provi-soire de l'instruction publique. Il sera également nommé membre de la commis-sion parlementaire des Finances.

ATTACHMENT b TO **32**[*]

The Thessaloniki Press Bureau to the Ministry of Foreign Affairs

neswpaper article from Indépendant   Thessaloniki, 4 February 1927

Title: "Le Gouvernement Accordera Une Subvention Aux Ecoles Israélites.
M. Michalacopoulos Appuiera Les Demandes de la Communauté".

Athènes 15 heures. -

On sait que le Conseil des Ministres aura à prendre une décision sur la subvention gouvernementale à accorder aux écoles israélites.

M.M. Kafandaris et Papanastassiou ont déjà déclaré à M. Bessantchi député de Salonique qu'ils appuieront la demande de subvention de la communauté israélite. M. Bessantchi s'est entretenu ce matin avec M. Michalakopoulos qui lui a textuellement déclaré ce qui suit:

"Non seulement j'appuierai avec le plus grand plaisir l'inscription d'un crédit au budget du Ministère de l'instruction publique pour les écoles israélites, mais encore j'y applaudirai des deux mains et serai exrêmement content de voir accorder une large subvention aux institutions scolaires de la communauté de Salonique."

On peut donc déjà considérer comme certain que la subvention demandée par la communauté israélite sera accordée d'autant plus rapidement que la majorité du cabinet s'y est déclarée favorable.

～≪≫～

33

D. Kalapothakis, Director, the Thessaloniki Press Bureau, to the Ministry of Foreign Affairs

confidential Press report   Thessaloniki, 8 April 1927

I have the honour to report that during March the Jewish Press raised once again the question of education and of the manner in which the Greek language is being taught in Jewish schools. The starting-point for this debate was the annual general assembly of the former pupils of the local schools of the World Jewish Alliance. The President of the Association of Former Pupils, Thessaloniki banker Mr Nehama, in his address, a summary of which was published in *Progrès* (I annex the issue of 1 March), drew the attention of the assembly to "the absolutely urgent need for a considerable section of the curriculum of the Jewish Community schools to be set aside for the teaching of the Greek language. The national language, which coming generations must learn in order to give Greece good Greek citizens who will, at the same time, be no less good Jews".

Mr Nehama went on to refer to the simultaneous teaching of various languages in the Jewish Community schools, pointing out that, as modern educational theory has demonstrated, the teaching of a large number of languages exceeds the brain-power of young children.

The assembly concluded by adopting a resolution expressing the wish "that the Government set up in each part of the town a large number of schools dependent directly on the Ministry so as to make it possible for Jewish children to enjoy the benefits of education without being obliged to submit themselves to serious sacrifices".

In speaking of the simultaneous teaching of a number of languages, Mr Nehama was alluding to the teaching in the Jewish schools where even in the primary classes, the languages which are taught are French (which the Jews regard as a *sine qua non*), Hebrew and Greek.

The words of the President of the Former Pupils of the *Alliance*, the resolution adopted by the assembly, and the subsequent articles published in certain newspapers applauding the views expressed by both stimulated violent protests and attacks by the Zionist Press and Zionists, who openly described those associated with the *Alliance* as enemies of Judaism. However, the latter group have raised the question in a specific manner: the Greek language, they claim, is essential for the Jews so as to allow them to make their living, but as it is taught now the desired result has not been achieved. The cause of this is the insistence of Zionists on devoting many teaching hours to Hebrew.

It should be noted at this point that those who advocate Hebrew are indeed referring to the ancient language of the Jews, which is their national language, and not to the Ladino which is usually regarded, and referred to, as their national language. However, while insisting on the Hebrew language, it is questionable how far they themselves are actually familiar with it. Rather than Ancient Hebrew, Ladino is regarded as their national language which they speak, write and which in general terms is their mother tongue. It is in this language that their newspapers are published and it is the language used by the Jews in general which reveals their nationality wherever they are present.

The Zionists could not, of course, defend Ladino when, as in the present case, they are opposed to the 'assimilators' who favour the dissemination and broader spreading and learning of the Greek language. Yet this would inevitably lead to the disappearance of Ladino and so, without their national language being affected, the distinguishing characteristic of the Jews – which is the survival of Ladino, and that alone – would be eliminated. Even now, when no restrictions are placed on the teaching of Hebrew so that more time could be allocated for the Greek language, Hebrew is neither learned properly, nor is there any need for it in the everyday lives of the Jews. However, they also put forward another argument, claiming that adopting the ideas connected with 'assimilation' of the language would mean to neglect Jewish education and upbringing, thus destroying the feeling of Jewishness.

In articles in *Pueblo*, the journalist Mr Veissi has pointed out quite clearly that "The years to come will be difficult, and it is not advisable that we should waste hour after hour learning a language such as Hebrew, which is of no use to anyone here" (*Pueblo*, 1 March).

And later (*Pueblo*, 19 March), in reply to the mouthpiece of the Zionist federation here, he wrote: "You have come too late to Hebraise the Jews. If the Hebrew language is so close to your hearts, why do you not use it in your families, why do you not teach it to your children? Why do you resist the replacement of Ladino with Greek? What use is it to us – to remind us of the Inquisition in Spain?"

The view advocated by the opponents of this position provided a clear picture of their intentions. In an article published in the *Pueblo* on 6 March (given the fact the other co-owner of *Pueblo*, M. Bessantchi, happens to be a Zionist), it was stated that Ladino should be replaced, but IN GOOD TIME [*sic*]. *La Verdad* (13 March) argued that the Jews should learn Greek AS A SECOND LANGUAGE [*sic*]. But given that the position of first language has never been occupied by Hebrew, nor could it be, it is obvious that the first language will be Ladino.

Mr Veissi in a series of further articles in *Pueblo* – to which I shall refer towards the end of this report – which cost him his removal from the newspaper - explained quite clearly why he insists on the broader learning of Greek by the Jews.

"If I speak about assimilation, I do so not out of Greek patriotism but for the sake of Jewish interests. I believe that in order for the Jews to be able to live here, they need to assimilate to the environment in which they live. The fewer barriers there are between Greeks and Jews, the easier it will be for us to live here. Our purpose is not to be ostentatiously patriotic, but to seek out ways of safeguarding the existence of the Jewish population. If assimilation is not the correct means of doing this, let us suggest another way" (*Pueblo*, 16 March).

"It is our duty to approximate to the Greeks as much as possible, so as to ensure that, as citizens of this country, we differ less from them. We should avoid noisy demonstrations such as those which occurred when Jabotinsky arrived. Interaction at school, in the army and in the mixed clubs will contribute to the elimination of many prejudices and misunderstandings. The Jews will feel more and more at home while the rest of the Greek community will gradually question this fact less and less" (*Pueblo*, 21 March 1927).

In connection with this debate, it should be noted that Mr Veissi found himself fighting this battle more or less alone in the Ladino Press, with the exception of one or two articles published in *La Verdad*. But neither that newspaper nor *Pueblo* belong exclusively to non-Zionist Jews. As a result, the articles in favour of assimilation published in both of them were rebutted in the same columns the following day.

As I noted at the beginning of this report, the signal for the start of the debate was given by *Progrès*, which in its issue of 1 March reported on what had happened at the assembly of former pupils of the World Alliance of Jews. Apart from the enthusiastic article carried by *Pueblo* on the same day, the *Indépendant* (4 March) and *Progrès* (6 March) published articles which - in muted terms, so as not to be accused of blatant hostility towards the Zionists - supported the view that the State should set up Greek state schools for Jewish children. *La Verdad* (3 March) replied in a strong article, as did *Renacencia Giudia* (4 March), the official mouthpiece of the Zionists, which under the headline 'Ecce Homo ...' launched an attack on Mr Nehama, President of the World Jewish Alliance.

In their replies, while violently opposing the 'assimilators', the Zionists pronounce themselves to be in favour of assimilation and to be working for it. But they want and seek assimilation as they perceive it and know it. This, obviously, is no way to make progress on the issue, since in the Jewish schools the Greek language will continue to be taught to a limited extent by comparison, on the one hand, to the dead Hebrew tongue and, on the other, to the basic teaching that Ladino requires. To these languages one has to add French, which they are careful to teach even in the classes of primary school.

"Why" – asked Mr Veissi – "should children be compelled to learn two languages on an equal basis when one of them is absolutely useless?"

During the debate, it was argued by the Zionists that preference should be given to the Community schools, where the Jewish soul is shaped and where good Jewish characters are moulded. In reply, *Pueblo* (4 March) explained that in Zionist fathers the paternal feeling is stronger than the Zionist one, causing them to send their children to schools where they can receive the learning necessary to make a living before their nationalism is cultivated. The columnist (Veissi) reported that one day he had interrupted Mr Florentin, a prominent Zionist and editor of *La Verdad*, who was delivering a speech in favour of the Hebrew language and the Talmud Torah school and asked him whether he [Mr Florentin] sent his son to that school. Mr Florentin did not reply, as it was common knowledge that his son attended another school.

Similarly, the Zionists argued (*Renacencia Giudia*) that they do not send their children to foreign schools, preferring the Altcheh private Jewish schools in Thessaloniki. In reply, *Pueblo* (2 March) published a statement from Mr Altcheh confirming that the opposite was the case.

The foreign schools were not brought into this long and detailed debate, with the exception of an (anti-Zionist) article in *La Verdad* (9 March) briefly outlining the type of propaganda practised (by nationality) in those schools and calling for the founding of sufficient Greek state schools to provide free education which would obviate the need for Jewish children to attend foreign schools. It was admitted, in the same article, that while 1,200 Jewish children (and possibly more) attend the foreign schools of Thessaloniki, only 80 attend Greek schools, and they receive support from an organisation.

The organisation in question is Béne-Bérith, whose work was praised in an article in *Pueblo* (6 March) by the Zionist Mr Bourla, who of necessity overlooked the harsh attack and criticism which that work had attracted six months previously in the columns of the official Zionist mouthpiece *Renacencia Giudia*.

In order to weaken the lively impression created by the articles of the 'assimilators', who had pointed out the inadequate teaching of the Greek language, Mr Kon, the inspector of the Jewish schools, presumably acting at the instigation of the Community Council (on which all the active members of the Zionist Federation serve), during a lecture at the Béne-Bérith Club shortly after the debate began (5 March), contended that sufficient time is set aside for the teaching of Greek (14 periods in the classes of the Asylum as opposed to 14 for Hebrew, and in general 12-17 periods in the classes of primary school as opposed to 10-12 periods of Hebrew). These figures served only to spark off fresh criticism on the part of *Pueblo*: "rather than familiarising Jewish pupils, who have more need than Greeks, with the Greek language, 50% of the teaching time in the classes of the Asylum and 37-50% of the time in the other classes is wasted purely and simply so that the gentlemen in the Zionist clubs can have the inner satisfaction of knowing that they are the people who run the community. Furthermore, it is doubtful whether the pupils leaving the school will know more than a couple of words of Hebrew."

Similarly, the *Indépendant* (7 March) expressed the opinion that it was an abuse to devote so many periods to the teaching of Hebrew, a language which may be beautiful but lacks practical benefits. The newspaper believed that rather than compelling young children to learn Hebrew for 14 periods a week, the teaching of the language ought to be confined to secondary schools, and for only a few periods a week, this system having the further advantage that the pupils would be in a position to benefit from the teaching.

The Greek-language Press hardly took part in the debate at all, with the exception of some isolated comments at the beginning in which it praised the work done by the Former Pupils of the Jewish Alliance. This was the result partly of the failure of the Greek Press to follow systematically Jewish developments and partly (this being the basic reason) of the fact that the debate immediately confined itself to the columns of the Ladino Press. After the article in *Progrès* (6 March), the French-language Press fell silent, in accordance with the tactics of the Jews, who generally and without distinction are agreed that discussion of matters which may present one part of the community in an unfavourable light should be carried out strictly within the 'family circle', which is possible because no non-Jews speak Ladino.

It is particularly noteworthy that the *Indépendant*, whose principal shareholder is the President of the Former Alliance Pupils (although its editor is the Zionist MP Bessantchi), kept silent, confining itself to the publication of a single article (4 March) and to comments on Mr Kon's lecture (7 March).

It is beyond any doubt that the debate conducted contributed to the efforts of those Jews who have declared themselves to be in favour of assimilation with the Greeks. However, it also provided an opportunity for the Zionists to step up their efforts and to succeed in bringing about, in the manner they desired, the long-awaited resignation of one of the editors of *Pueblo* (Bessantchi and Veissi) as a result of their opposing views on the matter in question. Sure enough, Mr Veissi left the *Indépendant* last week, and the newspaper is now in the exclusive owner-ship of Mr Bessantchi (Member of Parliament, elected thanks to the support of the Zionists), as *Renacencia Giudia* (1 April) hastened to announce with great bombast and intense satisfaction.

In parallel, efforts are being made to collect enough subscriptions to make possible the publication of the French-language *Opinion* on a daily basis (so far it has appeared irregularly), so that there will also be a French-language Zionist mouthpiece.

Although in its fear of being boycotted by the Zionists, *Progrès* has for some days adopted a policy leaning towards the nationalist views, it offers no guarantees as a loyal mouthpiece. The Zionists are unable to forget some of the articles it has published on the subject during the last two years. Similarly, Mr Bessantchi at the *Indépendant* would not be in a position, at some given moment, not to do the bidding of Mr Nehama (President of the Former Alliance Pupils).

⸻◈⸻

34

The Inspector of Primary Education in Corfu to the Ministry of Education

report   Corfu, 4 June 1928

Report on the Operation of School No. 3 (the Jewish Quarter) in Corfu

On the conclusion of the school year 1927-1928, we hereby duly submit a brief report on the operation of School No. 3 (the Jewish Quarter) in Corfu.

As you will be aware, this school functions under special conditions and for a specific national purpose. It aims at attracting all the Jewish children, who previously formed the most important body of pupils for the Italian schools here.

This year, the two schools – the two-class boys' school and the single-class girls' school – functioned as a co-educational three-class school, and we are absolutely delighted by the way in which it operated. Our aim, at all costs and in breach of the official curriculum, was to concentrate on the linguistic and national aspects and we have to admit that on these points there has been amazing and unexpected progress.

The systematic operation of these schools, in collaboration with the elementary school, will make it possible that in a few years' time the children of this large community will speak perfect Greek instead of the current mixed idiom of Spanish and patois Italian.

To give some idea of the progress made by the school in terms of numbers, we state below the number of pupils registered and examined during the years in which it has functioned:

School year	No. of pupils registered			No. of pupils examined			Elementary school
	Boys	Girls	Total	Boys	Girls	Total	-
1925-26	105	62	167	95	56	151	-
1926-27	117	74	191	102	72	174	52
1927-28	129	83	212	116	77	193	67

In other words, there has been a steady increase in the number of pupils.

To give some idea of the importance of these figures, it should be noted that in 1924 these schools were closed because the number of pupils attending them was no greater than 10.

We have reached this pleasant result thanks to a series of carefully-planned measures in which we had the willing assistance and valuable support of the Ministry of Education. The Ministry supported our effort, and ignored legislation in force, in order to help us in the promotion and amalgamation of the schools and the formation of the elementary school.

At this point we should not omit to mention the material support we have received during the past year from the Ministry of Foreign Affairs, acting through the local Prefecture. With its contribution of 25,000 drachmas we were able to supply the children with copybooks, abacuses and books, to distribute various prizes to almost all school children, and to provide material support for the Community treasury so as to support the Most Reverend Chief Rabbi Abraham

Schreiber, who has been a sincere friend of Greece and a valuable supporter of our efforts to promote the school.

Unfortunately, the Chief Rabbi has been compelled to depart from the Jewish community here. This obliges us to draw your attention to the question of his successor. A persistent rumour has circulated to the effect that the Chief Rabbi was removed at the instigation of Italian propaganda so that he could be replaced by a successor whose feelings are not pro-Greek. It has even been said that they will instal a Chief Rabbi with an Italian education!! (there is a Rabbinical University in Florence). Chief Rabbi Schreiber, by way of contrast, was German-trained and hostile to all things Italian.

In our confidential report No. 884, submitted last year, we described to you the activities of the former Chief Rabbi and recommended that he ought at all costs to be kept in his position, given that there was a rumour to the effect that he would be leaving because of a shortage of funds. In this respect, we recommended both in the above report and to the Minister Mr Argyros, when he visited Corfu, that material support ought to be given to the Jewish Community for the sole purpose of sustaining the Chief Rabbinate. The material support and fees paid by us to the pupils of the school are minimal in comparison with the generous allowances made by the Italian schools in the form of books, medicines, clothing, footwear, etc.

At the time of the most recent examinations, no support whatsoever was provided with the exception of eight bonds granted by the Mayor of Corfu, since the relevant credit from the Ministry of Foreign Affairs was delayed. However, we have promised that this oversight will be rectified in the very near future.

In order for the school to function still more effectively and with greater expedience, it should have an additional classroom, as dictated by the number of pupils and the unsuitability of the present classrooms. During the coming school year, we expect that the number of pupils will be still greater, since, on the one hand, we will have Primary Six next year and, on the other, the children born in 1922 will be starting school. Thus, we estimate that we will have 235-250 children in the primary school and 75-85 in the elementary school.

By its instrument No. 121 of 21 April of this year, our Supervisory Council proposed that the school should be divided into four classes.

We would like to request the Ministry most warmly to be good enough to provide us with its support this year, too, and order the implementation of our proposal so as to ensure that no irregularities, which may have adverse consequences, occur at the beginning of the school year.

It is a matter of national interest that this school should be supported for a few more years, and for that reason we must act in advance on every front so as to prevent a repetition of the regrettable phenomenon of 1924.

Even if financial considerations are thought to prevent the expansion of the school, we have the honour to report that, in Act No. 178 of 22 June of this year of the Supervisory Council, we indicated two schools which could be amalgamated, thus saving two teaching posts. If this proposal is put into effect, then the Ministry could order the expansion of Corfu School No. 3 into a four-class school.

That is the most important support we could receive from you in order to boost this school, and we are sure that the results will, in due time, prove to be in every respect extremely gratifying.

⇥◆⇤

35

D. Kalapothakis, Director, the Thessaloniki Press Bureau, to the Ministry of Foreign Affairs

Press report   Thessaloniki, 29 October 1928

I have the honour to report that the Thessaloniki newspaper *Progrès* carried an article in its issue of the 26th which notes with regret that none of the Jewish Members of Parliament for Thessaloniki has been appointed to the parliamentary committees, while, by way of contrast, the Muslim MP Halil Galip is among the members of the committee on state education.

In view of this, it was pointed out to *Progrès* and explained on the following day that the non-inclusion of the Jewish Members of Parliament on the committees in question was the result of the fact that they do not belong to any of the political parties and consequently were not proposed by those parties for membership of one or more of the committees. Consequently, this is not an expression of hostility towards the representatives of the Jews of Thessaloniki.

This explanation provoked a violent attack by *Flambeau* (27 October 1928) against *Progrès* for attempting to damage the prestige of the Members of Parliament.

⇥◆⇤

Attachment to **35**[*]

The Thessaloniki Press Bureau to the Ministry of Foreign Affairs

neswpaper article from Le Progrès   Thessaloniki, 26 October 1928

Title: "Aux Commissions Parlementaires Aucun Député Juif n'y Participe".

Les chefs de parti ayant remis au président de la Chambre la liste des députés de leurs groupes, M. Tsirimokos a constitué avant-hier les différentes commissions parlementaires. Nous avons eu le regret de constater que les noms des députés juifs de Salonique ne figurent nulle part, alors que nous avons rencontré des noms de députés turcs, notamment dans la commission d'instruction où siégera le veniséliste MP Halil Galib.

neswpaper article from Le Progrès   Thessaloniki, 27 October 1928

Title: "Les Commissions Parlementaires".
Pourquoi aucun député Israélite n'y figure

Le *Progrès* a rapporté hier que dans les commissions parlementaires constituées à la Chambre pour la nouvelle session aucun député juif n' y figure alors qu' un musulman fait partie de la commission d' instruction. Nous avons tenu à connaître les raisons de cette absence, et une personnalité fort au courant des choses parlementaires nous a fourni les explications suivantes: Les commissions parlementaires sont constituées par le Président de la Chambre sur proposition des partis, avec des membres désignés par ceux-ci. Or c' est ainsi que dans les précédentes législatures, les deux députés israélites, l' un cafandariste l' autre tsaldariste avaient été proposés par leurs groupes et amis à siéger au sein de différentes commissions. M. Isaac Sciaky était alors membre de celle de l'instruction des travaux publics. Il faut donc déduire que les deux députés israélites actuels, n' étant incorporés à aucun groupe politique, n' ont pas été proposés.

Celui qui nous a fourni ces explications a souligné qu' il ne faudrait donc pas voir en cette absence une exclusion quelconque qui ne saurait exister.

36

*D. Kalapothakis, Director, the Thessaloniki Press Bureau, to the
Ministry of Foreign Affairs*

report   Thessaloniki, 6 November 1928

I have the honour to report that the day before yesterday (Sunday) the
assembly of the Jewish Community convened for the last time. I referred to earlier
meetings in my reports Nos 4454 and 4740.

The Minutes of the meeting were published the following morning in the
French-language newspaper *Flambeau* (Zionist) and *Echo tis Thesssalonikis*
(anti-Zionist). From the report in the latter it would appear that the opposition
to the Zionists, represented chiefly by elements of the extreme Left, launched a
violent attack over educational issues. They insisted on the assimilation of the
Jewish pupils into the Greek school population, on the abolition of the fees
charged by the Community schools, and on the improvement of the position of
those teaching in them. The majority – that is, the Zionists – supported a motion
expressing confidence in those managing the Jewish Community's educational
policies and called for a greater part of the curriculum to be set aside for the
teaching of the Greek language, as well as of Hebrew. Despite the efforts made
by the Zionists to have the motion accepted unanimously, they were thwarted by
the obstinacy of the opposition, which insisted on the assimilation of the schools
of the Jewish Community with the Greek schools. As a result, the motion received
24 votes in favour and 8 against.

Flambeau published the motion passed by the assembly, which is as follows:

"The Community assembly notes with gratification the explanations given in
connection with the educational matters. It praises the expansion of Greek
education to all social classes and the retention of the Hebrew programme, which
is the reason for the existence of the Jewish schools. It approves the draft budget
tabled by the Community Council to increase the remuneration of the teaching
staff by a reasonable amount. It expresses its confidence that the Community
Council will, as it has promised and after studying the question, re-introduce free
education in the Community schools."

Despite the persistence of the opposition, those in charge of the Community
refused to provide any information in connection either with the actions of the
committee sent to Athens to mediate in favour of the abolition of the separate
electoral system, or with the reasons for the resignation from the Community

Council of the Thessaloniki banker Mr Moise Benveniste. Lastly, they were under no circumstances prepared to discuss or give any explanation with regard to the violent attack against those in charge of the Community contained in an article in *La Verdad* of Sunday morning. The Editor of the newspaper, former Member of Parliament Mr I. Sciaky, reviewed the entire situation that has come about in the Community, and stated that, although for three years now, the Community Council has been requested to account for its management, it has avoided doing so. What will happen, the columnist asks, when the revenue authorities appear and request a statement? In relation to the management of the Community, *La Verdad* claims that a man called Bitti who is one of those involved in the management – and whose name appeared recently in the Greek Press, which denounced that he had no place in the Jewish Community since he is neither a Greek citizen nor a resident of Thessaloniki – is managing 500,000 drachmas without any supervision because he is useful as a first-class Zionist electoral agent.

❈

37

The Director of the Thessaloniki Press Bureau to the Ministry of Foreign Affairs

Press report   Thessaloniki, 21 August 1929

Further to my report No. 4145 of the 19th inst., I have the honour to report that the polemic between the Greek and the Jewish Press over the question which has arisen in connection with the Jewish vote in the municipal elections of the 1st inst. has continued with some intensity. The Jewish newspapers reported in no uncertain terms, as soon as this became evident, that only two of their fellow-Jews will be members of the City Council. Although two Jews will serve on the Council and despite the allegation that the supporters of the winning candidate, Mr Manos, deleted the other Jewish candidates from the ballot paper, it is nonetheless the case that all the Jews on the list of candidates were successful, since six of them were among the 30 candidates who received the most votes. It may be true that five of the six were ranked between 21st and 30th, and that only the first 20 candidates serve on the City Council, but this does not mean that the Jews were treated unfairly. It is not possible, under a majority system, to ensure that they will be represented in proportion to their numbers, and by candidates ranked among the first in terms of their success rather than among the last. And if it had turned out that the Jews had occupied such positions among the successful candidates of the majority and of the minority as to elect five councillors from the majority and five from the minority, there would have been an outcry in the entire Greek Press, which would have accused the Jews of having succeeded in electing more councillors than the number to which they were entitled. Since the Jews vote as equal citizens and under the majority system, and since the City Council consists of the successful candidates from the majority and the minority, it is only to be expected that there will always be causes for friction and attacks in the Press, since the aim is that the representation of the Jewish community is in proportion to its numbers and any success in excess of that proportion will be seen by the Greek public as a provocation and, at the same time, as a hostile act.

I list below the most important articles published in the last few days, and submit them, attached hereto. However, most of the Greek-language newspapers have been recommending to the Jewish Press that the time has come for it to put an end to its polemics. Even the *Nea Aletheia*, which from the start has defended the Jewish population and has always avoided offending them, carried the following article in this afternoon's edition:

"We have a piece of sincere advice for the Jewish newspapers: the time has come for them to cease their protests and provocations. What is done, is done. They know as well as anyone else that what is done cannot be undone. The municipal elections were the cause of certain misunderstandings, but the result of the elections demonstrated that erroneous judgments and opinions had been put forward, something which the Greek newspapers were the first to admit with complete honesty and which provided the Jewish newspapers with the opportunity to have the last word.

"Do the Jewish newspapers expect any benefit from further articles in the same spirit of provocation and the same bitter and aggressive style? We think not, and for that reason we recommend once again to the Jewish newspapers that they should turn their attention to other matters in which they can promote the interests of the community whose opinions they interpret and friendly co-existence with those whose opinions we, the Greek newspapers, represent."

38

The Director of the Thessaloniki Press Bureau to the Ministry of Foreign Affairs

report   Thessaloniki, 3 October 1929

I have the honour to report that, as is apparent from articles published in yesterday's editions of the Thessaloniki newspapers *Progrès* and *Action*, the members of the Jewish community will demand or attempt to bring about, in implementing the provision of Law 4374 concerning the payment of salaries of the teachers in the Jewish schools (for which see my report No. 1919), that the teachers of the French language should be included. In this connection, *Action* reports that the inspector of primary schools, asked about the matter, replied that in his personal opinion all those teaching in the Jewish community schools, without exception, will receive salaries, apart from those teaching foreign languages if those languages do not form part of the curriculum of the state primary schools.

The publications in question are indicative of the insistence of the Jews that their children should also, in parallel with ancient Hebrew and Greek, be taught the French language even in the primary schools, that is, a total of three foreign languages apart from their mother tongue, which is Ladino. Their proficiency in foreign languages (French, Italian, etc.) is the reason why almost none of the Jews acquire the Greek education which is essential for the people of this city; the consequences of this are their inability to deal with current living conditions, their straitened means (attributed to other factors), and the large-scale departures for other countries, over which they are creating quite a stir.

ATTACHMENT TO 38

The Director of the Thessaloniki Press Bureau to the Ministry of Foreign Affairs

Press report   Thessaloniki, 29 September 1929

I have the honour to report that for some days the Jewish newspapers of Thessaloniki have turned their attention to the new law on education (Law 4374,

Government Gazette Vol. A, No. 296 of 28 August 1929), by which the teachers in the Jewish Community schools are assimilated to those of the state schools with the rank of Class B clerks and will receive state salaries of 1,000 to 1,200 drachmas per month. The first newspaper to announce this was *Action*, on the 22nd inst., and on the same day *Tiempo* reminded its readers than on a previous occasion the Jewish teachers had been invited to receive state salaries but had declined to do so.

The newspapers which have dealt with the matter since that time have referred to the fact that although these state salaries will not entail the complete abolition of the remuneration paid by the Community, they will contribute to the support of the Community education fund as well as improving the financial position of the teachers. Of course, *Action* wrote (on 25 September 1929), the state will supply these sums as a supplement to the salaries already received by the teachers. Such an increase could be seen as excessive at a time when the Community is faced with such needs. Consequently there is a need to seek out a compromise solution, with part of the increase being allocated to improving the position of the teachers. However, under no circumstances should the Community appropriate the entire sum.

According to *Tiempo* (25 September), the state support provided in this way will not lead to any reduction in the annual grant (of 1,200,000 drachmas) to the Jewish Community for its schools. It should be noted that in the past the newspapers have reported that although the grant has been paid regularly over the last 2-3 years, the salaries of the Jewish teachers have not been improved at all.

This is not the first occasion on which the state has declared its intention to support the Jewish schools by undertaking to pay the salaries of their Jewish teachers, given that the teachers of Greek (of both sexes) are supplied from among the staff of our educational system. A provision similar to that of Law 4374 was included in Law 3215, Article 11 (Government Gazette No. 217, Vol. A, of 6 September 1924). The leaders of the Jewish Community at that time declined to comply with the law, putting forward the argument that the salaries offered were inadequate. It would seem, moreoever, that they forbade the teachers to take advantage of that law. In the light of what was known at the time and has been made public later, their refusal should be attributed to the fact that such intervention on the part of the state in the affairs of the Jewish schools was undesirable, since paying the salaries of the Jewish staff involved control – at least the control of its members, who would have to be exclusively citizens of our state. Although the state's offer was rejected (despite the fact that the law could have been implemented regardless of the attitude of the Community Council and that it would have been a tremendous relief to the Community budget), the Jewish Press and the leaders of the Community have missed no opportunity to accuse the state of being unkind to the Jews in that it has not assisted them in the heavy task of education.

Sure enough, as noted above, an annual grant of 1,200,000 drachmas for Jewish education was decided 2-3 years ago, which from now on they consider as having no connection with the payment of the salaries of the Jewish teachers established by Law 4374.

The question naturally arises of whether the offer will once again be rejected. The Zionist Press has been silent on the entire issue. On 27 September *Pueblo*, owned by the Member of Parliament Mr Bessantchi, described as inaccurate the report (in *Action*) that there is to be an increase from 12 to 19 periods per week in the teaching of the Greek language as of the current school year, adding that the Community Council has not yet had an opportunity to turn its attention to Law 4374 and that it will act in concert with the education committee on this matter.

However, in an article published on the 25th inst., which I submit in translation, *La Verdad* reports that despite the economic crisis affecting the teachers in the Jewish schools and although their salaries are always 2-3 months in arrears, they are unwilling to accept salaries from the state treasury and that on this matter they are in complete agreement with the Community Council and the education committee. According to *La Verdad*, to accept these salaries would be a bad precedent, since the state would then be in a position, one day, to lay hold of the Community's assets which are used to maintain the Community schools.

In reply to *La Verdad*, *Action* (26 September 1929) expressed the view that since this is a serious question, the Community Council should not refuse to implement the law before it has consulted the Community Assembly. A refusal to implement the law would not only be to the detriment of the Community budget but would also have a political impact, since to decline the assistance offered by the state to the teachers would be an act of such significance that it would affect all the Jews.

Action returned to the matter in its issue of the 27th inst., reporting that the inspectorate of primary schools will display great tolerance in checking the academic qualifications of the Jewish teachers, on the basis of which they will be recruited. No one, it added, will be excluded from the payment of salary. If need be, a certificate of completion of studies in the Talmud Torah will be deemed sufficient. The newspaper goes on to express the view that the education committee ought not to appropriate the entire amount of the increase in the teachers' salaries provided in this way, reducing the increase, according to rumour, to a mere 10%. The greater part of the increase ought to be used to improve the teachers' living conditions.

Among the French-language newspapers, only *Progrès*, (24 September 1929) has dealt with the matter, simply announcing that under Law 4374 the Jewish teachers will receive salaries of 1,200 drachmas per month. The day before yesterday (27 September), it returned to the matter, reporting that the state's interest in the Jewish teachers had created an excellent impression in Jewish circles.

⌁

39

I. Minardos, Director, the Thessaloniki Press Bureau, to the Ministry of Foreign Affairs

Press report   Thessaloniki, 26 October 1929

I have the honour to report that all today's morning newspapers published the telegram from the Prime Minister addressed directly to them together with his communication to the Deputy General Governor of Macedonia (the Governor being in Athens), both texts dealing with the campaign against the Jews.

Of the only two Jewish newspapers published today, by reason of the Sabbath, the Communist *Avanti* describes the Prime Minister's intervention as "platonic", while *Progrès*, terms it a clear official disapproval of the anti-Semitic campaign launched by certain newspapers as a result of a commonplace incident. The Jewish community of Thessaloniki, it continues, cannot but be profoundly moved by the gesture made in their favour by the Prime Minister, who chose this day, the anniversary of the liberation of the city, to proclaim the absolute equality of all Greeks regardless of their origins and religious convictions.

Makedonia devotes its leading article to the Prime Minister's telegram, noting that as it contains strict instructions to civil servants it will appeal to the proud members of the rest of the population, who had risen in revolt against the anti-Greeks and would not wish to concede things to the head of the state. Nonetheless, the newspaper described the events of the past days as a warning to the elements of the population belonging to other races which will make them see reason. "Either they will acquire a Greek consciousness, identifying their interests and expectations with ours, or they will have to seek a home elsewhere, because Thessaloniki is not in a position to nurse in its bosom people who are Greeks only in name whereas they are the country's worst enemies. Thanks to those people, Greece has been unable to open negotiations with its neighbours and immemorial friends, co-operation with whom it deems of the greatest importance in its international relations."

Phos announced that the pupils are to hold fresh demonstrations today and stressed the need for a huge demonstration of all the school population with the slogan "Down with the foreign propagandists". A reply to publications of this kind came in the form of the following short article published in today's *Tachydromos*:

"Some newspapers are trying to exploit the question of the incident at the *Mission Laique* in order to increase their circulation. Unfortunately, they are striving to enlist the pupils in this endeavour. We assume that this undertaking is beyond reason, since rather than reducing the issue it ought to be used as a starting-point for more general and wholesome thoughts.

"Rather than engaging in attempts to increase their circulation, these newspapers ought to be trying to inspire the Greeks with love and appreciation of their country, their culture, their own value. Can our young people take such a course? If they can, they will deserve our congratulations. All the rest is just to make a stir and show off to serious-minded persons."

The Jewish Press – that is, the newspapers published yesterday evening and the Communist weekly *Avanti*, published this morning – replied to the Greek Press in the spirit of the previous days, as can be seen from the translated précis of their articles submitted with the present report. Today's *Makedonia* once more praises the delegation of the Jewish Community here for condemning the incident at the French School when (the day before yesterday) they visited Mr Papanastassiou, leader of the Democratic Union, who is in Thessaloniki. However, it is reported elsewhere in the same issue that the Community had denied this in the Jewish Press, in accordance with the standard tactics of the Zionists of presenting themselves as law-abiding citizens and advocates of assimilation to the Greek authorities and the Greek public and as intransigent and indefatigable fighters for the benefit of the Jewish public. Yesterday evening's *Indépendant*, however, contains a categorical assurance that the report in *Makedonia* is inaccurate, since neither the incident in question nor the subject of Sunday as a day of rest and the Thessaloniki town plan were touched upon, as that newspaper reported during the meeting with Mr Papanastassiou. The delegation, continued the *Indépendant*, could not condemn an incident that never took place. Nonetheless, the newspaper adds immediately below that the incident was of a kind very common in the schools, which those in the world of the Press, impelled by base motives, had magnified out of all proportion.

On the other hand, a short article in today's *Makedonia* concerning the *Indépendant* (which it did not name, referring to it as a French-language evening paper belonging to a Liberal Member of Parliament expelled from his party) accuses the newspaper of being in the pay of the French and describes Mr Bessantchi as a humble servant of the French Consulate.

⇥⊶

40

Haim R. Habib, locum tenens of the Chief Rabbi, and J. Cazes, President of the Jewish Community of Thessaloniki to the Prime Minister

memorandum   Thessaloniki, 24 December 1929

By its decision No. 437 of 12 July 1929, the Council of Ministers approved a joint proposal of the Ministers of Agriculture and Social Welfare and declared that an area of six thousand eight hundred and fifty square metres, located in Thessaloniki in the vicinity of the 'Adrianoupolites' settlement and belonging to the Jewish Community of Thessaloniki, was to be expropriated for the public benefit, that is, for the urban settlement of refugees in Thessaloniki.

Our Community was recently informed of this decision and, noting that the area for compulsory purchase constituted part of the Jewish cemetery of Thessaloniki, hastened, in its telegram of 12 November to Their Excellencies the Ministers of Agriculture and Social Welfare, to protest and to request that the expropriation decision be revoked.

Indeed, in implementation of the above decisions, the procedure for the determination of compensation for the area acquired by compulsory purchase began a few days ago. In view of this, we believe it is an essential duty resting upon us to submit, with all respect, the views of the Jewish Community on the question of this compulsory purchase, in the conviction that the Government will look upon them with its usual favour.

The area under expropriation is located entirely within the boundaries of the Jewish cemetery of Thessaloniki and is full of graves dating back hundreds of years. Among those graves are many belonging to wise Jews of international renown. These graves have been preserved intact for many centuries, constituting historical monuments of great value for the Hebrew people in general and for the Jews of our city in particular.

Regardless of the historical value of our cemetery, what is most important is the position of cemeteries in general in the Hebrew religion, which accords them unique significance. The Jewish religion expressly enjoins the most profound respect for the cemeteries of the dead, describing them as holy places (the Talmud, interpretation of Sacred Law, Treatise 'Meghila', page 29a and Code Shulchan-Aruch, Code of Sacred Law, Yore Dea, Art. 368, para.1) This respect has always been kept alive, and, as a result, the Jews regard cemeteries in the same light as temples. Indeed, at the most crucial moments facing the Jewish people and in their times of greatest danger, we as individuals and groups of people are accustomed to take refuge at the tombs of our ancestors, our fathers and our wise men the Rabbis, holding religious ceremonies within the cemeteries and invoking divine assistance and protection.

The use of these sacred places for other purposes is thus in itself a sacrilege for our religion, and the removal of the remains of our dead is absolutely forbidden, as stated in explicit references in our sacred texts, according to which "It is forbidden for a dead person or his bones to be moved from an honourable tomb to another honourable tomb, or from a dishonourable tomb to another dishonourable tomb, or as is self-evident, from an honourable tomb to a dishonourable tomb" (Talmud, Jerusalem – Moed Katan, Chapter 2, Code Shulchan Aruch, Yore Dea, Art. 368, para. 1).

It is plain from the above that the area subject to compulsory purchase is a piece of property belonging to the things *extra commercium* of divine justice (Talmud, Avel Rabadi, Chapter 14 and Sulhan Aruh, Yore Dea, Chapter 388, para. 31)[*sic*]. "A piece of ground destined for use as a cemetery and in which burials of the dead have begun may be neither sold nor distributed". As such, the ground must be exempted from compulsory purchase.

Furthermore, this is not the first occasion on which the question of the ex-propriation, for the public benefit, of Jewish cemeteries lying within cities has been faced by the Jews living in the states of Europe. A similar question arose in Vienna in 1898, when the City authorities wished to construct a tram line through the Vahrungen Jewish Cemetery, within the city limits. The compulsory purchase was cancelled when the Jewish Community successfully invoked the provisions of the Hebrew religion. Indeed, recognition by a provision of positive law was granted in Austria to the inviolability in perpetuity of the Jewish cemeteries (Founding Law of the Jewish Communities, paragraph 3). No question of the expropriation of Jewish cemeteries in the cities of France where Jews live has ever arisen precisely because of the sacred purpose of those areas, although instances of the need of compulsory purchase for the public benefit have occurred. As a result, the Jewish cemeteries at Bordeaux and Bayonne, in Alsace and elsewhere, have survived intact though they are no longer in use.

The above provides sufficient proof that the Jewish cemeteries are inviolable places in accordance with our sacred laws. It is obvious that this inviolability is fundamentally infringed by the decision approving the compulsory purchase of part of our cemeteries for the establishment of an urban settlement there. The magnitude of the offence that this will represent to the religious feelings of the Jews is such that the entire Jewish population is in a state of anguish since it is facing, for the first time, the possibility of the sacred laws concerning the Jewish cemeteries being violated.

The Chief Rabbinate and the Jewish Community of Thessaloniki have always been under the impression that the Government proceeded to take the measure in question in ignorance of the fact that the area destined for expropriation is used as a Jewish cemetery or, at the least, in reasonable ignorance of the sacred laws of the Jewish religion concerning the inviolability of cemeteries. For that reason, we are firmly convinced that the Government, having been enlightened on this issue, will hasten to lift the compulsory purchase which it has approved and restore matters to their previous state.

⊷⟐⟐⊶

4I

The President and the Secretary of the Zionist and Religious Organisation Misrachi to the Minister of Foreign Affairs

letter   Thessaloniki, 26 December 1929

The question of the recognition of Sunday as a day of rest in Thessaloniki, in connection with the desire of the Jews to be able to choose either Saturday or Sunday as their day of rest, will not be unfamiliar to you.

You will, of course, be aware that the united Jewish population of Thessaloniki has always honoured Saturday as its day of rest, since rest on the Sabbath is one of the commandments of Moses the Teacher of the Word of God and one of the most important foundations of the Jewish religion.

For 400 years, from the expulsion of the Jews from Spain to the present day, the Jews of Thessaloniki have never waived this commandment of their religion and have always closed their shops on Friday evening.

We believe that a constitutional, liberal and religiously tolerant state such as Greece ought to allow its citizens to rest on whatever day of the week they wish, the purpose of rest being one of a chiefly social nature.

We believe that it is a grave offence to the freedom of the human conscience to compel the Jews, in violation of their religious duties, to work on the Sabbath.

The Jews of our city have been faced with the dilemma of whether to rest twice a week, thus suffering excessive financial loss, or to violate their religious feelings by working on Saturday. Living as they do in a free state, they should not be compelled to choose the second option.

It is our duty to point out that the Jews in France, Germany, America and elsewhere are free to work on Sundays.

Examining the question at the local level, we believe that in view of the composition of the population of Thessaloniki in recent years there should not be even the slightest hesitation about allowing the Jews to rest on Sunday or Saturday, as they wish.

The majority of the population of Thessaloniki is of Greek origin. We are sure that if the Jews are granted the freedom to choose to work on Sundays this will be seen as very strong evidence that the Greek administration, in a liberal and tolerant spirit, is no longer concerned with the question of the Greekness of Thessaloniki, which is regarded as having been resolved long ago.

After examining the matter calmly, we have no doubt that Your Excellency will propose the following amendment to the law concerning Sunday as a day of rest, which has been tabled before Parliament for debate:

"The Jews are permitted to honour either Saturday or Sunday as a day of rest."

If this amendment is approved, you will see with your own eyes that the prestige of the nation will in no way suffer; on the contrary, Greece will be numbered among those states which wish to serve as models of religious tolerance for the civilised world.

In the hope that you will give due consideration to the contents of the present, please accept, Mr Minister, our best regards.

~⊷⊷~

42

D. Kalapothakis, Director, the Thessaloniki Press Bureau, to the Foreign Ministry

Press report   Athens, 14 February 1930

We have the honour to forward to you, from *Progrès* (Thessaloniki, 2 February), a report concerning a protest made in the name of the Thessaloniki Peace

League to the General Governor, the Mayor and the Chief of Police in connection with the acts of vandalism recently committed in the Jewish cemetery of Thessaloniki. They expressed the hope that when the perpetrators are found, they will be punished with extreme severity.

The League in question was founded during the visit to Thessaloniki last September of Monsieur Le Fouyer, one of the French delegates to the peace conference in Athens. The above protest constitutes the League's first appearance.

ATTACHMENT TO 42*

The Thessaloniki Press Bureau to the Ministry of Foreign Affairs

neswpaper article from Le Progrès   Thessaloniki, 2 February 1930

Title: "La question du cimetière israélite: Une intervention
de la Ligue de la Paix".

La Ligue de la Paix a pris une très louable initiative. A la suite des dernières profanations du cimetière israélite elle a formé une commission chargée de près de l' enquête qui a été ouverte par la police pour découvrir les coupables.

Cette commission formée de MM. Athanase Manos, Jean Ladas, Andoniades, Isaac Altcheh et Yomtov Yacoel, a visité hier successivement MM. Gonatas, Manos et Calochristianakis.

Les membres de cette commission ont fait part aussi bien au gouverneur général qu' au maire et au directeur de la police de la douleur causée aux membres de la Ligue de la Paix par les dernières profanations du cimetière juif. Ils ont remercié les autorités pour les mesures qui ont été adoptées afin de protéger le cimetière juif contre tout acte de vandalisme et exprimé l' espoir que les coupables des dernières profanations, une fois découverts, seront punis avec la dernière rigueur.

43

D. Kalapothakis, Director, the Thessaloniki Press Bureau, to the
Ministry of Foreign Affairs

Press report   Thessaloniki, 16 March 1930

In connection with the matter of the introduction of a complete day of rest on
Sunday for the butchers of the city and of the protests against this by the Jews, I
have the honour to report that in its issue of the 14th inst., the Ladino newspaper
La Verdad printed the following article under the title 'Victory for the Jewish
Tradesmen':

"We are pleased to announce today a news item that will be received with the
greatest joy by Jewish tradesmen. Despite the behind-the-scenes activities of
certain persons who allege that they represent the class of tradesmen, the law
concerning Sunday as a day of rest will not be enforced fully in Thessaloniki. The
Ministry of the National Economy has officially announced that this law cannot
for the moment be implemented in this city. Needless to say, the news will cause
particular pleasure among the Jewish butchers, who would have suffered the most
by the strict enforcement of the law concerning Sunday as a day of rest."

44

S. Gonatas, General Governor of Macedonia, to the Ministry of
Foreign Affairs

letter   Thessaloniki, 7 April 1930

In reply to your communication No. 3279 of 10 March 1930, which arrived at
the offices of the General Governance on the 20th ult., we have the honour to
inform you of the following:

The Jewish Community of Thessaloniki, which is a legal person under public
law, is governed by Law 2456 of the year 1920 concerning Jewish Communities.
The special by-law regulating matters affecting this Community was ratified by the

Decree of 12 April 1923, published in the appendix to issue No. 135 of 28 June 1923 of the Government Gazette. This by-law amended a subsequent decree dated 1 November 1925 and ratified by the Decree dated 26 February 1926 which was published in the appendix of issue No. 92 of 24 March 1926 of the Government Gazette. The second by-law contains provisions which contravene the standard law ruling the Jewish Communities.

The supreme authority of the Jewish Community here is the Community Assembly, which consists of 70 members. The Board of Management of the Community, elected from among the members of the Community Assembly, has 12 members.

The duration of the term of both the Community Assembly and the Board of Management is three years.

According to Article 16 of Law 2456 all Jews of foreign citizenship who are currently members of community councils may continue to take part and be elected as members of the Community Assembly for the next ten years.

For the elections of 6 June 1926, the Legislative Decree of 26 February 1926, published in No. 80, Vol. 1, of the Government Gazette (issued by the Pangalos regime), granted the right of vote to foreign nationals in Thessaloniki along with the right to be elected in a proportion of up to one third of the total number of seats. The foreign nationals recognised as eligible by Article 16, sub-para. 3 of Law 2456 were included in the above proportion.

New elections after the expiry of the three-year term of service were not proclaimed since, in accordance with the Statutes of the year 1926, the Assembly extended its mandate for a further six months.

As we have been informed, the Community Assembly of the Community here has already six members who are foreign nationals, while the Board of Management has two members of foreign nationality. In our communication No. 27940, we informed you about the amendments to Law 2456 which have been requested by the Jewish Members of Parliament and the Jewish Senator.

The Jewish Community and the foundations and services dependent on it appear to be in very straitened circumstances, hence the constant applications for state aid. Assistance of this kind has been provided only for education, in the form of a state grant of 1,200,000 drachmas provided in the last two years.

However, it is not possible to determine the precise current economic position of the Jewish Community, since the Community indulges in the contracting of loans by mortgaging its real estate while at the same time constructing new property and constantly calling for the financial support of Jewish charitable organisations in the United States. We are taking into consideration the budgets attached hereto, in French translation, for the years 1927 and 1929 of the

The Hirsch Hospital (today the Hippocrateion Hospital). It was inaugurated on 4 May 1908 thanks to the support of Baroness Clara De Hirsch and the tireless efforts of Dr Moise Misrachi. It served the Jewish community as a general hospital until 1940. Archive of the Jewish Community of Thessaloniki.

Thessaloniki 1938. The staff of the Hirsch Hospital. Archive of the Jewish Community of Thessaloniki, donated by Isaac Menache (Athens) and David Amir (Israel).

Thessaloniki 1938. In front of a building under construction in the courtyard of the Hirsch Hospital. From left to right the doctors: Sciaky (neurologist), Zac Allalouf (surgeon) Semberg (gynaecologist) Albert Menache (gynaecologist) and Cohen (gynaecologist). Archive of the Jewish Community of Thessaloniki, donated by Isaac Menache (Athens) and David Amir (Israel).

Community, the charitable institutions, and other entities which are subsidised by the Jewish Community of Thessaloniki.

A simple comparison of the tables for these two years (the general budget for the year 1927 is marked with the number 1 and the special budgets for that year with the numbers 2 to 13, while the budget for 1929 is marked 14 and the special budgets for that year by numbers 14 to 25) reveals the following:

The budgets for the foundations in the year 1927 do not include a budget for the Orphans' Fund, which does exist for the year 1929 (No. 25).

The sums of revenue and expenditure for special budget No. 12 in the year 1927 are entered on the general budget of the Community for the year 1929.

The budget for the year 1927 is in deficit to the sum of 1,907,781 drachmas, while the budget for 1929 is in surplus to the sum of 1,524,471 drachmas, which is noted as having been transferred to the account for the construction of new buildings. The question of housing is one of the most important problems with which the Jewish Community has dealt; the Jewish Press presents the State as concerning itself only with homeless Christians. However, the special budgets for

Residents of the Mair Aboav Jewish girls' orphanage of Thessaloniki in 1927. The orphanage was founded in 1925 and supported approximately forty residents who were trained as seamstresses or nurses. Shortly before the outbreak of the War, because of the financial situation, it was united with the Allatini boys' orphanage.

the year 1929 do not contain one for low-cost housing corresponding to budget No. 13 for the year 1927.

The principal Jewish charitable institutions for which special budgets are drawn up and which receive subsidies from the Community are as follows:

1) The Hirsch Hospital, which sets aside 55 free beds for destitute Jewish patients and 20 beds at moderate fees.

2) The Bikour Holim Urban Clinic, which provides free medical care and the necessary pharmaceuticals for 5,000 poor Jewish families.

3) The Carlo Allatini Orphanage, which has 50 male orphans who are also provided with education.

4) The Meir Aboav Orphanage, which has 35 female orphans who are also provided with education and vocational training.

5) The Insane Asylum, which has 50 destitute inmates.

6) The Matanoth Laevionim Canteen, which provides free lunches to 300 poor and orphan pupils of the Community schools.

The schools operated by the Jewish Community, for which support is also provided by the Greek State, number 8 complete primary schools and 9 single-teacher nursery schools. The number of pupils in these schools amounts to approximately 2,800, while the Greek teachers working in them and receiving salaries from the State number 42.

There are also 5 primary schools and 2 nursery schools in Thessaloniki which are subsidised by the World Jewish Alliance in Paris, with some 2,100 pupils and 18 Greek teachers. Some 1,000 pupils attend the 14 private schools, and there are two schools of commerce.

The Greek teachers work in accordance with the official detailed curriculum of the Ministry of Education and under the supervision of a Greek Inspector.

✦

45[*]

The Thessaloniki Press Bureau to the Ministry of Foreign Affairs

neswpaper article from l' Avanti   Thessaloniki, 10 May 1930

Title: "La Vie des Travailleurs Israélites Dans L' Armée Bourgeoise".

Il y a trois mois que les jeunes de la classe 1929 ont été contrôlés, et pendant l' expiement du sixième de leur détention militaire, ils ont déjà connu le militarisme de la classe exploitatrice. Il serait très long d' énumérer ici tous les faits qui nous ont été signalés, des faits qui montrent combien difficile est la condition de vie de nos jeunes frères. Signalons quelques-uns, ceux qui concernent les jeunes soldats israélites:

Des peines de 5 à 20 jours de prison pour un rien sur le simple plaisir d' un "décanéa", encouragé par son officier; des insultes et des coups pour le moindre manque d' attention aux palabres de la "théorie"; des cervées pour nettoyer les cabinets et d' autres principalement pour les juifs.

L' antisémitisme, a pris dans l' armée, pendant ces derniers temps un développement tel qu' il met même en péril la vie des soldats juifs. Signalons divers faits qui suffisent eux- mêmes à montrer que l' antisémitisme est officiellement exercé.

– Les jours de notre Pâque, pendant que les soldats juifs se trouvaient en permission, le "club des soldats" (la baraque "des frères chrétiens") a connu succès sur succès. Les soldats couraient en masse pour voir le cinéma que jamais pendant l' année le club ne leur offrait. Avec le cinéma il y avait d' autres attractions. Et ces moyens étaient mis en pratique dans le seul but de recueillir le

Moses Allatini *(1803-1882) was a doctor and important philanthropist who made a notable contribution to the community of Thessaloniki. Moses was the son of Lazaros Allatini, who moved to Thessaloniki in 1802. He created one of the largest industrial complexes as well as several smaller companies, establishing the Allatini family as one of the pre-eminent families in the trade and industrial fields during the 19th century.*

THE ALLATINI FAMILY

The founder of the family was the Italian Jew Lazaros Allatini, who settled in Thessaloniki in 1802, at a time when changing socio-political conditions were favouring the growth of trade and attracting large sums in Western capital to the East. Lazaros Allatini began his entepreneurial activities by importing goods from the markets of Europe. He then formed a partnership with Isaac Modiano – under the trade name of 'Modiano and Allatini' – and entered the flour and cereals market, establishing the first flour mill in Thessaloniki.[1] Lazaros Allatini died in 1834. The partnership with the Modianos broke up in 1880, and the family continued to trade under the name of Fratelli Allatini, expanding into banking (founding the Banque de Salonique), a pottery, a distillery, a brewery and an ice-factory.

The union of Lazaros Allatini and Anna Morpurgo yielded a son, Salomon, and two daughters. Moisis Allatini studied medicine and distinguished himself for the contribution he made to society; he used his science to help his fellow-citizens, and funded much of the cultural and educational development of Thessaloniki.

In collaboration with Youda Nehama, Moisis Allatini was instrumental in founding the schools of the Alliance Israelite Universelle (1873) and did much towards the reform of the Talmud Torah school. He also provided considerable support for the Greek schools of Thessaloniki. His charitable activities were rewarded with honours from the Ottoman, Italian, Austro-Hungarian and Greek governements.

The sons of Moisis Allatini – Lazaros, Emilios, Carolos, Ougo and Roberto – took over the reins of the business from their uncles Darios and Salomon Allatini and operated succesfully for some years. But the death of Carolos Allatini, upon whom the family enterprices had largely relied, and the loss of considerable sums of money on the stock market compelled the last members of the family to leave Thessaloniki in 1911, on the outbreak of war between Italy and Turkey. Thus ended, rather ingloriously, the history of an important family which dominated the economic and social life of Thessaloniki for a century and more.

1. This mill burned down in 1898 and a new and larger one, to a design by the Italian architect Vitapiano Poselli, was built on its site: "Le plus grand moulin de tout d' Orient", according to a period postcard. The mill in Antheon St, one of the best-known landmarks in Thessaloniki, was recently sold to the Sheraton chain for conversion into a hotel. Poselli also designed the villa for the Allatini family, the largest and most sumptuous in the city. It was used at various times as accommodation for the exiled Sultan Abdul Hamid and as the premises of the Aristotle University of Thessaloniki. Today it houses some of the departments of the Prefecture.

plus de soldats chrétiens possible auxquels parlaient divers "inconus" sur "la race maudite israélite, les sans-patrie, les bolchéviques, ceux qui veulent dominer le monde, ceux qui tuent les chrétiens en Russie" et toute une série d' idioties concernant la mort du Christ etc.

– Aucun journal, même bourgeois, n' est pas permi aux soldats de lire. Aucune immixation, aucune discussion sur la "politique". Le seul journal que leur est permi de lire et pour lequel les officiers déploient des efforts gigantesques pour inscrire des abonnés est la feuille de choux des officiers de réserve "Efedricos Agon". De ce qu' il écrit, en général, ce journal occupons nous dans un autre numéro. Regardons ce qu' il dit à l' égard de notre minorité. Il commence par attaquer l' "Avanti" parce qu' il "insulte" les galonnés; "les juifs ennemis de la patrie nous devons les frapper; les "trois epsilon" qui existent maintenant doivent mettre à la raison tous les juifs; la communauté juive aide l' "Avanti", pendant qu' elle se montre vénizeliste".

– Troisième fait caractéristique est celui du premier mai au Commandement de la Place (Frourarchion). Pour "assurer l' ordre" aucun juif ne devait être pris. Cette mesure est pour inculquer, particulièrement après les théories, au jeune travailleur ou villageois, l' inimitié contre le juif. Et au Commandement de la Place le jour du premier mai même après s' être renseignés qu' il n' y avait aucun juif parmi les soldats, on leur dit de frapper sans pitié les communistes, leur expliquant que ce sont les juifs qui provoquent les troubles, et que quand ils vont rencontrer quelque communiste dans la caserne, qu' ils le tuent sans qu' ils craignent rien. Cela veut dire que n' importe quel soldat qui sera aveuglé par l' antisémitisme, avec l' arme en main, se jette sur le premier juif venu et le frappe, le blesse, le tue.

Sous cette atmosphère vivent les jeunes soldats de la minorité juive.

A côté des exercices fatiguants, à côté de mauvais mangers, ils ont aussi l' oppression particulière en tant que Juifs. Et cette situation ira en s' empirant à mesure que la crise aigüe de plus en plus à la bourgeoisie et à mesure que se rapproche le déclenchement de la guerre.

Cette situation peut être changée seulement par la lutte révolutionnaire. On peut réagir avec énergie et sans attendre pour mettre un frein aux manoeuvres du militarisme sanguinaire. Les jeunes soldats juifs doivent s' organiser pour mener la lutte contre leurs exterminateurs. Ils doivent démasquer tous les "patriotes" qui ont pour but de dévier l' attention du soldat des pénibles conditions de vie qu' il supporte dans l' armée de la patrie des bourgeois. Ils doivent montrer les buts plus grands des buts guerriers, contre l' union soviétique, que la campagne anti-juive et anti-communiste poursuit.

Les jeunes communistes se trouveront à la tête de leurs luttes. Ils devront réaliser dans la caserne la lutte coordonnée, de tous les soldats, pour leurs revendications générales et particulières.

Les soldats juifs exigeront:
– Défense de circulation dans l' armée de l' "Ephedrikos Agon".
– Arrestation immédiate de tout agitateur antisémite.
– Liberté d' organisation et libertés politiques.

Pour mener leurs luttes ils doivent s' organiser en nommant une commission d' entre eux et en créant une large commission d' auto-défense dans chaque compagnie (loho).

⇥✦⇤

46*

The Thessaloniki Press Bureau to the Ministry of Foreign Affairs

neswpaper article from Tiempo   Thessaloniki, 19 May 1930

Title: "La Situation Des Juifs de Turquie: Demie Heure Avec Un Ancien Salonicien Installé A Stamboul".

Le hasard nous a fait rencontrer hier un de nos anciens amis instalés à Consple et que ses affaires personnelles l' obligèrent à venir pour quelques jours dans sa ville natale.

Profitons de cette présence inespérée pour lui demander certains renseigne- ments sur la vie en général des Juifs de Turquie.

Vous me demandez, nous replique notre ami, quelle est la situation en Turquie au point de vue économique? Sans être défaitiste, je vous dirai qu' elle n' est pas très brillante. La crise mondiale a aussi ses répercussions sur le marché turc. Le chômage est grand, et presque toujours des maisons des plus importantes de Consple déposent leurs bilans au tribunal ne pouvant plus faire face à la gravité de la situation.

Est - ce que la situation des Juifs est particulièrement critique?

– Sauf les capitalistes qui peuvent plus ou moins compter sur le lendemain, le reste de la population juive souffre en général.

– Combien de Juifs compte - t - il Consple?

– Cinquante mille si je ne me trompe.

– Existe - t - il à Stamboul un certain mouvement nationaliste juif?

– Mouvement nationaliste juif? Que dites - vous! Le citoyen turc qui ne s' occupe que de questions turques est déjà pousuivi comme "Traître à la Patrie" et à ce point de vue il est terrorisé.

– Pourquoi, car nous savons, lui disons - nous, que la communauté juive de Consple, malgré sa numérosité, n' a pas ses représentants à la grande assemblée "Nationale" d' Angora?

– Il n' y a pas de quoi. Les citoyens turcs ne votent avec pleine liberté de conscience. Ils jettent aveuglement dans l' urne le bulletin le gouvernement leur fournit.

– Notre interlocuteur avait un "Milliet" en caractères latins.

– A propos, nous lui demandons, quelle impression a fait en Turquie la réforme des caractères latins?

– Je vous dirai; cette réforme a ses partisans et ses ennemis. Mais selon l' avis de plusieurs intellectuels turcs, les caractères latins ont fait perdre à la langue écrite turque une grande partie de son charme.

Sur ces mots nous avons salué notre ancien ami en lui souhaitant bon voyage et en promettant de nous rencontrer à nouveau dans l' avenir.

47

D. Kalapothakis, Director, the Thessaloniki Press Bureau, to the Ministry of Foreign Affairs

Press report   Thessaloniki, 29 May 1930

I have the honour to report that some time ago the local weekly newspaper *Ephedrikos Agon*, mouthpiece of the Association of Reserve Non-Commissioned Officers of Macedonia and Thrace, embarked upon a systematic campaign directed against the Jews. This campaign, as it has been conducted, could be described as anti-Semitic *per se*, and, furthermore, was intended to attack those who are in charge of the Jewish community here, since it accuses them of being responsible for all the things they themselves put forward as reasons for the acceptance of various claims they have made.

Thus, *Ephedrikos Agon* published in its issue of 24 April extracts from an anti-military article taken from the Communist *Avanti*, and again in its next issue (27.4.30) in order to place the responsibility for the April 24th article on the Jews as a whole. The newspaper further, calls for the Jewish Community to issue an announcement deploring it. Otherwise, the organisation EEE (*Ethniki Enosis Ellas*), familiar from its short proclamations, will 'put them in their place'.

As soon as the brief article of 27 April appeared, I summoned Mr Antonios Kosmatopoulos, journalist, editor in chief of *Ephedrikos Agon*, and pointed out to him that it is unfair for the entire Jewish community to be held responsible for the articles published in *Avanti*. If the *Ephedrikos Agon* continues with the tactics it has adopted – out of a patriotic spirit and inclinations – the results will be the opposite to those intended, since the Zionists, who control the Jewish community, have repeatedly raised the spectre of the Communist menace, claiming that it can only be combated by Zionism - that is, by Jewish nationalism.

Continuing the tactics it had inaugurated, *Ephedrikos Agon* printed in its issue of 25 May, under the title 'Admire the Jews', an entire anti-military article published in the issue of *Avanti* dated 8 March, without stating that the article was taken from a Communist newspaper. The article in question, submitted to you in our report No. 1186, thus appears to have been written by a bourgeois Jewish newspaper. Indeed, the text of the translation is identical with that produced by us.

Fortunately, these publications have so far passed unnoticed by the Jews. It is clear that, otherwise, there would have been loud and noisy protests in all their newspapers, since all the Jews are represented as applauding such propaganda against the Greek Army via the Press.

While waging this campaign against the Jews – out of a spirit of excessive patriotism – *Ephedrikos Agon* also published a detailed account of the graduation ceremony of the Catholic French school here, emphasising that the Union of Reserve Officers had contributed to the success of the ceremony. However, it is common knowledge that such associations exist in all the principal foreign schools in Thessaloniki – which are often the target of attacks in the Press – and that their purpose is to advertise and support the work of the schools and to foster the maintenance, after graduation, of strong bonds between former pupils and the school and its mission.

I conveyed these observations, especially those concerning the improper manner in which the *Avanti* article had been used, to Mr Zannian, President of the Reserve Officers. I do not believe however that they will change their tactics, and sooner or later we are going to find ourselves facing a universal outcry in the Jewish newspapers, which will not fail to point out that while the Jews fulfil their military obligations to their homeland, the Greek reservists continue to have a hostile attitude towards them. Consequently, it would be expedient – if there are no objections – for the appropriate department of the Third Army Corps, to which it would appear from earlier publications in *Ephedrikos Agon* that the reserve non-commissioned officers feel themselves obliged, to point out to those in charge that the tactics being applied by their Press organ and the mishandling of matters concerning the Jews could at any time give rise to protests on the part of the Jews. Such protests, accompanied by strong articles in the Jewish newspapers, will give the impression to the rest of the world that there is an anti-Semitic current among us.

❖

ATTACHMENT a TO 47

The Thessaloniki Press Bureau to the Ministry of Foreign Affairs

newspaper article from Ephedrikos Agon   Thessaloniki, 27 April 1930

Title: "Let them Think Carefully".

Subsequent to the tactics being applied by the Jews and their newspapers, extracts from which we published in last Sunday's issue and in which they most foully insult the Greek officers, two things have to be done. First, the Jewish Community must issue an official statement denouncing these publications in *Avanti*, and second it must advise the Jews to stop buying that vile newspaper.

If these steps are not taken, we shall have no alternative but to support the national organisation EEE in achieving its objectives and to take it upon ourselves, as reservists, to put the comrades of *Avanti* – and their offices – 'in their place'.

Let the Jewish Community and those involved in *Avanti* think the matter over carefully.

❖

ATTACHMENT b TO 47

The Thessaloniki Press Bureau to the Ministry of Foreign Affairs

newspaper article from Ephedrikos Agon   Thessaloniki, 20 April 1930

Title: "The Jewish Communists".

In last Sunday's article, we dealt with our Christian 'comrades', if it can be supposed that they have not yet repudiated their religion. Today we shall be dealing with the Jewish Communists, who, protected by our culture, are undermining the foundations both of the state and of religion.

Apart from the other action taken by the Jewish comrades and their mouth-piece, the Communist newspaper *Avanti*, not a day goes by without their attacking the state and the officers.

Here is a paragraph from an article in *Avanti*:

"Let us put a stop to the terrorism and violence of the brass-hats, to the swearing and the beating, to the imprisonment and the fatigues, and let the frenzied brass-hats be prosecuted and punished".

And another:

"The workers in khaki, who will be called upon to attack their brothers, should fraternise with them and turn their guns on the brass-hats."

That, and much more, will be found in the notorious newspaper *Avanti*, and yet the authorities still allow it to appear and circulate freely. Is it permissible for a Jewish newspaper with obscure financial backing to insult our glorious officers and our state in such a vile manner?

What corruption, if the truth be told.

48

G. Papandreou, Minister of Education and Member of Parliament for Lesvos

Draft Legislation   Athens, 16 June 1930

Explanatory Report on the draft law 'concerning the amendment and supplementation of Law 2456 regarding Jewish Communities'

To Parliament

The ten years during which Law 2456 has been implemented have revealed certain defects in that law which have encumbered the smooth and normal functioning of the Jewish Communities in Greece. The most important of those defects necessitate the completion and amendment of some provisions of the said law.

Article 3 of Law 2456 is hereby replaced by a provision defining with precision the concept of membership of the Jewish Community. Given that the Jewish Communities are unions of persons of a fundamentally religious nature, it has been deemed correct to set this shared characteristic of religion as a substantive element in defining the concept of membership. Membership is defined, as can be clearly seen from the amendment of Article 6, regardless of the nationality of the members, since nationality is in no way connected with the cycle of activities of the Jewish communities.

The amendment of Article 6 lays down the qualifications of the members of the Community who are eligible for the Board of Management. The amendment introduces the principle that those who manage the Jewish Community must, as a rule, be Greek citizens. This condition becomes essential in the case of the members of the Community Council, who are charged with the responsible management of all the Community's affairs and are its lawful representatives.

Article 9 is supplemented with a provision removing the misinterpretation that has occurred in some Communities in connection with the application of the law regarding Chief Rabbis serving prior to its introduction.

Article 16 is amended so as to allow its implementation in accordance with the principle stated in Article 1 of the draft law, which states that the Jewish Communities are basically religious unions. Consequently, the members of these unions will be all the persons who are of Jewish faith and reside in the area of each Community. Such persons, having reached the age of 21 years, will be entitled to elect representatives to the Community Assemblies. The representatives who make up the General Assembly must, however, be Greek citizens.

This is the draft law submitted to your consideration which we have the honour to ask you to vote for.

16 June 1930

DRAFT LAW
Concerning the amendment and supplementation
of Law 2456 regarding Jewish Communities

Article 1

Article 3 of Law 2456 is amended as follows:

"All persons of Jewish faith permanently residing in the seat of the Community are automatically deemed members of the Jewish Community."

Article 2

Article 6 of the same Law is amended as follows:

"Each Jewish Community shall be administered by the Community Council elected from members of the Community Assembly who have reached the age of 25 years.

"The Community Council must consist of Greek citizens; established with each Community, it shall administer the assets and, in general, all Community affairs, in particular those of the charitable and educational institutions as well as of foundations for religious, charitable and educational purposes."

Article 3

The following provision shall be added at the end of Article 9 of the above Law:

"Those who, prior to the present Law, bore the title of Chief Rabbi and did not conform to the procedures of this Article and those statutes stipulated in particular for each Community, in accordance with Law 2456, Article 17, cease to be Chief Rabbis, retaining only the title and position of Rabbi.

The Chief Rabbi and the Rabbis must be of Greek nationality.

Article 4

Article 16 of the above Law is amended as follows:

"1. The supreme authority of each Community shall be the Community Assembly, to which the Chief Rabbi and the Community Council shall be accountable.

"The Community Assembly of each Community shall consist of a number of delegates, all Greek citizens, designated by the particular statutes of each Community and elected by male members of the Community over the age of 21 years."

All provisions contrary to the present Law are hereby rescinded, and the present Law shall enter into force as of the date of its publication in the Government Gazette.

49

D. Kalapothakis, Director, the Thessaloniki Press Bureau, to the Ministry of Foreign Affairs

Press report   Thessaloniki, 12 July 1930

I have the honour to submit, from the bulletin dated the 3rd inst. of the Jewish Telegraph Agency of Paris, a report from Thessaloniki on the right granted to Jews of foreign citizenship to vote in the elections of their Community Assembly.

The report in question could be described, without reservation, as malicious. The law of 1920 concerning Jewish Communities (that is, Law 2456) did not retain the existing system in force for a period of ten years, as the correspondent of the Jewish Agency reports. It did not permit all foreign citizens to elect and be elected. Article 16, para. 3 of the law simply provided that those foreign citizens who, at the time the law was passed, were members of the Community Councils (and those alone) might continue to take part in the Community Assembly and the Community Council. In other words, this was an exception applicable to 3-4 persons only, given that the Community Council has twelve members.

No question or demand for the recognition of equal rights for non-Greek citizens was raised. Consequently, Law 2456 established without reservation that only Greek citizens shall be involved in the administration of their community. The question of foreign citizens did not arise until 1926, when they succeeded in having the dictatorial government issue the Legislative Decree of 20 February 1926, by which permission was granted for the participation of non-Greek citizens on the occasion of the Community elections which took place on 6 June 1926.

The Jews having succeeded, first, in achieving final recognition of the participation of foreign citizens in the administration of the Community by declaring in Parliament, through their representatives, that the Community is religious in nature - while at their assemblies they state the opposite - the correspondent of the Jewish Agency now falsely assures his readers that the law of 1920 laid down that the Jews of foreign citizenship would have the right to elect and be elected for a period of ten years. This right is now restricted by the amendments passed by Parliament, the correspondent writes, and there are fears that this may be the starting-point for a fresh weakening of the community.

<hr />

50

Law 4837

Athens, 25 July 1930

Law 4837 concerning the amendment and supplementation of Law 2456 regarding Jewish Communities
The Hellenic Republic

Taking into consideration Article 75 of the Constitution, we hereby issue the following Law, passed by Parliament and the Senate:

Article 1

Article 3 of Law 2456 is amended as follows:

"All persons of Jewish faith residing permanently in the seat of the Community are *ipso jure* deemed members of the Jewish Community."

Article 2

Article 6 of the same Law is amended as follows:

"Each Jewish Community is administered by the Community Council which in turn will be elected from those members of the Community Assembly who have reached the age of 25 years.

"The Community Council shall consist of Greek citizens, established in the seat of each Community, and shall manage the assets and, in general, all the affairs of the Community, including, in particular, matters connected with the charitable and educational institutions and the foundations operated for religious, charitable and educational purposes."

Article 3

The following provision is added at the end of Article 9 of the above Law:

"Those who, prior to the present Law, bore the title of Chief Rabbi and have not conformed to the formalities of this Article and to the formalities of the statutes specially approved for each Community in accordance with Article 17 of Law 2456 cease to be Chief Rabbis, retaining only the title and position of Rabbi.

"The Chief Rabbi and the Rabbis must be of Greek nationality."

Article 4

Article 16 of the above Law is amended as follows:

"1. The supreme authority of each Community is the Community Assembly, to which the Chief Rabbi and the Community Council are answerable.

"The Community Assembly of each Community consists of a number of delegates, who shall all be Greek citizens, determined by the particular statutes of each Community and elected by all male members of the Community over the age of 21 years."

All provisions contrary to the present Law are hereby rescinded, and the present Law shall enter into force as of the date of its publication in the Government Gazette.

The present Law, passed by Parliament and the Senate and issued by us today, is to be published in the Government Gazette and applied as a state law.

In Athens, 17 July 1930

The President of the Republic   The Minister of Education
Alexandros Zaimis   G. Papandreou

51

G. Papandreou, Minister of Education, to the Ministry of Foreign Affairs

communication   Athens, 13 August 1930

In reply to your secret communication No. 9101, we have the honour to inform you that, in accordance with Article 3 of Law 4837, already published in the Government Gazette (issue No. 252), "the Chief Rabbi and the Rabbis must be of Greek citezenship". Furthermore, we have no knowledge, and neither we nor our competent department have given any assurance, that the Chief Rabbi of foreign citizenship to be appointed by invitation from abroad will be naturalised by a special law. Indeed, there has been no thought of taking such a measure.

52

D. Kalapothakis, Director, the Thessaloniki Press Bureau, to the Ministry of Foreign Affairs

Press report   Thessaloniki, 21 September 1930

I have the honour to report that the Jewish Press of Thessaloniki has reacted with reservation to the decision announced by the Government in Athens to the effect that five new primary schools for Jewish children will be opened in Thessaloniki since their attendance of foreign schools has been banned. The Jewish Community here, unlike the one in Athens, has avoided issuing an announcement stating its gratitude. By way of exception, *Progrès*, unlike the *Indépendant*, which refrained from any comment, printed a leader in yesterday's issue praising the decision taken by the Minister of Education. *Progrès*, welcomed the fact that rather than providing the Community with a new grant, as had been requested by the Community, in line with its educational policy, the Minister has chosen to have the state undertake all the costs involved in founding and maintaining the new schools.

However, reading between the lines of the statements made by the inspector of the Jewish schools of Thessaloniki to the newspaper *Progrès* (21/9/1930), upon his return from Athens, one can see that the manner in which the state has settled the issue is far from inspiring enthusiasm among the Jewish Community here. The evening edition of *Indépendant*, after giving a brief description of the manner in which these schools will operate, stresses that the Community will propose the headmasters and the staff teaching Hebrew to be appointed. The newspaper adds that the Community Council deemed it necessary to engage in a new exchange of views with the representatives of the state so as to confirm that the Community will have continuous control over the teaching of Hebrew – as, indeed, the Government had proposed.

While *Pueblo* and the *Indépendant* refrain from commenting on the relevant Government decision, *Action*, the mouthpiece of the Zionists who have split from those in the Community, has so far published two articles (on the 18th and 21st of September) forcefully arguing that these new schools are putting in jeopardy the education of Jewish children.

ATTACHMENT TO 52

D. Kalapothakis, Director, the Thessaloniki Press Bureau, to the Ministry of Foreign Affairs

Press report   Thessaloniki, 22 September 1930

Further to my report No. 5452 of yesterday's date, I have the honour to report that the Ladino newspaper *Pueblo* reports in today's issue the decisions taken yesterday during the meeting of the Jewish Community Council. In connection with the decisions regarding the five primary schools being founded by the Greek State for Jewish children, *Pueblo* makes the following comments:

"The Community Council, having heard the report of Mr Kon, inspector of Community Schools (who had returned from Athens), appointed a committee consisting of Messrs Leon Gattegno, M. Bessantchi, Moisis Ascher and Kon to contact Mr Dzoumeleas, inspector of education, who is expected here in two or three days' time, in order to settle various details. However, the Community

Council greeted with satisfaction the principle and general outlines of the new state Jewish schools, which will be subject to the control of the Community Council insofar as the teaching of Hebrew is concerned, and resolved to express its satisfaction in the form of an announcement to be published in the Press."

The Greek-language newspapers have refrained from commenting at any length on the solution provided for the question of Jewish education. Two days ago (20 September 1930), *Makedonika Nea* carried the following report:

"The Greek State has not hesitated to manifest its interest towards the Jewish minority. It extended its care to the education of Jewish children – for whose sake it is hastening to set up new schools, thus shouldering fresh economic burdens despite the crisis afflicting both the private and the public sectors. The unstinted interest on the part of the Greek State towards the Jewish population is proof of the paternal and affectionate way in which the State and the Government deal with the ethnic minorities in this country.

"Furthermore, the gratitude which the Jews expressed towards the Government and their Greek homeland, in view of this decision, is just proof of the manner in which the Jewish element has come to appreciate the attitude of the Greek State."

Makedonia, which is always on the look-out for ways to attack the Jews, carried the following article in today's issue:

"Although the Government has set up five Jewish primary schools in our city, our Jewish fellow-citizens continue to send their children to the foreign schools. To date, the number of children registered with the state primary schools has not reached even twenty. In view of this sad, but inevitable, observation, we have been asked - and we pass on the question – what point is there in the founding of the new schools?"

53

D. Kalapothakis, Director, the Thessaloniki Press Bureau, to the Ministry of Foreign Affairs

Press report   Thessaloniki, 14 October 1930

I have the honour to report that yesterday's morning Jewish newspapers reported the results of the Community elections held the previous day as follows:

Of the total of 6,201 votes cast, the candidates received the following:

Zionist Party	2,123 votes
National Union	1,724 »
Popular League (Communists)	1,015 »
League of Moderates	864 »
Professionals	327 »
Tisoret Israel (Zionists)	148 »
Total	6,201

Considering that 7,065 individual voting booklets had been distributed, it seems that 13% of the electorate abstained from the elections. However, if it is also borne in mind that to the more than 11,000 electors on the state Electoral Register, the foreign citizens who are entitled to vote in these elections have to be added, then it becomes apparent that at least 50% of those entitled to vote abstained from the recent elections.

In accordance with the above results, the Zionists will receive 24 of the 70 seats in the Community Assembly, the National Union 19, the Communists 11, the League of Moderates 10, the Professionals 4 and Tisoret Israel 2. In view of the fact that the first and last parties are Zionist, it is inevitable that out of the 70 members of the Community Assembly, 45 will be Zionists. However, considering the widespread annulment of voting rights, sorting of the ballots may change this picture. The comparatively lengthy process of sorting will not start until the day after tomorrow, given that tomorrow is the last day of the Succoth festival period. The election results indicate that the split in the official Zionist wing is quite serious, since against their 24 seats the opposition, the National Union, has won 19.

Pueblo (mouthpiece of the Zionists), said on 13 October 1930: "Triumph for the Zionist ticket. Despite all the gerrymandering, it wins first place". I submit, attached, a summary of this article, which ends as follows: "If yesterday's elections were a triumph of ethics over corruption, they were also a triumph of the national ideal over anti-Semitism in its various manifestations".

Action (National Union) is triumphant over its success in falling only 400 votes behind the Zionist Party - that is, it attracted a number of voters equal to at least 80% of the Zionist Party vote.

Progrès (14 October 1930) claims that in its view the new members of the Community Assembly should work hand-in-hand towards the election of a viable Council so as to allow the latter to bestow upon the entire Jewish population, so sorely tried of late, the ultimate happiness of guaranteeing prudent management of the Community's activities.

The *Indépendant* (13 October 1930) notes that if compared with the Assembly just dissolved, the newly elected Assembly consists of 45 Zionists (60%) as opposed to 30 (Zionists and Misrachists). This assertion is not accurate. In the same context, the newspaper reported the previous day that the last Assembly consisted of a total of 30 Zionists, 10 Professional People and 18 independents. At the elections of 6 June 1926, held with a restricted number of voters in view of the limit imposed by Decree (as sought by the Zionists), there were only two lists of candidates, those of the Jewish Union and of the Communists. In order to frustrate a Communist success, all the other parties and organisations formed a union and succeeded in electing 58 Jewish Union candidates as opposed to 12 Communists. The fact of the matter is that the Zionists were in all places – the Assembly, the Council, etc. – in the absolute majority and were able to arrange the affairs of the Community as they saw fit. In addition, there is the assertion even of the *Indépendant* itself – which now wishes to present Zionism as having scored a resounding success and in particular as having conquered new ground – in contradiction of what it printed two days ago. According to the *Indépendant*, (9 June 1926) of the 58 successful candidates at the elections 30 were Zionists, 5 were Misrachists, 2 were members of the National Union of Settlements, 12 were independents (members of the Béne-Bérith Lodge, etc.), 7 were Professionals and 2 were members of the Association of Graduates of the World Jewish Alliance. Recapitulating the results of both elections, we can see that compared with the 45 Zionists in the new Assembly, the previous one had 40. Over time it became possible for the Zionists to summon meetings whenever they wished to arrange matters in accordance with their views.

It is not expected that the Zionists will collaborate in the new Assembly. The opposition seceded from the Zionist Party not over matters of principle but for personal reasons. As the Communist organs frequently pointed out – and, indeed, as is very well known – this is a case of an attempt to satisfy personal ambitions by seizing the Community in order to pave the way for their entry at a later stage into Parliament or the Senate. Indeed, the *Indépendant* (13 October 1930) admitted the impossibility of co-operation between Zionists: "The selection of the new Community Council will not be an easy task. The two Zionist groups are divided by a very profound difference of perceptions and it is extremely doubtful whether they will be able to collaborate in the administration of Community affairs. Each group will try to collaborate with the other and smaller groups in order to attain an adequate majority."

Of the Communist newspapers, only *Popolar* has been published since the elections (12 and 13 October 1930). After reiterating the various Zionist abuses, the newspaper contends that there is a need to work together in the common struggle against their enemy for the sake of their claims. I submit a summary of the relevant articles in translation.

Although the Greek-language newspapers published detailed information about the results of the elections, they have refrained from commenting. Only the *Ephemeris ton Valkanion* carried the following comment in yesterday's issue:

"Yesterday's elections in the Jewish community gave the victory to the Zionists. That means that the spirit of narrow fanaticism continues to prevail among the majority of the Jewish population, while the advocates of assimilation are not gaining ground."

⎯⎯⎯⎯

54*

The Thessaloniki Press Bureau to the Ministry of Foreign Affairs

newspaper article from Action   Thessaloniki, 8 January 1931

Title: "Le Grand Rabbin Rebbi Benzien Ouziel et Notre Communauté."

Son Opinion sur le Nouveau Conseil.
Ce qu' il Pense des Ecoles Etrangères.
Il Viendra Nous Visiter à la Première Occasion"

Notre ancien grand rabbin, Rebbi Benzien Ouziel, aujourd' hui, grand rabbin de Tel-Aviv, suit toujours avec un vif intérêt la vie juive de notre ville. Il vient d' adresser à un des plus grands actifs membres de l' assemblée communale, une intéressante lettre de laquelle nous relevons les passages suivants:

"...Je reçois avec un intérêt passionné, toute nouvelle concernant votre communauté, que j' ai aimée du fond de mon âme et à laquelle je resterai attaché toute ma vie, n' importe où que je me trouve.

"J' ai lu ce qui s' est passé pendant les élections communales de Salonique. J' ai constaté que ce n'est pas seulement un changement de personnes qu' il y a eu, mais la nouvelle composition du conseil prouve qu' un nouvel esprit souffle ou est sur le point de souffler dans votre communauté.

"....Un événement réjouissant s' est produit en votre ville, que j' attribue aux mystères de la Providence, gardien de l' existence éternelle de notre peuple. Je veux parler de la défense de fréquentation des écoles étrangères. Vous connaissez, pour sûr, avec quel grand mécontentement, pendant mon séjour à Salonique je voyais une proportion très grande de pères de familles, et particulièrement les membres les plus considérés de la communauté, remettre les enfants en pouvoir d'étrangers. Toujours je me demandais ce que serait l'avenir de la communauté si la plupart de ses enfants l'abandonnent ... [sic] je voulais apporter un remède à ce mal, mais ceux qui pouvaient m'aider ne m'ont pas compris. D'autre part le temps limité que j'ai été parmi vous n'a pas suffi à réaliser mon désir. Maintenant, la chose a été faite par décret du Gouvernement, et aujourd'hui on a donné la possibilité au conseil d'élever les enfants des juifs, comme des hommes et comme des juifs fidèles. Grande est cette mesure, et dans la même mesure la responsabilité est grande. J'espère que ceux qui sont à la tête de la direction communale sauront être à la hauteur l'heure décisive. Je suis prêt à vous aider de loin en choisissant des instructeurs et des directeurs capables et dévoués, naturellement si on me le demande.

"Quant à la question de ma venue à Salonique, vous savez que j'avais voulu me consacrer complètement à votre communauté. J'ai été une fois et j'ai accepté à aller une autre fois. A mon plus profond regret, aujourd'hui je ne puis plus vous contenter. Vous comprenez très bien que chaque année qui passe m'enracine et me fait aimer beaucoup plus la Palestine. Aujourd'hui, je ne pense même pas quitter mon poste. Mon grand désir est de visiter une fois Salonique et cela je le ferai, si Dieu le veut, à la première occasion que je ferai un voyage en Europe...."

N.D.L.M.

De cette intéressante lettre de notre ancien Grand Rabbin, nous relevons que quoiqu'étant loin, Rebbi Benzien Ouziel, pense, comme nous, que les nouvelles écoles ouvertes pour les élèves qui fréquentent les écoles étrangères, devraient être des écoles à bases juives, comme le sont les écoles communales. Malheureusement, tel n'est pas le cas. Nous faisons ce que nous pouvons dans ce journal pour obtenir que la communauté avec l'aide du Gouvernement, et non pas le Gouvernement seulement, ouvrirait de nouvelles écoles pour les petits juifs. Nous n'avons pas été entendus. Nous sommes heureux, en connaissant l'opinion autorisée de Rabbi Benzien Ouziel sur ce problème, de constater que nous étions dans la voie juste et non ceux qui, pour inscrire des succès faciles à leur actif, ont ouvert la porte à l'assimilation et ont jeté le mépris sur nous.

55*

The Thessaloniki Press Bureau to the Ministry of Foreign Affairs

newspaper article from Action   Thessaloniki, 9 January 1931

Title: "Le Judaïsme de Salonique Sans Direction".

A pas de géants notre collectivité avance dans le chemin de la déchéance. Le niveau économique de la population ne cesse de baisser, et avec lui nécessairement, le niveau moral.

Cette collectivité qui, devant une situation rédoutable comme l' actuelle, devrait resserer ses rangs et marcher comme un seul corps, sous une même direction, se trouve aujourd' hui désemparée, plus que cela ébranlée! Une tendance tire d' une côté, un autre groupe tire de l' autre, ce que l' un fait, l' autre ne le trouve pas à son goût. Et aucune autorité n' est restée parmi nous, assez hors des haines et des intérêts, pour qu' elle puisse attacher et réunir les membres séparés de ce corps malheureux.

Dans d' autres temps aussi il y eut des luttes, mais il y avait une tête vers laquelle convairgeaient tous les séparés. Il y avait des grands rabbins dont le prestige et l' autorité imposaient le respect à tous. Les exclamations des lutteurs étaient modérées par la vénération et se taisaient au moins quand elles arrivaient jusqu' à son siège. Les intérêts, les passions, les haines ne se déchaînaient pas comme elles se déchaînent dans la sûreté du manque d' un frein.

En même temps que les Grands Rabbins, et après eux, il y avait des présidents de la communauté qui dirigeaient, qui savaient se faire entendre, sinon par leur culture, au moins par leur âge, leur savoir-faire, leurs qualités représentatives.

Aujourd'hui il n' y a rien! La juiverie de Salonique est sans direction. Au lieu d' une direction, plusieurs directions qui se choquent les unes contre les autres. Entretemps, la construction séculaire de cette communauté, de cette collectivité tombe et se détruit. Son faste passé, comme la mer quand le clair de la lune manque, se retire et ne laisse pas à découvert que des restes inconnus.

Une direction! La communauté a besoin d' un Grand Rabbin et d' un Grand Rabbin supérieur en tout. Seul un grand rabbin peut mettre de l' ordre dans nos affaires, seulement avec un grand rabbin à la tête nous pouvons défendre nos intérêts, on peut tenir autant qu' il y a possibilité, à cette population de glisser insensiblement vers l' abîme.

Depuis des années nous entendons que ces questions soient reglées! Le vieux conseil, à la fin de ses jours, a envoyé un représentant en Europe. Qu' y a-t-il eu ensuite? Personne ne le sait! Qu' a fait le conseil actuel? Personne ne le dit!

Que le conseil laisse de côté toutes les questions de second et troisième ordre pour lesquelles il perd de vaines réunions. Et qu' il se consacre, en tout premier lieu, à régler la question du grand rabbin. Tous les sacrifices qu' on ferait pour mettre à la direction de notre communauté un homme de valeur et de prestige, pouvant se faire entendre et pouvant arbitrer, ne sont rien devant la contribution qu' il peut apporter, à retenir notre marche vers le gouffre.

❦

56[#]

The Director of the Thessaloniki Press Bureau to the Ministry of Foreign Affairs

report   Thessaloniki, 5 July 1931

I have the honour to report, on the occasion of the events which for the last ten days have held Thessaloniki in a state of turmoil and have caused such a sensation throughout the country and abroad, that, since the events were the result of the tactics adopted by the Greek and Jewish Press, with the Maccabee association as the pretext, this is not the first time in recent years that similar fierce battles have been fought in the Press here nor is it the first time that the Greek Press has dealt with the association in question. In the present instance, of course, a third factor intervened: the patriotic organisations of Thessaloniki. These organisations, too, were not the subject of Press attention for the first time. Over the last two years, I have repeatedly reported to you articles in connection with the leaflets distributed with particular frequency at the time of the major Christian festivals and attributed by the Jewish Press to the *'Ethniki Enosis Ellas'* ('Hellas Patriotic Union', EEE), whose real title, according to the Communist newspaper *Avanti*, is *'Ellines Exontosate Evraious'* ('Greeks Eliminate Jews'). Although leaflets of this kind have not appeared for many months, EEE has repeatedly intervened on numerous occasions in the form of announcements, the most

---

Owing to the poor quality of the copy, some of the dates in this document indicated [?] cannot be regarded as established with certainty.

important of which were those referring to the lecture delivered by Abraham Recanati, to the cinema film *King of Kings*, and to the Press campaign over the article by Mr Bessantchi,

It will be evident from the above that this was not the first occasion on which all those in the front line of events of the last few weeks had been involved in matters of a similar nature. However, it was the first occasion on which the situation developed in such a way and on which it proved impossible to confine the issue to squabbling in the Press and the distribution of patriotic leaflets.

Looking back over the Press of Thessaloniki during the last seven years, we will see that the Maccabee sports association, which was founded under the inspiration of the Maccabees of Bulgaria, who visited Thessaloniki shortly after the declaration of the Turkish constitution of 1908 and were admired for their soldierly bearing (*Renacencia Giudia* Thessaloniki 3.12.28, Press Bureau 307/11.2.27, review *El Maccabeo* 5591, Press Bureau 2141/5.4.31), has the principal objective of boosting the Hebrew patriotic feelings of Jewish youth and is one of the media which help convey Zionist national ideas. Sport is used as a medium for conveying the true purpose being aimed at.

Mr David Florentin, an active member of the Zionist Federation of Greece and at this moment its delegate to the World Zionist Congress in Basel, recently toured Greece, where he took action to achieve the formation of a league of Jewish Communities throughout the state and to study the situation from the Zionist point of view, recorded his impressions in *Renacencia Giudia* (Thessaloniki, 6.1.31 [?], Press Bureau 160 12.1.31[?]): "We can expect valuable results both in Kavala and in Serres and Drama, where there are teams of Dararim Maccabee which constitute branches of those in our city. There is also a strong Maccabee team in Komotini. However, they need support so that they can survive and this is the task of their brother organisations in Thessaloniki."

Mr Florentin omitted to mention that a Maccabee team had, at that time, recently been set up in Xanthi, too. *Progrès* (Thessaloniki, 26.9.27) published an announcement from the Maccabee Scout Troup of Thessaloniki, and a few days later *Phos* (Thessaloniki, 8.10.27) carried a detailed report from Xanthi describing the ceremony held to mark the formation of the group, attended by our authorities there, while Lieutenant C. Stavroulakis, General Governor of the Scout corps – according to *Phos*, owned by the Scout organisation - delivered an enthusiastic address approving and encouraging this nationalist initiative on the part of the Jews.

More recently, too, we have had another example of an attempt to set up a special sports association for Jewish young people and thus to remove them from any contact and interaction with young Greeks. In Kavala, there does not seem to have been any separate Jewish sports association with the exception of the Jewish Scout troop, the existence of which was known to us from the article by Mr Florentin cited above. However, when, last December, the Maccabee football team of Thessaloniki visited Kavala, an association under the same name was established there by means of the resignation of the Jews from our associations entitled Philippos, Heracles and Pavlos Melas (*Action*, 4.1.31, Press Bureau 83/4.1.31). Mr Nehama, the Italian Consul in Kavala - presumably an Honorary Consul - donated a considerable sum to the Maccabees of Kavala, as was reported by *Progrès* (24.2.31), for the purpose of supporting the football team.

The Maccabees, in their efforts to alienate the members of their association from any contact or involvement with Greek athletes, were responsible for the formation of a separate Scout troop of purely Jewish membership by compelling the Jewish Scouts to resign from the Scout Troop of Macedonia. There was no prohibition on the formation of this new troop of Jewish Scouts, who immediately began to appear wearing special uniforms which bore no resemblance to Scout uniforms and marching through the streets of the town singing Jewish songs, etc. This gave rise to discussions in the Press and painstaking negotiations to bring about the return of the Jews to the Greek Scout Troop.

The Maccabees then demanded recognition of their right to wear special uniforms and to use the Scout flag with the Jewish emblem affixed to it, and they also laid claim to a whole series of other rights of lesser importance which would have made it more than plain that there was nothing in common between the Greek Scouts and the Jewish Maccabee Scouts. Although even some of the Jews disagreed with the tactics of the Maccabees, neither the article criticising this action published in *Progrès* on 8 May 1925 nor the refusal of the Jewish team Amaach to secede from the Greek Scouts was sufficient to shake their persistence in applying the plan they had decided upon.

In the meantime, no opportunity was lost of emphasising that this association, allegedly devoted to sport, had the principal mission of boosting and elevating the nationalist sentiments of its members.

On his visit to Thessaloniki in December 1926 Mr Jabontinsky, leader of the Revisionist Zionists, was greeted as follows by the now Editor of *Action*, Mr Elie Frances (*Opinion*, 26.11.26):

"The young people who have paraded before us were raised in a spirit of profound and passionate Hebrew patriotism. They know that they are here to protect the sacred rights of our people. With faith and enthusiasm, they have accepted the altogether military discipline we have imposed upon them because they are aware that we expect of them not only their physical development but also the moulding of their souls in a revolutionary spirit."

When Elie Veissi, in the following day's *Pueblo* (24.11.26), strongly criticised these words of Mr Frances, the latter replied, also in *Pueblo* (28.11.26), to the effect that by the reference to the revolutionary spirit, etc., he intended to emphasise that the Jews should leave behind the old spirit of servility, that they should abandon the earlier type of Jew who was incapable of defending his rights, and that they should replace it with the new type of Jew who is aware of his worth as an individual, who is proud and ready to defend his personal honour and the honour of his people.

Further, Elie Frances wrote a lengthy article in *Renacencia Giudia* (3.12.26) about the Maccabees, in which he stated:

"The work of the Maccabees is not confined only to spreading a love of sport and gymnastics among young people. They have also been brilliantly successful in providing healthy patriotic education for their members, and I regard this as being one of the organisation's greatest claims to glory."

When the Maccabees announced the establishment of a branch in Xanthi, they published a statement that its aims would be to foster the moral, physical and patriotic education of its members.

In parallel, however, the disputes in the Press had not come to an end. The Greek Press certainly did not provide the pretexts for them, and in most cases was the victim of provocation. By proclaiming and issuing assurances that they would return to the Greek Scout troop, they [the Jews] succeeded in taking part in the parade of the Thessaloniki garrison on the first day of the New Year 1926. They appeared in all their glory, with their band in the lead, with their cyclists, and their boys' and girls' teams. Indeed, the teams were led by a First Lieutenant. Unfortunately, on the day in question our Scout Troop sent only a small group to the parade, and this was used by the Jewish Press and in particular by *Progrès*, which, noting the importance of the impression created by the presence of the Maccabees, reported *inter alia* (3.1.26) that 150 Maccabees had paraded as opposed to 20 Greek Scouts. *Makedonia* (4.1.26) replied, and so a short-lived campaign in which other newspapers participated began, but this would have been avoided if the provocation intended to exploit the participation of the Maccabees had not taken place.

This was followed by a period of more or less continuous interest in the Maccabees on the part of the Greek Press. The Union of Journalists, which has its offices above the *Dionysia* Cinema, held an exhibition of handicrafts by pupils from the schools of Thessaloniki in which the Maccabees took part. No one who visited the exhibition will be able to forget the appalling Greek in which the captions giving the names, etc., of the exhibitors on the exhibits were written. This is further proof of the achievements of the Jews in matters of Greek learning, and of how slanderous it is to allege that they avoid learning the language of the state!!! They may not have been subjected to attack on this matter on the part of the Greek Press, but their participation in this exhibition was far from failing to provide reasons for such an attack. Just as not a single Maccabee could be found to write the captions to the exhibits in correct Greek, so it seems to have been impossible to compose in Greek a letter written to *Makedonia*, which had protested over the fact that a Greek association was corresponding in French with the local Press (6 February 1926). Without questioning the facts of the matter, the Jewish newspapers engaged in a campaign against *Makedonia*, alleging that the responsibility for the incident lay with the chief reporter, Mr Vardis, who told the bearer of the letter that there was no need to find someone to translate it into Greek because he would do this himself. But why should the letter not have been sent in Greek in the first place?

A few days later, Mr D. Charitopoulos, now General Secretary of EEE (the Hellas Patriotic Union), published in *Makedonia* (19 February 1926[?]) a strong article under the headline "The Jewish Scouts under the mask – Macedonia and Thrace to be flooded – setting an example for the Communists".

Some weeks later, *Makedonia* launched a fresh attack, in reply to *Progrès*, which, advocating the need for a generous municipal grant to the Maccabee band, had added that unless such a grant was received the band would not take part in the 25 March celebrations. In two very sharp notes, *Makedonia* (23.3.26) stated *inter alia* that the appearance of the Maccabees in public ought to be banned.

The extent to which those in charge of the association are aware of the fact that they are Greeks and that their duty is to be of service only to what is Greek is demonstrated by the manner in which Scouts are sent to, and participate in ceremonies and meetings held by the foreign communities here. When the Italian community organised fencing matches in the King George Gardens on 2 July 1927, quite a number of Maccabee Scouts lined up at the entrance and saluted the dignitaries as they arrived, inspiring, together with the presence of numerous other Jews, a column in *Makedonia* (4 July 1927).

After lengthy and painstaking efforts, it ultimately proved possible to bring the Maccabees back into the ranks of the Greek Scouts. Although their troop still retained its autonomy, at least the different uniforms disappeared, though the once-ostentatious parades through the streets are still carried out. *Progrès* (17 August 1928) reported the reunion, publishing the relevant announcement. However, a few days before this, the French-language newspaper *Echo tis Thessalonikis* (27 July 1928), a merciless opponent of nationalist tendencies among the Jews, proceeded to make some rather peculiar revelations. It disclosed that the Maccabees had insisted that the Corps of Greek Scouts should report to the International Scout Association in London, and asked whether it would be possible for the Jewish Scouts to swear allegiance to both the Greek and Jewish nations. The answer was in the negative, since the Scouts are not intended to pursue any political end whatever, and in addition, that if the use of the name 'Maccabee Scouts' had any political implication in Greece, then it ought to be dropped.

It is perfectly plain from the above account that Greek public opinion has repeatedly concerned itself with the Maccabee association, allegedly of a purely sporting nature, and that the Maccabees had acted provocatively before. But if it is true that this was not the first time that there had been cause for campaigns in the Press against the Maccabees, then it is equally true that such campaigns, of an equally fierce nature, repeatedly took place between the Greek and Jewish Press. It is not, of course, possible to state positively which side is responsible. However, it cannot be denied that the Jewish newspapers, while they were always in possession of more facts and occupied a position of advantage by comparison with the Greek papers, nonetheless adopted a stance of intransigence and, in general, did not employ tactics such as to lessen the friction and bring the debate to as rapid an end as possible on all occasions.

If the Greek newspapers very frequently made use, in their attacks, of pretexts which were far from serious and often groundless, then the Jewish newspapers ought to have remembered that not a line of the Greek Press escapes the Jewish public, while the writings of the Ladino Press are always completely unknown to Greek journalists and the Greek public. The battle in the Press is completely unequal. When the Jewish Press describes as slanderous the charge that linguistic assimilation is, supposedly, not being pursued, it is of course not unaware that the official Zionist mouthpiece (*Renacencia Giudia*) has repeatedly described as unpatriotic the education of Jewish children in Greek schools. In general, the Zionists have never been disturbed by the prospect of sending their children to foreign schools when it was not possible for them to obtain an education in Jewish schools. Nor was the Jewish Press unaware, when proclaiming to the Greek public that it was pioneering the purely Greek education of the younger generation, that the Zionists did not see the matriculation of three (Jewish) Béne-Bérith scholars at the University of Thessaloniki as praiseworthy and failed to comprehend how this served the interests of the great mass of the Jewish population of Greece (*Renacencia Giudia*, 26 October 1928). Although three years have elapsed since then, the attitudes have remained the same, given that the idea launched at that time by the Zionists – that the Béne-Bérith scholars should not be sent to Greek commercial schools but should be registered at state teacher training colleges so as to lead to the emergence of a body of Jewish teachers of the Greek language

The Boy Scout Troop of the Maccabee Physical Education society of Thessaloniki posing in front of the National Bank building in 1937. The Macabees were founded in 1908 and had sections for soccer, basketball, boxing and table-tennis. Archive of the Jewish Community of Thessaloniki, donated by Vital Aelion.

to replace the Greeks now working in the Jewish community and other schools – has now begun to be implemented.

These are matters which the Jews handle only through the Ladino Press and which thus escape the attention of the Greek Press and public, whose tactics would otherwise be different from the current approach, which is, however, always described as provocative and slanderous.

I would have to write at considerable length if I had to report on even a few of the fierce debates in the Press during recent years. Taking all the facts into consideration, no one could deny that the Jewish newspapers have always been provocative. In 1927, then General Governor Mr Kalevras, made through me a request that *Progrès* should not reply to an article in *Tachydromos*, with which it had become embroiled in a dispute in which other newspapers were already taking part, so as to bring the dispute to an end. Although the General Governor, in his request, was agreeable to a reply to *Tachydromos* being published in the Ladino

Press, for the sake of appearances in the eyes of the Jewish public, the request was denied and *Progrès* returned to the battle still more forcefully the following day.

During the period of the Pangalos dictatorship, use was made of prohibition orders issued by the military authorities to end such disputes in the Press, which tended to create enmity between the two communities.

The Jewish Press alleges that *Makedonia* is the only newspaper which systematically launches attacks on the Jewish population. Although perhaps it is true to say that the newspaper in question takes a broader and more frequent interest in Jewish affairs, the Jewish journalists should not forget that there was a period when it refrained from covering this subject and when they themselves held an attitude of great respect towards it. This was the period in which the election of Mr Mallah as Senator for Thessaloniki was supported and achieved (1928) with the backing of the Liberals. Those Jews who assert that only *Makedonia* has engaged in such campaigns are mistaken, since during the last few years *Tachydromos*, too, has repeatedly become involved in battles with them, while it was impossible that other newspapers should remain indifferent in the face of the ferocity and provocativeness of the Jewish journalists.

Makedonika Nea, regarded as favourably disposed towards the Jewish population in view of the position they adopted during the Maccabee affair, contained a strong article directed at Mr Bessantchi, the Member of Parliament, on 3 November 1928, an extract of which follows:

"Our friend Mr Bessantchi could and should be somewhat more moderate in his judgments and criticisms – not to say more respectful. When those whose ambition it is to present themselves as leaders and parliamentary representatives of the Jewish population of Thessaloniki conduct themselves in public life in the way his letter – not to mention other evidence – presents him, then it is very natural that a measure of discontent should be observed among some classes, at least – and the best classes, at that – of the Jews in connection with their condition under Greek administration.

"It is a mystery to us why some of the leaders of the Jewish community – with our friend Mr Bessantchi in the forefront – should ignore the truth of this and should create isolation, talking about Turkish (!) sovereignty in order to make tacit comparisons with Greek rule.

"Mr Bessantchi, his associates and those who share his views certainly ought to understand that, by conducting themselves in this manner, they are doing the Jewish community a disservice, bearing in mind that it is unthinkable that what we once did, in the years on which they look back with such nostalgia, should be repeated today to our detriment. Patience and toleration have their limits."

To conclude, there can be no doubt that one day the pretexts which arise so often for friction and fighting between the two categories of newspaper in Thessaloniki will no longer be confined solely to the columns of the newspapers. This is particularly the case when the issue involved is the revival of a question which caused a stir in public opinion a year ago and showed the Jews to be lying and deceiving Greek public opinion. However, what happened now could have happened two months ago, when it was revealed that Mr Abraham Racanati, President of the Misrachi, during his lecture on the film *King of Kings* which was so provocative that it attracted members of the EEE – who were forcibly removed by the police – referred to the crucifixion of the Saviour as follows: (*Action*, Thessaloniki, 22 April 1931)

"Our opponents have used this myth about the crucifixion to poison people's minds and to arouse passions against us over the last 2,000 years. And this lie, taught to young Christians and disseminated everywhere, from generation to generation, has been the cause of anti-Semitism among the masses of the people, and it is to this lie that we must attribute most of the misunderstandings between Christians and Jews, the incitement of hate in all forms against us, and the constant oppression and pogroms."

A summary of this was included in the announcement from EEE (published in *Tachydromos*, ... [sic] May 1931) in reply to the Directorate of Police, which had issued an official assurance that nothing insulting to the Christian religion had been said during Mr Racanati's lecture. If the Greek newspapers had actually been inspired with anti-Semitic feelings, they could easily have made capital out of the above, republishing it in huge headlines and demonstrating to religious believers that the Jews were insulting their faith. However, what did not happen then took place in the present instance over the Maccabees.

The news of a conference of Maccabees in Sofia was first mentioned in the newspapers of Thessaloniki on 1 September 1930, when the French-language newspaper *Flambeau* published a special report from Sofia, signed by R. Pardo, describing in detail the inauguration of the Second Maccabead of Bulgaria, which had taken place there with great formality. The same report was published in the Ladino newspaper *Action*.

On the following day (2 September 1930), *Makedonia* published a report from Sofia compiled here from the Bulgarian newspapers, which also mentioned the speech of Chief Rabbi Hananel, who had spoken about Macedonia. No comment or observation from the Jewish Press followed. On the following day (Thessaloniki, 3 September 1930), returning to the proceedings in Sofia, *Makedonia* published what had been said by the delegate sent by the Maccabees as a message to the Conference of the Macedonian Youth Movement, taking place in Sofia at the same time. This Maccabee delegate, by the name of Arditti, delivered a speech assuring the Bulgarian Macedonians that the Jews of Bulgaria would not cease to fight for the cause until the flags in the conference hall were flying from Divri to Beles and from Skopje to Thessaloniki over an independent Macedonia.

Makedonia (Thessaloniki) commented that the Jews of Bulgaria are at liberty to arrange their affairs as they wished. However, it called upon their fellow-Jews in Greece to sever all bonds with them, criticising in still stronger terms the fact that the Jewish newspapers here had given space to reports referring to festivities during which the above things were said. Lastly, it called upon the Maccabees of Thessaloniki to change their name by way of protest, given that there are Maccabee *komitadjis* in Bulgaria.

The *Indépendant* replied sarcastically on the same day (3 September 1930) to *Makedonia*, and called into question the accuracy of the latter's information. It asserted categorically that there is no relationship of any kind between the Maccabees of Thessaloniki and those of Sofia. If, it added, there were any chance relations between the two sports associations, then they were of a purely sporting nature, as would be the relations between Greek and Bulgarian sports associations.

Makedonia returned twice to the issue (5 and 7 September 1930), provoking from the *Indépendant* sarcastic comments indicative of the fact that the newspaper had been displeased to see revealed what their fellow-Jews in Bulgaria had been saying.

The dispute in the Press ended there, without it becoming known that a representative of the Thessaloniki Maccabees had been present at the meeting in Sofia. However, the dispute was not confined to these two newspapers. The *Ephemeris ton Valkanion* (3 September 1930) called *inter alia* upon the Maccabees of Thessaloniki to state openly and plainly whether they agreed with their colleagues in Bulgaria and with the *komitadjis*, providing evidence – not merely of an academic nature – of the points on which they disagreed.

The *Eleftheron Vima* (Athens, 1 September 1930) expressed its surprise that the self-styled Jewish Zionists of the Maccabee Association should have been among those who attended the conference of the Macedonian Youth Movement, and concluded by doubting whether the Zionists of other countries would collaborate with those in Bulgaria, although it said that our own Zionists have never declared themselves to be ready to lay down their lives for Greece and its rightful causes. Yet whilst the disputes and the campaigns in the Press were in full swing, *Action* (Thessaloniki, 4 September 1931) published another report from Sofia, giving details of the festival of the Bulgarian Maccabees.

Quite a number of months went by, and the question had been forgotten. Despite their failure to adopt an unreserved attitude during the debate in the Press in the first days of September, and despite their obvious displeasure over the revival of the question, what was of primary importance was that the Jews had asserted that they were completely unaware of what had taken place in Sofia – over which, even so, there was no shortage of enthusiastic reactions, since even after the disclosures made in the Greek Press, a Jewish newspaper could be found which was prepared to publish a relevant report from the Bulgarian capital. However, while the *Indépendant* (3 September 1930) had assured its readers, in the most unambiguous terms, that there was no relationship of whatever kind between the Maccabees of Thessaloniki and the Maccabees of Bulgaria, the annual review of the Maccabee Association *'El Maccabeo'* (No. 1 of the year 5697), in an article describing the Association's activities, revealed that it had been represented at the festival in Sofia. There follows the relevant extract, in translation:

"The attention of our Board was attracted by the activities and the progress made by the Maccabees in other countries. We followed with great interest the proceedings of the convention of the World Union of Maccabees, to whose Presidium we deemed advisable to address a message of solidarity as well as a memorandum about past and present activities of the Maccabees of Thessaloniki, with the intention that we, too, should succeed in joining the ranks beneath the banner of the Union so that we may be inspired by their brilliant example and collaborate very closely with them in furthering the shared ideal of the physical and moral elevation of the Jewish youth in a strictly patriotic spirit. The President of the Union of Maccabees replied most cordially to our application for membership, welcoming us enthusiastically and inviting us to send a delegation from our Board to the festival organised by the Maccabees of Bulgaria, which took place from the 27th to the 31st of August last. Taking into account the overall significance of our collaboration with the World Union, we hastened to accept the invitation and sent our friend Mr Isaac Cohen as a delegate to Sofia, with the mission of entering into negotiations with Dr Rosenfeld, member of the Presidium of the World Union, and of examining the possibility of organising, during the course of the year 1931, a display with the participation of Maccabees from all over the Balkans. Our readers will later be able to enjoy a fine article by Mr Cohen on what he saw and did during his stay in Sofia."

No such article has yet been published. From the report published in *El Maccabeo*, however – of which you were informed in my report No. 2141 of 8 April – it is clear that the presence of a Maccabee delegate in Sofia was deliberately suppressed, both when the *Indépendant* asserted in such a categorical manner, amid its ironical replies to *Makedonia*, that there was no relationship of any kind between the Maccabees of Thessaloniki and those of Sofia even after the return of Mr Isaac Cohen to Thessaloniki. Not only was no protest made, as it ought to have been, over the fact that having set out to attend a sports festival he found himself a participant in a political event – and, indeed, one addressed to an organisation which is regarded as law-abiding, and declares itself to be so – but, on the contrary, his mission to Sofia is included in the proceedings of the association and referred to as one among those with noteworthy and meaningful accomplishments. And all this as if nothing unusual or irregular had occurred and as if the dispute in the Press which I have described in detail had never occurred.

It has to be noted, however, that *El Maccabeo* was published, as it is every year, in Ladino, that is, in a language which is not accessible to the Greek public, and thus the Greek public would have been unaware of the Isaac Cohen affair. Unfortunately, this did not happen, since months later *Makedonia* found out about the revelation contained in *El Maccabeo* and, unable to discover exactly what had been written – or even the name of Isaac Cohen, the delegate who went to Sofia – was the first to report the news in its issue of 20 June of this year. Despite the ungrounded and irrelevant additions about the alleged arrival of *komitadjis* in Thessaloniki, what *Makedonia* had to say about the matter was accurate, since it is a fact, first, that a representative of the Maccabees was present in Sofia at the festival at the end of last year, and second, that a representative at that festival attended the conference of the Macedonian Youth Movement (another organisation belonging to the *Komitato*), taking place in Sofia at the same time and, in the name of the Maccabees, made the declaration about the hoisting of the Bulgarian flag even over Thessaloniki.

Although there was still time, even at the eleventh hour, for the Maccabees to have done what they ought to have done last September, on the return of Isaac Cohen – who may have been informed only then of what had been said in Sofia – and something they did not do even when publishing their annual review, the Jewish Press replied immediately and in the same strong terms which the *Indépendant* had used last September, insulting and denouncing *Makedonia*.

Progrès (21 June 1931) reprinted the entire article from *Makedonia*, stating (falsely) that the presence in Sofia of a Maccabee representative from Thessaloniki had not been kept secret, and that it was unthinkable that they should have been absent from the meeting in Sofia, attended by 2,000 Jewish athletes who concerned themselves only with sport. The article concludes, most insolently, with the statement that the readers of *Makedonia* would be the first to laugh at such nonsense, unworthy of a newspaper claiming to be serious. According to this newspaper, then, the seriousness or otherwise of a Greek newspaper is judged to lie in its failure to disclose that Greek citizens had been present, as delegates, at a convention during which wishes to the detriment of the integrity of the Greek State were expressed, and that an authorised person had been sent, in the name of the convention, to convey its greetings and express the same feelings to a conference consisting of people among whom the gangs sent out against Greek territory are formed.

The other two Ladino morning papers, *Action* and *Pueblo* (21 June 1931), also dealt with the question. The former attacked *Makedonia*, stating *inter alia* that the presence of Mr Cohen in Sofia had been a formality, and that his visit had no connection with the feelings of the *Komitadjis*, while the latter said, ironically, that the seriousness of *Makedonia* could be judged by its report that nuns were planning to collaborate with the *Komitadjis*.

Among the Jewish evening newspapers, the *Indépendant* (21 June 1931), under the title 'Storm in a Teacup', counter-attacked *Makedonia*, claiming that Mr Cohen would not have been in a position to understand what had been said in Sofia because the statements in support of the *Komitato* had been made in Bulgarian, while the *Tiempo* described the report in the above-mentioned newspaper as childish.

On the following day, Monday 22 June, *Action* wrote that the presence of a Maccabee representative from Thessaloniki at the Sofia festival was perfectly natural and that it could not be seen as in any way connected with the speeches delivered by the Bulgarian Maccabees. *Pueblo* expressed its displeasure over the appearance of the "famous reservists", who although being aware that the whole fuss had been started by a single newspaper in order to create a cheap impression, had nonetheless issued a resolution attacking the Maccabees. The resolution in question had been passed by the reserve non-commissioned officers of Macedonia and Thrace and had been published in the evening papers the previous day.

On the same day, *Makedonia* (22 June 1931) dealt more widely with the question and published a lengthy announcement from the Maccabee Association asserting, contrary to what had been stated in the review *El Maccabeo*, that Mr Cohen had not had a meeting in Sofia with Dr Rosenfeld, the representative of the World Union of Maccabees. However, the announcement refrained from protesting over the fact that statements in favour of the Bulgarian *Komitato* had been made in the presence of the Maccabee delegate from Thessaloniki and from deploring these statements.

However, *Makedonia* also published and commented on a statement by the Minister of the Interior confirming that the Government was aware of the activities of the Maccabees. This statement had first been published in the *Ephemeris ton Valkanion* (21 June 1931), in a report from Athens. The Jews of Thessaloniki described the statement as forged and were heard to call for the prosecution of the newspapers which had counterfeited it here in order to inflame the populace. This accusation is not accurate, since the statement by the Minister of the Interior had been published in *Proti* (Athens, 21 February 1931) and was passed on to Thessaloniki after that publication.

Apart from *Makedonia*, this statement was also commented upon in other newspapers. The *Ephemeris ton Valkanion* (21 June 1931) wrote:

"The Minister of the Interior has stated that the activities of the Maccabees are known and are being watched. In view of this official confirmation of a regrettable fact, we believe that measures should be taken to ensure that the gentlemen in question know that any treacherous action on their part will be ruthlessly stamped out.

"If they wish to become friends and collaborators of the *Komitadjis*, they need do no more than emigrate to the country where the *komatidjis* live, where they can collaborate with them freely."

Under the title 'Their Pride and Joy', *Makedonika Nea* (22 June 1931) carried the following comment:

"If the Jewish organisation 'Maccabees' is actually guilty of anti-Greek activities, as the Minister of the Interior stated, then one wonders why the competent authorities have not yet hastened to dissolve it. In cases in which our existence as a nation is threatened, there is no place for sympathy or mercy. If these 'Maccabees' were in another state and if they plotted against it, they would not only be dissolved: they would be expelled beyond its borders, if not sent to prison."

The *Indépendant* published in the evening of 22 June called for an investigation to be carried out to determine the liability of the Maccabees and observed that if anything particularly serious had happened the authorities would not have waited ten months before taking the appropriate action.

On the morning of 23 June, *Makedonia* carried the leader attached to the present report, under the title 'Let us Settle the Accounts', while *Progrès* also in a leader ('The Light') referred to accusations based on dangerously slanderous rumours which were causing a deeply regrettable upsurge of public feeling. "The time has come", added the newspaper, "to shed light on this poisonous atmosphere"; below, it stated that in the event of the investigation, which it demanded with all its powers, uncovering a loathsome plot, the perpetrators of such unpatriotic action should be punished, whoever they are.

Both Ladino newspapers were equally forceful and provocative in their morning issues of 23 June, persisting in ignoring the real situation. While admitting as a fact that a representative had been present in Sofia when the Bulgarian Jews were expressing themselves in favour of the Bulgarian *Komitato* and the autonomy of Macedonia, *Action* (23 June) saw it as disgraceful that they were obliged to defend themselves to the authorities over such a base accusation.

Thus, faced by the general outcry on the part of Greek public opinion, the Maccabee Association had not only failed to issue an announcement deploring what had been said in Sofia in the presence of its representative but continued to speak of slander plots, etc., and to demand the intervention of the judicial authorities so as to determine whether the Maccabees were liable, and if so, how.

The General Governor, Mr Gonatas, asked about the issue by journalists on the afternoon of the 21st, and in particular whether he had formed an opinion subsequent to the particulars submitted to him by the Jewish Community, stated (*Nea Alitheia*, 23 June 1931) the following:

"I believe the Jewish Community ought to have issued an announcement, since it was in possession of more information, in order to clear up the matter, as they explained to me yesterday. I have formed the opinion that the representative of the Maccabees sent from here did not take part in the discussions held in Sofia, and I hope that the Jewish Community will issue the relevant announcement – today, at that – to set matters right."

In fact, no such announcement was issued, while on the evening of the same day the first anti-Jewish leaflets were distributed by the members of the National Student Union, giving rise to noisy incidents which disturbed the centre of the city. In a telegram to the Havas Agency, a young Zionist – using the signature of its regular correspondent in Thessaloniki – described these incidents as the first anti-Semitic disturbances since the arrival of the Jews from Spain in 1492.

I attach hereto the issues of *Makedonia* and *Progrès* for 24 June, which, as might have been expected, dealt at length with the events of the preceding evening. *Makedonia* published, *inter alia*, the text of the leaflets distributed (those of the National Student Union, which, though provoked by the Maccabee Association, make no mention of it in their text), the statement of the General Governor, various announcements, including those of the EEE, the Veterans, etc., and, lastly, a lengthy announcement from the Jewish Community which, though refraining from repudiating what had been said in Sofia, described the event as lacking in substance.

Progrès, publishing more or less the same announcements as *Makedonia*, carried a large headline describing the leaflets as the result of the Press campaign and in its leader called for the uncovering of those responsible for the whole affair and their strict punishment.

Pueblo (24 June 1931) commented that for the first time in 500 years Thessaloniki had heard cries of "Down with the Jews!", while *Action* argued that the General Governor, and not the Jewish Community ought to have issued an announcement, in order to put Greek public opinion on the path of truth and clear the Jews of the slanders hurled at them. "If", the newspaper added, "he was not convinced that it was a conspiracy, then he could have urged calm while promising to announce the results of the investigations".

Inevitably, one is amazed by the perseverance of the entire Jewish Press in avoiding the issuing of an announcement, even one from the Maccabee Association, simply expressing protest over the fact that a representative of theirs attended a sports meeting in Sofia and that, in his presence and without his knowledge (since it was alleged that everything in Sofia was said in Bulgarian), his fellow-Jews had made statements against the integrity of the state of which he happened to be a citizen.

The attack on the offices of the Maccabees took place on the evening of 24 June, and their Vice President, Herrera, who was injured, made a statement to *Nea Alitheia* (28 June 1931) to the effect that at the moment of the attack the Board of Management was meeting in order to compose an announcement. Needless to add that, on the following day (25 June), all the Press devoted whole pages to accounts of the events and the tone of the Jewish newspapers had become ferocious. *Makedonia*, continuing to play the leading role in the struggle, relied on what had been said by the Member of Parliament Mr Bessantchi in the parliamentary debate of 22 June in order to proclaim that the charge made from the very first had now been admitted: in other words, that a Maccabee representative from Thessaloniki had been present in Sofia. In parallel, *Nea Alitheia*, which as of the previous day (24 June) had insisted on the need for the Jewish Community to issue an announcement, published a leading article on 25 June (attached hereto) which made an impression among the Jewish public, who are used to reading, as in the past, only words of flattery in the newspaper in question. "In view of the presence of the Maccabees at the Sofia conference", the newspaper continued, "and of their participation in, and toleration of, matters of an unpatriotic nature, it was unthinkable that the lively and vigorous souls of the Greek youth should remain unmoved and undisturbed, or that they should remain indifferent in restrained tolerance. No one imagined that."

The other Greek newspapers, although avoiding articles directed against the Jews of the type carried by *Makedonia* or even *Nea Alitheia* – and in some cases even defending them and openly condemning what had been done to them – nonetheless reported the incidents very widely and did not omit to publish various announcements, telegrams, etc. supporting the patriotic organisations and congratulating them on their attitude.

Makedonika Nea (26 June), which was the newspaper most sympathetic to the Jews, did not fail to express disapproval of the tactics of the *Indépendant*:

"Although we can understand the bitterness with which the *Indépendant* comments on the regrettable incidents of the last few days, we cannot explain why it has involved the Liberal Party in such sorry events by claiming that the sign for the uprising was given by an agent of that Party.

"If we admit that a Liberal newspaper happened to comment in sharp terms on the question of the Maccabees, then the *Indépendant* would also have to accept that other Liberal newspapers in the city deplored the events. Whatever the case may be, party politics has nothing to do with the sad events, as our French-language colleague knows better than any one – which is why we are so surprised at the allusions in its article of yesterday's date."

In the meantime, *Makedonia* was still keeping its intense campaign going, as can be seen from the issues attached hereto. Some of its short articles, in any case, are characteristic. In reply to an article in *Progrès*, praising the services performed by the French-language newspapers, *Makedonia* published the following comment (on 28 June):

"In a long article defending the Jewish community, *Progrès* explains which, and how many, services are provided to the nation by the French-language newspapers published by Jews. Let us be allowed to say that we have our reservations about this. French-language newspapers published by fanatical Jews which at any time and on the slightest pretext present the Jewish population as having been dealt with unfairly and persecuted and which send telegrams with monstrous lies abroad are anything but Greek and do anything but benefit the country. The question of the French-language newspapers should be raised as widely as possible, and it shall be."

On the statement made by Herrera, the Vice President of the Maccabees injured in the attack of 24 June (*Nea Alitheia*, 28 June 1931), *Makedonia* published the following comment the next day (29 June 1931):

"Herrera, the injured Maccabee, told a reporter from *Nea Alitheia* in connection with the participation of the Maccabees in the festivals and conferences held in Bulgaria that the Jews of Bulgaria are Bulgarians who have a great love of Bulgaria, while the Jews of Greece are Greeks who love Greece equally greatly (?) and so on and so forth. All the Maccabees are brothers and support one another. That is to say, *viz.*, *videlicet*, in other words, Mr Herrera is telling us that the Jews are not Bulgarians nor Greeks, nor Germans nor Chinese: they are Jews only, living in conventional fashion and, with masterly powers of acting, deceiving everyone and everything. Wherever they find themselves, they are in agreement with the powers that be – and Mr Herrera is not far from the truth."

I submit, attached hereto, the announcement from the Jewish Community and of the Jewish Associations and Organisations denying that they had asked for the dissolution of the Patriotic Organisations and the relevant comments from *Makedonia* (28 June 1931). I also submit articles by the Thessaloniki lawyers Messrs K. Economou (*Indépendant*, 26 June 1931), Spiliakos (*Progrès*, 27 June 1931) and I. Varvitsiotis (*Phos*, 28 June 1931) defending the Jewish community and expressing their sympathy for it. I also submit the article published in Greek in the Ladino newspaper *Action* on (.....June) [*sic*] by the journalist Mr Alexandros Orologas praising the work and patriotic feelings of the members of the Maccabee Association.

Regardless of the seriousness of the subsequent sad and bloody actions against the Jewish population, the tactics of the Jewish Press continue to be the same as those employed since the first day, with the guideline of describing as slanders, provocation of the Jews, etc., the fact that the Greek Press made use of a disclosure in a Jewish newspaper published in Thessaloniki to the effect that the festival or conference held in Sofia last year during which the Jews of Bulgaria declared themselves in favour of the autonomy of Macedonia and the conquest of Thessaloniki, was attended – notwithstanding the assurance to the contrary given last year – by a representative of the Maccabees, who, not having protested at the time, continued to refuse to do so even when Greek public opinion – rightly or wrongly – took to the streets and engaged in acts of violence.

57

Y. Calochristianakis, Police Director of Thessaloniki, to the Ministry of the Interior

confidential/ secret report   Thessaloniki, 10 July 1931

Action taken by the Jews subsequent to the recent incidents:

I have the honour to report the following action taken by the Jews of our city subsequent to the recent incidents.

1) On the day following the burning of the huts in the Campbell district, a group of Jews of Serbian citizenship visited the leather merchant Arouestis, a Jew and a Serbian citizen, and after a discussion it was decided that they should make their way to the Yugoslav Consulate seeking its protection, and a committee of five, chaired by the said Arouestis, was appointed for this purpose. The committee presented itself to the Yugoslav Consul General, to whom they explained the fears in the minds of the Jews of Serbian citizenship who are residents of Thessaloniki.

The Consul General evinced great interest and told the committee that he would immediately proceed to make the appropriate representations. If Serbian citizens were among the Jews who were beaten or suffered other loss or damage, the Consul General asked that a list of their names should be submitted to him, but according to my information no such list was submitted.

2) Furthermore, various Jews of Italian citizenship visited the Italian Consulate and sought the protection of the Consul, while a group led by Isaac Tivoli, who

until two months ago was pharmacist in the Community pharmacy in the Campbell district and was dismissed from his post by order of the General Governance, presented themselves to the Italian Consul and asked the Consul to allow them to raise the Italian flag on their houses and shops. The Consul received them kindly but forbade them to raise the flags, advising them to go about their business in complete peace of mind, since the competent Greek authorities would do their duty. On the other hand, if any persons had suffered damages, they should present themselves at the Consulate and declare their losses so that he could take action for them to receive compensation.

When the Italian Consul's reply and attitude were discussed by the Jews, they were disheartened, since for years they have been deluding themselves with the hope that any serious incidents committed against them would be followed by sharp intervention, especially from Italy. It has not been ascertained whether any statements were submitted to the Italian Consulate by Italian citizens who suffered losses.

3) Even on the first day of the incidents, the Jewish Community was extremely active, and after the arson in the Campbell district, for reasons of expediency and to avoid comment, it established Mr Kon, inspector of Jewish schools, in the Hirsch Hospital with instructions to prepare the relevant reports and, in general, to produce an account of the recent events.

For this purpose, Kon was allocated a special office which outsiders were forbidden to enter and where he received successive visits, all day, from various Community officials, each bringing the particulars which he had assembled.

All the Jews who alleged that they had suffered losses of any kind were examined in detail and in depth by the Community officials.

Among the Jewish victims was a certain Romano, employee of the Press Bureau of the General Governance and resident of the Campbell district, who was attacked in his home. After beating him up as well as his wife, the assailants took away 3,000 drachmas and various valuables. They also strip-searched the local midwife, but found nothing.

It was the intention of the Community officials that the said Romano should present himself to the investigating magistrates and testify in detail about the events, since they had the impression that as he receives a salary from the State and is a stated friend of Greece, he would refrain from presenting himself or, if he did so, would not testify in detail. So that the Community would not appear to be an interested party, it used third parties since it realised that Romano was not inclined to curry favour with the Community, and employed the following method:

Since Romano was receiving treatment, as a casualty, in the Hirsch Hospital, the Community introduced into the Hospital and installed in his room the healthy brother of the Community employee Yacoel, with the obvious purpose that, during conversation with Romano, he should extract from him the entire series of events so that he could later be used as a witness. This move was unsuccessful, however, since according to information received by the department, Romano made no disclosures whatever.

4) On the 4th inst., the American journalist George Agronsky arrived in Thessaloniki from London, as an emissary of the Jewish Press Agency in London, and made his way to the Jewish Community to study the situation that had arisen.

Community officials were immediately placed at his disposal and, with them, he toured all the points in the city where incidents had taken place. He repeatedly visited the Hirsch Hospital, where he had long discussions with the officials who had been charged with investigating the events and with Kon, in his office. With Kon, he drew up a lengthy telegram in which he greatly exaggerated the events, going as far as to describe a whole series of rapes, which may have been prompted by the strip-searching of the midwife in Romano's house.

5) The headmaster of the Altcheh private school asked Agronsky to obtain a cash grant from the Jewish National Capital to support the teaching of the Hebrew language, and Agronsky promised his willing support.

I report the above with the request that you be good enough to take this information into consideration and issue the appropriate instructions. I would also like to state that if the reports submitted by Agronsky are published in the Greek Press, the current calm will certainly be succeeded by a fresh wave of high feelings.

❦

58*

C. Xanthopoulos, Consul General in Buenos Aires, to the President of the Emile Zola 2a Lodge

letter   Buenos Aires, 11 July 1931

Dear Mr President

On 7 July, the Consulate General received a letter from you accompanied by a memorandum on the recent events in Thessaloniki with the request that the memorandum be forwarded to His Excellency the President of the Hellenic Republic.

Having the honour to be the sole representative of Greece in the Republic of Argentina today, I feel the obligation, in view of the eminent destination of your memorandum, to explain to you the thoughts which a reading of your memorandum provoked in me.

I was unable without bewilderment and sorrow to read the phrases contained in the memorandum about massacres and vandalous persecution of the Jewish population of Thessaloniki and about the alleged toleration of such acts by those whose mission and duty it is to prevent them.

Such judgments, in view of the fact that we have only incomplete information by telegraph about the facts, are in no way justified where Greece and its Government are concerned. It is known the world over that in Greece, a free and democratic country *par excellence*, the Jewish community enjoys complete liberty and is subject to no restrictions whatever of a religious, civic or political nature, while it lives and has always lived in harmony with its Greek fellow-countrymen both in pre-War and in post-War Greece. Proof of this, *inter alia*, is to be found in the fact that shortly before the regrettable events to which you refer, the President of the Jewish Community in Thessaloniki sent a telegram of thanks to His Excellency the Prime Minister expressing his gratitude for the particular care which the Greek State devotes to the Jewish Community.

It will certainly have escaped your attention that the telegrams referring to the incidents in question noted that the local authorities had taken all the measures dictated by circumstances [...] [*sic*]

Against such a background, how could it even cross anyone's mind that the events were tolerated by those whose mission and duty it was to prevent them?

59

S. Gonatas, General Governor of Macedonia, to the Ministry of Education

confidential report   Thessaloniki, 30 July 1931

We have the honour to inform you that, in implementation of Law 4837 (Government Gazette No. 252/25 June 1930), Article 3 expressly states that "the Chief Rabbi and the Rabbis must be of Greek nationality", the Ministry of the Interior (Central Aliens Service) has already ordered the expulsion of one Rabbi who was a Serb citizen, which has already taken place, while two Rabbis in Thessaloniki, also Serb citizens, are to be expelled for the same reason.

It should be noted that Yugoslavia, whose laws also prohibit foreign nationals from serving as Rabbis in Serbia, has recently expelled a Rabbi who was a Greek citizen.

Now, the two Members of Parliament belonging to the Jewish Community here and Senator Mallah, wishing to retain Abraham Kamhi, one of the Rabbis scheduled for expulsion, in the service of the Community in view of his outstanding qualifications in the art of circumcision and of his preaching to his congregation, would like to interpret the above Article in such a way as to mean that the word "be of" should include the concept that the foreign rabbis will be allowed to remain in service here after an application to acquire Greek citizenship – in other words, that they will be able to serve during the three-year period which it is required should elapse between the application and the acquisition of citizenship, which Rabbi Kamhi is willing to ask for.

If such an interpretation – which they claim was given by the Minister when the law was before Parliament – is given, it will facilitate their intention of bringing rabbis into Greece from other countries at any other time, and also a Chief Rabbi, since they have already stated that no suitable candidate for that post, with Greek citizenship, is available.

In bringing the above to your attention, we would be grateful if you would be good enough to inform us of your views on the matter.

<hr />

ATTACHMENT TO **59**

C. Stephanopoulos, Legal Adviser, Ministry of Education, to the Directorate of Religious Affairs of the same Ministry

report   Athens, 2 October 1931

In reply to the communication from the General Governor of Macedonia forwarded to me, in which the question is raised of whether in order to acquire Greek citizenship it is required that three years should elapse from the date of the relevant declaration of the applicant, with particular reference to the Chief Rabbi of Macedonia, *et al.*, together with the return of the relevant document-ation, I have the honour to express my opinion on the subject, which is as follows.

In view of the expulsion from Macedonia of a Rabbi who is a Serbian citizen on the orders of the Ministry of the Interior, and of the imminent expulsion of two more Rabbis of Serbian citizenship, the General Governor of Macedonia, acting on the recommendation of the Jewish Members of Parliament and the Senate from Thessaloniki, insists that Rabbi Kamhi should remain in Greece without fail in view of his outstanding qualifications in the art of circumcision and of his preaching to his congregation, and recommends, for this purpose, that Article 3, para. 2 of Law 4837, which states that the Chief Rabbi and the Rabbis must be of Greek nationality, be given the interpretation that such persons may reside in Greece after the date on which they have submitted their application to acquire Greek citizenship without the elapse of the three years period required by law, particularly in view of the fact that, during the passage of the above law, that interpretation was given by the Minister of Religious Affairs.

A review of the Proceedings of the parliamentary session of 17 June 1930, at which Law 4837 was passed after a single reading, has revealed no statement by the competent Minister giving an interpretation to which such a meaning could be attached and entitling the Rabbi in question to remain in Greece as of the date on which he submitted his application for Greek citizenship.

According to the provision of Article 15 of the civil law of 28 October [...] [sic], any person wishing to be naturalised as a Greek shall be obliged to declare this intention to the municipal authorities of the place in which he wishes to reside and, after that declaration, to reside in Greece for two years, in the case of persons of ethnic Greek descent, or three years, in the case of persons of other descent, etc., attaching the certificates required by law, and, in addition, to take the oath required of Greek citizens, finally acquiring Greek citizenship only after he has taken that oath. However, in accordance with the provision of Article 1 of Law 3842 (G.G. 197) of 1911, amending the relevant provisions of the above Law, the naturalisation as a Greek citizen of any alien may take place by Royal Decree prior to the elapse of the time limits set above by Article 15 of the civil law.

In view of all the above, I am of the opinion that the naturalisation of the above Rabbi could take place without the elapse of the three-year period if, after the preliminary procedure required by law has been completed, a Decree were to be issued granting him Greek nationality, thus, after his taking the oath, making him finally a Greek citizen. In this way, the desired solution will be facilitated in a lawful manner.

60

S. Gonatas, General Governor of Macedonia, to the Political Office of the Prime Minister

confidential report   Thessaloniki, 21 November 1931

It is common knowledge that the old Jewish cemetery in Thessaloniki occupies an enormous area which, according to the City Plan and the University complex prepared by the French engineer Hébrard, is destined to become a park and university campus.

It is also common knowledge that whenever this issue has been raised since, there have been vigorous protests on the part both of the Ladino Press here and from Paris, where a considerable number of Jews from Thessaloniki have settled. These protests are based in part on the strict provision of their religion which forbids the disinterment of the remains of the dead in perpetuity and in part on the fact that since the cemetery of Thessaloniki contains the old tombs of distinguished Jews it ought to be classed as an archaeological site.

Last year, the question was revived once more when it was decided to demolish the Aghia Photeini district which abuts on the cemetery so as to create the city park, and there was once more an outcry and protesting.

Now, a few days ago, the Senate of the University visited me and informed me that one of the buildings provided for (that of the Department of Physics) is to be erected as rapidly as possible, and that, when constructed on the site provided for by Hébrard, it will occupy a small part of the Jewish cemetery. The Senate asked for my help in the negotiations with the Jewish Community to make the said site available.

I invited the President of the Jewish Community and the Jewish Senator and Member of Parliament to a private meeting and explained to them the urgent need in which we find ourselves to use a small part of their cemetery. I also provided them with a drawing of the small space which will be required, asking them to inform me of the formalities which would be required in order to obtain its cession.

They admitted to me, in confidence, that, as individuals, they recognise the needs of the living as being superior to those of the dead and that the price of the piece of ground would enable them to meet many of the urgent needs of the community. However, they declared themselves unauthorised to reply to me and stated that they would bring the matter before the Community Council. They were afraid that because of their canon laws it would not be possible for the Community to give its consent, and so all that remained was for us to occupy the area without it.

Since that time, the Community has not given us its answer.

However, the Ladino Press has been dealing with the matter every day since then, and we were informed by it that the Community instructed the Rabbinical Council to examine the question. The Council, on the one hand, dismissed in principle the request for the sale of part of the cemetery as being in contravention of the sacred rules, and, on the other, conducted an on-the-spot investigation which revealed that the part of the cemetery we have requested contains the grave of a rabbi regarded as a sage. Naturally, the Jewish Press, relying on this expert opinion of its clergymen, has since opposed any thought of expropriation with still greater vehemence. We submit, attached hereto, extracts from these articles. The Jewish population, however, has to date evinced no displeasure.

It emerges clearly from this that the Community's response will in no circumstances be affirmative since even those who inwardly accept our views are incapable of stating this in public, considering that doing so would incur the wrath of the Jewish masses, who would be incited in this direction by their political opponents.

It thus remains for us to determine whether we should occupy the site required for the construction of the new University building, having in this case to face the passive resistance of the Jewish population here and general obloquy, or whether we should back down, abandoning the extension of the University and cancelling the creation of the park.

The space which is to be occupied is small and is located at the edge of the cemetery, adjacent to the University building already standing, and its use would constitute a starting-point and precedent for the further use of the whole area in the future. Measures will be taken for the removal and safekeeping of the inscribed plaques and we shall certainly comply with any formalities which may be recommended to us.

We unreservedly agree with this point of view, but since this is a question which may create difficulties – of a moral rather than a substantive nature - for the Government, we considered it essential that we seek your opinion before taking any action.

The Committee of Jews will bring the same issue to your attention on its arrival in Athens.

61

The Prefect of Corfu to the Director of the Prefecture

confidential order   Corfu, 13 January 1932

Further to our confidential order No. 115 of 23 December last and in accordance with order No. 28849 of the Ministry of Foreign Affairs, please pay the sum of two thousand five hundred (2,500) drachmas for the salary of the Chief Rabbi for the month of January 1932 out of the sum of 80,000 drachmas for the educational needs of the Jewish School.

62

The Thessaloniki Press Bureau to the Ministry of Foreign Affairs

report   Thessaloniki, 19 January 1932

The Eighth Zionist Conference of Greece
(Thessaloniki, 25-27 December 1931)

The annual conference of Greek Zionists, meeting in Thessaloniki for the eighth consecutive year, took place on this occasion after a break of two years, on the day set some weeks before – that is, on Friday 25 December 1931 (Christmas Day) – and lasted three days. The proceedings of the conference were declared closed late on the evening of Sunday 27 December.

The French-language Press devoted very little space to the work of the conference, implementing the tactics faithfully complied with of not releasing to non-Jews details of what is discussed and decided at Jewish 'national' meetings of this kind. Similarly, the contents of the daily Jewish Press were not sufficient to allow one to form an opinion of what exactly had taken place at the conference. As a result, we were compelled to rely on the comparatively detailed information provided by the weekly *Renacencia Giudia*, organ of the Zionist Federation of Greece, which gave a detailed account of the Eighth Conference in its issues of 1 and 8 January 1932, published after the Conference had taken place.

The conference of 25-27 December 1931 was not as interesting from the point of view of the discussions which took place as its predecessor (30-31 March 1930). The opposition did not attend this conference. It consisted of delegates belonging to the Zionist Federation, which organises each of the conferences. Those who split away from the Federation two years ago (these included the Member of Parliament D. Matalon, who died some months ago) did not attempt to take part in this conference. They were repeatedly mentioned during the course of discussions, particularly in connection with the *Artsenou* Zionist association they have founded. It was emphasised, in passing, that there is a need to enlighten the members of that Association, and that any concessions to them must be avoided.

After noting the fact that the conference was attended by Mr Fischer, authorised representative of the Jewish National Fund, who arrived quite a few days before the conference began, it should then be emphasised that the most detailed and lively discussions were those connected with the affairs of the Jewish Community. We deal with this part of the conference at length because what was said demonstrates yet again that the Zionists will always do anything in order to remain within the Community. However, their struggle is not an easy one this time, given the existence of the said opposition. It was recognised on this occasion, nonetheless, that without a Community in the hands of the Zionists or without control of whatever happens in it, nothing is possible for the Zionists. The address delivered by Mr Bessantchi shows that his positions are in no way different from what they have always been. On this occasion, too, he proclaimed, as he had at the Sixth Conference (2-4 February 1929), that for the Zionists to fail to involve themselves in the administration of the Community was tantamount to suicide, and that the Zionists would be willing to surrender the Community to their opponents as long as the latter were agreeable to the implementation of the Zionist educational programme.

"Since a large number of Jews will always remain in the Diaspora, it is our duty to ensure that their patriotic feelings are strengthened. In order to achieve that, it is necessary that we should rear their children, from a tender age, in a Jewish atmosphere."

THE INAUGURAL ADDRESS BY MR MALLAH

The conference opened with an inaugural address by Senator Mallah, President of the Zionist Federation, who confirmed what the Zionists have always maintained – namely, that Jewish nationalism is growing and gaining ground only in those places in which the Jews live in difficult conditions, and that, in contrast, efforts to promote it have failed wherever the Jewish population is prosperous.

Thessaloniki 1932. Inaugural ceremonies for the Saul Modiano home for the aged, which continues to serve the community to this day. In the first row from the left: the President of the Jewish Community, Jakob Cazes, the deputy Chief Rabbi, Haim Habib and the director of operations of the Allatini Moses Morpurgo Foundation. In the second row: first from left, Senator Ascher Mallah, and, fifth, Senator Albert Tchénio. Recanati Archive, Israel.

Prosperity, he continued, can be assumed to exist in those countries in which assimilation has taken place. For the purpose of comparison, one could point to countries such as France or Britain on the one hand, or, on the other, Poland, the Baltic states, and Romania – in particular, the territories newly annexed to that country.

The beginning of Mr Mallah's speech included the following words: "However, we can see our movement growing and progressing with particular success among those masses which today seem to find consolation for their sufferings of all kinds in our movement for the renaissance of Judaism and in the tendency towards a life of freedom. In these conditions, it must be noted that this gives us renewed strength."

The President of the Zionist Federation then referred in his speech to the attempts made to undermine the Federation's task, to the work of the Zionists in general, to his trip to Palestine last year and, lastly, to the departure for Palestine of many fighters for Zionism from Thessaloniki. But, he added, they are being replaced by new and eager forces which are continuing their work. "It is our ambition", he concluded, "to offer the Federation in Greece, the organisation entrusted with the task of the Jewish renaissance and of the reconstruction of our Jewish national home in Palestine, as much support as possible".

LETTERS OF GREETING

After the election of the Presidium of the conference, whose members included Mr Mallah himself, various letters of greeting to the delegates were read out. The first, from the office of the Chief Rabbinate of Thessaloniki, called upon the delegates to be firm and persevering in their mission and not to be downhearted by any difficulties or obstacles. Courage and firmness, noted the letter, are among the unique qualities of man, and each of us ought always to bear in mind the commands of the Bible (the relevant point in the Pentateuch being quoted), which, during this week, urge us to model ourselves on the immortal David, who undertook with complete success the task of unifying and consolidating the Jewish people on earth.

The Jewish Community expressed its hope that the conference be fertile in its results for the national ideal and confirmed, *inter alia*, that it watches with the closest interest all developments intended to strengthen and extend what has been achieved in Palestine together with the efforts to reinforce the great movement towards national renaissance.

The letter from the teachers of Hebrew (towards the dissemination of which great efforts are being made) in the Community schools included the following extract: "The teacher of Hebrew, creator and supporter of the effort for Jewish liberation, understands perfectly that the only path leading to the physical and spiritual health of the Jewish people is that which involves the dissemination of Jewish education. Today, more than in the past, that problem ought to occupy its rightful place at the Zionist conference, since it is impossible to speak of Zionism without Jewish education."

IN MEMORY OF THE DECEASED - MR FISCHER

After the greetings had been read out, Mr David Florentin, Deputy President of the Zionist Federation, listed the members who had died during the previous year, including the poet Joseph Eliya, who, although described by a section of the Greek Press as a Communist, had proved himself to be an enthusiastic Jewish nationalist. Suffice it to confirm this that he bequeathed his library to the Jewish Federation of Greece. Mr Florentin said, in his speech, of Joseph Eliya that although he had lived amid a Greek environment he had remained until his last moments loyal to his ideal.

Mr Florentin continued his speech by presenting to the conference Mr Fischer, representative of the Jewish National Fund and resident of France, who had arrived in Thessaloniki on 20 December (Press Bureau Bulletin No. 7141 of 22 December 1931). "We hope", said Mr Florentin, "that the presence among us of Mr Fischer will open up new horizons of action for us, in terms both of the National Fund and of Zionism in general". Mr Florentin did not omit to refer to the practical work accomplished by Mr Fischer in France in favour of the Jewish National Fund.

Taking the floor, Mr Fischer – who in an article in the *Indépendant* (Thessaloniki, 22 December 1931) had explained that Zionism, non-existent in France before the War, was undoubtedly gaining ground thanks to the Jews of Alsace and Lorraine and to those who had flooded into France from Eastern Europe and the Balkans after the War – said that despite the difficulties experienced by Zionism, the spark of nationalism, far from being extinguished, was growing stronger and stronger. The Jewish world had realised that the Zionist ideal was no longer a Utopia but a need, one whose complete fulfilment depends on us. He concluded with a reference to the desire on the part of the Zionists of Greece to demonstrate their strength and vitality by founding a settlement in Palestine consisting of Jews from Greece.

POLICY IN PALESTINE

In the lengthy political report then read out by Mr Florentin, *rapporteur* on Zionist policy, he argued that the best policy to be followed is the avoidance of discussions with the Arabs, with whom, he said, we should be seeking some way of reconciliation. He added that we should be striving to create a favourable atmosphere in the circles of the League of Nations and among other peoples, enlightening the world about the need for a Jewish national home. He also argued that attempts should be made to co-operate as fully as possible with Britain, without which, he said, the Balfour declaration can never be implemented.

THE ACTIVITIES OF THE FEDERATION

The work of the conference continued in the evening of the same day with a presentation by Mr Isaac Angel, in the name of the Board of Management of the

Joseph Eliya *(1901-1931) was the greatest Greek poet and philosopher of the Jewish faith. He was born in 1901 in Ioannina, where a representative Jewish Romaniot community flourished. Well trained in ancient Hebrew literature, and a speaker of four languages, Eliya translated the Song of Songs, excerpts from Job and Isaiah, Deuteronomy, the Book of Psalms and works by contemporary Jewish poets. He died young in 1931, of typhoid in Athens. In his home town a commemorative bust has been erected in his honour and a street has been named after him.*

Zionist Federation, of a detailed report on its activities throughout the year. A considerable part of the report was devoted to the split in the Zionists which had occurred at the time of the Community elections (October 1930). Mr Angel stressed the importance of the victory which the Federation had won thanks to the purity of its intentions and the loyalty of its supporters (a Pyrrhic victory, since it did not gain the Federation an absolute majority), despite the many obstacles put in its way. He continued by describing the efforts of those who split away from the Federation (and whose mouthpiece is the Ladino newspaper *Action*) to form a new Federation and the *Artsenou* Zionist Association, the principal objective of which has been to cover up various ambitions and events completely irrelevant to the Zionist movement. Moving on to discuss the efforts made in order to persuade the members of *Artsenou* to re-join the Federation, Mr Angel reported that the administration of the Association had reported to the Central Zionist Committee in London, explaining the reasons for which they had founded their Association. The Zionist Federation was obliged to submit a report of its own explaining in detail the *Artsenou* affair, and, as the *rapporteur* asserted, its views were fully accepted in London. He concluded his reference to the split by expressing his hope that the moment would come for the members of the Association to return to the straight path of Zionism.

In the section of his speech dealing with propaganda action, Mr Angel reported on Mr Florentin's tour of the Jewish communities of South Serbia during the past year and to the fact that, at a banquet held in early February of the previous year by the Municipality of Thessaloniki in honour of the delegates to the Balkan Conference, Mr Mallah had proposed a toast to Palestine and the Jewish people.

To conclude, Mr Angel remarked that they should be satisfied with the achievements of the past year. "We have, at least, the pleasure of knowing that we were able to keep our organisation afloat amid a fierce storm and to guide it to a safe harbour. The dark clouds are now on their way to being dispelled. A period of fruitful work is now beginning. New forces, many of them present here, are working with us, drawn by the beauty and nobility of our ideal. We expect much of them for the future. Together, we shall continue our activities, and our reward will be to see our organisation strong, respected and united."

ZIONISTS AND THE COMMUNITY

Mr Angel's report was followed by a wide-ranging debate revolving principally around the need for a Zionist presence in the Community. The report on this debate is almost exactly as published in *Renacencia Giudia*.

The second speaker during the debate, Robert Raphael, referred first to the negligence which the Zionist Federation had displayed in its work inside Greece, demonstrating this by the fact that the representatives from Greece at the present conference were fewer in number than in the past. Athens and Kavala had sent no representatives at all this year. The speaker went on to refer to the question of the Community, saying that he found the attitude of the Zionist members of the Community Council too passive, which according to him was a great mistake and entailed serious responsibilities. If, he said, the Zionists do not take part in the administration of the Community, then no effective Zionist work can be done. It is impossible to educate the masses if the operation of the Community schools cannot be controlled. It is the duty of the Zionists to take an interest in the Jews of the Diaspora, since only a strong Jewish Diaspora can create a strong Palestine. And since there will continue to be Jews in Thessaloniki, then the Zionists do not have the right to be indifferent towards the Community. It should remain always under their control so as not to leave a door open to those with ideas and thoughts opposed to Zionism.

Mr Albert Sciaky observed that the Zionists of Greece ought not to be represented by persons resident in Thessaloniki, who are unaware of the course of the Zionist movement in each city.

Mr D. Hazan, agreeing with Mr Raphael on the question of the Community, recommended that the Board of Management of the Zionist Federation should work actively towards the organisation by the various Zionist associations of classes in Hebrew, which should be taken by as many people as possible so as to achieve better results.

Mr R. Raphael declared himself to be amazed to hear at the conference that there was no point in the Zionists involving themselves with the Community, since the schools belonged to the Community and the school curriculum was under its control. (The delegate who had indirectly argued the opposite view was Mr Hananel Naar).

Mr Jacques Beza said that since the Zionists are not free to implement their programme, since they see obstacles being put in the way of their work, since they note that the Community is on its way to bankruptcy and they themselves are not allowed freely to act in the appropriate way, it is impossible for them to take a share in the responsibility for ambiguous situations. They should thus resign from the Community Council and remain on the alert to serve on it again as soon as effective work becomes possible. He continued by declaring himself to be opposed to any consultations with the opposition (Zionists), since any unduly hasty reconciliation would leave the door open for renewed internal quarrels.

Mr Isaac Amarillo said that without new elections it would be impossible to expect anything from the existing Community Council.

CONTINUED DISCUSSION ABOUT THE COMMUNITY

At the session which took place in the evening of Saturday 26 December, the debate about the work of the Zionists in the Community continued. Adolfos Arditti said that the Community was an instrument for Zionism and that there was a need for the conference to take decisions about our work in the Community, while those decisions should be written into the Charter of the Federation.

J. Beza criticised the work done by the Federation in the Community, saying that if it was impossible to implement the Federation's programme in the Community, then the efforts of the Zionists should be confined to scrutinising the affairs of the Community.

Mr D. Florentin explained the immediate need for the Zionists to involve themselves in the work of the Community, saying that all over the world the Zionists strove to secure majorities in the Communities. It is impossible, he said, to conceive of good Zionist work without widespread representation of the Zionists in the Community. We are not paying enough attention to this point, but to hesitate means hesitation about the work of Zionism.

THE SPEECH OF MR BESSANTCHI

D. Florentin, seen from any point of view one of the most eminent Zionists, was succeeded on the rostrum by Mr M. Bessantchi, Member of Parliament, who is also in favour of the continuation of the work of the Zionists in the Community. Since, as he said, a small number of Jews will always remain in the Diaspora, it is our duty to ensure that their patriotic feelings, too, are boosted. And if we are to achieve that result, it is essential that we should rear them in a Jewish environment from a tender age.

The Jewish Member of Parliament for Thessaloniki continued as follows:

"It is our duty to continue our effort to sustain a powerful race to serve as the reservoir from which Palestine is supplied. As a result, the task of education and schools must always be among the concerns of the Zionists. The truth of the matter is that we have not done what we ought to have achieved as a result of disagreements and of the lack of organisation which we found when we took over the Community. But it is our duty to work to implement our programme in its entirety."

After admitting, in a manner of speaking, that, given the current dispute among Zionists, work in the Community is impossible, Mr Bessantchi went on to say that efforts should be made to co-operate with the opposition and form a Board on strong foundations consisting of persons caring for the interests of all, and for their own interests. Then, he said, Zionism will be able to demonstrate that it is a living, not a decaying, organism.

Other delegates took the floor on the question of participation in the Community, and in particular of whether the Zionists ought to remain in it or withdraw, and Mr Bessantchi ultimately declared himself to be in favour of reaching an agreement with the opposition or, if this should prove impossible, the holding of fresh elections.

The debate closed with another speech by Isaac Angel, who replied to the criticisms that had been made of his report. Our aim, he said, is always to achieve co-operation with the forces outside the Federation, on condition that they are honourable. It would be possible for a campaign of enlightenment to be undertaken among the members of *Artsenou* (founded by the Zionists who split away from the Federation, and whose representatives did not take part in the current conference), but not by means of concessions harmful to the principles of Zionism. He went on to say that if the necessary work in favour of the Jewish National Fund had not been carried out, this was the result of the fact that they had been absorbed by the disputes. The same factor lay behind the delay in working on the Zionist women's associations.

The session closed with the reading by David Florentin of a report on the problems in Palestine and on the founding there of a settlement of Jews from Greece.

THE LAST SESSIONS

The conference met in three more sessions.

The first of these (fourth in order) took place at 11 p.m. on the same day (Saturday 27 December 1931). At it, the lawyer Yomtov Yacoel read a report on the work done in Greece by the Jewish National Fund.

At the fifth session (held in the afternoon of Sunday 28 December 1931), Member of Parliament Bessantchi read out a message in Hebrew from the Zionist Central Executive Committee (based in London) dealing with the political and economic position of Zionism. His reading was greeted with loud applause.

Isaac Florentin read a report on the Zionists' problems of propaganda and organisation.

At the last (sixth) session, held on Sunday evening, reports were read from the committee responsible for the Federation's budget, which was approved after some discussion, from the committee responsible for the organisation's newspaper *Renacencia Giudia*, and from the committee for amendment of the statutes, and, lastly, the resolutions were read out. This was followed by a ballot to elect the new General Council and Board of Management of the Zionist Federation.

The following members were elected to the General Council: Ascher Mallah – David Florentin – M. Bessantchi – Albert Frances – Dr A. Nissim – Hananel Naar – Isaac Amarillo – Isaac Angel – Yomtov Yacoel – Salomon Djahon – Ascher Moisis – Samuel Amarillo – Jacques Beza – Robert Raphael – Isaac Florentin – Salomon Itsaki – Israel Nahmia – Salomon Bitti – Leon Amaratzi – Simon Bourla – Adolfos Arditti – Sam Beza – Alfredos Ben Sion – Albert Sciaky – Moisis Matzaris – Samuel Ferenta and Aaron Florentin.

The new Board of Management, with eleven members, will consist of Ascher Mallah – M. Bessantchi – David Florentin – Isaac Angel – Yomtov Yacoel – Jacques Beza – Adolfos Arditti – Isaac Florentin – Robert Raphael – Isaac Amarillo and Albert Frances.

THE CLOSE OF THE CONFERENCE

After the elections, Mr Mallah wished 'bon voyage' and success to Mr Sabbethai Pelosov, one of the delegates, an active official in the Union of Young Judaeans, who was leaving the following day to settle in Paris, where, as he said, he will be continuing his efforts in the Zionist cause. He was also wished 'bon voyage' by Mr Angel, who asked him to take news of the conference to his friends in Paris, last stop, as he put it, on the road to Palestine.

Declaring the conference closed, Mr Mallah praised the fruitful results achieved by it thanks to the spirit of sincerity and cordiality that had prevailed throughout its duration. He also addressed a heartfelt appeal to all the delegates to keep up their efforts in every area during the new Zionist year just beginning.

The conference closed amid what *Renacencia Giudia* described as general rejoicing and to the sound of the *Atikva* (the Jewish national anthem) and of Zionist songs which stimulated powerful enthusiasm.

I attach hereto, in French translation, the resolutions approved by the conference, including that concerning the participation of the Zionists in the administration of the Community. By it, all the Zionists are called upon to provide close support for those administering the Zionist Federation in the event of action and sacrifices being demanded of it in order to obtain the triumph of its principles in the Community administration. At the end of the resolutions, the new Board of Management was called upon to organise the Zionists in the Community Assembly into a group run by a committee consisting of members of the group, in accordance with the principles of the General Council of the Federation, the implementation of which is assigned to the Board of Management.

I also attach hereto (from *Renacencia Giudia* of 8 January 1932) the report read by Attorney Y. Yacoel during the evening session of the conference on 26

December 1931, concerning the activities in Greece of the Jewish National Fund. This is followed by the debate on the report, from which it is clear that the contributions to the Fund have been scanty in the extreme, given that they are optional, and that in order for any action to be effective these contributions will have to become compulsory, as a kind of taxation.

Nothing has been published about the installation of the new Board of Management of the Zionist Federation. However, this ceremony did in fact take place on Sunday 3 January. Senator D. Mallah was once more elected President, with Mr D. Florentin as Deputy President.

According to *Renacencia Giudia* of 8 January, the inaugural session also saw the election of the various committees of the Federation, of which we report the following:

Committee for community work: M. Bessantchi, D. Florentin, Ascher Mallah, Dr Herrera, Y. Yacoel, S. Bourla and Robert Raphael.

Editorial Committee of *Renacencia Giudia*: David Florentin, Isaac Florentin, Isaac Angel, Salomon Bitti, Adolfos Arditti and Salomon Itsaki.

Maccabee Scouts Committee: Albert Sciaky, Isaac Salem, Paul Tazartes, Danil Saia, Isaac Florentin and Salomon Itsaki.

According to the newspaper, the new Board of Management turned its attention in particular to the reinforcement of the finances of the Federation and to the publication of *Renacencia Giudia*, which, it would appear from what was said at the conference and from the proclamation addressed by the Board after its installation to the Zionists of Greece, is also undergoing a financial crisis. It would appear from this that there is not even much enthusiasm about ensuring that the weekly Ladino paper is published.

63

I. Minardos, Director, the Thessaloniki Press Bureau, to the
Inspector of Primary Schools of Thessaloniki

Press report   Thessaloniki, 23 March 1932

I have the honour to inform you that the following item was published by the Ladino newspaper *Tiempo* in its issue of yesterday's date (22 March 1932):

"Various parents have reported to us that at the state Jewish school in Depo the Jewish pupils took part in the Christmas tree ceremony, accompanied by one of the teachers of Hebrew. In the same school, the little Jews are obliged not only to take part in daily prayers but also to recite them. As a result, there are Jewish pupils who make the sign of the Cross in the most natural manner. In some circles, these schools were a source of joy; but rather than rejoicing, we ought to be weeping bitterly over the situation that has arisen for our school-children. Where are the religious authorities? What are those in charge of the Community doing?"

In another column, the same newspaper reports that while these events were taking place in a school which is Jewish in name but Christian deeper down, Hebrew occupied the second position at the opening ceremony of the Talmud-Torah school. "That was not all", it adds, "but the only decoration that could be found was a large wooden cross! May God protect us from anything worse."

———❖———

ATTACHMENT TO 63

The Inspector of Primary Education of Thessaloniki to the Editor of the Tiempo newspaper

letter   Thessaloniki, 4 April 1932

By virtue of the law concerning the Press, please publish the following, on the same page and in the same typeface, as a denial of the report about No. 46 Jewish School published in your issue of 22 March:

a) It is not true that a Christmas tree ceremony took place at No. 46 Jewish School. On 30 December, in the presence of the Jewish teachers, a New Year ceremony was held and gifts were distributed among the poor children. The ceremony was prepared by the teachers after consultation with the Inspectorate of Schools.

b) It is not true that Jewish pupils attend prayers along with the Christian children or that they make the sign of the Cross. The Jewish pupils attend separate prayers with the Jewish teachers.

———❖———

64

C. Diamantopoulos, Director, Directorate of the Press, Ministry of Foreign Affairs, to the B Directorate for Political Affairs of the same ministry.

report   Athens,18 July 1932

We have the honour to forward to you, attached hereto, a report from Paris published in the Ladino newspaper *Tiempo* of Thessaloniki which, in referring to the possibility of the migration of 'Oriental Jews' to Palestine, gives a picture along general lines of the current state of the Jewish population in Turkey.[*sic*]

Thessaloniki, 7 July 1932

Newspaper article from *Tiempo* entitled: The Current State of the Jews in Turkey

The newspaper carried a lengthy report from Paris concerning the possibility of the migration of 'Oriental Jews' to Spain, given that the 'Western Jews' have already put down roots in their home countries. The correspondent continues as follows:

"Let us focus our attention on the Jews of the East – of Turkey, that is – who constitute a solid group consisting of 100,000 Jews from Spain. They are industrious entrepreneurs with broad and vigorous minds, good appearance and natural and moral elegance who for centuries have been proving themselves as capable of the creation of wealth and prosperity. However, since 1912 this solid population has been dislocated: the Balkan Wars, the World War, changes of government, the economic decline of Thessaloniki, Smyrna and Constantinople, and Turkish nationalism have all combined to displace the Jewish population from the field of their most brilliant achievements and to ruin them. Now they lack the intensity of power and action which was once theirs.

"Nonetheless, systematic and widespread emigration would create a major political danger for this population. Kemalist Turkey has severed all its bonds with the traditions of Old Turkey. It is an absolute and jealous master. Two years ago, the Jews of Turkish citizenship were accused - quite groundlessly - of having sent an assurance of loyalty to the King of Spain. It proved completely impossible to convince anyone that this accusation was a gross slander. It is not difficult to imagine what impression would be made by the emigration of the Jews to Spain – no matter how little that emigration took place *en masse* – and what kind of death would await those Jews who, voluntarily or otherwise, remained in Turkey. They are already seen as second-class citizens, and in such circumstances they would decline into a still more humiliating state, becoming the object of even more widespread contempt."

65

The Prefect of Corfu to the Ministry of Foreign Affairs

report   Corfu, 8 July 1932

In connection with your communication No. 5187, I have the honour to report that as it emerges from the report on the management of the Jewish Community for the financial year 1929, submitted to the Prefecture, the Community has an annual revenue, from various sources, amounting to 202,909.35 drachmas. This sum is spent on various items in total. In our opinion, No. 9129 proposal of this Prefecture (dated 5 October 1929) concerning the payment of a sum of 2,500 drachmas per month for the salary of the Chief Rabbi of Corfu and of a once only amount of 10,000 drachmas per year for educational needs ought to be approved.

The granting of this amount will also satisfy the Community.

However, we would be grateful if, for the reasons stated in the above report No. 9129 from the Prefecture, the payment were made by the Prefecture. In this case, the Prefecture will transfer the sum of 10,000 drachmas against a statement of account and after consultation with the President of the Jewish Community and the headmaster of the school, which is a public school of the Greek State, the sole difference being that it is attended by only 280 Jewish children and that a Rabbi is paid to teach Religion.

66

The Thessaloniki Press Bureau to the Ministry of Foreign Affairs

Press report   Thessaloniki, 9 October 1932

Title: The Education of Jews and the Zionists

(The article translated below is from the official organ of the Zionist Federation of Greece in Thessaloniki. It has been published in connection with the results of the elections of 25 September 1932. It is evident that the Zionists attach enormous importance to the education of Jewish children. Also manifest are the efforts made by them to ensure that this education should be entirely in their hands.)

From *Renacencia Giudia*, Thessaloniki, 7 October 1932

The newspaper published, under the title 'Zionist Policy in the Diaspora', a lengthy article expressing its deep sorrow over the failure of the Jewish representatives in the previous Parliament and Senate to gain re-election.

According to the newspaper, the recent parliamentary elections, with their unfortunate results for the separate Jewish association, proved that we cannot remain indifferent as to the persons who will represent the Jews in Parliament. While we had as Members of Parliament and Senators individuals who inspired confidence for their devotion to the Jewish people, their dedication to public affairs, and their abilities, we were able to believe that matters would develop by themselves in the most natural manner, without any need for intervention on our part. The elections of 25 September demonstrated in a positive manner that our duty is to intervene actively in the electoral contest.

Speaking in general terms, the columnist then remarks that it is the central duty of all Zionists to work for the reconstitution of Palestine as well as also to mould the characters of the people of the Diaspora, since such moulding will make a significant contribution to reconstituting Palestine.

The conquest of hearts and the education of the masses for the sake of national renaissance, he continues, have to be carried out by means other than direct ones. The Press and the Zionist organisations are not enough. By its tactics, the Community can either foster or impede the task of enlightenment: everything depends on the persons who are in charge of it.

The article continues as follows:

"Our presence in the administration of the Community is, therefore, essential if we wish the Community to do everything in its power for the Jewish people... But the Community is not free to do as it pleases. Its educational work is, to some extent, under the control of the state. Unless our parliamentary representatives have taken to heart the views which we would like to see prevailing in the Community, they will be unable to defend those views before the state authorities. They will make one concession after another, particularly since such concessions will cause them no grief whatsoever. Our Members of Parliament are also our representatives before public opinion. What they say and what they do is generally said and done on behalf of all of us. No Jew conscious of his identity would be in favour of misconceptions being created by people who present the Jews as being prepared to obliterate their individuality and vanish into the non-Jewish sea surrounding them. Consequently, it is unthinkable that there should be even one Jewish Zionist familiar with the meaning of Zionism who would fail to elect his Members of Parliament from among those who adopt an attitude in their Jewish lives consistent with our general principles. Our participation in the parliamentary elections is thus essential, and, indeed, with the separate electoral system, inevitable. ... Zionism is not purely a Palestinian affair. Zionism is Jewish. Jews who become Zionists do not cease to be Jews: on the contrary, they become something more than Jews. As Jews, they have not only the right, but also the duty to act in such a way that their beliefs are obvious in every facet of Jewish life. This has to be fully understood unless we wish to see the Jewish community of Thessaloniki go into rapid decline."

Note from the Press Bureau: This article was published in Ladino in the *Renacencia Giudia*, despite the fact that one page of that newspaper is published in Greek for the purpose, *inter alia*, of providing a way in which the Greek public can see and understand their true beliefs and not believe the false and slanderous things written against Zionism. As can be seen from the issue of the Zionist organ attached hereto, the page in Greek is very far from achieving this aim.

⇥⬥⬥⬥⇤

67

V. Dendramis, Director, Press Directorate of the Ministry of Foreign Affairs, to the Ministry of the Interior

note   Athens, 20 October 1932

We have the honour to forward to you, attached hereto, a leaflet printed by the Panhellenic Anti-Communist and Humanitarian Social Union which has circulated here. The principle from which the said Union sets out in order to support the national economy is, of course, praiseworthy, but the manner in which the recommendation is made may create misunderstandings on the part of foreigners in general and of the minorities living in Greece – however tiny they may be – since it raises the question of religion as well as that of nationality. It will, of course, not escape you that matters connected with the establishment and labour of foreign nationals are governed by international conventions based on reciprocity, and you will agree that the creation of xenophobia in this manner might have unfortunate consequences for the Greeks who are resident in other countries.

As a result, we believe that it would be expedient for the appropriate department of your service to advise the organisation in question to avoid recommendations of this kind, which could be confined simply to urging a preference for Greek products.

(From the Panhellenic Anti-Communist and Humanitarian Social Union)

DO NOT
Go into shops which are not GREEK
DO NOT
Use foreigners in your business
ALWAYS PREFER
Greek products
GREEKS, NEVER FORGET
That every drachma you give to foreign workers or spend in shops not owned by GREEKS and CHRISTIANS leaves the country for ever!
LET THE WATCHWORD OF ALL OF US BE:
Greek money only for Greek products and to Greek shops!

68

The Director of the Thessaloniki Press Bureau to the Ministry of Foreign Affairs

Press report   Thessaloniki, 20 December 1932

I have the honour to report that the Jewish Press has attributed particular importance to the presence here of the Jewish envoy Dr Senator, who arrived on the 11th of the month and, after staying for five days, left on the morning of the 16th for Zagreb.

As you may be kind enough to see from the cuttings from French-language Jewish newspapers and translated Ladino newspapers attached hereto, Dr Senator had meetings with all the Jewish organisations, visited the Jewish quarters and schools, and informed himself about the situation regarding his fellow-Jews in Thessaloniki. He gave assurances that he will do everything possible to facilitate emigration to Palestine and that he will exert all his influence towards ensuring the assistance of large Jewish organisations in other countries in strengthening and improving the position of the Jews destined to remain here. In the case of those who are to migrate to Palestine, he recommended that they choose the port of Haifa, which is expected to have a great future and which possesses a hinterland entirely in Jewish hands. The idea was also raised of establishing a tobacco industry in Palestine, with experts and labourers from among the Jews of Thessaloniki being employed for this purpose.

It is interesting to note the opinions which Dr Senator expressed concerning the Jews of Thessaloniki. He asserted that he would be working for them not only because of the unhappiness that afflicts them, but also because of supreme national interest. According to him, the Jews of Thessaloniki possess vigorous national forces and treasures of Jewish vitality. They could emerge as a factor of national revival. In saying this, Dr Senator was thinking of the moral decline to be observed among the Jews of other countries, and particularly in Constantinople, where the sight of the Jewish community is enough to rend the heart. There, the decline is moral as well as material. There are almost no Jewish schools. The concept of the 'Jewish brand' has disappeared. The Jews of Thessaloniki are fortunate not to have experienced such decline.

Where emigration is concerned, there are no exact figures for the number of Jews who have left Thessaloniki for Palestine. According to D. Florentin, whom Dr Senator described as the representative of the Jewish Agency in matters connected with emigration, approximately 5,500 Jews left Thessaloniki this year. However, according to *Terre Retrouvée* of Paris (*Progrès*, 13 December 1932), the number was barely 2,000. That newspaper also reported that the emigrants have shifted considerable amounts of Jewish capital from Greece to Palestine.

On his departure, Dr Senator - who met the members of the consular corps at a reception at the house of Mr A. Mallah - stated that the number of entry permits to Palestine for the current half-year will be increased from 100 to 110.

Dr Senator's departure was marred by a sharp protest from the Zionist organisation Misrachi, caused by the fact that more than half the members of the committee set up to distribute the 110 permits are Zionists of a general nature.

Misrachi has also protested to the headquarters of the Zionist organisations abroad.

⎯⎯✦⎯⎯

ATTACHMENT TO 68

The Thessaloniki Press Bureau to the Ministry of Foreign Affairs

newspaper article from Pueblo   Thessaloniki, 14 December 1932

Dr Senator on the Jews of Thessaloniki

(The following extract is from a leading article published by the newspaper *Pueblo* in connection with the presence in Thessaloniki of an envoy of the Jewish Agency Executive Committee) [sic]

Dr Senator's visit to the Jewish quarters left him with a bitter impression. The sight of hundreds of families living under unhygienic conditions moved him deeply. Speaking to a group of friends, he said that the unhappiness he had observed among the Jews of Thessaloniki was worse than that of the Jewish masses of Eastern Europe. That was why he had promised to exert all his influence towards facilitating the emigration of Jewish families to Palestine and, if possible, towards securing the assistance of the large Jewish organisations abroad in order to invigorate and improve the situation of those Jews destined to remain in Thessaloniki. And he added:

"It is not only the misfortune of the Jews of Thessaloniki that has impelled me to take up their cause. A supreme national interest dictates the action in their favour I intend to take. To my mind, the Jews of Thessaloniki may be called upon to play an important role in the movement for the migration of the Jewish people. A hundred years ago, the Sephardic and Ashkenazim Jews were approximately equal in number. Today, 92% of the world's Jews are Ashkenazim. In Germany today, the Jewish population is around 600,000, but assimilation, mixed marriages, proselytism and the disputes within the Jewish communities are wreaking such havoc that there is a fear of their number falling to about 200,000, out of 65 to 70 million, within the next twenty or thirty years. Besides, at any moment, this population is in danger of being absorbed. The Jews in the United States are in a better situation, but when I last visited that country my impressions were very discouraging because of the rapidity at which assimilation is proceeding. On the contrary, the Sephardic Jewish communities are healthier from the national point of view, and this is particularly true of Thessaloniki. I was in Constantinople, where I saw something that rends the heart: there, the decline of the Jews is not only material, but moral as well. There are almost no Jewish schools. Jewish education is non-existent. That is a vanishing population. It was there that I realised that in Thessaloniki you have living national forces. Of course, there are shortcomings and disputes, as in every country, but I am convinced that you also possess a wealth of Jewish vitality. If you succeed in blending the values of European culture, which it would be impossible to dismiss, with the moral values of Judaism, the Jews of Thessaloniki will be in a position to play an important role in the regeneration of the Jewish people. They could become a factor in the revival of the nation. That is one more reason for which the Executive Committee of the Jewish Agency is interested in your city."

69

The Director of the Thessaloniki Press Bureau, to the Ministry of Foreign Affairs

Press report   Thessaloniki, 31 December 1932

I have the honour to report that, as announced by the Jewish newspapers, the ninth annual conference of the Zionists of Greece has been convened for the 28th, 29th and 30th of January next. I submit, from yesterday's issue of the *Renacencia Giudia*, mouthpiece of the Zionist Federation, the programme for the conference, published in Greek. In its Ladino section, the newspaper also published an article reviewing the work accomplished by the Zionists here during the past year. In connection with the manner in which Zionism is adapted to conditions here, the article contains the following passage:

"This is the best proof of the fact that Zionism here really is a living force which does not cling to specific persons or depend upon ephemeral conditions, but is capable of taking everything in its stride, according to circumstances at any time. All this is surprising, particularly in view of the fact that, during the year, our Federation lost a considerable amount of its strength because of the departure of many of its best associates. However, new forces are constantly joining us and in a few years' time there will be fresh faces in charge of the local movement without its work having suffered in any way during the period of transition. The Board of Management and the various committees of the Federation have been seriously examining this question and are making every effort to ensure continuity in the Zionist work being done here. Private lessons in Zionist ideology and history have begun, thanks to active members of our associations. An encouraging start has been made on the issuing of Zionist publications which will be useful in spreading and deepening a knowledge of the Zionist idea among young people. Closer contact has been established between the Board of Management and the various committees here and abroad. Thanks to the Greek-language section of our news-paper, a new spirit and new activities have begun to develop among the associations and communities of southern Greece. The work accomplished in this manner is of the kind with which we ought to be highly satisfied. Despite the departures and the economic crisis, our associations have strong foundations today and most of them have seen their membership increase significantly in the last year."

❧

ATTACHMENT TO 69

The Thesssaloniki Press Bureau to the Ministry of Foreign Affairs

newspaper article from Renacencia Giudia					Thessaloniki, 30 December 1932

Title: "The Ninth Conference of the Zionists of Greece"

The Ninth Conference of the Zionists of Greece will meet in Thessaloniki on 28, 29 and 30 of January next.

The conference, whose purpose is to examine all the Zionist work done during the past year and to set the guidelines for Zionist action in Greece during the coming year, can be considered the most important of the conferences we have held so far.

The development of Zionist work in Greece on all issues and, in particular, in connection with the question of emigration to Palestine, should attract the attention of the delegates, who, as a result, will have to seek more efficient means which would permit a greater flow of emigration and even the establishment of many of our emigrants as farmers.

In Greece, Zionism has become more than just an ideological movement without a specific and immediate purpose: it is also a vital need for a large section of our population.

The ninth Conference of the Zionists of Greece could not of course ignore this point, which is one of the most important on its agenda.

Fifty delegates are expected to take part in the Conference.

The Agenda of this important Conference is as follows:

1) Inaugural address.
2) Election of the Conference Board.
3) Election of committees.
4) Reading of messages addressed to the Conference.
5) Report of the Committee of Scrutiny (ratification of mandates).
6) The Jewish people in the Diaspora and in Palestine.
7) Report on the activities of the Board of Management during the past year.
8) Report on 'propaganda' and 'organisation'.
9) Report on the work accomplished in Palestine.
10) Committee reports (*Renacencia* budget, amendment of the Charter).
11) Zionism and local politics.
12) Zionist participation in the Community.
13) Resolutions.
14) Election of the General Council.
15) Election of the Board of Management.
16) Closing address.

70

The Director of the Thessaloniki Press Bureau to the Ministry of Foreign Affairs

newspaper article from Pueblo   5 January 1933

I submit attached hereto, in French translation, the leading article published in the Ladino newspaper *Pueblo* (Thessaloniki, 2 January) and have the honour to report that the Jewish Press has for years been cultivating daily the persistent idea that emigration is the only way out of the difficult economic position in which the Jewish population of Thessaloniki finds itself. Given that, under the current circumstances, such emigration is generally not possible without securing in advance residence and work in other countries, those departing will encounter difficulties similar to those which emigrants to Spain had to face (see the letter to the *Indépendant* from a person from Thessaloniki living in Barcelona, on which my report No. 93: indeed, it was this letter which stimulated the attached article from *Pueblo*).

Although it is some time since the recommendations of our consulate in Barcelona were published in the Jewish Press, some of the Jewish newspapers persist in reporting that such Jews as have made their way to Spain – from Kavala, in particular – have succeeded in making a living.

Even if this is partially true, given that a similar piece of information was also issued by the police in Kavala, it does not mean that work or favourable conditions are available there for all.

The article in *Pueblo* is the second to inform the Jewish public of the true situation after spending so many years telling its readers that emigration is the only source of salvation. A month ago, *Action* (22 December 1932) carried a lengthy article arguing that attention should also be paid to the part of the Jewish population which would not be emigrating and must therefore be in a position to cope with making a living here under local conditions.

71

The General Governor of Macedonia to the Ministry of Foreign Affairs

confidential report   Thessaloniki, 14 February 1933

In connection with your confidential communication No. 13626 of 10 December 1929 and 9913 of 19 August 1930, I have the honour to inform you that today I received a visit from the President of the Jewish Community of Thessaloniki accompanying Dr Koretz, preacher in the synagogue at Charlotten-burg, who arrived yesterday and is a candidate for the post of Chief Rabbi here.

In a short address, Dr Koretz expressed his good sentiments towards Greece, as an admirer of the spirit and learning of ancient Greece, and said that he would be pleased to serve in Greece if his appointment is approved.

After complimenting the Chief Rabbi on his learning and on the knowledge for which he has distinguished himself in Germany, I said nonetheless to the President and the members of the Community that the Greek Government would consider with particular pleasure the election of a Greek Jew as Chief Rabbi. This would demonstrate the patriotism of the Community, while it is in the interests of the Community itself that its spiritual leader should be a Greek citizen, in view of the self-evident prestige that his capacity as a Greek Chief Rabbi would confer upon him in the eyes of the authorities. A similar need in the case of the Greek Catholics had long been discerned by the Holy See of the Vatican, which appointed Mr Philippousis, a Greek by descent and citizenship, as the Catholic Archbishop in Athens.

The President of the Community, putting forward the explanation that the local rabbis are deficient in learning, expressed – as did the candidate for the post – their willingness to apply to the Greek Government for the naturalisation of the said foreign national by special act, particularly in view of the fact that he is willing to lawfully relinquish his foreign (Polish) citizenship and all other bonds with Germany and Poland.

On this question, I told them that, since I was not aware of the views of the Government, I could neither reply nor discuss such an issue but that I would willingly pass on this proposal on the part of the Community and the interested party.

However, I made it clear to them that the view I expressed should not be taken in any way to imply any lack of favour towards the prospective Chief Rabbi, whom we hold in high esteem, but that it was a matter of principle by whose implementation the prestige of the State is secured and the interests of the Greek Jews, in the best sense, are safeguarded.

The said prospective Chief Rabbi, who has studied divinity and philosophy in Germany, is aged about 40 years and speaks Hebrew, Yiddish and French, in which language he will preach this coming Saturday in the Beth Saul Synagogue here.

After holding meetings with the Jewish organisations and visiting the Jewish charitable institutions he will return to Germany, departing towards the end of this month, so as to make his way back, with his family, on condition that a final agreement between himself and the Community as to his employment has been reached. We attach hereto the statement he made to the Jewish newspapers on his arrival.

Regardless of the decision to be taken in principle by the Government in connection with the question of his nationality, it would not be inexpedient if the Greek Embassy in Berlin, which issued the visa for his Polish passport, were to be asked to provide information about him.

We shall be grateful if you have the goodness to inform us of your views on the above.

The Matarasso family in 1917.
Archive of the Jewish Community of Thessaloniki,
donated by Isaac Menache (Athens) and David Amir (Israel).

Performance of the theatrical association *La Bohéme* in 1903-1904.
Archive of the Jewish Community of Thessaloniki,
donated by Armando Modiano.

M. Navaro and Daisy Nissim in Thessaloniki circa 1920.
Archive of the Jewish Community of Thessaloniki,
donated by Armando Modiano.

Thessaloniki 1930.
Picture from the wedding of Yehouda and Merkada Allalouf .
Archive of the Jewish Community of Thessaloniki, donated by Rosa Allalouf, Athens.

Thessaloniki 7 July 1925. The engagement of Lazaros Sefiha and Daisy Matalon,
parents of the current President of the Jewish Community of Thessaloniki, Andreas Sefiha.
Archive of the Jewish Community of Thessaloniki, donated by Armando Modiano.

Thessaloniki, 1930s. Picture depicting Germaine Matalon and Lazaros Sefiha. The young boy in the centre is the current President of the Jewish Community of Thessaloniki, Andreas Sefiha. Archive of the Jewish Community of Thessaloniki, donated by Armando Modiano.

1930s record label promotional advertising.
From left: Medi Kune and Rene Matalon.
Archive of the Jewish Community of Thessaloniki, donated by Armando Modiano.

1930s Thessaloniki. Picture from the wedding of Salvador Sarfaty and Linda Modiano.
Sarfaty was originally from Larissa, and stationed in Thessaloniki as an army doctor.
Archive of the Jewish Community of Thessaloniki, donated by Armando Modiano.

March 1948. Celebration of Purim at the child care centre
of the Jewish Community of Thessaloniki.
Archive of the Jewish Community of Thessaloniki, donated by Isaac Menache (Athens), David Amir (Israel).

Panteleimon I′, Archbishop of Thessaloniki, with Rabbi Sabbethai Azaria
and members of the Jewish community of Thessaloniki.
Archive of the Jewish Community of Thessaloniki.

Prime Minister Constantine Karamanlis, visiting the Israeli stand at the Thessaloniki
International Fair in 1959, greets Rabbi Sabbethai Azaria.
Donated by Alice Tiano Saias.

Andreas Papandreou visits the Israeli stand
at the Thessaloniki International Trade Fair in 1964.
Alice Tiano Saias archive.

Festivities at the Jewish Community kindergarten circa 1960.
On the right is the author and director of the community services, Barouh Chibi.
Archive of the Jewish Community of Thessaloniki.

72

P. Dragoumis, General Governor of Macedonia, to the Ministry of Foreign Affairs

cover letter   Thessaloniki, 10 April 1933

We have the honour to submit to you, attached hereto, memorandum No. 162 from the Jewish Community of Thessaloniki together with an application from Mr Hirsch (Cevi) Simha Koretz, Polish citizen, resident of Berlin, without supporting documentation, and we request that you decide in this matter as you see fit in consultation with the Ministries of the Interior and Education.

In its memorandum, the Community explains the reasons for which it will be employing, as of 1 May of this year and for five years, the said foreign national as its Chief Rabbi and, given that, in accordance with Article 3 of Law 4837, the Chief Rabbi (and all Rabbis) must be Greek citizens, requests that the said person, as stated in his own application, be granted naturalisation in Greece by special act.

It should be noted that Article 1 of the Legislative Decree of September 1925 (Government Gazette, Vol. A, No. 247 of 11 September 1925), invoked in the above memorandum, was cancelled in its entirety by Law 3442, No. 1 (Government Gazette, Vol. A, No. 313 of 28 December 1927).

ATTACHMENT a TO 72

The Jewish Community of Thessaloniki to the General Governor of Macedonia

memorandum   Thessaloniki, 29 March 1933

As you will be aware, the post of Chief Rabbi of our community has been vacant for approximately ten years. The absence of a religious and spiritual leader of the large and cohesive mass of the Jews of Thessaloniki is detrimental to our community in a variety of ways.

The religious and moral education of the Jewish population, and of its young people in particular, has been seriously retarded precisely because of the absence of a suitable person who, by the prestige stemming from the office of Chief Rabbi and thanks to his own breadth of learning, would be able to guide the masses of the people in honourable directions and to contribute to their general improvement.

Our Community Council, setting out from these beliefs, in conformity with the provision of Article 9 of Law 2456 'concerning Jewish communities', and after studying the matter carefully from every point of view for two years, has arrived at the decision to employ as Chief Rabbi to the Jewish Community of Thessaloniki Mr Hirsch (Cevi) Simha Koretz, of Polish citizenship, now Rabbi to the Jewish Community of Berlin, who possesses all the qualifications to take up that post, holding a doctorate from the Faculty of Arts of Vienna University and being in his final year of study both at the Rabbinical Seminary of Vienna and the School of Advanced Hebrew Studies of Berlin.

The Community Council's decision was submitted for approval to the Community Assembly, which, lawfully convened under the provisions of Articles 57 and 58 of the internal regulations of our Community, approved, by the lawful majority, the employment of Mr Hirsch (Cevi) Simha Koretz as Chief Rabbi to the Jewish Community of Thessaloniki for a period of five years commencing on 1 May 1933 and authorised the Community Council to submit the relevant application of appointment to the Ministry of Education and Religious Affairs.

However, in order for this appointment to take place, it is necessary that the above prospective Chief Rabbi shall have been granted Greek nationality, in advance, in accordance with Article 3 of Law 4837. As can be seen from his application, submitted together with the present, he is willing to acquire the said nationality. However, in view of the exceptional nature of the present case, it is clear that the provisions to be appplied are not the ordinary provisions of civil law on naturalisation dealing with the previous residence of the applicant in Greece, but the extra-ordinary provisions of the Legislative Decree of 10/11 September 1925 'concerning modification of the provisions concerning the naturalisation of foreign nationals'.

Bearing the above in mind, we have the honour to submit the present, respectfully requesting that the legal measures be taken by the Ministry of the Interior, in connection with the naturalisation of Hirsch (Cevi) Simha Koretz under the extra-ordinary provisions of the Legislative Decree of 10/11 September 1925, and by the Ministry of Education and Religious Affairs, in connection with the issuing of the Decree appointing the said person as Chief Rabbi to the Jewish Community of Thessaloniki, as of 1 May 1933, in accordance with the provisions of Law 2456, Article 9, and Law 4837, Article 3.

ATTACHMENT b TO 72

*I. Politis, Greek Ambassador in Berlin, to the Greek Ministry of
Foreign Affairs*

confidential letter   Berlin, 11 March 1933

In reply to your communication No. 1389/21/14 of 21 February, I have the
honour to report to you that information obtained confidentially by the Embassy
from the German authorities in connection with Mr Hirsch Koretz presents him
as an enthusiastic and extremely active Zionist made still more dangerous by his
administrative abilities and his eloquence as a speaker. However, I believe that
in fairness I should add that both Mr Koretz' Polish nationality and the general
anti-Jewish attitude prevailing in the ruling circles of Germany today may, to some
extent, have influenced the judgement of Dr Koretz outlined above.

ATTACHMENT c TO 72

*I. Minardos, Director of the Thessaloniki Press Bureau, to the
Ministry of Foreign Affairs*

Press report   Thessaloniki, 2 May 1933

As I had the honour to inform you in person, the issue of the *Indépendant*
published this afternoon announces that Dr Koretz, the Chief Rabbi-elect of
Thessaloniki, will be arriving here on 11 May, that is, on Thursday of next week.
   In view of the promise given that Dr Koretz would not be arriving here before
the question of his nationality had been settled, I am of the opinion that the Jewish
Community is attempting to present the Government with a *fait accompli*. It thus
appears that the information reported by *Progrès* (15 April), to the effect that Dr
Koretz would be taking up his duties as Chief Rabbi during the second half of
the month that began yesterday (Press Bureau communication 904/17.4.33), was
accurate.
   In announcing the arrival of the Chief Rabbi, the *Indépendant* also touched on
the question of Dr Koretz' nationality, as follows:

"It is hoped that between today and the 11th of the month the question of formal legitimation of the appointment will have been concluded. As readers will be aware, the Government is demonstrating the best intentions so that the entire Jewish community of Thessaloniki will acquire the spiritual leader its importance deserves. It is very likely that a delegation from the Community Council will proceed to the border to receive Dr Koretz."

From the information in the Jewish Press I have at my disposal, it would appear that the question of Dr Koretz' nationality has not yet been settled. In my communication No. 991/25.4.33, of which a copy was sent to you, I conveyed the information that the President of the Jewish Community was to travel to Athens to report and explain matters to the Prime Minister, in view of the difficulties which have been encountered over the question of the naturalisation of the Chief Rabbi. *Progrès*, dealing with the action taken by the President of the Community in Athens, reports, as can be seen from the cutting attached hereto (28 April 1933), but goes no further than noting, where results are concerned, that matters are proceeding in a satisfactory manner, with the Government displaying the best of intentions. It is to be hoped, adds the newspaper, that it will not be long before the matter is resolved.

—◆—

<h1 style="text-align:center">73</h1>

I. Politis, Greek Ambassador in Berlin, to the Greek Ministry of
Foreign Affairs

letter   Berlin, 3 May 1933

With reference to your communication No. 1989/A/21/IY and further to my communication No. 561 of 11 March, I have the honour to inform you that Dr Hirsch Koretz, having recuperated from an illness, intends to leave Berlin, with his family, in late May for the purpose of settling in Thessaloniki and, as he informed the Director of the Consular Bureau of the Embassy, will be taking up the duties of Chief Rabbi of that city. Dr Koretz added that he had received a letter from the President of the Jewish Community of Thessaloniki to the effect that he will be granted Greek citizenship within the next few days.

On this occasion, I believe it is expedient to remind you that four years ago –
if my memory serves me well – the Greek Government categorically refused to
accept the appointment of a foreign national as Catholic Bishop of Corfu.

⟶✦⟵

74

*The Director of the Thessaloniki Press Bureau to the Ministry of
Foreign Affairs*

Press report   Thessaloniki, 5 August 1933

At a moment at which the Jewish newspapers of Thessaloniki are continuing
to publish articles on the impoverished condition of the Jewish population and the
exceptional circumstances in which the Community finds itself, preventing it from
granting aid to the many members of the lower classes afflicted by misfortune
and misery, I have the honour to report that it would not be inexpedient to glance
at the news items in the Jewish newspapers which concern the manner in which
the Community is administered.

In accordance with Article 47 of the by-laws of the Jewish Community of
Thessaloniki in force, the general budget of the Community was to be submitted
for approval to the Community Assembly by the end of March each year. The
by-laws originally determined that the budget should be submitted by the end of
December, but the amendments to them made (by the Royal Decree of 26
February 1926) altered this to the end of March.

However, although we are now nearing the middle of the second half of the
year, it was not until its meeting on 3 August that the Community Council
completed its approval of the budget for the financial year that began on 1 January. The budget thus approved must now also be approved by the Community
Assembly, which, having adjourned until the end of September, will now be
convened in extra-ordinary session within the next fortnight.

This is not the only occasion on which similar delays and irregularities have
occurred in the submission and approval of the Jewish Community's budget.
Protests have frequently been carried in the Press. As concerns the financial
position, if *Progrès* (16 July 1933) is correct, the budget for the current financial
year will show a deficit of 250,000 drachmas, which will be met by applying a
variety of measures, including the reduction by 10% of the salaries of the

Community employees, who reject such a measure and have recommended other ways of raising funds.

According to the same newspaper, the management of the unleavened bread, for which flour and sugar are imported duty-free (this year, the Community of Thessaloniki has imported 31 tons of these items), was expected to produce a surplus of 100,000 drachmas but actually showed a deficit of 150,000 drachmas. The surplus, together with the 20% increase in the Community levies, was to have been used to pay the salary of Dr Koretz, employed as Chief Rabbi.

On the other hand, it should be noted that while, in accordance with the Community by-laws in force, as ratified by the Royal Decree of 12 April 1923, elections for the new Community Assembly ought to be held in the autumn (the Feast of Tabernacles), they are now to be postponed until Passover next year. The postponement will be based on a resolution of the present Community Assembly, by virtue of Article 10 of the said by-laws, as supplemented (by the Presidential Decree of 26 February 1926), which provides that, in exceptional circumstances, the Assembly can prolong its mandate for a further year, at a maximum, etc.

The reason for the postponement of the elections is the fact that the process of debating and approving by the existing Community Assembly the amendments which are to be made to the by-laws – amendments which appear to be radical – has not yet been completed. Although the need for this was recognised immediately after the last elections (in the autumn of 1930), and despite the fact that both the Community Council and the Assembly have dealt with the matter, the Assembly's debate on the amendments is taking place extremely slowly.

There are those who say that failure to draw up the amendments in question, which have to be approved by Presidential Decree, cannot be deemed a reason to postpone the Community elections, in accordance with the spirit of the aforementioned amendments of 1926 to the Community by-laws in force.

The previous Community elections, which ought to have taken place in the autumn of 1929, were again held a year later. That was because when the mandate of the previous Community Assembly expired, it was judged that elections ought not to take place before Law 2456 concerning Jewish Communities had been amended, so as to allow Jews of foreign citizenship to be among the electorate, as was in fact the case in July 1930 by virtue of Law 4837.

To date, it has been observed that the failure – due exclusively to those administering the Community – to complete the process of drawing up and approving the amendments to the Community by-laws cannot be deemed an 'exceptional case'; similarly, four years ago, it was observed that since the participation of the foreign nationals in the Community elections was a vital issue, it ought to have been anticipated and implemented in good time, since otherwise the provision of Article 10 would not have been applicable.

⎯⎯◆⎯⎯

75

The Minister of Foreign Affairs to the General Governance of Macedonia

confidential letter   26 September 1933

In connection with the report from the General Governance of Thessaloniki submitted to this Ministry on 31 July of this year and concerning the emigration to Palestine of Jews from Thessaloniki, with particular reference to the views of Mr Ascher Mallah, Senator and President of the Zionist Federation, in connection with the full support of the Jewish Community by the City of Thessaloniki and the State, we have the honour to inform you that we do not find this approach practicable, for the following reasons:

The Greek Government, which views with regret the fact that its Jewish citizens are compelled to emigrate by reason of the economic crisis, is, unfortunately, unable, as a result of the current difficult circumstances, to assist them by granting them the sums of money required. However, even if circumstances permitted this, we do not know whether the sums involved would actually be used for the purpose for which they were granted. Furthermore, the British authorities in Palestine may refuse to permit the final settlement of Jews belonging to the lower social classes and lacking the means to provide for themselves. It might be more expedient if the Jewish organisations in Thessaloniki were to be advised to make direct contact with the leaders of the Jewish movement in London so that the matter can be placed, jointly, in its full dimensions before the British Government. We would be grateful if you would be so kind as to inform us of your views on this matter, sounding out informally the local leaders of the Jewish community, if you deem it advisable.

⎯⎯◆⎯⎯

76

P. Dragoumis, General Governor of Macedonia, to the Ministry of Foreign Affairs

confidential report   Thessaloniki, 3 October 1933

In reply to your communication No. 8819 A.21/IY, we have the honour to inform you that we completely agree with your views, particularly in view of the fact that the Greeks, by numerical proportion of the population, are suffering more from the economic crisis than the Jews. The study published and the relevant report were, in any case, a news item. The complaints about "inaction" are constantly being made, given that while in earlier times, under Ottoman rule, the Jews were in control of commerce, they now feel – naturally enough and as was to be expected, in view of the ethnic composition of the city's population – that they are being displaced by, or having to compete with, the Greek population, in the form of a struggle for survival to which the general economic crisis and poverty now have to be added.

As for emigration to Palestine, the special committee here is in constant contact with those in London and in Palestine, acting at times on its own initiative in issuing the Jews of Thessaloniki with the quota of immigration permits by profession, given that the Jewish population here is not agricultural. As a result, the number of permits is comparatively low, but even so emigration, though on a small scale, goes on smoothly. Now, however, the numbers of those wishing to go to Palestine, even for a visit, have been reduced.

77

The representatives of the Union of Jewish Communities of Greece, of the Council of the Jewish Community of Thessaloniki, of the Chief Rabbinate and of all the Jewish organisations

resolution   Thessaloniki, 22 November 1933

Having taken cognisance of the measures which the Colonial Office and the Palestine Administration are intending to take and which tend to:

Reduce Jewish emigration to Palestine by issuing a very small number of immigration permits, precisely at a moment at which there is a major shortage of working hands and at which the greater part of world Jewry, and that of Germany in particular, is in a quandary and has turned its gaze upon Palestine, which it considers as the sole means of salvation;

Lead to the persecution of those immigrants who have entered the country as visitors and have settled there after securing the means by which to support themselves;

Paralyse the tourist trade, which is the prime source of prosperity for the entire country, with the issuing of laws creating difficulties for that industry and making its growth almost impossible:

BELIEVE

that this attitude is dictated by factors other than economic ones and that it is entirely contrary both to the spirit and to the letter of the Mandate in Palestine, which sets up an obligation for the mandatory power to favour the development of the Jewish National Home;

PROTEST

Strongly against this blatant contravention of the principle that the Jews returning to Palestine are doing so by right and not under tolerance, a principle which has been recognised by the League of Nations;

REVOLT

Strongly against the inhuman measures which are being introduced for the purpose of driving out the Jews living in Palestine without being a burden on anyone;

DEMAND

The abolition of these measures, which endanger the work of the reconstruction and development of Palestine and which may bring the entire Jewish people to the point of despair;

PROCLAIM

Once more their unshakeable determination to continue, in the strongest possible manner, the struggle for the recognition of the Jewish rights on Palestine, as stated in the Mandate;

DEMAND

With the greatest possible persistence that emigration to Palestine be freed of restrictions;

EXPRESS

Their conviction that Britain will see itself as having the duty to comply with the obligation it has undertaken towards the Jews and towards the League of Nations of facilitating, by every means, the founding of a Jewish National Home in Palestine; and

INSTRUCT

That a committee serve the present Resolution upon the Greek Government in the person of His Excellency the Minister and General Governor of Macedonia, upon the Government of Great Britain in the person of its representative in Thessaloniki, and upon the Mandate Commission of the League of Nations in the person of the Minister of Foreign Affairs.

───※───

78

The Directorate of Police in Thessaloniki to the Gendarmerie Headquarters

report   Thessaloniki, 8 December 1933

Jewish propaganda: 'Zionism'

I have the honour to report that at about 11 a.m. on 3 December 1933 a meeting of the above Association was held in the *Apollo* Cinema and attended by approximately 600 persons, the majority of them school pupils and youngsters.

The opening of the meeting was declared by Moses Barzilai, General Secretary of the Cheire Misrachi, who, speaking in Hebrew from a manuscript, criticised the British policy being implemented in Palestine. The next speaker was Joseph Abenyez, General Secretary of the Misrachites, who, speaking in Ladino – also from a manuscript – explained the threat hovering over Palestine in terms of persecution of the Jews and, in conclusion, recommended to his audience that they display calm, courage, unity and solidarity.

The next speaker was Salomon Ruben, General Secretary of the Revisionists, who, speaking in Ladino from a manuscript, accused the British authorities of persecuting the Jews in Palestine and concluded by stating to the audience, *verbatim*, "the time has come for the Jewish Revolution and they should be ready to resist".

The meeting approved a lengthy resolution of protest containing the following points:

1) An end to the displacement from Palestine of Jewish immigrants.
2) Free entry for Jews into Palestine.
3) Strict implementation of the Balfour agreement, etc.

A committee was elected from among the audience to deliver the resolution, of which copies will be sent to the Greek Government, the British Government (via its consulate) and the Minorities Office of the League of Nations through the Minister of Foreign Affairs of Greece. At this point, the meeting broke up quietly. The Army Corps here has received a copy of this report.

79

D. Kaklamanos, Greek Ambassador in London, to the Greek Ministry of Foreign Affairs

cover letter   London, 14 February 1934

I have the honour of forwarding to you, attached hereto, a copy of a letter addressed to me by the Executive of the Agudas Israel World Organisation expressing its concern over news reaching it in connection with the difficulties allegedly facing Jews in Greece, and in Thessaloniki in particular, who wish to observe the Sabbath.

ATTACHMENT TO 79[*]

H. A. Goodman, Agudas Israel World Organisation, to D. Kaklamanos, Ambassador in London

letter   London, 7 February 1934

Dear Sir,

The Executive of this Organisation, a world wide universally organised representative of Orthodox Jewry, is somewhat perturbed at the recent response concerning difficulties which may be placed in regard to Sabbath observing Jewish merchants and shopkeepers in Greece generally, and particularly in the town of Thessaloniki.

In many countries, including Great Britain, special provision is made for observant Jews whose premises are closed on the Sabbath and who are, under certain conditions, permitted to trade on Sundays.

I am sure that the High Government of Greece will facilitate Jewish religious observance, and protect freedom of conscience, and I should be grateful if the purport of this communication could be conveyed to the department concerned for its sympathetic consideration.

I would be happy of an opportunity for reassuring my executive in regard to this matter.

⟩⊷⟨

80

P. Dragoumis, General Governor of Macedonia, to the Ministry of Foreign Affairs

report   Thessaloniki, 2 April 1934

In connection with your communication No. 1823/A/21/IY and subsequent to our communication No. 337 (from the Press Bureau), we have the honour to inform you that no difficulties are placed in the way of observance of the Jewish Sabbath in Greece and, consequently, in Thessaloniki.

In Greece, as in all other states, Sunday has been established as a day of rest for many years, as is common knowledge, and, in this instance, the Jews are free to open or close their shops on Saturday.

It should be borne in mind that out of a population of six and a half million, the Jews of Greece do not number more than 65,000, of whom approximately 40,000 reside in Thessaloniki (whose total population is 250,000).

Sunday as a day of rest was recently extended only to groceries, at the insistence of the majority of grocers and their employees, without any protest from the Jews, who did not ask to be exempted from the measure until after it had been introduced, a request which could not be satisfied since it would have led to a competition between Christian and Jewish grocers. A similar request on the part of the butchers and their employees that Sunday as a day of rest should also be extended to butchers' shops was not accepted despite the fact that it was submitted by the majority of those concerned, because the Jewish butchers are closed all day on Saturday, for specific religious reasons, and the introduction of a complete day of rest on Sunday would have been financially damaging to them – which was

not the case with the grocers, most of whom ceased to observe Saturday closing
years ago.

—◆—

81

*E. Papandreou, Director, the Thessaloniki Press Bureau, to the
Ministry of Foreign Affairs*

confidential report   Thessaloniki, 29 May 1934

We have the honour to inform the Ministry that the elections of the Jewish
Community took place on 27 May.

The election campaign conducted in the newspapers over the last few weeks
was a tough one, partly because of the number of parties contesting the administration of the Community and partly because of the differences between them on
the levels both of principles and of personalities.

The parties which put up candidates were as follows:
1) Zionists
2) Moderates
3) National Action
4) Independents
5) Suburbanites I
6) Suburbanites II
7) Popular
8) Corporations
9) Concord

The manifestos of each of these parties were approximately as follows:
1) Manifesto of the Zionist Party: retention of the ethnic identity of the Jews
within the Greek entity, and a completely law-abiding attitude towards the Greek
State.

One of the principal points in the Zionist manifesto is the teaching of the
Hebrew language in its modern form and not just as a religious language, so as to
ensure that young Jews wishing or needing to go to Palestine are better qualified
to make a living there. For this purpose, the Zionists are of the opinion that the
teaching of the Hebrew language ought to be directed by a school inspector
familiar with modern educational methods and in particularly with the teaching of

Hebrew. This person (the inspector) ought to be recruited abroad, and thus of necessity will be a foreign national.

2) Manifesto of the Moderates: The Moderate party is a more political formation whose objective is to defend the interests of the Jews of Thessaloniki. It is inspired by the principles of the Universal Israelite Alliance and believes that the solution to the problem facing the Jewish community of Thessaloniki is the elimination of any differences other than those of religion between the Jews of Thessaloniki and the Greeks and the exclusive dedication of the Community to the Jews of Thessaloniki. The Moderates believe that although, of course, the Jews of Thessaloniki should not cease to take an interest in the Jewish nation in general and in the Jews of Palestine in particular, their prime consideration should be their own future, in accordance with local conditions and in complete concord and absolute equality of rights with the other Greek citizens.

On the question of the teaching of Hebrew, the Moderates hold the view that it should be taught as a religious language. However, for electoral reasons, they recently went some way towards espousing the views of the Zionists, though without precisely defining their attitude to the issue.

3. Manifesto of the National Action Party: The manifesto of this party is inspired by approximately the same principles as the Zionists. In view of its composition (it consists of three different organisations), it, too, is a Jewish national party whose object is the maintenance of the Jewish identity.

4. Manifesto of the Independents: This party consists of a small number of middle-class Jews who do not wish to take an active part in political disputes.

5. Manifesto of the Suburbanites I Party: This party consists of residents of the Jewish suburbs and its objective is to protect their interests. In particular, its aim is to release the residents of those suburbs from the obligation to pay rent for the cottages which the Jewish Community and the City of Thessaloniki have constructed for them.

6. Manifesto of the Suburbanites II Party: as above.

7. Manifesto of the Popular Bloc: This party is probably a front group for the Communists.

8. Manifesto of the Corporations Party: This party seeks to defend the interests of the Corporations (guilds).

9. Manifesto of the Concord Party: of no significance.

The most important of the above nine parties in terms both of the number of their supporters and of the eminent Jews who belong to them are the Zionists and the Moderates.

The fiercest struggle was fought out between these two parties, and the newspapers were full of charges and counter-charges. The Zionists accuse the

Moderates of having repudiated the national ideals of the Jewish nation and of following, by their programme of assimilation, what might be called a cosmopolitan policy. The Moderates, on the other hand, accuse the Zionists of having impeded the development of the Jews of Thessaloniki and of damaging their rights and, in particular, their political rights within the Greek entity, thus, by their sterile policy, encouraging the trend to restore the separate Jewish electoral college in elections to Parliament and the Senate.

To summarise, it could be said that the Zionists are Jewish nationalists and that the Moderates tend to favour assimilation.

In accordance with the results of the elections, the 50 seats of the members of the General Assembly of the Jewish Community were distributed as follows among the above parties:

1) Zionists:	votes	2,989,	seats	21
2) Moderates:	votes	1,376,	seats	10
3) National Action:	votes	437,	seats	3
4) Suburbanites I:	votes	512,	seats	4
5) Suburbanites II:	votes	165,	seats	1
6) Popular Bloc:	votes	1,106,	seats	8
7) Independents:	votes	261,	seats	2
8) Corporations:	votes	153,	seats	1
9) Concord:	votes	71,	seats	0

Since none of the parties won an absolute majority, the General Assembly will of necessity consist of a coalition of various parties, and the consultations among the parties to this end have already begun.

82

The Greek Consulate in Adrianople to the Greek Embassy in Ankara

report   Adrianople, 3 July 1934

I have the honour to report to you that the situation prejudicial to the Jews which has recently come into being in Thrace is worsening with each passing day. Criminal elements are going around the Jewish shops and threatening the shopkeepers that if they do not close they will be beaten – to the point where this poses a risk to their lives. The most unpleasant aspect of the situation for us is that the persons threatened in this way include two small merchants who are Greek subjects. The Chief of Police, whom I have visited, claimed that he knew nothing, pretending to complete ignorance of the situation! What is certain is that the decision to drive out the Jewish population here, numbering 7-8,000 people and relatively prosperous, was taken in the House of the People. According to the plan, the Jews will be terrorised by roundabout means of all kinds, with the toleration of the authorities, and compelled to leave Thrace by, as it were, their own will. The plan may make provision, later, for the Jews to be forced to scatter throughout Asia Minor in such a way as to prevent them constituting, from now on, concentrated and economically powerful communities. The Ottoman Bank here, which I visited today, was crowded with Jews seeking to close their accounts in view of their imminent departure. The acting Italian Consul (there has been no consul for some time) told me that so far the Jews here who are Italian subjects have not been harassed, but on the other hand this was not the case in Üzün Köprü, where one of the two resident Jews was frightened into leaving.

Please be so good as to inform me of any instructions you may have where the Greek citizens are concerned.

⤛⬦⤜

83

The Greek Consulate in Adrianople to the Greek Embassy in Ankara

report   Adrianople, 4 July 1934

Further to my communication No. 103 of yesterday's date, I have the honour to report that the exodus of the Jews, in their hundreds, continued throughout the day yesterday. They are all panic-stricken. The Italian Consulate has received instructions from the Italian Embassy to facilitate the departure of the Jews of Italian citizenship, possibly even lending them money. Learning of this, the Greek Jews descended upon the Consulate requesting money. As I am aware, this is impossible, particularly in view of the fact that our citizens, most of whom are poor working people, as a rule share their accommodation with relatives who are Turkish subjects, and the latter might exploit the situation in order to benefit from any financial assistance. Nonetheless, allow me to suggest that it would be just to grant these persons passports free of charge, if you so approve. I would therefore be grateful if you would inform me, by telegram and as soon as possible, whether you approve this suggestion, bearing in mind that these unfortunate people are being driven by the terror which has overcome them to abandon everything here and suffer great losses. Although so far no one has come to any harm, all of them – in view of the threats they have heard – have closed their businesses and locked themselves up in their houses. Allow me to repeat that they are making their way to the Consulate in search of financial assistance to depart for Greece.

❧

84

D. Kapsalis, Consul General in Istanbul, to the Greek Embassy in Ankara

report   Istanbul, 5 July 1934

I have the honour to inform you that Aaron Samuel Cazes, Jewish merchant, Greek citizen, established at Saranta Ekklesies [Kırklaleri] in Thrace since 15 May 1933, presented himself at this Consulate General this morning and stated that he had been compelled to leave in haste yesterday and seek refuge here in order to escape the persecution of the Jews by the local populace. Mr Cazes reported to me that at 9.30 on the night of 3 July a group of pupils from the secondary school began to roam the streets of the Jewish quarter throwing stones at the houses. The group of boys was joined by the people of the town and soldiers without weapons, and the enraged crowd burst into the houses of the Jews, which they looted, insulting and manhandling the tenants. In this way, the rioters reached the house in which Mr Cazes has his apartment and looted the apartment of his son-in-law. Mr Cazes had time to lock the door of his apartment and escape via the window and the roof to a family of friends. The persecution of the Jews continued throughout the night, and on the morning of the following day, 4 July, the terror-stricken Jews began to leave the town by rail, taking refuge in Constantinople. Mr Cazes estimates that about 400 Jews left Kırklaleri, and that no more than 100 have remained there.

Mr Cazes, who has a commercial establishment in Kırklaleri, stated to me that although he had left Kırklaleri without money and has commercial obligations which he is bound to honour, he dare not return to Kırklaleri because his life and that of his wife are in danger, and he requested that the Embassy act as it thinks fit so as to ensure that his merchandise, located in his shop on Cumhuriyet Cadesi, be sent to him by the city authorities. Mr Cazes added that after the persecution of the Jews only assurances from us to the effect that he is in no danger will convince him to return to Kırklareri in order to look after his affairs.

Since the Prefecture of Kırklareri comes under the region of the jurisdiction of the Adrianople Consulate, I am, unfortunately, unable to take any action addressed to the Prefecture of Constantinople.

According to the information I have assembled, similar anti-Jewish riots have also taken place in Çanakkale, Gallipoli, Raidestos, Adrianople and other towns in Thrace. I am informed that the Jews of those places are leaving their homes in panic. They have received no instructions to do so from the authorities. In such of the above towns as the anti-Jewish action has taken the form of persecution, as in Kırklaleri, the Jews are terrorised by means of anonymous letters, the boycotting of their businesses, and veiled threats from their neighbours. The Jews of Constantinople have had no trouble so far.

As I noted, the authorities have not expelled the Jews from any towns. However, it seems certain that the anti-Jewish movement was organised and was tolerated, to say the least, by the authorities, subsequent to a campaign in the Press begun not long ago by the nationalist periodical *Mili Inkipal*. It has taken place along the Dardanelles, which Turkey intends to fortify, and in the provinces close to the border in Thrace, in which the presence of non-Turkish elements is undesirable. Irresponsible groups are undertaking the implementation of Law 2510, which I dealt with in my report No. 897 of 4 July.

━━◆━━

85

K. Sakellaropoulos, Greek Ambassador in Ankara, to the Greek Ministry of Foreign Affairs

report   Neohorion, Bosporus, 12 July 1934

The anti-Semitic movement which took place along the Dardanelles and in various parts of Eastern Thrace two weeks ago has given rise to various comments, especially in connection with the purpose which it was intended to serve.

The government version, according to which the anti-Jewish activities – which in some districts seem to have become a real pogrom – were caused by various irresponsible organisations on which the authorities were unable to impose order immediately, has been greeted with considerable scepticism among those who are familiar with affairs in Turkey. The authorities in Turkey, and in particular the superbly-organised police force, only fail to impose order when that is not their actual purpose. In the present instance, it is not simply questionable whether the authorities of the State sincerely attempted to protect the Jews; it is almost certain that what happened was precisely the opposite.

In these circumstances, it is generally believed in foreign circles in Turkey that the anti-Semitic riots were provoked and encouraged by the People's Party for the purpose of compelling the Jews to leave certain crucial parts of the Turkish State.

Although official denunciation of the action was forthcoming and measures were taken in favour of those driven from their homes by the Minister of the Interior, who visited Thrace in connection with the events, this simply means that it did not prove possible to carry out the plan in a manner which would have preserved appearances, and that a bad impression was created abroad, and especially in Soviet Russia. Furthermore, despite the official condemnation and the measures in favour of the victims, the purpose for which the anti-Semitic movement was intended has already been accomplished, at least in part, and will most likely be completed in the near future. Not all of those who have been compelled to leave their homes will return to them, and such people as do return will probably not be planning to live permanently in places from which they were expelled and in which, of course, they no longer feel themselves to be safe. It follows that whatever happens, the Jewish population of Thrace and the Dardanelles will drain away.

The removal of the Jews – the only alien element in the Turkish population of these provinces – seems to be part of a more general programme to whose application the Turkish Government has recently been applying itself with assiduity. The bringing of the Prefectures of Thrace under an Inspector-General armed with wide powers was justified, not long ago, as being intended to foster the re-organisation and development of that region, which, having undergone many vicissitudes during the long years of war, was abandoned and neglected after it. However, it would seem that first priority among the concerns of the Turkish Government is the need to secure the European territories against external threats of all kinds. By exaggerating – as even many Turks will admit – the hazards which the general state of affairs could create, the government in Ankara has for some months been channelling much of its attention and resources into the defence of the country. Major movements of troops and changes in the commands of these units have been taking place in the last few days. Thrace is being strengthened, with significant increases in the numbers of troops there, and there are those who claim that the construction of works of fortification in Thrace and the Dardanelles has already begun.

I am not in a position to know whether, and to what extent, all the things being said about this are exaggerated, but it is my duty to note that the Russian Ambassador believes – or at least says he believes – that it is out of the question for the Turks to fortify the Straits since, *inter alia*, to do so would be superfluous: even without fortifications, Turkey would in time of war not lack the means of giving the Dardanelles sufficient protection. However, it can be confidently assumed that Turkey, which, as we all know, is increasing its defence expenditure in general, will be paying particular attention to the Dardanelles and Thrace.

86

The Greek Embassy in Bucharest to the Greek Ministry of Foreign Affairs

newspaper article from Apararea Nacional   Bucharest, 7 August 1934

Title: "The Jews and the Monarchy in Greece".

In its issue of 29 July, *Apararea Nacional* (National Defence), the semi-official anti-Semitic organ of the National Defence Club headed by Professor A. Cusa, carried the following article:

"As we all know, in opposition to its fundamental doctrines, the Freemasons look favourably on the restoration of the Habsburgs, since the young Otto, candidate for the throne, was raised in the spirit of Freemasonry and is a good servant of the campaign of isolating nationalist Germany.

"In Greece, too, the Jews and the Freemasons are financing the royalist party, whose leader has become Prime Minister of the country.

"A report which the Jewish newspapers published on their front pages makes evident to us the reasons why international financial circles look favourably on the restoration of the monarchy in Greece.

"When in Thessaloniki recently, Mr Tsaldaris replied to a delegation from the Jewish community which had come to welcome him by saying, 'I am pleased to talk to "my Jewish friends", whose virtues and love of work and progress I particularly appreciate'.

"And so Tsaldaris, the leader of the Greek royalists, the man who introduced such harsh measures against the Hellenic National Union, reveals who he really is and says 'my friends the Jews' – who must certainly be friends also of Mr Tsaldaris' patron.

"In other countries, too, the Jews have become monarchists, because monarchies restored with the help of the Jews are not restored only to serve Jewish interests: by incriminating the principle of monarchy, they also prepare the way for the Marxist revolution."

87

P. Rossettis, Ministry of Foreign Affairs, to the Prime Minister's Office

letter   Athens, 3 October 1934

With reference to your communication No. 11863 of 24 July concerning the emigration to Palestine of Jews from Thessaloniki, we have the honour to inform you that some time ago we informed the General Governance of Macedonia of the fact that in the current difficult economic circumstances, the Greek Government is unable to provide financial support for emigration of this kind and that the Jewish organisations of Thessaloniki should make direct contact with the Jews in charge of the Zionist movement so as to prevent the British authorities from obstructing their settlement in Palestine.

88

The Minister of Foreign Affairs to the Ministry of the Interior

letter   Athens, 24 October 1934

In forwarding to you, attached hereto, a copy of a telegram under the same reference number sent by us to the General Governance of Thessaloniki in reply to a query submitted to us by telegram, we have the honour to inform you that, after a fresh review of the question, we have decided to suspend the orders issued by that telegram and to permit the disembarkation in Thessaloniki of the Jewish passengers of the steamship *Velos*, on condition that, on the one hand, they furnish the written guarantee of their competent diplomatic or consular authorities in Greece to the effect that, after the said persons have remained in Thessaloniki for a period of time not exceeding one month, they will be permitted to return to their home countries and, on the other, that they pay a cash guarantee representing the cost of repatriation of each one of the said persons.

According to information supplied to us by a Jewish Senator who has taken an interest in the above issue, most of the Jews on the *Velos* are Polish, a smaller number are Romanians and a very few are Czechoslovak. In discussions with the said Senator, we pointed out to him the need for the granting of a written guarantee ensuring the right of repatriation from the Polish and Romanian Consular authorities in Greece, but not from the Czechoslovak authorities, since in a telephone conversation with the Czechoslovak Chargé d' Affaires here, we received an assurance that there will be no difficulty over the return of these Jews to Czechoslovakia, since they are regarded as Czech citizens.

In informing you of the above, we have the honour to request that you be so kind as to take the appropriate action.

DOCUMENTS
DURING AND AFTER THE SECOND WORLD WAR

Readers will observe that there is a gap in the documents between 1934-1943. This is the result of destruction of documents by the Axis occupation forces and the losses due to the dismissal of the MFA staff, on which see the note on p. 425.

89

The Commercial and Industrial Chamber of Athens et al to S.
Gotzamanis, Minister of Finance and of the National Economy.

appeal   Athens, 20 March 1943

Minister

We the undersigned Chairmen of the commercial and industrial institutions and organisations have the honour to appeal to you to take action in the matter of the task begun by the Occupation Authorities of the concentration of Greeks who are of the Jewish faith and their transportation beyond the borders of Greek territory.

Since the Jews have never wished to constitute an element alien to the Homeland and have readily performed the same services and made the same sacrifices as the rest of its children, we believe it to be our duty not only as Greek fellow-citizens but also as organisations which include in our ranks a large number of distinguished Jewish businessmen, industrialists and professional people in general, to express our warm sympathy towards these fellow-citizens and in an awareness of the inexorable conditions of war which our Country is currently enduring to put forward a proposal which in the present circumstances we believe will be for the Occupation Authorities a solution capable of implementation – that the Greek Jews now being displaced beyond the borders of Greek territory should be concentrated and remain on Greek soil in specific centres to be determined by the Occupation Authorities.

By this proposal, the cruel expatriation of thousands of Greeks whose very existence may be endangered by the inevitable hardships of displacement will be avoided, while, on the other hand, the objective pursued by the Occupation Authorities is ensured.

In the hope, Minister, that as our immediate superior as Minister of the National Economy and of Finance, you will favourably accept our proposal and duly put it before the Prime Minister with a view to the swift and timely settlement of this very serious issue by the Occupation Authorities, we have the honour to be

Yours very truly

A. Poulopoulos
Chairman of the Commercial and Industrial Chamber of Athens

I. Terzakis
Chairman of the Association of Greek Industrialists and Craft Industrialists
T. Lekatsas
Chairman of the Association of Joint Stock Companies
D. Vassilopoulos
Chairman of the Commercial Association of Athens

—◆—

90

Archbishop Damaskinos and other eminent Greeks to
C. Logothetopoulos, Quisling Prime Minister

letter   Athens, 23 March 1943

Prime Minister

The Greek people have recently learnt with understandable surprise and
distress that the German and Military Occupation Authorities have begun to
implement in Thessaloniki the measure of the gradual displacement of the Greek
Jewish element beyond the country's borders and that the first groups of the
displaced persons are already on their way to Poland. This distress of the Greek
people has been all the more profound since:

1. According to the spirit of the terms of the armistice, all Greek citizens were
to receive the same treatment by the Occupation Authorities regardless of race
and religion.

2. The Greek Jews have not only proved themselves valuable factors in the
country's economic performance, but have generally shown themselves law-
abiding and fully cognisant of their duties as Greeks. Thus they have shared the
common sacrifices for the Greek Homeland and have been in the front line of
the battles which the Greek Nation has fought in defence of its indefeasible
historical rights.

3. The observance of the law by the Jewish element in Greece precludes in
advance any charge of its involvement in activities and acts capable of threatening,
even at a distance, the security of the Military Occupation Authorities.

4. In the national consciousness, the children of our common Mother Greece
are seen as indissolubly united and equal members of the body of the nation,
regardless of any religious or denominational difference.

5. Our Sacred Religion recognises no discrimination, superiority or inferiority based upon race or religion, teaching that "there is neither Jew nor Greek" (Gal. 3: 28), any inclination towards the creation of any discrimination deriving from racial or religious difference thus being condemned.

6. Our common fortunes in days of glory and in times of national adversity has forged upon the anvil of Greek nobility of soul indissoluble bonds between all Greek citizens without exception, to whatever race they may belong.

We are not ignorant, of course, of the profound opposition which exists between New Germany and the Jewish element, nor is it our intention to be apologists for or even judges of world Jewry and of this or that activity on its part in the sphere of the major political and economic problems of the world. What is of interest to us today and disturbs us deeply is the fate of our 60,000 Jewish fellow-citizens, whose nobility of feelings and humanitarian disposition, the progressiveness of whose ideas and whose economic activity, and, most important of all, whose unimpeachable patriotism we have come to know during a long co-existence in slavery and in freedom. Of this patriotism an incontrovertible witness is the large number of victims which the Greek Jews have offered, without complaint or hesitation, on the altar of duty towards a common homeland endangered.

Prime Minister

We are certain that the Government thinks and feels in the same way as all the rest of the Greeks on this matter. We further believe that you will already have made the necessary representations to the Occupation Authorities for the suspension of the distressing and pointless measure of the displacement of the Jewish element in Greece. We hope, moreover, that you have signified to the powers that be that such harsh treatment of Jews who are Greek subjects in contrast with Jews in Greece of other nationalities renders even more unjustified and consequently morally unacceptable the measure implemented. If considerations of security are put forward to justify it, it is our view that it would be possible for solutions to be proposed and preventive measures taken, such as the confinement of the active male population only (excluding old men and children) in a certain area of Greek territory under the surveillance of the Occupation Authorities in such a way that their security would be safeguarded - even though against a hypothetical danger - and the class of Greek Jews would escape the dire consequences of the displacement with which it is threatened. It is needless to note that to the above measure the rest of the people of Greece would be ready to add without hesitation, if this were required, its absolute guarantee in favour of its suffering brothers.

We hope that the Occupation Authorities will realise in good time the pointlessness of the persecution in particular of the Greek Jews, who are among the most peaceable, the most law-abiding and the most productive elements in the country. If, however, against all our hopes, they stubbornly persist in their policy of displacement, we consider that the Government, as the holder of the residual political power in the country, should take up a clear position against the acts being carried out, leaving to the foreigners the entire responsibility of the manifest injustice being committed. No one, we believe, is entitled to forget that all the acts of this difficult period, even those which lie beyond our wishes and our power, will one day be investigated by the Nation for the due apportioning of the judgement of history. And in the moment of judgement, the side of the moral responsibilities which the rulers have shouldered even for the acts of the powers that be will weigh heavily in the conscience of the Nation if they omitted to express, by a noble-minded and courageous gesture, the entirely reasonable indignation and the unanimous protest of the Nation at actions which vitally affect its unity and honour, such as the displacement of Greek Jews now beginning.

We have the honour to subscribe ourselves

Damaskinos
ARCHBISHOP OF ATHENS AND ALL GREECE
S. Dontas
PRESIDENT OF THE ACADEMY OF ATHENS
E. Skassis
RECTOR OF THE UNIVERSITY OF ATHENS
I. Theophanopoulos
RECTOR OF THE NATIONAL METSOVIAN POLYTECHNIC
G. Nezos
RECTOR OF THE ÉCOLE SUPÉRIEURE OF ECONOMIC AND POLITICAL SCIENCES
M. Karzis
CHAIRMAN OF THE MEDICAL ASSOCIATION OF ATTICA AND BOEOTIA
P. Anastassopoulos
CHAIRMAN OF THE ATHENS BAR ASSOCIATION
C. Antonopoulos
CHAIRMAN OF THE ASSOCIATION OF NOTARIES PUBLIC OF ATHENS AND THE AEGEAN
Georgios Karantzas
CHAIRMAN OF THE JOURNALISTS' UNION
T. Synodinos
CHAIRMAN OF THE SOCIETY OF GREEK WRITERS
M. Argyropoulos
CHAIRMAN, GREEK AUTHORS

A. Karas
CHAIRMAN OF THE TECHNICAL CHAMBER OF GREECE
S. Chalkiadakis
CHAIRMAN OF THE ATHENS PROFESSIONAL CHAMBER
K. Nevros
CHAIRMAN OF THE UNION OF GREEK CHEMISTS
A. Tsitsonis
CHAIRMAN OF THE ATHENS PHARMACISTS' ASSOCIATION
I. Kareklis
CHAIRMAN OF THE ATHENS DENTISTS' ASSOCIATION
K. Papadoyannis
CHAIRMAN OF THE ATHENS CRAFT INDUSTRY CHAMBER
M. Kalantzakos
CHAIRMAN OF THE PIRAEUS PHARMACISTS' ASSOCIATION
M. Moridis
CHAIRMAN, GREEK ACTORS
L. Karamertzanis
CHAIRMAN OF THE PANHELLENIC PHARMACISTS' ASSOCIATION
D. Petropoulakis
CHAIRMAN OF THE PIRAEUS COMMERCIAL CHAMBER
D. Vassilopoulos
CHAIRMAN OF THE ATHENS COMMERCE ASSOCIATION
T. Sperantzas
GENERAL DIRECTOR OF FIRST AID SHELTERS
D. Mantouvalos
CHAIRMAN OF THE PIRAEUS MEDICAL ASSOCIATION
A. Poulopoulos
CHAIRMAN OF THE ATHENS CHAMBER OF COMMERCE AND INDUSTRY
M. Rodas
REPRESENTATIVE OF THE UNION OF GREEK THEATRE AND MUSIC CRITICS
I. Terzakis
CHAIRMAN OF THE UNION OF GREEK INDUSTRIALISTS
M. Apostolou
GENERAL SECRETARY OF THE PANHELLENIC DENTISTS' ASSOCIATION
M. Romantonis
CHAIRMAN OF THE KALLITHEA MEDICAL ASSOCIATION

91

Archbishop Damaskinos and other eminent Greeks to Gunther von
Altenburg, Ambassador, the Reich Plenipotentiary for Greece

letter   Athens, 24 March 1943

Your Excellency

We, the undersigned, are not seeking in this letter to interfere in any way with matters of the general tactics of the German Authorities in this country or anywhere else, but simply to submit certain thoughts to you, on the occasion of an issue which in recent days has held the entire society of Greece in a state of surmise and emotion, being certain that you will examine them in a spirit of profound good will and even more profound understanding.

The issue in question is that of the expulsion from Thessaloniki of the community of Jews of Greek nationality who, for a very long time, entirely lawfully integrated into the institutions of this country, not only never gave occasion for complaint on the part of any Greeks, but, on the contrary, always set an example of serious and co-operative solidarity with them and, at moments of crisis, proved themselves to be capable of self-denial and self-sacrifice in their country's cause.

Let it be noted in this connection that the Jews in question never competed, even in the narrow circle of their private interests, with us, but, on the contrary, a spirit of responsibility towards Greece as a whole never deserted them, thus enabling us to observe that most of them belong to the ranks of the poor.

It should be also noted that the Jews in Greece have a mentality which differs from that of the Jews in Germany, and that they do not even know the language of their co-religionists in Poland, where they are being sent to live.

Having taken all this into consideration, and, further, bearing in mind that throughout the entire length of Greek history our relations with the Jewish community have always been harmonious and smooth - from the depths of antiquity through the time of Alexander the Great and his heirs, down all the eras of tolerant Greek Orthodoxy to the framework of our recent life as a nation – we believe that in Your Excellency's high capacity as regulator of affairs in our country during the present war, you will not hesitate to espouse our present request and decide that the expulsion of the Jewish community from Greece shall be suspended, at least on a temporary basis, until the question of the Jews in Greece can be studied in the light of a special and thorough research.

In putting forward our request, we invoke the powerful advocacy of recent historical fact *per se*, which relates that at the time of the surrender of the city of Thessaloniki, and subsequently of all Greece, the terms of the relevant protocols included one according to which "The Occupation Authorities undertake the protect the life, honour and property of the inhabitants", surely implying in that term that there would not be at any time persecution of Greek citizens, regardless of their religion, race and birth, and, consequently, that the theory of racial or religious division would not be in any way applied in Greece.

Further support for this argument is to be found in the clear statement made shortly afterwards by General Tsolakoglou, whom the Occupation Authorities had then appointed as Prime Minister of Greece, who expressly announced that "the Jewish question does not exist in Greece nor will it ever be raised. All Greeks, going about their business peaceably, can be sure that their honour, their lives and their property are under the protection of the Occupation Authorities and the Government."

Your Excellency,

Just a few days ago, Berlin radio broadcast a talk by a German journalist and friend of Greece which was a true hymn to the traditional virtue of Hospitality, as practised among Greeks in all circumstances, and even towards those who are supposedly its enemies. Yet how can that same people, into whose hearts two thousand years of Christianity have instilled the principle of responsible love, fail to feel pain when it sees its very brothers, snatched away from the altars of their shared home, which over so many years they had embraced with boundless trust and a spirit of irreproachable solidarity towards us?

Your Excellency,

In the name of those sublime ideas which the Greek spirit and the high culture of Your homeland have elevated to the status of watchwords of universal prestige and incontrovertible authority, we beg of you that the suspension of the expulsion of our Jewish fellow-citizens which we have requested be implemented as soon as possible, and we assure you that the entire Greek people will be in a position to appreciate in the due manner the magnificent historic gesture you will have made.

With the greatest respect

ARCHBISHOP OF ATHENS AND ALL GREECE	Damaskinos
THE PRESIDENT OF THE ACADEMY OF ATHENS	S. Dontas
THE RECTOR OF THE UNIVERSITY OF ATHENS	E. Skassis

THE RECTOR OF THE OF ÉCOLE SUPÉRIEURE ECONOMIC AND POLITICAL SCIENCES	G. Nezos
THE CHAIRMAN OF THE ATHENS BAR ASSOCIATION	P. Anastassopoulos
THE PRESIDENT OF THE MEDICAL ASSOCIATION OF ATTICA & BOEOTIA	M. Karzis
THE PRESIDENT OF THE CHAMBER OF TRADE AND INDUSTRY	A. Poulopoulos
THE PRESIDENT OF THE TECHNICAL CHAMBER OF GREECE	A. Karas
THE PRESIDENT OF THE ASSOCIATION OF NOTARIES PUBLIC OF ATHENS AND THE AEGEAN	K. Antonopoulos
THE GENERAL SECRETARY OF THE PANHELLENIC DENTISTS ASSOCIATION	K. Apostolou
THE PRESIDENT OF THE DENTAL ASSOCIATION OF ATHENS	I. Kareklis
THE PRESIDENT OF THE GREEK UNION OF CHEMISTS	K. Nevros
THE PRESIDENT OF THE PHARMACISTS ASSOCIATION OF ATHENS	A. Tsitsonis
THE PRESIDENT OF THE PANHELLENIC ASSOCIATION OF PHARMACISTS	L. Karamertzanis
THE PRESIDENT OF THE UNION OF MORNING NEWSPAPER JOURNALISTS	G. Karantzas
THE CHAIRMAN OF THE GREEK ACTORS	M. Moridis
THE GENERAL DIRECTOR OF FIRST AID SHELTERS	T. Sperantzas
THE PRESIDENT OF THE MEDICAL ASSOCIATION OF KALLITHEA	M. Romantonis
THE PRESIDENT OF THE ATHENS CHAMBER OF CRAFT INDUSTRY	K. Papadoyannis
THE PRESIDENT OF THE ATHENS COMMERCIAL ASSOCIATION	D. Vassilopoulos
THE PRESIDENT OF THE ASSOCIATION OF GREEK WRITERS	T. Synodinos
THE GENERAL DIRECTOR OF THE SOCIAL SECURITY FOUNDATION	C. Agalopoulos

92

Report of P. Kontopoulos, student of chemistry, private

report   Cairo, 15 September 1943

'Concerning the persecution of the Jewish Greek citizens resident only in German-occupied northern Greece and certain islands'

The persecution of the Jews began in Thessaloniki, the centre of the Jewish population of northern Greece, in mid-February 1943 by means of specially-dispatched German Police forces belonging to the SS Battalions which had already swept away the Jews of all the other European countries conquered by the Germans.

The measures taken against the Jews were comparatively mild at first, reaching their climax in June 1943, when the Jews were openly tortured before the eyes of all the Greek population.

Measure 1: The Jewish Community, whose President was Albert Hasson and whose members included many eminent personalities (including Chief Rabbi Koretz), handed over to the Rosenberg Gestapo Battalions all the registers of the Jewish Community of Thessaloniki. This was the greatest mistake made by the Jews, since it was the beginning of the disaster that came upon them later.

In the meantime, the Gestapo had commandeered a very fine two-storey building which was handed over to the Jewish Community for use as its offices. The Germans also supplied the Community with two motor vehicles, one eight-seater and one five-seater taxi.

Measure 2: Two weeks later, all the Jews of Greek citizenship were instructed to present themselves at the offices of the Jewish Community, where they were issued with Stars of David, yellow in colour, measuring approximately 10 x 10 cm., and bearing their register number in the centre. All Jews, regardless of sex and age (over the age of 3 years), were obliged to wear the Star. All the Gestapo's orders were issued to the Jews solely and exclusively via the Jewish Community, and not via the Greek newspapers.

For the time being, the Rallis (Greek) Government appeared to be completely ignorant of the situation.

Measure 3: Five days later, all the Jews were instructed to assemble within five districts selected by the Jewish Community. This assembly had to take place within 4 days and at least 5 persons had to live in each room. Of the districts

View of the Jewish cemetery in Thessaloniki after it was destroyed by the Nazis in December 1942. The cemetery covered an area of 357,246 square metres. Today, the location is occupied by the facilities of the University. Archive of the United States Holocaust Memorial Museum, Washington DC.

selected, three were exclusively Jewish (Baron Hirsch, 151 and 6) while the other two, in the centre of the city, were also inhabited by very many Greek families.

This move was the first hardship to which the Jews were subjected, because in early March, a time of continual rain and amid the cold, they were compelled to leave their houses and assemble as best they might, usually in the basements of houses – and in conditions of severe crowding, given that there was a complete shortage of housing in view of the German requisitioning. The Jewish houses and shops were sealed by the Germans, who held these buildings in their own exclusive possession.

At this time, the Germans issued an order forbidding the Greeks to undertake the protection of Jewish property and to engage in commercial transactions of any kind with them.

Measure 4: Once the Jews had been enclosed within the above areas, and after three days had elapsed, an order was issued forbidding all Jews from leaving these areas. The streets leading to the outside world were guarded by Greek gendarmes and Jewish civil guards. Entry into the areas was permitted to all the Greeks, who began to pass supplies to their Jewish friends and to help them in all possible ways.

Measure 5: Special detachments of the Jewish militia, escorted by Germans, were sent to all the cities of northern Greece, Thrace and the Greek islands to bring all the Jews living there into the Jewish camps in Thessaloniki.

Measure 6: Under the escort of Jewish civil guards and with special permission from the Germans, all the Jews owning shops were taken into the city one by one, every day, to hand over their keys to the German authorities. The Germans immediately began to empty and strip the most important Jewish shops. The Jewish goods were loaded on whole convoys of German trucks and taken to the German warehouses.

Measure 7: Deportation to Poland. The first group was from the Baron Hirsch camp, which was closest to the railway station and was the only camp to have been surrounded with barbed wire and guarded only by German soldiers. The first train was loaded with approximately 3,000 persons of all social classes, regardless of sex, age or condition of health. The Jews were loaded on to the train like animals, 70 persons being crammed into each ordinary goods wagons of the Greek railways. It was at this point that the Jewish militia began its dreadful work of extortion and treachery. On that day, its members mercilessly whipped all those who delayed in boarding the wagons or were unable to do so by reason of age or ill-health.

The Jewish militia, with a strength of some 200 men, consisted largely of Jewish refugees from Poland, German Jews and other scum from Thessaloniki.

The Germans had promised the members of the Jewish militia that they would be the last to leave Thessaloniki and that, depending on the services they offered, they might escape being sent to Poland. This was a tempting promise, and it led them to commit the worst atrocities against their own compatriots while at the same time it did not save them from the fate of the other Jews of Thessaloniki. The deportations began to follow one another at short intervals: an area would be evacuated and its inhabitants moved to the Baron Hirsch camp, where the selection was made. The richer Jews of Thessaloniki were subjected to frightful tortures by the Jewish militia to make them reveal where they had hidden their gold. All the Jewish gold came into the hands of the Germans, without exception. Many of the rich Jews died in prison, while others were shipped off for further action. During this period, the Jewish militia had turned the Baron Hirsch camp into a brothel, and the German officers of the Gestapo with their instruments, the Jewish civil guards, indulged in all-night orgies there.

The remaining Jewish real estate was turned over to the Property Office of the National Bank of Greece and such merchandise that was left was put into the hands of Greek custodians, most of whom were Gestapo puppets. The general administration of Jewish property and affairs was undertaken by a department of the General Governance of Macedonia under the direction of Mr Panou; in other words, while the Jewish property was apparently turned over to the Greeks, I do not think that anyone would believe that the rapacious Fascists would have missed such rich plunder.

In these circumstances, the Greek people did as much as they could to help their brothers the Greek Jews, and more than just a few Greeks are still rotting in prison, awaiting trial, in the German concentration camps. In addition, many Greeks adopted Jewish children, and equally as many are still hiding Jewish families, at the risk of their own lives. Special mention should be made of the action taken by the Metropolitan Bishop of Thessaloniki, who called on the German military commander and begged him, on behalf of all mankind, to make the measures taken against the Jews and their deportation more humane. The military commander's answer was that his orders came from a higher authority and he was completely powerless to intervene. The general attitude of the Greek population, and of the Greek guerrillas (EAM), who took into their ranks their comrades-in-arms from Albania, was outstanding. I do not think that there could ever be a Jew who would dare to complain about the Greek population. Nor would it be possible to find anyone who believed either the Axis propaganda to the effect that the Jews, when asked, declared themselves dissatisfied with the Greeks, or the report published in the German newspaper *Pariser Zeitung* of Paris, according to which the Germans, behaving charitably even towards their enemies the Jews, made trains available to rescue them from their Greek oppressors (mid-April).

Some incidents did, of course, occur, but they were caused solely and exclusively by organs of the Gestapo.

The Greek soul did its duty and is proud of the fact, and the humanitarian sentiments of the Greeks won the admiration even of the German conquerors.

Likewise the Italian Consulate managed to save quite a number of Greek Jews who could prove that a member of their family had - even at some time in the past - borne Italian citizenship.

The Jews of Thessaloniki who had Italian citizenship were not included in the German persecution, but by order of the Germans to the Italian Consulate they were sent to Athens on a special train. The Spanish Jews were also exempted at first, but after the Greek Jews had been removed they, too, were included in the plan and, indeed, were treated in an even more barbaric way.

The names of the principal traitors and organs of the Jewish militia are as follows:

President of the Jewish Community of Thessaloniki: Albert Hasson
General Secretary: Albala
Pharmacist, member of the Council: Edgar Cunio
German Jew: Marcel Heftel

Chief Rabbi Koretz was a traitor by reason of his criminal cowardice, as were many others whose names are known to all the population of Thessaloniki but escape me. Of the 50,000 Jewish inhabitants of Thessaloniki, it has been calculated that 4-5,000 saved themselves by taking refuge on Mt Olympus and in Athens.

As we were informed unofficially by the Germans, the Jews of Thessaloniki, once they had been taken across the frontier, were all murdered by poison gas in special bath-houses.

—◦◦◦—

93

M. Sakellariadis, Consul General for Palestine and Trans-Jordan, to the Greek Ministry of Foreign Affairs in Cairo

document   Jerusalem, 6 November 1943

I have the honour to submit, attached hereto, a letter from the 'United Committee in Favour of Greek Jewry' of Tel Aviv, by which that organisation conveys a resolution taken in public session of its members, which I also have the honour to attach.

I did not omit to inform the Jews who visited me in this connection of the matters dealt with in my report to the Royal Ministry of Foreign Affairs No. 1302 of 2 October 1943.

—◦◦◦—

ATTACHEMENT a TO 93*

The President, M. Carasso, and Secretary, A. Altcheh, of the United Committee in Favour of Greek Jewry to the Consulate General of Greece in Jerusalem

letter   Tel-Aviv, 2 November 1943

Monsieur le Consul Général

Nous avons l' honneur de vous présenter par notre délégation la résolution adoptée au cours de la grande réunion publique tenue le Samedi 30 Octobre à Tel-Aviv, dans la vaste salle du Cinema Ophir et organisée par notre Comité.

Nous vous serions obligés si vous vouliez bien porter la susdite résolution par la voie la plus rapide à la connaissance du Gouvernement Central Hellénique.

Nous vous présentons, Monsieur le Consul Général, l' expression de notre haute considération.

ATTACHEMENT b TO 93*

A. Mallah, President of Assembly, United Committee in Favour of Greek Jewry

extracts from resolution   [without specific date] 1944

.....[*sic*]

h.   Soulignent avec la plus grande satisfaction l' attitude humaine de la population de Grèce envers les Juifs et réitèrent leur prière de continuer à les assister dans toutes les circonstances et par tous les moyens en leur pouvoir;

i.   Expriment leurs plus vifs remerciements au Gouvernement de la Grèce Libre pour le message émouvant lancé au Peuple et au Clergé de Grèce l' invitant à soutenir les Juifs et les défendre contre les agressions de l' ennemi;

j.   Prient le Gouvernement Hellénique de proclamer d'ores et déjà que toute la législation faisant une discrimination entre citoyens Chrétiens et Juifs est considérée comme nulle et non avenue et que les Juifs seront restaurés dans leurs droits et que tous leurs biens leur seront restitués.

94

Directorate of Special War Services (Bureau II A)

report   [without specific date] 1944

Information Concerning Atrocities Against Greek Jews in Greece

German measures against the Jews
Information of 17.9.42

Announcement

Further to the announcement of the General Governance of Macedonia concerning the assembling of the Jews of Thessaloniki in Eleftherias Square on 11 July 1942, only those isolated in their homes by reason of the cases of epidemic typhus which have occurred will be deemed to be justifiably absent.

By order of the German Authorities
Thessaloniki, 10 July 1942

The Jews deemed by order of the Commandant of Thessaloniki and the Aegean to be obliged to provide labour and under record numbers:

57	61	64	65	70	76	87	91	92	98	106	107
145	201	205	206	214	216	227	230	237	239	240	242
243	245	247	253	256	257	258	259	260	272	274	277
278	286	287	290	292	295	297	298	303	304	330	407
410	448	452	458	480	701	729	768	841	863	874	876
880	895	920	924	944	945	956	962	967	978	987	999
1001	1002	1005	1017	1018	1019	1020	1022	1024	1025	1032	1040
1041	1042	1045	1047	1051	1064	1065	1068	1069	1107	1108	1210
1271	1284	1288									

are hereby summoned

to present themselves for work.

These persons will present themselves at the Depot on Sunday 26 July at 6 a.m.

The items of clothing and bedding which these persons are obliged to bring with them may not exceed 10 kilograms.

FORCED LABOUR FOR JEWS

Information of 5.11.42

The Thessaloniki newspaper *Apoyevmatini* carried the following item on 5 September 1942:

"By order of the Germans, the Jews holding the following numbers from among those registered and obliged to work on 11 and 13 July in *Eleftherias* Square are to present themselves, without fail, on Sunday, the 6th inst., at 8 a.m., at the *Nissim* School in Thessaloniki (48 Velissariou St.) so as to be transported to the location in which they are destined to work. Each of the persons summoned may bring with him up to 20 kilos of luggage [the numbers follow, as above].

This announcement was also published by the newspaper *Nea Evropi*, Thessaloniki, 13.9.42.

The Liaison Bureau (Verbindungsstelle) of the Jewish Community of Thessaloniki hereby summons all male Jews aged 18-45 years who, for whatever reason, did not present themselves on 11 and 13 July of the current year in Eleftherias Square in order to be registered, to present themselves, in person, at the premises of the Bureau (44 Vassileos Irakleiou St, third floor) by 15 September at the latest to be issued with the proper work cards. Those who fail to present themselves before the above date will be severely punished.

Thessaloniki, 9.9.42

The German Military Commandant of Thessaloniki and the Aegean hereby announces that as of 31 August of the current year a special committee of the Jewish Community of Thessaloniki has been instructed to set up a Bureau which will deal with all matters relating to the Jews enlisted for compulsory labour. This Bureau bears the title Liaison Bureau – Labour Recruitment Department (Verbindungsstellearbeiteinsatzamt) and will have its premises at 44 Vassileos Irakleiou St., third floor.

Thessaloniki, 8.9.42

Information of 5.11.42

According to information from Thessaloniki, until 2-3 months ago the Jews had not suffered any persecution or pressure from the Germans.

Recently, however, one of the Bavarians established in Greece, by the name of ..., [sic] presented himself in Thessaloniki and, since he had undertaken the construction of a road from Katerini to Larissa through the Tempe defile, requested the help of the Germans in finding labour, and the Germans thought of enlisting the Jews of Thessaloniki. The German authorities thus decided to subject the Jews aged 18-45 years to forced labour in order to construct the road. The richer Jews disappeared, moving to other parts of Greece and to Athens in particular, while 9-10,000 of the poorer Jews presented themselves and were registered. Subsequently, however, a committee formed from among these Jews determined the capacity of each of them and on that basis set the sum for which the compulsory labour could be bought off, which varied from 1-7,000,000 per person.

Information of 21.1.43

On 9.12.42, the newspaper *Apoyevmatini* of Thessaloniki published the following announcement:

"All Jews belonging to the call-up classes of 1943, 1944, 1932, 1930, 1929, 1928, 1926 and 1925, that is, all those born in the years 1922, 1923, 1911, 1910, 1909, 1908, 1907, 1906, and 1905, must present themselves between 8 a.m. and 3 p.m. on 10 and 11 December of the current year at Synagogue 151 to be issued with Civil Mobilisation Cards in accordance with the summons of 5 December 1942.

Thessaloniki, 8.12.42

Thessaloniki, July 1942. Nine thousand male Jews between the ages of 18 and 45 were ordered to gather in Eleftherias Square in Thessaloniki. After being tortured and humiliated publicly, they were forced to hard labour. In October 1942, in order to relieve these men from the forced labour, the Jewish Community of Thessaloniki had to pay 2.5 billion drachmas in ransom to the German authorities. Archive of the Jewish Community of Thessaloniki, and the Beth Hatefutsoth Museum, Tel Aviv, Israel.

From the Bureau of the Jewish Community of Thessaloniki

According to information dating from approximately the same period, the purpose of mobilising the Jews was the construction of various projects, particularly of a defensive nature. Wealthy Jews donated 3,500,000,000 drachmas to the Germans - 1,000,000,000 of it in cash - and they thus succeeded in exempting the Jews from this service. Shortly afterwards, however, a new summons called up 10 age groups of Jews and Greeks, indiscriminately, for work on fortifications.

According to information received in mid-December, the Germans have carried out widespread civil mobilisation in the Peloponnese. The persons mobilised in the Nafplio and Kalamata areas are employed in the construction of fortifications.

According to information dating from 6.4.43, the real property belonging to the Jews has been confiscated. It will be distributed as follows: 1/3 to the Germans, 1/3 to the Jewish community, and 1/3 to the Greek state.

According to information dating from mid-April 1943, the only family of Jews living in Chios has been removed from there.

On 22.6.43, the newspaper ... [sic] carried the following report:

"The Greek General Governor of Macedonia has set up a service to manage the Jewish property confiscated by the German authorities. The houses of the Jews are deemed to have been confiscated and will be be used to accommodate refugees, etc.

Information of 15.5.43

A clandestine newspaper circulating in Greece carried the following report, inter alia, on 15.3.43:

"Last month, the Germans began to take terrible measures against the Jews of Thessaloniki. They have compelled the Jews to wear yellow badges so that they can be identified, forbid them to use telephones, trams, as well as to enter cinemas, theatres and other public places, and have restricted their movements by imposing a 5 p.m. curfew."

The newspaper reports that 60% of the property of the Jews has been looted by the Germans, who have burnt the Jewish quarter of Rezi-Vardari.

Most of the Jews of Thessaloniki have disappeared, and men, women and children, regardless of social class, are constantly being deported to Poland.

Greek public opinion is appalled by the martyrdom of the Jews. The Church of Greece and the political leaders have protested against this unprecedented persecution.

According to information dating from 2.7.43, the Jews of Orestiada and the Evros area in general were loaded into 48 box-cars, with 80-90 people in each car, and sent to Thessaloniki. By the time the train reached Poroia, seven people had died.

German Persecution of Jews in Greece

Athens (information of 8.12.43)

In late September 1943, it became known that members of the Rosenberg Commission and SS units specialising in carrying out its orders had arrived in Athens.

By the end of September of the current year, no measures of persecution against the Jews of Athens had been taken.

Around 18-20.9.43, the Gestapo asked the Rabbi of Athens for lists of the

Picture from the same gathering. Archive of the United States Holocaust Memorial Museum, Washington DC .

members of the community and also of its Board of Management (the leading Jewish citizens), setting a 48-hour deadline.

When they heard of this, the Jews left their houses and went into hiding.

The Rabbi did not present himself to the Germans, but disappeared with the help of nationalist Greek secret organisations.

After this, the Germans began to loot the houses which the wealthy Jews had abandoned. The people of Athens displayed the greatest sympathy for the suffering Jews. Complete strangers helped to hide the Jews who were homeless. The services rendered by the Greeks were such as to cause it to be said that despite the persecution of the Jews by the Germans, only one Jew was arrested.

On 5.10.43, the newly-arrived SS commander, Major-General Strupp, issued a proclamation ordering all the Jews to return to their homes within 24 hours and to register with the Jewish Community. The Jews of Spanish, Turkish and, in general, foreign nationality of neutral countries were exempted from this rule. The Italian Jews, who had not been persecuted in Thessaloniki and had been moved to Athens, and the Jewish residents of Athens of Italian nationality received the same treatment as the Jews of Greek nationality.

The time limit for presentation and registration was from 5.10.43 to 11.10.43. The Jews of foreign nationality were to present themselves on 16.10.43. Jews of this category were not convinced that they would continue to escape persecution. The Spanish Jews did not present themselves for registration until they had received assurances from their Embassy that a representative of the Embassy would be present during the course of registration.

A rumour circulated to the effect that only 200 Jews, of Greek and other nationalities, had presented themselves for registration.

This demonstrates that the Greeks provided the Jews with effective assistance, despite the fact that the German order imposed an immediate death penalty on all Jews found hiding, while the concentration camps lay in wait for the Greeks who hid them.

The Greek police, which is under the direct orders of the Germans, was recently instructed to take part in the persecution and apprehension of the Jews. However, there is no evidence that they complied with this command.

Damaskinos, Metropolitan Bishop of Athens, received an undertaking from the Germans - after repeated representations - that the following persons would be exempt from persecution:

a) young Jewish children

b) Jewish war-wounded

c) categories of Jews who had given their services to the Greek State.

However, the Jews were not convinced by this promise, since the Germans had also asked for lists of names of the individuals in these categories.

The professional organisations of Athens have assisted their Jewish members in every way possible.

- Thessaloniki (information of 10.7.43)

Subsequent to orders from the German Authorities in Thessaloniki issued between 15 and 28 February 1943, the Greek Jewish residents of Thessaloniki – men and women alike – were compelled to wear on their chests a special yellow badge bearing a serial number, to abandon their houses and gather in specially determined zones (ghettos) in the city, where sanitary and living conditions were generally appalling, and to make statements of their possessions, including even their clothes. Immediately afterwards they were compelled to abandon their shops, offices and businesses, with all the goods and commodities of all kinds in them. Both their real property in general and their immovable property were classified as 'hostile' and placed in receivership.

Once these measures against the Greek Jews had been completed (and it should be noted that none of the measures was applied to Jews who were not of Greek nationality), they were informed in the afternoon of 14.3.43 that they would all be deported to Poland. Sure enough, on that same morning the Jews residing

Commemorative picture of Myriam Benrubi before her wedding in the Jewish ghetto of Thessaloniki in March or April 1943. Deportation of Jews to concentration camps had already begun. Her father, Isua Benrubi, wears the easily discernible yellow star on his chest. At the time there was a tremendous increase in weddings, often exceeding 100 per day. This phenomenon is indicative of the search for security in order to face the uncertainty of the presumed migration to Crakow. Archive of the Jewish Community of Thessaloniki, donated by Isidore Benrubi, USA.

in one of the assembly zones (ghettos), numbering some 10,000 souls, found themselves surrounded by barbed wire and guarded on all sides. They were told to be ready for immediate departure to an unknown destination.

The news reached Athens the same morning and profoundly shocked public opinion.

His Reverence the Archbishop and a number of other personalities, and Greece as a whole, headed by the Orthodox Church and expressing itself through the political leaders and the presidents of organisations of all kinds, protested to the Government and demanded that the Prime Minister and his associates should intervene to suspend this unprecedented persecution.

However, all these representations went unanswered, and thus on 16.4.43, 2,700 men, women, old people, infants, handicapped and injured persons were packed like crates, 60-80 at a time, into box-cars of the type normally used for transporting animals and left Thessaloniki without luggage and with one *oka*[*] of bread each. That was the only provision made by the Germans for the six-day trip facing the persons being exiled in this manner. The box-cars were sealed from the outside before the train departed.

After the announcement of this first shipment, the representations to the Greek Government and the International Red Cross on the part of the political leaders, the Archbishop, the presidents of organisations, etc., multiplied in number. A great wave of human solidarity swept through the people of Athens, and protests and resolutions were conveyed to the Government. There were calls for the Prime Minister to leave immediately for Thessaloniki so that once on the spot he could take active measures to stop the disaster while at the same time providing the Jews with as much help as possible.

In the meantime, similar shipments of between 2,000 and 3,000 persons each continued to leave at intervals of 2-4 days, under the indifferent eyes of the General Governor of Macedonia, who appears not even to have taken the trouble to make an official report to the Government on what was occurring.

By 29.3.43, 5 shipments had taken place, involving some 13,000 persons or more than 1/4 of the entire Jewish population of Thessaloniki.

According to rumours, the box-cars were opened for the first time at Skopje, so that corpses could be removed. In all the box-cars, it was said, there were many persons dead or dying, while several other occupants had been driven mad by the horror of the experience.

In the meantime, the number of those in Thessaloniki committing suicide in their despair rose by the hour.

---

* One *oka* is the equivalent of 1,280 grams.

In addition to these shipments, the German police arrested 1,500 Jews in the streets of the ghetto and shipped them off to forced labour in Thessaly and Central Greece, not permitting them even to notify their families.

Faced with the mass outcry of the Greek people over these terrible happenings taking place under the indifferent eyes of the General Governor of Macedonia and the other state authorities, the Government appears to be under the impression that it has done its duty by sending two written protests to the Reich Plenipotentiary and by taking a decision, in principle, that one of its ministers and a university professor should make their way to Thessaloniki. Their departure, however, has been repeatedly deferred, and it is not known whether their journey has ultimately taken place.

- Ioannina (information dated 7.1.44)

Since September 1943, the German occupation authorities have been applying measures which put pressure on the Jewish community of Ioannina.

After pressure had been exerted, the President of the Jewish Community delivered to the Germans a list of names of the Jews together with their assets.

As a first compulsory tax measure, the Germans then demanded from the Jews, and received, 300 beds to meet the needs of a newly-established German military hospital.

The general conduct of the Germans towards the Jews is rapacious. Since the arrests began, many of the Jews have fled to the guerrilla refuges in the mountains, where they receive care and protection.

- Didymoteichon (Prefecture of Evros), May 1943

In late April 1943, a senior German officer arrived in Didymoteichon and, gathering the Jews at the garrison command, subjected them to a beating.

On 4.5.43, all the Jews of Didymoteichon were loaded on to box-cars, the men, women and children being placed, 80 at a time, in separate cars. Each Jew was entitled to bring effects to a total weight of 30 kilos. During the loading, three persons died of heart attacks. The destination of the train was not announced, but may be Poland. It is believed that these Jews will be eliminated during the course of the journey (see also Bulletin No. 38 of the Directorate of Special War Services).

In the districts of Orestiada, Didymoteichon and Soufli, the Germans assembled all the male and female residents and, having stripped them of all their valuables and maltreated them by beating, they shaved the heads of the men and women and removed their clothing, making the men dress up in women's clothing in order to humiliate them. Then they were all taken to the station in Alexandroupolis and loaded, like beasts, into box-cars, 80 per car. The Metropolitan Bishop of Didymoteichon, out of sympathy for the Jews and despite the prohibitions of the Germans, attempted to relieve and comfort them by supplying them with water, which was a very valuable commodity at the time of entrainment. The scene was most moving, and all the Greeks shut themselves up in their houses, unable to face the tragic scenes taking place before their very eyes. All the shops, possessions and houses of the Jews were confiscated by the Germans after they had first been looted, most of the furniture, utensils and valuables being dispatched to Germany.

- Athens, 30.9.43

In Athens, the Greek people were in a better position to help the persecuted Jewish refugees from Thessaloniki, perhaps because the capital was under Italian command. For the time being, the persecution has gone no further than the imposition of crushing compulsory taxation on the Jewish merchants of Athens.

- Athens, 7.1.44

In Athens, a German order has been issued imposing the death penalty on any Christian Greeks who hide Jews. Even so, the Jews receive protection and are facilitated in various ways in escaping to the Middle East or joining the guerrilla bands.

After the disappearance of the Rabbi (who is said to have been taken to a place of safety by a band of guerrillas), a large black circle was placed over the door of the Synagogue and a star of David inscribed within it. This is explained as a declaration of persecution to the death upon the Jews.

- Thessaloniki, 15.9.43

The Jewish Community, whose President was Albertos Hasson and among whose members were eminent personalities such as Chief Rabbi Koretz, have handed over to the Rosenberg Battalions of the Gestapo all the registers of the Jews of Thessaloniki.

The Gestapo has given the Jewish Community a fine two-storey building in which to instal its premises and the Germans have also put two taxis at the disposal of the Jews.

The persecution of the Jews began, in the form of mild measures, in mid-February 1943 and culminated in June 1943.

Two weeks after the delivery of the registers, all the Jews of Greek nationality were instructed to make their way to the Community offices and be issued with the familiar yellow stars.

All the orders against the Jews were issued by the Germans via the Jewish Community and not through the Greek Government or the Greek newspapers. Five days later, all the Jews were assembled by the Germans in three districts: that of Baron Hirsch, No 151, and No 6, which had been exclusively Jewish, and two in the centre of the city, where many Christian families had also lived. The removal of the Jews to these districts, in the midst of the bad winter weather at that time of the year, was the first hardship they had to undergo. The Jewish shops, etc., were sealed by the Germans. At about the same time, a German order forbade the Greeks from taking the property of Jews into their safekeeping and prohibited any commercial transactions with them.

The Jews thus enclosed within these city blocks were forbidden to leave the area. Greeks were allowed to enter the area, and they were thus able to supply and help the Jews.

Special detachments of the Jewish militia, accompanied by Germans, were sent to all the towns of Northern Greece, Thrace and the islands, in order to bring the Jews established there to the camps described above.

The Jews themselves handed the keys of their shops over to the Germans, who used whole convoys of trucks to convey the goods in the shops to German warehouses.

The first shipment of Jews to Poland set out from the Baron Hirsch camp, near the railway station. It had been surrounded with barbed wire and was exclusively guarded by Germans. Approximately 3,000 persons of all social classes, sex, age, etc., were loaded, like animals, 70 at a time, on to box-cars belonging to the Greek Railway Company.

On that day, the Jewish civil guards mercilessly whipped all those who were slow in boarding the cars.

The Jewish militia is 200 strong and consists of Jewish fugitives from Poland, German Jews and scum from Thessaloniki itself.

The Germans have promised these men that they will receive better treatment, and they will probably escape deportation to Poland.

As a result, they committed the most frightful atrocities against their fellow-Jews, and even so, they did not escape the fate of the others.

The Jewish gold came into the hands of the Germans.

Many wealthy Jews died in prison.

During these days, the Germans had turned the Baron Hirsch camp into a brothel, where all-night orgies took place.

The remainder of the Jewish assets was delivered to the real estate office of the National Bank of Greece.

The overall management of Jewish assets and Jewish affairs was undertaken by a department in the General Governance of Macedonia – apparently, of course, since it seemed very doubtful that the voracious Nazis would pass up such rich plunder.

Many Greeks are today in an appalling state in prison because they helped the Jews.

The Metropolitan Bishop of Thessaloniki took an admirable interest in the

Jews, repeatedly visiting the German Military Commander in the hope of obtaining more humane measures and transportation conditions for the Jews.

The Jews of Thessaloniki who were Italian citizens were exempted from the persecution, and by order of the Germans to the Italian Consulate were moved to Athens in a special train.

The Jews of Spanish nationality were treated in the same way as the Greek Jews.

Of the approximately 50,000 Jews who lived in Thessaloniki, it is estimated that only 4-5,000 survived by fleeing to the mountains or to Athens.

According to certain information from German sources, when the Jews of Thessaloniki had crossed the Greek border, they were murdered by poison gas in special bath-houses.

The names of those who acted as traitors to their fellow-Jews are as follows:

1) Albertos Hasson, President of the Jewish Community of Thessaloniki.

2) Albala, General Secretary of the Jewish Community of Thessaloniki.

3) Edgar Cunio, pharmacist, Member of the Board of Management.

4) Marcel Neutel, German Jew

and Chief Rabbi Koretz, whose criminal cowardice made him a traitor to his fellow-Jews (see DSWS report of 29.10.43).

- Thessaloniki, 30.9.43

As a result of the inhuman persecution they have suffered at the hands of the Germans, the Jewish element of Thessaloniki is now almost non-existent. Terrible rumours have been heard about the fate of those deported to Poland. On the way, they were stripped completely naked by the Bulgarians. It is highly unlikely that they ever reached their destination. Just before the trains departed, the Germans snatched a number of girls from the arms of their parents to put them to work in the military brothels.

- Thessaloniki, 3.10.43

The Chief Rabbi of Thessaloniki was persuaded to submit lists of names of the Jews of Thessaloniki including children as young as six years. After this, the Germans ordered all the Jews to wear on their chests the familiar distinctive yellow star, measuring 14 cm. across, bearing within it the serial number of each Jew. They were forbidden to use the tram or go about in the main streets of the city, and in cases of absolute necessity only could circulate when accompanied by members of the police force formed from among the Jews themselves by order of the Germans. There was a special ban on the opening of Jewish shops, which fell into the hands of the Germans and were looted. The Germans then encircled the various city blocks in the Jewish quarters of the city and herded the Jews into a block of the Jewish quarter near the railway station, which they had previously evacuated. The assembled Jews were kept there for a fortnight and then loaded

Picture of Lilian Menache, daughter of Dr Albert Menache, who died at the age of 16 in the gas chambers of the Birkenau concentration camp. Archive of the Jewish Community of Thessaloniki, donated by Isaac Menache (Athens) and David Amir (Irsael).

on to a train, 60-80 people being packed into each box-car. The train set off for an unknown destination after the Germans had sealed every box-car. Old people, infants, pregnant women and the inmates of the various Jewish old people's homes were loaded on to the cars as if they were animals. An empty oil can was placed in each box-car to be used as a latrine, together with another can full of water. The Greek people helped the Jews in a variety of ways. Despite the ban imposed by the Germans, many Jewish children were adopted by Greeks.

In order to attract the Greeks to adopt an anti-Semitic attitude, the German propaganda promised that the property of the Jews would be distributed among the refugees from Thrace. No Greek voluntarily presented himself to request a house or any other asset belonging to a Jew.

According to information received to 22.10.43, the Greek Quisling Government has taken no measures against the Jews. There has never been discrimination between the Greek Jews and the other Greeks.

The foodstuffs, medicines, etc. sent by the United Nations were distributed equally among the Jews and the other Greeks.

According to the census of the Greek population carried out in 1928, there were 72,791 Jews in the entire country.

Those deported from northern Greece today number approximately 45,000.

Daily newspaper *Haboker* (Tel Aviv 10.5.44)

Headline: "Greeks help Jewish compatriots"

"Refugees recently arrived from Greece have much to say about the many forms of help which the Christian Greek population has given to the Jews of Greece despite pressure from the Germans. Many instances are known in which Greeks have risked their own lives in order to save Jewish compatriots in danger of falling into Nazi hands and being transported."

The daily newspaper *Davar* carries the same report, under the headline "The sons of Greece aid the persecuted".

The daily newspaper *Hatzofeh* also carries the report, under the headline "Greeks defend Jewish compatriots".

All three newspapers publish the news item in a prominent position on the front page.

12.5.44 The Jewish newspapers publish a telegram from London (Jewish News Agency) containing a statement from the Duke of Alba, Spanish Ambassador in London, to the effect that "the Spanish Government is doing everything possible to protect the Jews who are Spanish citizens and residents of Greece.

"The necessary measures have been taken to put a stop to the transportation of Jews to Poland."

13.4.44   Humanitarian feelings in Greece

The daily newspaper *Ha' Aretz* ('The Land', Tel Aviv) publishes a lengthy report from Constantinople on the subject of the admirable humanitarian feelings of the Greeks towards the Greek Jews, who are being brutally persecuted by the Germans. The newspaper's correspondent cites many examples demonstrating that hundreds of Greeks risked their lives by hiding Jewish refugees in their homes and sharing with them the last crusts of bread they had. He then draws attention to the aid granted to the Greek Jews by the Greek clergy and by the guerrillas, who facilitated the Jews in every possible way in their flight from Greece.

14.5.44   The Jews of Greece

The daily newspaper *Davar* (Tel Aviv) today carries a statement broadcast on the Greek programme of London radio to the effect that most of the Greek Jews had been deported to Yugoslavia and Czechoslovakia after the confiscation of their property. SS Commander Burgen was named as the champion persecutor of Greek Jews.

The daily newspaper *Hasman* (Tel Aviv) publishes a note on the help granted by the Greeks to their Jewish compatriots during their persecution by the Nazis, and comments:

"The Jewish people all over the world notes with the greatest satisfaction this conduct on the part of the heroic sons of Greece, whose spiritual values continue always to set an example of civilisation and humanity."

7.5.44 The daily newspaper *Ha'Aretz* (Tel Aviv) carries a lengthy report from Beirut on the arrival in Syria of a group of Greek-Jewish refugees whose accounts included the following passage:

"We owe a perpetual debt of gratitude to the Greek patriots who saved us and fed us, endangering their own lives. The Greek captain of the small boat which brought us refused to take money for our passage, and he distributed among us the best of whatever he had.

"In Athens, the Germans were assisted by the three sons of the Recanati family (Jews), who discovered Jews in hiding and stole their money and possessions. These traitors and spies thus enriched themselves at the expense of the blood of their unfortunate brothers."

The news about the three sons of the Recanati family has made a great impression here, given that Mr Leon Recanati, manager of the Palestine Discount Bank, is the leader of the Greek Jews here. The Quisling Rallis has organised a gang of 4,000 Greeks, called 'the Evzone Division', whose mission is to discover Jews and murder Greek patriots hiding in the mountains.

On the other hand, all the Press (including the *Palestine Post*) carries on the front page the news from Beirut of the arrival in Syria of a group of Greek Jews who had been saved by Greek guerrillas from the hands of the Nazis.

19.5.44   The magnanimity of the Greek people

The daily newspaper *Davar* (Tel Aviv) publishes a lengthy special telegram from its correspondent in Geneva describing the atrocities committed by the Nazi conquerors against the Greek Jews and the help the Jews received from the Greek population. The telegram adds:

"The Jews are full of gratitude to the Greek people for the generosity and nobility of their feelings. Such fraternity among fellow-citizens had never before been reported in history. Any Jew who asked for help received whatever he needed and was given accommodation and food.

"Despite the German threat that any Greek hiding a Jew would be shot, the Greek people are still hiding and defending their Jewish fellow-citizens with unbounded loyalty."

This telegram was carried on the front page in bold type print. *Davar*, organ of the Labour Party, is the most important newspaper in Palestine.

23.5.44 The daily newspaper *Hamaskif* (Tel Aviv) carries an article referring to the official announcement made by the Greek Government in Cairo in connection with the state of the Jews in Greece. This report refers to the persecution of the Greek Jews and to the help they received from the Greek population.

According to information dated 22.6.44, 1,200 Jews from Corfu have been sent to Germany and are being held there as Greek hostages.

Athens: Information of May 1944

The Jews of various nationalities (Greek, Spanish, Portuguese) arrested in Athens and various other parts of the country (Epirus, Corfu) in late March 1944 were brought to Athens and on the night of 1 April were taken in closed trucks to the Rouf railway station in Athens. There they were packed with suffocating tightness, 80 or 100 at a time, into 37 closed box-cars to be sent north. The box-cars were sealed, and gangs of station workmen put barbed wire and planks of wood across the slit windows. People were piled on top of one another: pregnant women, children, invalids and old people, all calling for help. But the German guards brutally drove away anyone who attempted to approach the box-cars. In separate though equally crowded box-cars were the Jews of Spanish nationality. Their windows were not blocked, and the Germans allowed their Ambassador to give them a little food.

Representatives of the International Red Cross, learning of the departure of the Jews who had been arrested, hastened to the station with food parcels. The German guards at first forbade them to give any assistance, but after the representatives had protested and persevered, permission was granted for the parcels to be distributed when the train had been closed up and was departing.

With great difficulty, the Red Cross representatives managed to push a few of the food parcels through the bars. In the end, although the Red Cross representatives followed the train, in cars, as far as Menidi, they were able to distribute only 400 food parcels.

⋆⋙⋆

95*

World Jewish Congress

report   [illegible] February 1944

Note:

We are presenting in the following pages a number of reports on the fate of Greek Jewry, which reached us from various sources.

The information they convey has been difficult to assemble. Greece does not lie on the beaten tracks. It is not in the limelight of political and military events.

These reports make us realize that the Germans, in their determination to wipe the Jewish population off the face of the European continent, did not overlook Greek Jewry.

But there is another, brighter aspect to this tragic chapter in our chronicles of last year: It gives further evidence of the determination of the subjugated peoples to thwart the fiendish Nazi plan, often at the risk of life and liberty.

Thus these sad reports also inspire hope; the hope that, thanks to the efforts of courageous Gentiles, many a Jewish child hunted by the Gestapo Searching Squads, many a Jewish man or woman, believed dead or deported, will be found saved.

Let us cling to this hope.

Table of Contents

I. Notes on the Present Situation of Greek Jewry by A.L. Molho
II. Report of a Refugee from Athens.
III. Athenians Protect Jews from Nazis (A News Item).
IV. Anti-Jewish Atrocities in Occupied Greece (A News Item).
V. Athenian Jews Rescued (A News Item).

Notes on the Present Situation of Greek Jewry
By A.L. Molho

Cairo, October 12, 1943

THE ANTI-JEWISH MEASURES AND THE QUISLING GOVERNMENTS.

No anti-Jewish legislation has been passed in Greece. At the beginning of the
occupation, it seemed indeed that the Nazis had put vigorous pressure upon the
government of Logothetopoulos, then in power, so as to bring about the
enactment of the 'Aryan paragraph'. The Quisling Prime Minister, however, knew
how to avoid taking the initiative. It is difficult to ascertain exactly the motives of
such an attitude on the part of a 'collaborationist' who showed himself in other
questions to be a servile valet of the Hitlerites. It is nevertheless believed that Mr
Logothetopoulos did not wish to oppose the popular sentiment which was
definitely hostile to any racial discrimination. The violent demonstrations that
have taken place in Athens against the illegal application by the occupation
authorities of persecution measures against the Jewish population of Macedonia,
demonstrated *a posteriori* that any and all official measures against the Jews were
likely to provoke very serious troubles all through the country.

It isn't known whether similar pressure was brought to bear by the Germans
upon the Quisling Governments that have succeeded the one of Mr
Logothetopoulos. The fact remains that up to the month of February of this year
the Jews of Greece have enjoyed, both *de jure* and de facto, the same status as
any other Greek citizens. The measures which have been adopted from the above
date on against the Jews of Salonika and entire Macedonia were originated
exclusively by the German occupation authorities. They acted, according to their
own admission, in conformity with very precise orders received by them from high
quarters. The Greek Authorities have obstinately refused to identify themselves
with these measures. The Orthodox Church raised its voice against them.
(Memorandum of the Archbishop-Primate of Athens to the German authorities).
The leaders of the political world as well as the professional and popular
organizations, have outright identified themselves with this protest. The pressure
of Greek public opinion has been so mighty that the Quisling Prime Minister, Mr
Ioannis Rallis, has been obliged to declare that he was going to intervene on
behalf of the Jewish element. It is not known whether he has kept his promise. In
any case, it hasn't manifested itself officially.

THE RELIEF SENT TO GREECE AND THE JEWISH CITIZENS.

The aid of the United Nations to the Greek people consists in monthly shipments representing on the average 15,000 tons of wheat and other general merchandise. The distribution of this aid is being performed through the intermediary of a committee of the International Red Cross. Up to the present time there has been no report of any discrimination whatsoever to the detriment of the Greek citizens of the Jewish faith.

However, taken as a whole, the Jews find themselves in an inferior position, and this is because of the following main reasons:

a) They cannot profit from the rations distributed by the workers' kitchens because workers constitute but the smallest minority of the entire Jewish population in Greece.

Besides, opportunities to work are being denied to the Jews in the factories where these kitchens are functioning, as these factories are under the absolute control of the Germans.

b) Certain police ordinances regulate the movements of the Jewish citizens in such a manner that is impossible for the latter to precede [sic] to procure provisions. Such ordinances it is true, have been passed and applied in those regions of Greece that find themselves under Bulgarian control, and namely: in Eastern Macedonia and Western Thrace where the Jewish population is relatively considerable. Up to the Jewish expulsion from the above two regions they were forbidden to go to market before ten a.m., while the traffic hours for them had been fixed as from 6 to 9:30 a.m. The Jews were obliged then either to resort to the black market or else to die from starvation. And, it seems, this was exactly the goal pursued by the Bulgarians. A great number of confiscations of Jewish properties has been justified by the fact that the persons in question have had recourse to the black market.

Some figures

When war was declared, Greek Jewry consisted of about 100,000 persons. The majority of this Jewish population (about 60,000 persons) was concentrated in Salonika where they comprise 1/4 of the total population.

The remaining 40,000 Jews were scattered, in more or less important agglomerations, all throughout the national territory. There were about a dozen communities worthy of mention, as for instance; Corfu in the Eptanisos, Ioannina in Epirus, Kavala, Florina, Verria and Castoria in Macedonia, and lastly, Volo, Larissa and Triccala in Old Greece.

The Jewish community in Athens deserves particular mention because of its rapid and considerable growth due to a series of special circumstances.

Up to the economic crisis of 1928 Athens counted very few Jewish families.

The transformation of a part of the Greek capital from commercial to industrial purposes, has attracted the influx of a considerably large number of Jewish capitalists of Salonika to Athens and Piraeus. As everyone ought to know, these are the two principal industrial centers of Greece.

Thus the Jewish community of Athens counted already in 1939 more than 4,000 members. This figure however, gives but a faint idea of the importance of this community. Owing to the economic, social and even intellectual qualities of its members, it began to rank as second in the Greek Consistory, the place of first rank being always held by the Jewish community of Salonika.

The entrance of Greece into the war brought in its wake a new growth of the Jewish population of the capital. In fact, fleeing the very frequent aerial bombardments of Salonika, a considerable number of Jewish families, belonging for the most part to the high and middle bourgeoisie, have escaped to Athens where the dangers of war were considerably less.

The arrival of German motorized troops to the Greek-Bulgarian frontier (March 1, 1941) has accentuated this movement. The Jews, as it was natural, have not escaped the panicky feeling of entire Macedonia because of the proximity of the Nazis and the evident imminence of their aggression. All those who have had the means (for it was very difficult to procure railroad tickets, and a trip by automobile between Salonika and Athens costs on the average 150,000 drachmas or about 300 lbs. [sic] sterling) hastened to find shelter beyond the Olympus – that is, in the capital. The number of Jews who succeeded on that occasion in reaching Athens is estimated at 5,000. The immigrants this time were, with but very rare exceptions, people in easier circumstances.

A third Jewish migration towards Athens manifested itself at the beginning of this year when it became clear that the Germans were about to undertake a wholesale deportation to Poland of the Jewish communities from Northern Greece. From the approximately 5,000 Jews who succeeded in their escape from Salonika, a few hundreds have been picked up in the mountains by the Greek partisans. The remainder have escaped to Attica.

Bearing equally in mind the number of Jews of Italian nationality that had been evacuated to Athens by the Italian consulate of Salonika one may, without fear of mistaking oneself, evaluated the present Jewish population in the Greek capital as 20,000 persons.

Thus, Athens has become the most important Jewish community in entire Greece. Salonika, as everyone knows, has no longer at present even a single Jew.

As to the total Jewish population in the entire of Greece, it probably does not exceed 30,000 persons. From a total of 100,000 Jews who lived in Greece at the beginning of the war, 65,000 or a little less have been deported to Poland, and the remaining 5,000 have been arrested and sent to labor camps in the interior of Bulgaria.

JEWS OF FOREIGN NATIONALITY

There was in Greece a very considerable number of Jews of foreign nationality. Jews of Turkish or Bulgarian nationality were rather rare. On the other hand, there were a large number of Jews of Italian or Spanish nationality.

The position of Jews of foreign nationality has in some respects been much better than that of the Greek Jews. For example, the Italian occupation authority, in spite of the existence of racial laws in Italy, had favored up to a certain point their compatriots of Jewish faith. Among others, they have obtained their exemption from being deported to Poland. When the Germans insisted that the presence of no matter what kind of Jews in the important military zone of Salonika was intolerable, the Italian Consulate took upon itself the evacuation of its Jewish compatriots to Athens.

As to the Jews of Spanish nationality, the attitude of the Nazi occupation authorities has been contradictory. At the beginning, the Spanish Jews had enjoyed a favorable regime when compared with the regime suffered by their co-religionists of Greek origin. They had also been excluded from the deportation measures. But this attitude suddenly changed. In their turn the Spanish Jews were called and deported to Poland. It seemed even that the Nazis had treated them with much more cruelty than they had the Greek Jews. This strange behavior is accounted for as an indirect consequence of the disappointments the Hitlerite circles have experienced in the Spanish attitude towards the war.

JEWISH REFUGEES FROM GREECE

We have no information of any kind concerning the arrival in Istanbul of Jewish refugees from Bulgaria. We only know that the attitude of the Bulgarian authorities towards the Jews, and above all towards those Jews of the Greek provinces that are provisionally being controlled by the Bulgarians, has been as inhuman and as ferocious as that of the Nazi authorities themselves. It is therefore more than probable that the Jews of Greek provinces, as well as those of Bulgaria proper, had attempted to escape their miserable fate by crossing, imperilling their lives, the Turkish frontier. Let's on this occasion remark once more that the measure of Jewish deportation to Poland has been applied just as vigorously in Eastern Macedonia and Western Thrace, which are being administered, as we have already said above, by the Bulgarians.

As far as the Greek Jews are concerned, a very small number of them have been able to reach Turkey. The Ankara government treats them on an equal footing with the other Greek refugees. Generally, after a brief internment, these refugees are being asked to choose a frontier of their convenience, across which to be driven back. Naturally, they demand then to be taken to the Syrian frontier as the French authorities of that country admit them without difficulties.

In Syria, the Jewish refugees of Greek nationality are being taken care of by the Greek Ministry of Assistance. Jews of military age are naturally mobilized for service, whereas, others are being sent either to Palestine or to Egypt where they are being maintained by the Greek government exclusively. Let us stress here that the Greek military authorities, giving themselves a full account of the sufferings endured by their compatriots of Jewish faith in occupied Greece, are doing everything to keep them up physically and morally. During a long period they are being excluded from difficult tasks and are being accorded long terms of convalescence. It is reasonable to state that common sufferings have still more strengthened the ties of brotherhood between the Greek nation and its Jewish citizens. These latter are deeply affected by the brotherly and sincerely liberal attitude demonstrated generally on their behalf by all the Greek authorities.

Report of a Refugee from Athens

Istanbul, October, 1943

After the Germans had issued an order to the effect that all Jews have to register, those who had provided themselves in advance with identification cards of Greek Orthodox people, found hiding places with their Gentile friends. It must be granted that the inhabitants of Athens have behaved more humanely than did the population of Salonika. It is, therefore, to be hoped that a substantial number of our people will be able to save themselves from the Germans.

There were cases when, in order to obtain a hiding place, one had to pay from one and a half to two million drachmas monthly. There were other cases where a deposit of L50 or even L100 in gold was demanded in advance. This was to identify [sic] the person furnishing the hiding place in case he were seized by the Germans and sent to a concentration camp as punishment.

The organization EAM has recruited many among us, and those who know English were sent to headquarters. Others (young people mainly) fled to the mountains in order to join the Andartes, or else went to those regions which are known as "Free Greece". The greatest number, however, has fled to the mountains into the region of Kapirnissia [*sic*], while others went into Evia, in the hope of finding a way to sail, even if illegally. The EAM, which has organized several transports, demanded that each of the well-to-do Jews support two of our destitute co-religionists. It distributed among the population of Athens circulars asking that the Jews be granted all possible aid and support. Just to cite an example: In Evia, from where we were to sail, the Andartes let only Jews board the ship, and on the strength of our oath permitted us to continue our journey.

Fifty to sixty people, chiefly those who could find no hiding place or who were afraid, are said to have registered during the five-day period following the announcement of the German order. As a consequence, the Germans tacitly prolonged the deadline for registration until the 17th. But there were people who registered even on the 18th without being punished.

The Germans handed out white identification cards without a photograph, giving the name, address and occupation of the card-owner and a list of the days when he had to report. In one case, a sick man was allowed four extra days in which to report. Those who were married to Greek women received brown cards.

It is believed that because the population of Athens strongly resents the anti-Jewish measures, the Germans will proceed less vigorously than they did at the beginning in luring the Jews from their hiding places.

Up until October 20th not a single Jewish store was looted except that of Alhadeff (immediately after the withdrawal of the Italian authorities) and still more recently, that of Eliezer Salomon and a depot at number 60 Kipsali St. Furniture, however, has been removed from many apartments, as for instance, from those of Salomon Kamhi, Joseph Danon, Soriano, Benzennana, Asseo. It must be observed that in cases where Jews had their Greek friends take over their apartments, declaring that the latter had purchased all their belongings, nothing was touched.

Our fellow Jews might suffer only, should the Germans announce a reward to those who report them. Such an attitude would be the consequence of the famine prevailing in Greece.

At the instigation of the Greek Archbishop it was preached in the churches that Jews should be aided, and he intervened with the German authorities in order that children younger than 14, as well as persons married to parties of the Greek orthodox faith, should be exempted from the strict anti-Jewish regulations. It seems that his intercessions were successful. Still, I believe that the only real solution for our people would be immigration [*sic*] to Palestine. For as time goes by our Greek friends, afraid of coercive measures, might be influenced to change their tactics.

The committee of the Jewish community, organized by the German authorities, is composed of Moise Seizky and Hadjopoulos and another person whose name is not known to me. As you may have learned, Rabbi Barzilai fled to the mountains, and burned all documents when he was asked by the Germans to furnish the list of 25 of the most distinguished Jewish citizens.

Athenians Protect Jews from the Nazis

Guerrillas Help Them to Escape

The story of how the people of Athens protected their Jewish fellow-citizens from Nazi persecution has been told to the Istanbul correspondent of the "Daily Express" by one of the 17 Greek refugees who have reached Turkish soil.

On October 25, said the refugee, the German military government of Athens sent for the Chief Rabbi and ordered him to prepare a complete list, with addresses, of all the 12,000 Jews in the capital.

He made no secret that this was a preliminary step to the expulsion of the entire Jewish population to Poland under the usual ghastly conditions of sealed trains.

Lists Burned

While preparing these lists the chief rabbi mentioned the new order to some of his Greek friends, who sent word to the head of the Greek underground patriot organization.

The night before the lists were to be ready a small party of Greeks broke into the rabbi's house, burned the lists, and moved the Rabbi to a mountain village, so that he should not suffer from his failure to produce the lists.

On October 31 the Germans published in the Athens papers an order to all Jews to report themselves by November 4.

By that date only 268 out of the 12,000 had presented themselves. The rest had hidden in Christian households, despite the German threat of the death penalty for hiding them.

After only two days in hiding a group of 17 was guided by night to a remote village near Marathon, and hidden in a cattle shed.

Orders by Radio

The following night they were taken across to an island where patriot forces were in control.

Three nights later a guide told them that his leaders had been in radio touch with the Allied authorities in the Middle East, and that he had received instructions to help them escape and to give them money.

The same day they were put aboard two caiques, in which they came to Izmir in Turkey.

Hellas - London, November 26, 1943

Anti-Jewish Atrocities in Occupied Greece

The Greek people react vigorously against the German plan to exterminate the Greek Jews.

London, December 1943

The Germans can truly boast of the thoroughness and astounding rapidity with which they carried out their plan to exterminate the Jews of Macedonia and Thrace.

Within four months, from the beginning of January till the end of May, most of the Jews in these regions were completely stripped of their belongings and were sent, 80 in one car, by railroad to Poland. According to an official report of 50,000 Salonika Jews, 13,000 had already been evacuated by the beginning of May.

The Greek population has reacted vigorously against the measures of persecution enacted against the Greeks of Jewish religion. Professional and popular organizations of Athens took steps with the Puppet Government to induce it to intervene on behalf of the Jews. The leaders of political parties joined, requesting the immediate departure of Mr Rhallys to Salonika in order that he take the necessary steps on the spot. The Church has not remained silent either. The Archbishop-Primate of Athens, Mgr. Damaskinos, composed and signed a memorandum branding in strong terms and in the name of Christian morality, the cruel measures taken against the Jewish population.

As for the conditions under which the evacuation of the Jews had been carried out, it is sufficient to quote the underground paper *Nea Genea* (issue of May 15, 1943):

"We shall not report the innumerable humiliations, the robberies, the brutalities and the murders perpetrated by the Germans against the Salonika Jews. The story below is quite sufficient to degrade Nazism forever.

"When the wagon which transported Salonika Jews to Polish Ghettos was opened at the point of destination, half of the travelers were found to be dead. Fifteen had gone mad. Only one was able to stand. The train had left Salonika seventeen days earlier. In the freight car, painted black and barely adequate for 50 persons, the Germans had jammed 68 Jews of the first convoy, among whom were old men of 90 years, pregnant women, women who have been forcibly separated from their husbands, 10-12 year-old children, etc.. On leaving Salonika, these unfortunates had a small parcel containing food for two days, and some water. The wagon had no toilets and had been sealed before the departure."

Athenian Jews Rescued

Greeks' Heroic Help

An official report on the situation of the Jews in Greece, which has been issued by the Greek Government in exile in Cairo, describes in detail how 15,000 Athenian Jews were "spirited" away by the population under the very noses of the Gestapo and brought to temporary safety despite the most vigorous steps taken by the Germans.

The report also discloses that at least 50,000 of the 60,000 Jews of Salonika have been deported and that Western Thrace and Eastern Macedonia are completely "judenrein."

Many Greeks who aided Jews were caught and severely punished, the report states. After serving their sentences they were not released but held as hostages. Armed bands of Greek patriots took a leading part in rescuing Jews, and 4,000 Jewish war veterans from Salonika have joined the forces of the Front of National Liberation.

Some weeks after the capitulation of Italy, members of the Rosenberg Commission, charged with the task of exterminating European Jewry arrived in Athens. They demanded from the Chief Rabbi of Athens, Dr. Itzhak Barzilai, a list of the members of the community. The Chief Rabbi pleaded that the lists were incomplete and obtained a respite of three days for their delivery. Instead of preparing the list, however, he destroyed all the records of the community and "disappeared," as recently reported briefly in the *Jewish Chronicle.*

Jewish Population "Vanished"

This "breathing space" enabled the patriots to make arrangements for the rescue of the Jews of Athens. Within a week the entire Jewish population of the city vanished. Jewish families were dispersed in non-Jewish homes, almost every Christian home in Athens, the Piraeus, and the suburbs taking in one Jew. There they remained hidden while the patriots, with the aid of religious and civil functionaries, as well as Greek police secretly affiliated to resistance organizations, prepared false identification cards, enabling the Jews to pass as Christians.

The Nazis, the report continues, then issued a decree warning the Jews to return to their own homes and to report to the police in the district of their ordinary domicile. Those failing to comply with this order were threatened with the death penalty. A second decree required the heads of all families to notify the police immediately of the identity of every person in their household who was not a member of their family. Only 300 reported.

Christian families adopted hundreds of Jewish children, passing them off as their own to prevent their deportation. Others who had relatives living in the countryside escorted Jews there for safe refuge.

The Jewish Chronicle
December 3, 1943.

──◆──

96

M. Sakellariadis, Consul General for Palestine and Trans-Jordan, to the Greek Ministry of Foreign Affairs in Cairo

cover letter   Jerusalem, 1 March 1944

I have the honour to submit to you, attached hereto, a copy of the translation from the Hebrew of a letter from the General Federation of Jewish Labour in Palestine expressing sentiments of gratitude to the Greek people for their noble behaviour in protecting the Jews in Greece.

──◆──

ATTACHMENT TO 96*

D. Ramez, General Secretary of the General Federation of Jewish Labour in Palestine, to M. Sakellariadis, Greek Consul General for Palestine and Trans-Jordan

letter   Tel Aviv, 23 February 1944

Dear Sir,

At the last plenary session of our Executive Committee, we had the opportunity of hearing an eye-witness account of the kindness shown by the people of Greece to their Jewish fellow citizens, at the time when the calamity of Nazi deportation was visited upon them.

We knew at the time about these happenings in a general way, but the facts as related to us on this occasion have aroused in us the strongest feelings of esteem and admiration.

We consider it a duty and an honour to express these feelings through you to the Government of Free Greece and to the Greek people in its homeland, to its sons and daughters, its aged and its children.

We shall ever cherish in our hearts the memory of these great humane deeds in the dreadful darkness of these days.

97

G. Christodoulou, Consul in charge for Palestine and Trans-Jordan, to the Ministry of Foreign Affairs

confidential letter   Jerusalem, 1 June 1944

Concerning the attitude towards the Jews of the Greek population in occupied Greece

Your telegram No. 4311 of 7 May 1944

I have the honour to inform you that a few days after receiving your telegram I had a meeting, in accordance with your instructions, with Mr Epstein, a senior official in the Jewish Agency, who has recently returned from Cairo.

I talked to Mr Epstein about the news items which appeared in the Press here in early May of this year – items which were unfavourable to the Greek people and according to which the Greek population supposedly betrayed Jews in hiding to the German authorities. The reports go on to say that more than 2,000 Jews had been apprehended by the Germans in this way. I made it clear to Mr Epstein, who had already been briefed on the matter by Mr Pappas, our Chargé d'Affaires in Cairo, that the publication of such news items, which are manifestly inaccurate, surprised me because they are in such dissonance with the pro-Greek articles frequently carried in the Palestinian newspapers to date.

Mr Epstein agreed with me, and told me that, as he had been able to establish, the news item in question was relayed here by the New York correspondent of the Jewish News Agency, who had in turn received it from another correspondent in Cairo. According to Mr Epstein, the Jewish News Agency does not have a permanent correspondent in Cairo, and thus it is difficult now to check the original source of the item. A journalist of American or other nationality passing through Cairo in late April may have reported the item to America, relying on carelessly-collected information or misled by persons whose objective is to slander everything Greek.

However, regardless of how the question arose, Mr Epstein declared himself willing to set matters right immediately. He promised me that he will use Palcor, the official Jewish News Agency here, to channel information to the Palestinian newspapers about the admirable and extremely courageous support which the Jews being persecuted in Greece received from the entire Greek people. Such information will completely overshadow the adverse impression in Jewish public opinion of Palestine created by the first news item.

Mr Epstein added that, in his opinion, such a tactic would be infinitely preferable to the publication of an official denial in the newspapers of Palestine, which would give rise to debate and dispute.

Sure enough, a few days later all the newspapers of Palestine retracted their initial statements, carrying information highly favourable to the attitude of the Greek people towards the Jews. Some of them published detailed descriptions of the assistance rendered to the Jews by the Greek Orthodox Church and the Greek people in general and of the manner in which the Greek guerrillas and the population of the Greek countryside had rescued the persecuted Jews. Some of these articles are true hymns to the attitude of the Greeks in this respect.

To conclude, it should be noted that in his inaugural address to the Conference of the 'Misrachi' religious organisation, Dr Herzog, Chief Rabbi of Palestine, stated the following, *inter alia*:

"The Jewish Palestinian people and, with them, the Jewish people of the United States, of Britain and of the entire world, would like to express their heartfelt thanks to the Greek Orthodox Church, and, in particular, that of occupied Greece, for the moral and material assistance it has given to the persecuted Jews, and also for the understanding which the worthy leaders of that Church have displayed towards the sufferings and problems now concerning the Jewish people." The Chief Rabbi's words were received with general approval and greeted with loud applause.

In my communication No. 66/D/6 of today's date I am forwarding to you a special Palestinian Press bulletin devoted to this subject. In it, I have assembled, in translation, both the articles unfavourable to Greece published in early May and the later ones, of an opposite point of view, published in the Palestinian newspapers either under the inspiration of Mr Epstein or in some other manner, in which gratifying praise is expressed of the attitude of the Greeks towards the Jews during the present War.

98*

*News Bulletin issued by the Greek Information Office of the Greek
Embassy in London*

London, 6 June 1944

About two thousand Jewish inhabitants of Athens, of Greek and foreign nationality, were sent by train to Poland by the Germans during May 1944.

Since October 1943, when measures of racial persecution were extended to Athens, the systematic persecution of the Jews was begun by the Gestapo. During this period the Greek population has shown a remarkable solidarity towards the escape. Many Jews have escaped to the mountains, where they joined the guerrillas, while others have reached safety in the Middle East, with the aid of the Greek population. The Germans made no exception with regard to Jews of foreign nationality (Spaniards, Italians and Turks) in spite of protests on the part of foreign ambassadors.

The conditions under which these victims of German barbarism were transported were terrible. The trucks into which, men, women and children, healthy and sick alike, were loaded, were of the type normally used to transport coal and wood, and had only one entrance which closes hermetically with an iron bar, and a small railed window at the top corner. The Germans closed even this small window with barbed wire, thus making impossible any communication with the outside. These Jews had to remain two whole days in the trucks which remained at the railway station before the train started on its journey. During this time one died, and a woman gave birth to a child without any medical assistance. No food or water was given to these Jews during this time.

When informed of what was happening, the Greek Red Cross immediately sent to the railway station some lorries with food to be distributed to the Jews by nursing sisters, but the officers in command of the guard refused to open the doors of the railway trucks, saying they had orders to forbid any communication with the Jews under transport. The only concession made was to remove temporarily the barbed wire of the windows, through which the nursing sisters threw whatever they could into the trucks.

99

G. Christodoulou, Consul in charge for Palestine and Trans-Jordan,
to the Ministry of Foreign Affairs

telegram   Jerusalem, 13 June 1944

I have received information from various sources to the effect that certain Greek employees at the Aleppo camp for Greek refugees – more specifically, Warrant Officer Apostolatos and Corporal Papazian – have been displaying anti-Semitic sentiments. Jewish refugees recently arrived from Greece have already reported the unfortunate incidents suffered by them at Aleppo to the official Jewish circles here, which have decided to release details both to the Palestine Press and to the English and American Press, thus causing a sensation comparable to the issue of anti-Semitism in the Polish camp. I have taken action to forestall these publications here, but I believe it is expedient that I should draw your attention to the matter so that you can conduct the appropriate investigation to discover how much truth there is in the allegations, whose repetition in the near future I cannot preclude.

—◦◦◦◦—

ATTACHMENT a TO **99**

P. Dragoumis, Undersecretary of Foreign Affairs, to the Greek
Ministry of Welfare in Cairo

report   Cairo, 17 June 1944

We have the honour to inform you that various complaints have reached us about the conduct of certain Greek employees of the *Aleppo* camp.

More specifically, it has been alleged that Warrant Officer Apostolatos and Corporal Papazian have displayed anti-Semitic sentiments towards the Jewish Greek refugees in transit through the camp.

Bearing in mind that such action is contrary to the beliefs of the Greeks as a whole, who not only have always displayed sympathy and affection for their Jewish compatriots but have also, in recent times, undertaken at risk of their lives to hide and protect them from the murderous frenzy of the Germans, we would be grateful if you could act so as to remove the above persons from the *Aleppo* refugee camp and severely punish them and all others who may be responsible for misconduct towards the refugees in transit through it.

⊷◆⊷

ATTACHMENT b TO 99

A. Demertzis, Infantry Lieutenant, to the Greek Ministry of Welfare in Cairo

report   Aleppo, 9 July 1944

'Concerning the allegations against Warrant Officer Emmanouil Apostolatos and the civilian Vassilios Papazian'

In execution of your order No. 2/17/27.6.44, attached to communication No. 15741/17.6.44 of the Ministry of Foreign Affairs, I have the honour to report the following:

I. The detailed research and oral investigations carried out by the undersigned reveal that Warrant Officer Emmanouil Apostolatos has never given rise to complaints on the part of the refugees in general and that always and in all cases he has conducted himself in a manner befitting a Greek officer. The allegations made against him by a certain Jew are certainly the result of base motives on the part of the person making the complaint, who did not receive from the officer in question the service which he believed he ought to have received.

The sentiments of the above officer towards the refugees, without exception, and towards the Jewish Greeks in particular are those of an individual who is fully aware of his mission.

II. The civilian Vassilios Papazian, of Armenian descent, serves in this camp wearing the badges of a British sergeant without holding any such rank and is paid a salary by M.E.P.P.A. He was the protegé of the former Camp Commander, Captain Harrison, who, despite your duly communicated orders Nos. 11552.30.7.43 and 1551/18.4.44, did not proceed to dismiss him. This individual has repeatedly given cause for complaint, in connection with your above orders, which were issued subsequent to reports from us.

Now, subsequent to the installation as Commander of this camp of Lieutenant Bennet, orders of dismissal have been communicated to the three members of the Papazian family – father, son and daughter – but have not been carried out because they are subject to the approval of the 9th Army.

In view of the above, please take the appropriate action to obtain approval for the dismissal of the above persons, whose continued presence in the camp administration is deemed to be highly damaging.

ATTACHMENT C TO 99

P. Skeferis, Ambassador, Greek Ministry of Foreign Affairs in Cairo, to the Greek Consulate General in Jerusalem

document   Cairo, 8 August 1944

In reference to your telegram in connection with the complaints voiced by some Greek Jewish refugees over alleged misconduct towards them in the *Aleppo* refugee centre on the part of Warrant Officer Apostolatos and Corporal Papazian, we hereby forward to you, attached hereto, a copy of a report from the said refugee centre demonstrating that insofar as the allegations concern Warrant Officer Apostolatos, they are groundless. We shall take action to ensure that the decision already taken to transfer Corporal Papazian, who does not belong to the Greek Army, is carried out.

100

G. Christodoulou, Consul in charge for Palestine and Trans-Jordan, to the Ministry of Foreign Affairs

communiqué   Jerusalem, 15 July 1944

Concerning the attitude of the Greek population in occupied Greece towards the persecuted Jews

(Our communications Nos 22/D/1 and 66/D/5 of 1 June 1944).

I have the honour of informing you that a few days ago I received a letter from His Reverence Ouziel, Chief Rabbi of Palestine, in which he expresses his cordial thanks for the attitude adopted by the Greek population and the Orthodox Church of Greece towards the Jews who were the victims of persecution in occupied Greece.

I attach hereto and send to you, for your information, a copy of this letter, which, as you will observe, is highly complimentary to our country and the Greek people.

Similarly, I attach hereto the text of my own letter of thanks which, in reply, I addressed to His Reverence the Chief Rabbi.

ATTACHMENT a TO 100*

Benzien Meir Hay Ouziel, Chief Rabbi of the Holy Land, to G. Christodoulou, Consul in charge for Palestine and Trans-Jordan

letter   Jerusalem, 10 July 1944

Most Honoured Sir

I have heard very frequently from the Press of the consideration and compassion in which the Greek Nation excelled towards the Jewish people in their great tragedy in occupied Greece.

Now some refugees who arrived here from Greece tell me with much praise of the brotherly help extended to them by the Greek people in Salonica and Athens, who gave them shelter, food and clothing from the little they possessed and smuggled them to places of safety out of the reach of the enemy. All this was done without regard to the dangers involved, and some have paid for this with their lives.

These immigrants also express undoubted praise and admiration for the Archbishop of Athens who did everything possible, physically and morally, in his instructions to and influence on all the Churches and clergymen to preach compassion and give assistance to their Jewish brothers, and in his protest and defence before the authorities with courage and strength that adds to him and his Nation honour and praise.

Ever since I stayed in Salonica in the darkest hour of the Greek Nation during the war against Anatolia I learned and respected the noblesse, courage and humane qualities of the Greek people. And now on hearing these reports I become all the more full of praise and admiration. I therefore hereby express to

Benzien Ouziel, Chief Rabbi of Thessaloniki (1921-1923) and Sephardic Chief Rabbi of Israel (1939-1953). Recanati Archive, Israel.

you, in my name, in the name of all your subjects who escaped and are escaping death and in the name of the whole Jewish Nation my most sincere thanks to the whole Greek Nation and its great spiritual leader for this brotherly help which will remain and be remembered for ever in the annals of Israel and the world.

And with this I express my hopes and sincere prayer for the restoration of the Greek Kingdom and State to its former freedom and glory.

ATTACHMENT b TO 100*

G. Christodoulou, Consul in charge for Palestine and Trans-Jordan, to Benzien Meir Hay Ouziel, Chief Rabbi of the Holy Land

letter   Jerusalem, 15 July 1944

Your Eminence

I was deeply moved by your kind letter No. 1031 of 10 July 1944, in which you expressed, with such eloquent words, your admiration and gratitude towards the Hellenic Nation, for the support granted to our suffering Jewish brothers during the present War.

My compatriots in occupied Greece are now enduring themselves one of the most appalling tragedies of History and suffer all the horrors of enemy occupation. Therefore, the Greek people have not the possibility of doing more, as they would wish, in favour of the Jews of Greece, persecuted by the barbarous invaders of our Country. Nevertheless, everybody in Greece seeks to help, as much as he can, his Jewish fellow Countrymen, and we Greeks who have the privilege to live on a free soil, note with the utmost satisfaction this sentiment of sincere fellowship, developed and strengthened during these times between Greeks and Jews.

I wish to tell you that I hasten to send a copy of your letter to my Government and I am sure that they will highly appreciate the noble feelings towards the Greek Nation expressed by your words.

In the meantime, I beg your Eminence to accept my warmest and heartiest personal thanks, as well as the renewed assurance of my highest consideration.

IOI

G. Christodoulou, Consul in charge for Palestine and Trans-Jordan, to the Ministry of Foreign Affairs

telegram   Jerusalem, 20 July 1944

Further to my communication No. 166, I have the honour to inform you that yesterday's issue of the *Palestine Post* carried a fresh report from Cairo describing, inaccurately and in unfavourable terms for the Royal Government, the suspension of talks between it and EAM.

Text of report will be sent by next post. Today, I took advantage of some meetings with Jewish circles to draw their attention to the unfortunate impression this publication by semi-official Jewish agency will make on Greek Government, particularly at moment when it, and entire Greek people, are displaying such interest in the Jews of Greece. Received promises that appropriate recommendations will be made to editors of newspaper.

Mr Epstein, senior staff member of Jewish Agency, left for Cairo today and told me he will consult with Ambassador Pappas on the matter.

IO2

D. Pappas, Ambassador of Greece in Cairo, to the Greek Ministry of Foreign Affairs

extract from minutes   Cairo, 18 September 1944

I have the honour of submitting to you, attached, for your information, an extract from the Minutes of the session of 16 August of the Community of Greek Jews of Egypt (Cairo), signed by its President, Mr Iossif Bessos.

Extract from minutes of the session of 16 August 1944 of the Committee of Management of the Greek Jewish Community.

The Chairman took the floor and spoke as follows:

"On the basis of the report read by the General Secretary of our Community and of the discussion which has taken place on that report, please allow me to submit for your approval my conclusions, which, if accepted, will in the future constitute the general policy of our Community.

"These conclusions can be summed up as follows:

"1. We must oppose the doctrine of world Jewish Nationalism and refuse to join any international organisation whose purpose is to represent the Jews anywhere in the world, with the right to speak to states and governments in their name.

"2. The Greek Jews will remain forever completely dedicated to their Motherland.

"3. We must request the Government of our country to ensure, as in the past, equality among the citizens, without discrimination by religion.

"4. We must support, in general, the rights and dignity of individuals.

"5. We must claim the protection and defence of political, civil, religious, economic, social and educational equality, without any discrimination by religion.

"6. We must attempt to develop co-operation with other organisations which hold similar beliefs in order to protect and improve the situation of Jews in other countries.

"7. We must collaborate in disseminating the ideals of the general fraternity of all citizens.

"8. We must accede to the Balfour Declaration, with the following reservations: 1) that the existence of a Jewish home in Palestine will not have any adverse impact on the free exercise of the political and civil rights of persons of the Jewish religion resident in other countries, and 2) that none of the rights of the non-Jewish populations of Palestine will be harmed.

"9. We must request from the Government of our country that, in good time, it grant its support, in consultation with the British, for:

a) the protection of Jewish settlement and migration to Palestine and the safeguarding of freedom in the growth and development of that country;

b)   the protection and support of the fundamental rights of all the citizens of Palestine;

c)   the protection and support of the sacred lands.

103

D. Pappas, Ambassador in Cairo, to P. Dragoumis, Under-Secretary of Foreign Affairs

letter   Cairo, 20 September 1944

Minister

I have the honour of submitting to Your Excellency, attached hereto, a copy of a letter addressed to me by Mr I. Bessos, President of the Greek-Jewish Community of Cairo. I do not know whether there are copies of this letter and of the texts which accompany it, and are of particular significance, in the Ministry archives, for which reason I attach them to the present. The texts in question are two resolutions, one passed by the Jewish American Committee and the other by the World Jewish Congress. Both resolutions are from extremely important organisations, but that which is of greater value to us is the resolution of the Jewish American Committee, since that Committee has political influence on the members of the Senate and, through them, has a considerable impact on the foreign policy of the United States. Mr Bessos' success in this matter is far from negligible, and I consider it unfortunate that the events which took place in May were not followed up as they should have been in order to keep the active friendly sentiments towards us at a usefully high level.

When at last the Government moves to Athens, it would be expedient to continue with the friendly relations so successfully commenced.

ATTACHMENT a TO 103

I.Bessos, President of the Community of Greek Jews in Egypt, to D. Pappas, Ambassador in Cairo

letter   Cairo, 8 July 1944

Your Excellency

We have the honour of enclosing herewith, for your information, a copy of the letter we are sending today to His Excellency the Prime Minister in connection with the two resolutions in favour of the Greek people given to me in America by two large Jewish organisations, together with copies of the resolutions in question.

Please be assured, Your Excellency, of our highest esteem.

ATTACHMENT b TO 103

I.Bessos, President of the Community of Greek Jews in Egypt, to G. Papandreou, Prime Minister

letter   Cairo, 8 July 1944

Your Excellency

During my stay in the United States of America, I considered that it would be both practically possible and extremely beneficial for the Greek cause if an interest in Greece were to be stimulated among the Jews resident in the various States of the USA, numbering some 4 1/2 million people who are prominently placed in society, in both economic and political terms.

On this basis, I began to work methodically and intensively, and, exploiting my personal acquaintance with some leading Jews, I made direct and continuous contact with the persons in charge of the various organisations. By means of discussions, reports and lectures within these organisations, I managed to praise the activities and self-sacrifice of our fellow-Greeks on behalf of the Jews in Greece, and as a result these organisations expressed, by wholehearted resolutions, their thanks and boundless gratitude to two of the main Jewish organisations in New York, the Jewish American Committee and the World Jewish Congress, which, in turn, drew up the two resolutions which, on their instructions, I have the honour to enclose herewith.

The former of these two organisations may be known to you as being one of the wealthiest and most powerful organisations in America, and it is in close contact and collaboration with the Administration of the United States.

Our Community in Egypt is in close contact with both these organisations, and we have already exchanged special envoys.

We are at the disposal of the Government, if it should ever deem that the co-operation of these organisations is required.

Please be assured, Your Excellency, of our highest esteem.

ATTACHMENT C TO 103*

*Dr M. Porlzweig, Political Department of the World Jewish Congress,
to I.Bessos, President of the Community of Greek Jews in Egypt*

letter   New York, 11 May 1944

Dear Mr Besso

At the request of my colleagues, I am glad to be able to convey to you the
terms of the following resolution in which the sentiments of our Executive
Committee are expressed.

'The World Jewish Congress takes the opportunity of the presence in New
York of the president of the Egyptian Hellenic Jewish community to place on
record its profound admiration for the heroism with which the Greek people have
resisted and continue to resist the aggression of the common enemy of democracy
and civilization. The Executive of the Congress is deeply convinced that this heroic
resistance, through which the Greek people held up the advance of Axis forces
in the Balkans for many months, was a contribution of incalculable value to the
ultimate defeat of the enemy in the Near East.

'The Executive recalls with profound gratitude that in the midst of this historic
struggle for human right and national independence, the Greek people did not
forget to extend fraternal help to Jewish citizens who were the victims of an
especial discrimination practiced by the enemy. The self-sacrifice with which
members of the Greek resistance movement have rescued large numbers of Jews
from deportation and death, will never be forgotten by the Jewish people in whose
records these acts of heroic and fraternal succor, often performed at the peril of
life itself, will find a permanent and honored place.'

'The Executive takes this opportunity also to recall that attempts by foreign
influences to import anti-Semitism into Greece have invariably been defeated by the
living power of an immemorial tradition of human right, which has been the most
effective protection of the equal rights of Jewish citizens in Greece. The Executive
is convinced that the experience of the common suffering and the inspiration of a
common hope will bind the Jewish citizens of Greece even closer to their fellow
citizens of the other communities. In a liberated homeland they will unite in the
reestablishment of an independent Greece on the basis of justice and respect for
human right which will guarantee to all its inhabitants full participation in the rights
and obligations of citizenship irrespective of racial origin or religious affiliation.'

'The Executive requests Mr Besso in his capacity as president of the Egyptian Hellenic Jewish Community to convey the text of this statement to the Greek Government.'

As you will see, it is the request of the Executive that you be good enough to convey the above statement to your Government.

May I also take this opportunity of conveying to you personally our sense of deep obligation for all you have done to help us increase our knowledge and understanding of the situation in Greece and in the Near East, in so far as Jewish interests and hopes are concerned. Please be assured that we shall always retain the pleasantest recollection of your visit and that we look forward to an uninterrupted collaboration through you with the community of which you are the distinguished representative.

——◆——

ATTACHMENT d TO 103*

J. Proskauer, President of the American Jewish Committee, to I.Bessos, President of the Community of Greek Jews in Egypt

letter   New York, May 9 1944

Dear Mr Besso

Your visit to the United States, in your capacity as President of the Greek Jewish Community in Egypt, has allowed us to substantiate in detail what we already know about the situation of the Jews in Greece and their relations with their non-Jewish Greek brothers. The Nazis in Greece have remained true to their traditions of oppression and extermination; the Greeks have remained true to their traditions of freedom and brotherhood. They have resisted every German attempt to enlist their sympathy and aid against the Jews. At great risk to their own persons they have shielded Jews from deportation, kept Jewish children in their own homes as though they were their own, and aided escaping Jews to make their way out of the country or to join the underground armed forces.

The American Jewish Committee expresses to the Greek Jewish Community sympathy for the outrages it has suffered and admiration for the courage and stead fastness with which it has resisted. For the Greek nation as a whole the American Jewish Committee shares entirely the common feeling of the American people: respect for its valor, sorrow for its sufferings and hope for its speedy liberation.

The American Jewish Committee requests the Greek Jewish Community in Egypt to communicate these sentiments to the proper Jewish organisations as well as to the Greek Government - in exile.

❖

104*

Benzien Meir Hay Ouziel, Chief Rabbi of Holy Land, to the Jewish Community of Athens

letter   Jerusalem, 19 October 1944

Nos Chers et Précieux Frères!

C'est avec nos coeurs brisés que nous vous avons suivi dans votre terrifiant état de poursuites diaboliques de la part de l' oppresseur le plus cruel que l' Histoire ait jamais connu. Pendant que vous erriez de ville en ville ou de village en village, nos esprits ébahis vous suivaient dans une imagination frappée de stupeur. Mais l' apogée de cet état de choses nous survint quand l' ennemi tyran exécute l' exil total de la grande population Juive de Salonique pour les envoyer aux camps d' extermination!

De notre Terre Sainte nous exclamâmes auprès des Autorités Démocratiques dans le Monde entier d' employer toute leur influence et de mettre en pratique tout moyen qui pourrait mener à la salvation de nos malheureux Frères.

Mais le Tout Puissant exauça vos cris pitoyables et mit fin à cette période obscure de l' occupation barbare. Les glorieuses troupes hellènes [*sic*] et Alliées ont libéré la belle Capitale qui sera suivie bientôt de Salonique et du Pays tout entier, et nos précieux Frères (qui sait le nombre des survivants!) avec toute la brave Nation grecque respirera l' air de la Liberté.

Je désire exprimer en mon nom et au nom de Vos confrères qui ont eu l' honneur et la chance d' immigrer en Terre Sainte, mes plus chaleureuses sympathies pour les familles souffrantes. Nous attendons impatiemment le jour où Vous seriez venus chez nous et avec des forces unies reconstruirions notre Terre Promise.

Combien ont dû être considérables vos pertes en âmes et biens durant ces années de ravage et de pillage. Les Synagogues et autres Etablissements religieux souillés par des bêtes profanes, vos maisons et magasins vidés. Mais grâce aux vaillants partisans grecs - parmi lesquels s' y trouvait un assez grand nombre d' entre vous - qu' ont pu quelques traces d' une Population prospère encore subsister.

Je formule encore une fois le voeu à ce que nous soyons privilégiés de vous voir chez nous travaillant côte à côte pour rétablir notre Vie Nationale indépendant, ce qui menera à notre Geula complète.

105

Z. Benzonnanas, Jewish Community of Athens, and A. Molho, Jewish Community of Thessaloniki, to the Prime Minister

telegram   27 October 1944

From this hospitable country in which they have taken refuge as a result of the inhuman persecution to which they were subjected by the barbarous conquerors, and in expectation of their return to their beloved homeland, the Councils of the Jewish Communities of Athens and Thessaloniki address to the Government and the people their most brotherly greetings on the occasion of the first celebration, in liberated Greece, of the anniversary of 28 October STOP On this day, remembering the epic of the Albanian campaign and the feats accomplished during the Greek resistance, we turn our thoughts reverently to our heroic fallen compatriots, among whom were so many of our co-religionists STOP We shall always remember the heroic solidarity and protection towards the Jewish community shown by all the Greek people during the darkest hours of the mass persecution of the Jews STOP As a symbol of our gratitude and of the very close brotherhood between Christians and Jews, we are sending through you to the city of Athens, the birthplace of culture and freedom, a flag to be raised above the City Hall on each anniversary of 28 October STOP It is our wish that the imminent complete liberation of our homeland should be the beginning of a new era of glory and prosperity after the victorious termination of the war imposed upon it and we are convinced that we shall soon see all our national aspirations fulfilled.

106*

J. Romanos, Counsellor, Greek Embassy in London, to the Secretary of the World Jewish Congress

letter London, 10 November 1944

Dear Sir

In reply to your letter of the 7th instant, reference W/L/176, I beg to inform you that the telegram which we have received from Athens confirms the news of a publication by the Greek Government of a Law cancelling Laws 1977/44 and 1180/44 regarding the restitution of Jewish property.

We have also heard that on the 2nd of November the Greek Prime Minister, Monsieur Papandreou, received the Chief Rabbi, who was accompanied by the members of the Central Board of the Jewish Community in Greece. The Chief Rabbi and the President of the Community expressed the cordial congratulations of the Jewish world to the Prime Minister of the National Government on accomplishing the liberation of the country without bloodshed, together with their thanks for the concern and sympathy manifested towards the Jews of Greece who have been hard hit.

Monsieur Papandreou listened attentively to the requests put forward by the Jews, and assured them that he would do everything in his power to afford relief. He added the assurance of his government's solicitude for them which has already been demonstrated by the restitution of Jewish property on the Government's initiative.

107

Government Gazette, Vol. 1, Issue No. 11

Athens, 10 November 1944

Law No. 2
Concerning the rescinding of Laws 1977/44 and 1180/44 and return of Jewish property.

We, George II,
King of the Hellenes
On the proposal of our Cabinet, have resolved and decree the following:

Article 1

1. Laws 1977/44 and 1180/44 are hereby rescinded.

2. All items of property of all kind belonging to Jews and now, in accordance with the provisions of Law 1180/44, under the management of the Greek State and located in the warehouses of the Department for the Management of Jewish Property, or in private warehouses or elsewhere shall be restored to their lawful owners by the same procedure as that under which they were originally received. These items will be restored without the deduction of the 10% withholding tax on each Jewish property in favour of the person informing the State of its existence, in accordance with the relevant decisions of the Minister of Finance, but with a 5% withholding tax to settle advance payments made, in accordance with the provisions of Law 1180/44, by the Treasury to cover the expenses of the said Department and to meet its operating costs.

3. Property subject to any control or investigation on the part of the Greek State which, its quality as Jewish property not yet having been established, has not been deemed to have been confiscated and thus subject to the provisions of Law 1180/44, shall be released from any commitment or other obligation towards the Greek State stemming from the said Law 1180 and shall be restored to those who are now in possession of it, with all injunctions of any kind taken to protect it by the above Department being lifted under the same procedure as the one by which the measure was originally imposed.

4. A decision to be issued by the Minister of Finance will define the manner of the disposal of those Jewish items of property surrendered by the army of occupation to the Department for the Management of Jewish Property without naming their owners when ultimately such identification does not prove possible.

Article 2

1. The Department set up by Law 1180/44, rescinded hereby, will continue henceforth to be under the General Directorate of Public Accounting and shall have as its purpose the implementation of the provisions of the present Law together with the performance of all other services and the settlement of all other matters assigned to it by Decree of the Minister of Finance.

2. The staff of the Department, headed by a senior official of the General Directorate of Public Accounting, shall consist of employees of the Directorate or employees of other departments of the Ministry of Finance or other Ministries, such employees being seconded by decision of the Minister of Finance or of the appropriate Minister.

All items of expenditure connected with the operation of the Department and already disbursed by the Treasury shall be charged against the Jewish properties in accordance with the provision of Article 1, para. 2.

3. The managers of Jewish property appointed by virtue of Law 1180/44, rescinded hereby, shall continue, until their replacement by decision of the Minister of Finance, to manage the Jewish properties until their restoration to their lawful owners.

Any Jewish properties not restored for lawful reason and justified cause shall continue to remain under the management of the Greek State, with the State's managers acting in this case as receivers for the owners of the said property.

The fees of the managers shall be determined by decision of the Minister of Finance.

All matters arising from the implementation of the present Law and all other details shall be settled by decision of the Minister of Finance.

Article 3

The present Law shall enter into force as of its publication in the Government Gazette.

In Athens, 26 October 1944

George II
The Cabinet
Prime Minister
G. Papandreou
The Members

N. Abraham, F. Manouilidis, P. Hatzipanos, A. Svolos, I. Tsirimokos, N. Askoutsis, S. Stephanopoulos, I. Zevgos, K. Maroulis, D. Kontos, P. Rallis, P. Kanellopoulos, P. Fikioris, G. Kartalis, K. Vlachothanassis, P. Dragoumis, P. Garoufalias, A. Angelopoulos, E. Theologitis.

108

G.A. Christodoulou, Consul in charge for Palestine and Trans-Jordan, to the Greek Ministry of Foreign Affairs

confidential report   Jerusalem, 21 November 1944

'Concerning the appointment of Boards of Management for the Jewish Communities of Athens and Thessaloniki'

I have the honour to inform you that, according to information which has come to my attention, the Greek Jews now resident in Tel Aviv and other Palestinian cities learned with surprise and displeasure, from announcements in the Press and on the radio, the names of the persons appointed by the Greek Government as members of the Boards of Management of the Jewish Communities of Athens and Thessaloniki.

Their displeasure stems firstly from the prevailing opinion that the Greek Government ought not to have proceeded to these appointments without at least consulting the Jews who have fled from Greece to Palestine, who today number many thousands and are the largest cohesive section of the once-populous Jewish Communities of Greece.

The second and more serious reason for displeasure with the persons in question lies in the fact that most of the new appointees belong to Left-leaning groups which are known for their anti-Zionist beliefs. Given that, as is generally acknowleged, 75% of the Jews in Greece are Zionists, it is believed that those who belong to that movement ought not to have been completely ignored. In the present case, the Greek Government is seen as having acted in approximately the same manner as the Bulgarian Government, which has also, as you will be aware, assigned the management of Jewish affairs in Bulgaria to non-Zionists, despite its loud proclamations abroad of its good intentions towards the Jews.

109

D. Pappas, Ambassador in Egypt, to P. Dragoumis, Minister of Foreign Affairs

letter   Cairo, 17 November 1944

Minister

By its confidential communication No. 510/D/1 dated the 6th inst., the Consulate General in Jerusalem reported to the Ministry on the displeasure caused in Palestine by the *ex officio* appointment by the Greek Government of Boards of Management for the Jewish Communities of Athens and Thessaloniki.

I believe it is expedient that I remind Your Excellency that neither you nor the Ministry are responsible for these appointments and that, when I was unofficially informed at the time that Mr Tsatsos, then Minister of Justice, had decided to take such action, I drew your attention, by oral report, to the danger of misunderstanding to which we were about to expose ourselves.

I would now like to add that the impact of the displeasure felt in Palestine has made itself felt here, too, in the same form. It is believed that the Government had ulterior motives in hastening to appoint Community Council members so as to have them as obedient tools for totalitarian solutions – while, as you will be aware, Mr Tsatsos' motives were quite different. I have given the appropriate clarifications to those who have been complaining here.

I shall convey similar instructions to Mr Christodoulou, but allow me to propose that such instructions should also be issued by the Ministry.

⋙

I I 0

Directorate of Special War Services to the Greek Legation in Cairo

note   [without specific date] 1945

Concerning the action taken by the Greek Government in favour of the Jews and the gratitude expressed by the Jewish authorities and organisations

In October 1943, the Greek Prime Minister, Mr Tsouderos, in an address by radio urged the people of Athens to give all possible support to their Jewish fellow-citizens in an attempt to frustrate the enemy's measures to eliminate the Jews.

On 15 October 1943, Mr Shertok, secretary for Foreign Affairs of the Jewish Agency – in practice, the Foreign Minister of the Jewish Government – sent a telegram from Jerusalem to the Greek Chargé d'Affaires in Cairo, Mr D. Pappas, expressing his thanks and those of his colleagues for this radio broadcast.

The resolution adopted at its session of 30 October 1943 by the Tel Aviv United Committee in Favour of the Jews of Greece, bearing the signature of its Chairman, Mr Ascher Mallah, states, *inter alia*, the following:

"The Jews of Tel Aviv, meeting on Saturday 30 October 1943 in public session in the large hall of the Ophir Cinema, with the participation of Mr David Ben Gurion, Chairman of the Executive Committee of the Jewish Agency of Palestine, and deeply moved by an account of the atrocities committed by the Nazi occupation authorities against the Jews of Greece and of the mass deportation of the Jews of Thessaloniki, Macedonia and Thrace ... hereby declare themselves to be greatly satisfied by the philanthropic attitude of the population of Greece towards the Jews, reiterate their plea that the Jews should continue to receive this assistance, ... [*sic*] and express their cordial thanks to the Government of Free Greece for the moving message it has addressed to the people and clergy of Greece urging them to help the Jews and protect them from the attacks of the enemy."

On 26 December 1943, a service of intercession for the salvation of the Jews and Greeks being persecuted in Greece and for the liberation of the country was held in the Great Synagogue, Cairo. After the religious ceremony, the Greek Prime Minister, Mr Tsouderos, addressed the Chief Rabbi of Egypt and the President of the Jewish Community of Cairo as follows: "The Hellenic Government, in wholehearted sympathy with the sufferings of the Jewish people, fully agrees that the Jews of Greece should receive all possible help. All Greek governments, in compliance with the unadulterated feelings of the Greek people, have always provided tangible evidence of their positive attitude towards, and care for, the Jewish element of the population". Speaking during the ceremony, Mr Rene Kattaui Bey, President of the Jewish Community of Cairo, said, *inter alia*: "The Jews of Greece and all the world will never forget everything that the Greek people have done in their favour. We owe them a debt of gratitude not only for the fraternal assistance they have rendered our co-religionists, but also for the example they have set for the rest of the world and, above all, for the hope of a better world to follow victory which they instil in our troubled hearts."

On 30 March, Prime Minister Tsouderos made the following statement, on the occasion of the recent appeal by President Roosevelt: "On 24 March, President Roosevelt issued a highly important announcement denouncing before the civilised world, once more, the crimes committed by our bloodthirsty enemies, who, concentrating their ferocity on the Balkans and Hungary, are continuing to massacre and subject to the slow death of hunger thousands of human beings. The language used by the President in addressing the United Nations was the language of relentless justice, which will not be long in bringing to punishment those guilty of these unprecedented crimes, together with their satellites and henchmen. President Roosevelt's declaration is also an expression of sublime human solidarity towards all the victims of these atrocities. The Hellenic Government, entirely sharing the feelings of the American leader, hereby appeals to the Greeks to give particularly careful consideration to his recommendation that the allied peoples of the Balkans should help in the rescuing and escape to neutral or friendly countries of the Jews, who are threatened with renewed inhuman persecution, and of all other victims of the Nazi tyranny."

In his communication to the Ministry of Foreign Affairs No. E 656 of 10 April 1944, Mr Kaloyannis, Director of the Royal Consulate General in Constantinople, states that Mr C. Barlas, head of the Jewish Agency in Constantinople, visited him and asked him "to convey to his Government cordial thanks and feelings of profound gratitude for the philanthropic and moving attitude displayed by the Greek population to the Jews of Athens and the surrounding area." Mr Barlas informed Mr Kaloyannis that the information coming to his attention had confirmed "that the interest and mercy shown by the Greek population in helping the Jews had reached the point of self-sacrifice", adding that, although he was aware of the entirely friendly attitude which the Greek population had always adopted towards the Jews, he was sure that the action taken by the Royal Government had greatly contributed to encouraging the Greek population in this direction, despite the fact that they themselves were subject to persecution and that to take any interest in the Jews might seriously worsen their own position vis-à-vis the occupation authorities.

At an official banquet held on 15 April 1944 at the Waldorf Astoria Hotel in New York by the Jewish organisations of America in honour of Mr Iosif Bessos, the Chief Rabbi of the United States, using words chosen with particular care, expressed the admiration of all the Jews for the Greek people in view of their heroic resistance, and, promising aid and solidarity in the near future, voiced his profound gratitude for the attitude of the Greeks towards the Jews of Greece.

In his inaugural address to the Conference of the 'Misrachi' religious organisation, Dr Herzog, Chief Rabbi of Palestine, stated the following, *inter alia*:

"The Jewish Palestinian people and, with them, the Jewish people of the United States, of Britain and of the entire world, would like to express their heartfelt thanks to the Greek Orthodox Church, and in particular that of occupied Greece, for the moral and material assistance it has given to the persecuted Jews, and also for the understanding which the worthy leaders of that Church have displayed of the sufferings and problems the Jewish people are now undergoing".

The Chief Rabbi's words were received with general approval and greeted with loud applause.

The Tel Aviv daily newspaper *Haboker* (10.5.44) carried the following report under the headline: "Greeks help Jewish compatriots": "Refugees recently arrived from Greece have much to say about the many forms of help which the Christian Greek population have given to the Jews of Greece despite pressure from the Germans. Many instances are known in which Greeks have risked their own lives in order to save Jewish compatriots in danger of falling into Nazi hands and being deported." The daily newspaper *Davar* carried the same report, under the headline "The sons of Greece aid the persecuted".

The daily newspaper *Hatzofeh* also carried the report, under the headline "Greeks defend Jewish compatriots".

All three newspapers published the news item in a prominent position on the front page.

The daily newspaper *Ha' Aretz* ('The Land', Tel Aviv, 13 April 1944) publishes a lengthy report from Constantinople on the subject of the admirable humanitarian feelings of the Greeks towards the Greek Jews, who are being brutally persecuted by the Germans. The newspaper's correspondent cites many examples demonstrating that hundreds of Greeks risked their lives by hiding Jewish refugees in their homes and sharing with them the last crusts of bread they had. He then draws attention to the aid granted to the Greek Jews by the Greek clergy and by the guerrillas, who facilitate the Jews in every possible way to escape from Greece.

The daily newspaper *Hasman* (Tel Aviv, 14 May 1944) published a note on the help given by the Greeks to their Jewish compatriots during their persecution by the Nazis, and commented: "The Jewish people all over the world notes with the greatest satisfaction this conduct on the part of the heroic sons of Greece, whose spiritual values continue always to set an example of civilisation and humanity."

The daily newspaper *Davar* (Tel Aviv, 19 May 1944) published a lengthy special telegram from its correspondent in Geneva describing the atrocities committed by the Nazi conquerors against the Greek Jews and the help the Jews received from the Greek population. The telegram added:

"The Jews are full of gratitude to the Greek people for the magnanimity and nobility of their feelings. Such fraternity among fellow-citizens has never before been reported in history. Any Jew who asked for help received whatever he needed and was given accommodation and food.

"Despite the German threats that any Greek hiding a Jew would be shot, the Greek people are still protecting and defending their Jewish fellow-citizens with unbounded loyalty."

The daily newspaper *Hamaskif* (Tel Aviv, 23 May 1944) carried an article referring to the official report published by the Greek Government in Cairo in connection with the state of the Jews in Greece. This report describes in detail how the Greek people saved the Jews from the Gestapo clutches and how, despite the draconian measures, these Jews were hidden.

In June 1943, the Greek Jews living in Palestine sent the following resolution to the Hellenic Government: "We, the Jews of Greek origin, meeting in public session in the hall of the establishment called 'Kantimar el Tel Aviv', having taken cognisance of a report from the committee for the aid of Jews in Greece, including information about the state of the Jews in Greece,

hereby resolve

a) That the competent Council be hereby authorised to submit to the Hellenic Government an expression of gratitude and admiration for the heroic attitude of the Greek people in resisting the measures to eliminate the Jews introduced by the Nazi authorities; b) That we appeal to the Hellenic Government to encourage, with all the means at its disposal, the Greek people to be watchful and protect the Jews who are victims of the Nazi occupation in Greece."

In June 1944, Mr David Revez, General Secretary of the 'Istanteruth' Great Zionist Labour Organisation of Palestine, sent the following letter to the Consul General of Greece in Jerusalem:

"During the last meeting of the plenary session of our Executive Committee, we had an opportunity to hear from an eye-witness a report on the nobility demonstrated by the people of Greece towards their Jewish fellow-citizens when they underwent the hardships of deportation at the hands of the Germans.

"We already possessed some information about this, of a general nature, but the narrative we heard filled our hearts with strong sentiments of appreciation and admiration.

"We believe it to be both our duty and our honour to express, through you, these sentiments to the Government of Free Greece and to the Greek people.

"We shall always keep within our hearts the memory of these supreme demonstrations of humanitarianism, which shine brightly in the terrible darkness of the days in which we live."

III

Greek Cabinet

note   [without specific date] 1945

On matters pending in connection with the Jews and requiring immediate settlement

A. Ministry of Education.
A draft law concerning the manner in which the Jewish Communities will be reconstituted and concerning the establishment of a Central Board of Jewish Communities to co-ordinate the task of rehabilitating and welfare of the Jews is pending with this Ministry. Please arrange for the speedy passing of this draft law, which is ready.
B. Ministry of Finance.
1) The Jewish assets in Macedonia and Thrace are still in the state of confiscation ordered by the Germans and under the management by the Greek State

introduced by Law 305/43. German Law 305/43 must be rescinded immediately, without the slightest delay, so as to make it possible to restitute the assets to their destitute Jewish owners when they present themselves.

2) A draft law prepared by the Central Board of Jewish Communities concerning the founding of an organisation to manage the abandoned Jewish assets by means of the systematic assembly, safeguarding and management of assets which are currently scattered here and there is pending with the Ministry of Finance. The process of studying and approving this draft law should be speeded up so as to prevent any further drain of the Jewish assets.

3) A memorandum from the Central Board concerning the exemption from receivership of the assets belonging to Jewish citizens of hostile states, as has been done by the Governments of all the Allied countries, is pending with the Ministry of Finance which has requested the views of the Ministry of Foreign Affairs on this issue. We would be grateful if this question could be resolved favourably and immediately, in accordance with the precedent established by the Venizelos Government during the first European War, when, by instrument No. 358 *ter* of Session XXXIX of the Cabinet, it exempted the assets of Jewish subjects of hostile states from the implementation of Law 1073 concerning receivership, etc.

C. Ministry of Justice.

By the Rent Moratorium Law under publication, tenants who are subjects of hostile states are exempted from protection. For the same reasons, Jews ought not to be subject to the exemption from rent moratorium protection.

D. Ministry of Foreign Affairs.

1) We would request that the committee whose formation is being studied and which will establish itself in Belgrade to supervise the repatriation of the Greeks deported to Germany and elsewhere should include a Jewish representative of the Central Board of Jewish Communities, given that some 60,000 Jews from Greece are among those deported.

2) The Palestine Jewish Red Cross (Maken David Adom), which is a department of the International Red Cross in Geneva, has requested from the Greek Embassy in Cairo that permission be granted for the arrival in Greece of a three-member Committee headed by Mr Jacob Czernowitz which will provide care on the spot for the surviving Greek Jews. Please ensure that instructions are sent by telegram to the Embassy in Cairo to the effect that they issue the required permission.

3) As you will be aware, the Jews who were subjects of Axis states lost their citizenship as a result of legislative or administrative measures taken by the Axis governments. More particularly, the Jews of Italian citizenship in Greece renounced their Italian citizenship during the war in Albania. Please ensure that

general measures are taken so that these persons, who are in effect without nationality, should obtain Greek nationality.

4) Please ensure that the Ministry of Foreign Affairs continues to make representations to the governments of the liberated countries of Central and Eastern Europe for their help in finding the 60,000 Jews deported from Greece by the Germans and in facilitating the repatriation of the survivors.

E. Ministry of Welfare.

As you will be aware, the Jews constitute a special category of citizens who have undergone persecution and suffered war damage, looting, etc., as a result of which they are in need of special care in connection with their return to their homes in the Greek provinces, the distribution of clothing, footwear, etc., and special ration books for the destitute so that they can obtain food. Please ensure that the Committee co-ordinating the relief agencies (ML, UNRRA, the Red Cross, etc.) classes the Jews who have undergone special hardships in the appropriate category so that they can receive the relief corresponding to that category.

F. Ministry of Labour.

A memorandum from the Central Board of Jewish Communities concerning the re-appointment to their positions in German and Italian companies (Austro-Hellenic, Victoria Berlin, the Italian-Hellenic Bank, Adriatic, etc.) of Jewish employees in Greece who, in implementation of the Axis laws concerning racial protection, were dismissed from these positions, is pending with the Ministry of Labour. Please ensure that the relevant measures are taken.

—◦◦◦—

112

C. Amantos, Minister of Religious Affairs and National Education, to the Ministry of Foreign Affairs

communiqué   Athens, 26 March1945

We have the honour to inform you, in reply to your communications Nos. 17.3108 and 2600 of the current year, that subsequent to consultation with representatives of the Jewish communities a law 'concerning the reconstitution of the Jewish Communities' has been submitted to the Cabinet for approval. By that law, Community Boards are appointed to administer the Communities until Boards can be elected in accordance with the basic law, No. 2456/20. A Central

Board of Jewish Communities to co-ordinate matters and issue expert opinions until the date of the elections is also appointed. Both the Board founded in Cairo by virtue of Law 3290/44 and the Central Board formed in Athens by Ministerial Decision No. 40741/20.11.44, about which displeasure and turmoil has broken out abroad, are abolished by the above law, submitted for approval, and the objections will thus be overcome by the law when it is promulgated.

━━◆━━

II3

G. Lambrinopoulos, Under-Secretary to the Prime Minister, to the Ministries of Foreign Affairs, Supply, Agriculture, and the National Economy

cover letter   Athens, 19 April 1945

Minister

    We have the honour to forward to you, attached hereto, a copy of the matters discussed between the Prime Minister and the chargé d'affaires for Foreign Affairs of the Jewish Agency, Mr Shertock, and shall be grateful if you will undertake to look into the issues which fall within the field of responsibility of your Ministry, bearing in mind the Government's policy that these matters should be examined in a favourable light and that they should, if possible, be settled rapidly.

    Please inform the Cabinet of the results of your investigation.

━━◆━━

ATTACHMENT TO II3

The Political Office of the Prime Minister

minutes

Matters discussed by the Prime Minister and the chargé d'affaires of the Jewish Agency, Mr Shertock, at their meeting of 15 April 1945.

    1) Mr Shertock congratulated the Prime Minister and, in his person, the entire

Greek people on the liberation of Greece and then thanked him for the support and protection the Jews had received from the Greek people during the persecution to which they had been subjected.

2) Mr Shertock requested that Greece should continue to manifest an interest in the progress of the Jews and that it should facilitate the movement to Palestine of the Jewish children aged 8-17 years who have been orphaned as a result of the persecution. For this purpose, the representatives of the Jewish Agency will be asked to issue group passports.

3) Mr Shertock called for the moral support of the Government in providing training in farm work for young Greek Jews so as to enable them to move to Palestine with farming experience and contribute to the development of agriculture there. In this respect, the Greek Government could propose to UNRRA that facilities (in the form of farming implements, seed, etc.) be given to the Jewish children being educated as above for the above purpose.

4) Those of the young Jews intending to migrate who have military service obligations should be allotted a status equal to Greeks who are permanent residents of other countries and consequently should be released from their obligation to bear arms.

5) Jewish Palestine greatly wishes to see the development of its commercial and cultural relations with Greece, and for that purpose has already founded a Palestine Office in Athens. It is convinced that the development of such relations is also in the Greek interest.

6) In order to assist voluntary emigration from Greece to Palestine in general terms, there is a need for the free management of Jewish property, currently restricted by Law 305/43, to be restituted to the Jews.

114

M. Pesmazoglou, Minister of Finance.

ministerial decision   Athens, 31 May 1945

Decision
(concerning the restitution of Jewish property to its rightful owners)
The Minister of Finance
Having taken into consideration: a) the provision of para. 2 of the single

Article of Law 337/45 'concerning the rescinding of Law 205/43, etc.', and b) the provision of Article 2, para. 4 of Law 2/1944 'concerning the rescinding of Laws 1977/44 and 1180/44, etc.',

hereby resolves:

1. The restitution of the Jewish properties held by the Department for the Management of Jewish Properties (DMJP) or other agency shall take place on the application of the Jews concerned and shall be carried out by teams appointed on each occasion by written order of the head of the DMJP and consisting of three tenured civil servants under the instructions of the civil servant of the higher grade. When the Jewish properties are being delivered by the teams, the presence of a Magistrate or other judiciary officer, appointed on each occasion by the President of the Court of First Instance, shall be indispensable. The presence of the judicial authority is purely of an administrative nature and the procedure laid down by the provisions of the Code of Civil Procedure will thus be avoided.

For each restitution, a protocol of delivery and receipt shall be drawn up in quadruplicate, describing the property in detail, and shall be signed by the officials composing the team, the judicial officer and by the person taking delivery of the property.

2. In the case of the restoration of items under the management of custodians appointed by the Thessaloniki DMJP, or by the former German occupation authorities, by the former Government Representative in Thessaloniki, or by another authority, this will be carried out by the said custodians on the written instructions of the DMJP in the presence of a team of three tenured civil servants constituted under the procedure of the foregoing paragraph and including, compulsorily, one representative of the Jewish Community of Thessaloniki appointed by a communication from it. In this case, the work of the team will not be confined solely to being present when the items in question are restored by the custodians, but will also extend to ensuring that the items held by the custodians are fully described in the relevant protocol at the time of restitution and to confirming that the items returned are of the same quantity as those inventoried when first received by the custodians and that the items are the same as those stated in the relevant protocols or other items equivalent to those items. In the event of the original receipt of the items on the part of the receivers having taken place without a protocol, the same team will undertake, on its own responsibility, the task of identifying the items of property placed under custody in the name of the Jew concerned, on the basis of all evidence which may assist them in this task.

3. In the cases of the foregoing paragraphs, the teams will submit to the DMJP, in execution of the instructions they have received, written reports containing every detail in connection with the restitution of property carried out. Obviously,

the protocols of delivery and receipt drawn up for the act of restitution will bear the signatures of the custodian, of the members of the team, of the representative of the judiciary and of the person taking delivery of the property. The protocols will also state in detail (by type of object, quantity, etc.) the items of property initially received by the custodian, the items now restored, the items sold by the custodian, the time and manner of the sale of the items, and the fate of the amounts collected, together with all other relevant details.

Of the four copies of the protocols of delivery and receipt - which, as stated above, must describe the items of property in detail by category, type, weight, etc., – one copy will be given to the person taking delivery of the items, one copy will be retained by the custodian and the remaining copies will be submitted to the DMJP in the form of a report from all the members of the team stating all details of the act of restitution.

4. In the event of the custodian of the property being absent, for whatever reason, and failing to present himself despite having been invited to do so, in order to be present for the act of restitution in accordance with the above, the team is obliged to take the appropriate action to carry out the instructions it has received, taking all the measures necessary to execute the instructions as fully and rapidly as possible, and shall be entitled to forcibly open any building in which the act of restitution, etc., is to take place.

5. In the case of the restitution of Jewish property outside the district of the city of Thessaloniki, the procedure outlined in our circular order No. 197/21.2.45 to the Prefects of the State, which shall be communicated to the General Governance of Northern Greece and the Prefectures of Macedonia under it, is to be followed, with the sole difference that the competence assigned by the said order to the Central Department for the Management of Jewish Properties (CDMJP) will be undertaken by the Thessaloniki DMJP. To the committee provided for in the said circular order for the restitution of Jewish property which is to be set up in each region by the competent Prefect, will be added one Jew appointed by the appropriate Community or, in the absence of such Community, by the Prefect. We hereby determine that each of the members of the said committees will receive a fee of five hundred drachmas for the complete processing of each Jewish case.

6. The withholding of the percentage of 5% in favour of the Greek State, as determined, will be applied only to the movable things of all kinds restored and not to real estate property. In order to calculate this percentage, the DMJP shall ask in writing the Commercial Association or the Chamber of Commerce and Industry or any other competent service to recommend special experts to assess the value of the movable things to be restored to the Jews. The percentage will be deducted prior to each act of restitution, in kind or in cash. The assessment will always be made in drachmas, in the presence of the teams constituted as

above and of the judicial official, and special reports will be drawn up by the experts and submitted by the teams to the Department as part of their report.

The same procedure shall be applied to the estimation of the value of items of property which may have been separated from the remainder and given by certain state departments to third parties as a reward for their declaration and the taking over by them of Jewish property during the occupation. In this case, the separate proportion of 5% in favour of the State will not actually be deducted, but will be offset, proportionally, against the sum given to the person surrendering the property, if this sum were in excess of 5%.

7. The property will be restored either to the possessor in whose hands the property was held at the time of confiscation and taking over of the property by the DMJP, or to the owner of the property in person, with the written consent of any lawful holder, or to the trustee appointed in accordance with the provisions of Law 2631/40 for owners who are missing and absent, subsequent, obviously, to the full legitimation of all the above persons.

Restitution of the property to its owner will be carried out with the written consent of any lawful holder of the property, in accordance with the above.

Obviously, the above beneficiaries may be represented by proxies. In the case of proxies, the following points must be borne in mind in each case: a) That powers of attorney drawn up after the termination of the enemy occupation fully legitimate the mandatory; b) That powers of attorney drawn up between 12 September 1939 and 31 December 1942 should, in principle, be deemed to be valid unless the instances in law that would invalidate the power of attorney apply. Powers of attorney drawn up between 1.1.1931 and the end of the occupation will not be taken into consideration with the exception of those drawn up in unoccupied countries.

The contents of para. 7 of the present shall also apply to the rest of the territory of Greece.

8. In the case of real property belonging to Jews whose administration has actually been undertaken by the DMJP, the act of restitution will be made, on the basis of a protocol, either by any custodians who may have been appointed, subsequent to a written instruction, or directly to the owners by the Department. Property belonging to synagogues or other Jewish charitable institutions will be restored immediately, as a matter of priority, without any need of special request. This will also apply to the movable property owned by such institutions.

9. In the event of the State not having been involved in any way whatever and for whatever cause in the taking over and management of Jewish property, the DMJP shall also not be allowed to intervene in any way and the Jewish owners concerned will take delivery of the property belonging to them in the normal manner, without any procedure whatsoever.

10. Until the date of the restitution of the property as above, the DMJP will continue to collect the rent on the Jewish buildings and will carry out as mandatory for the Jewish beneficiaries all the lawful acts of maintenance and management of the property if it has actually been placed in the management of the State. Rent and all other revenue from the property shall be deposited with the Consignments and Loans Fund in the name of the beneficiary Jew and shall be rendered at the time of final restitution of the property.

11. The custodians of Jewish property shall be restricted to the management of the Jewish property until its restitution. Thus, they are not entitled to proceed to sales of the property or substantive alterations to it.

Within ten days from the date on which the protocols of delivery and receipt of the property under their management are drawn up, the custodians will be obliged to submit, via the DMJP, to the Central Department for the Management of Jewish Property in Athens a report describing in detail the course of their management. To this report they shall attach all proofs (documents, etc.) showing the manner in which they have managed the property. A more specific decision shall be issued by us determining matters in connection with the auditing of such management and the final release of the custodians in question from any obligations and liabilities.

12. A committee consisting of A. Kyriazis, President of the Court of Auditors of the General Governance of Northern Greece, as Chairman, of C. Youlis, Chief Manager of State Services and Legal Persons under Public Law, the Head of the Department, the Chief of Police of Thessaloniki, the President or the Deputy President of the Commercial Association of Thessaloniki, and three Jews recommended by the Jewish Community of Thessaloniki will be set up in the DMJP. The *rapporteur* and clerk to the Committee will be DMJP employees appointed by the Head of the Department and will be university graduates with the rank at least of *rapporteur.*

The responsibilities of this committee will be: a) on the basis of applications from Jews interested or on its own initiative, to investigate and ascertain the items of property received, in whatever manner, by the former occupation authorities or those collaborating with them, under a procedure to be determined by a more specific decision issued by us, and b) to examine the particulars, of all kinds, held by the DMJP in connection with the Jewish items of property (valuables in general, merchandise, furniture, domestic utensils and fittings, etc.), handed over at various times to the above Department by the German occupation authorities, whose owners are unknown, to identify, on the basis of the applications submitted by Jews interested or on its own initiative, the owner or holder of the said items of property, and to issue reasoned decisions on the restitution or otherwise of such items of property.

This Committee shall meet outside working hours at a place and time appointed on each occasion by its Chairman and the clerk shall keep detailed minutes of the meetings. The Chairman and the members of the Committee shall receive, for each session, fees of one thousand drachmas each, the *rapporteur* will receive a fee of five hundred drachmas and the clerk a fee of four hundred drachmas, to be charged against the Jewish properties.

13. Property of all kinds belonging to Jews of foreign nationality which was confiscated in whatever way and came under the management of the Greek State shall be restored to the persons as determined in para. 7 by the procedure laid down in the present.

These acts of restitution shall be carried out either by the DMJP or by any custodians who may have been appointed by it, on the basis of a protocol in quadruplicate. In the case of movable things, restitution will always take place in the presence of a team of employees in accordance with the provisions of paras. 1, 2, 3 and 4 of the present.

14. A committee of consultants consisting of the Head of the General Directorate of State Accounting, as Chairman, of the Director Class A of the General Directorate of State Accounting, of G. Zarifopoulos, Director Class A of the said Directorate, of G. Nikolaidis, President of the Council of State, of Ioannis Foukas, holding the rank of Director Class A of the General Directorate of State Accounting, of the Head of the CDMJP, and of two Jews recommended in writing by the Central Board of Jewish Communities of Greece, shall be set up in the CDMJP.

The task of this committee will be to supply its expert opinion on any matter which may arise in the course of the implementation of the laws issued in connection with the Jewish property and to supervise the restitution, in general, and disposal of it. The matters to be examined will be brought for discussion by the Department, whose head will serve also as *rapporteur*. The clerk of the committee will be appointed by the Head of the Department. The members of the committee will receive, as a fee, two thousand drachmas per session up to two and the clerk will receive one thousand drachmas. Meetings of the committee will be convened by the Chairman, who will determine the place and time of the meeting.

15. To the committee set up in the CDMJP by virtue of our Decision No. 147/10.2.45 shall be added, as members, C. Stamelos, Director Class A of the General Directorate of State Accounting, C. Karteroulis, holding the rank of Director Class A of the General Directorate of State Accounting, and two Jews recommended by the Jewish Community of Athens. The fee of the members, *rapporteurs* and clerk of this committee and of the managers of Jewish property appointed by virtue of decisions issued by us is hereby doubled.

The task of this committee shall also be, by virtue of applications from Jews interested or on its own initiative, to investigate and ascertain the items of

property belonging to Jews taken over in whatever manner by the former occupation authorities or those collaborating with them, under a procedure to be laid
down by a more specific decision on our part.

16. The CDMJP, the DMJP and the committees of civil servants set up by the
Prefectures in the provinces by virtue of our Decision No. 197/45 shall also
undertake to continue the management of the property of Jews who have not
presented themselves for its restitution and of the property which, for whatever
reason, has not actually been brought under the management of the Greek State,
after it has first been ascertained that none of the lawful representatives, as
determined by para. 7, of the owner has presented himself in order to ensure the
management and care of the property. The Greek State will continue to manage
this property, which shall be deemed to have been abandoned, acting as the
mandatory of its owners until the final restitution of that property. In the case of
management of abandoned Jewish property undertaken in this manner by the
State, the latter may appoint special managers who shall be civil servants, civil
pensioners, or Jews, as determined by a particular decision.

17. In the case of joint-stock companies whose assets were confiscated during
the course of the occupation by virtue of the relevant laws as having been deemed
Jewish property, restitution will be carried out on the basis of special decisions.

⊷⊰⊛⊱⊷

115

*G. Christodoulou, Consul in charge for Palestine and Trans-Jordan,
to the Ministry of Foreign Affairs*

confidential report   Jerusalem, 27 June 1945

'Concerning articles in Jewish newspapers dealing with the Jews of Greece'

I have the honour to inform you that throughout the months which have
elapsed since the liberation of Greece, the Jewish Press of Palestine has not ceased
to deal with the state of the Jewish community in Greece.

Firstly, the newspapers of Jerusalem have repeatedly carried articles describing
the pitiable state into which the once-flourishing Jewish communities of Greece
have declined. Furthermore, the departure from here, for Greece, of a delegation
headed by Mr Czernowitz of the Red Star of David and of the Jewish (Palestinian)

Aid Group to Greece delegation (in association with UNRRA) provided the occasion for the publication of quite a number of articles appealing to the Jewish people to support their co-religionists in Greece, who had suffered much and were in some cases destitute. The Zionist newspapers have often stressed the need for a certain number of the Jews remaining in Greece, and of orphaned Jewish children in particular, to be moved to Palestine and settled there.

In connection with this point, I believe it is expedient to report to you the contents of an article which appeared recently in the socialist newspaper *Davar* of Tel Aviv, in the form of a correspondent's report from Athens.

"The Zionist movement", wrote the newspaper, "is developing satisfactorily among the Jews of Greece. In Thessaloniki, there is already a branch of Haluts" ('Pioneers' - an organisation whose purpose is to train young people who intend to move to Palestine) "and a Jewish school with 70 pupils has been opened.

"In other Greek cities, Zionist Associations have been formed, and active propaganda and other work is being carried out by Haluts and the 'Hatehia' ('Rebirth') Zionist Youth Movements. There is great enthusiasm in these organisations.

"Preparations are complete for the inauguration of the exhibition of Palestinian products. A Zionist Library in the Greek language has been established, and three issues have already been published on Zionism and Palestine.

"This widespread activity receives great support from the Jewish army officers from Palestine who are now serving in Athens, Thessaloniki and the provincial cities of Greece".

I would like to take this opportunity to report to you the main points of an article which appeared some time ago in the Tel Aviv newspaper *Hamaskif*, which, by way of contrast, talked of the extensive conversion to Christianity of Greek Jews, who proclaim their desire not only to stay in Greece but also not to return to the Jewish religion:

"Many Jews who remained in Greece", wrote *Hamaskif*, "have embraced Christianity, entering the Greek Orthodox Church. Many of them state quite openly that they will never return to Judaism, adding that they are convinced that the tragic fate of the Jews will never change, consisting of persecution, pain, famine and death".

The newspaper adds that, according to these Christianised Jews, since their lives were saved thanks to the help granted to them by the Orthodox Church and thanks to the papers with which they were supplied and which certified that they had embraced the Christian religion, it would be immoral to spit now in the wells whose water had saved them from death at the most tragic moment in their lives.

In brief, the newspaper states the following as possible reasons to explain this mentality on the part of the Christianised Jews:

1) fear of the future; 2) the anti-Semitism still prevailing in Europe; 3) reluctance to believe the promises of the Democracies, and 4) the closing of Palestine to Jewish immigration.

❈

116*

Doctor Léon Cuenca, Reservist Health Officer of the Hellenic Army, to the Greek Legation in Berne

letter   Lausanne, 3 July 1945

Messieurs

Faisant suite à notre entretien verbal avec Messieurs Nahum at Jahannides, avant quelques jours à Lausanne et sur leurs désirs je vous confirme par ce petit rapport les quelques passages importants de notre entretient au sujet des israélites hellènes.

Depuis mars jusqu' à fin avril 1943 45.000 israélites de Grèce (Thessalonique) furent transportés par le corps spécial des S.S. allemands aux camps d' Auschwitz (Haute-Silésie) où 10.000 seulement, choisis parmi les femmes et hommes comme les plus solides, furent répartis dans les différents camps d' Auschwitz, tandis que les autres 35.000 furent agazés et leurs corps brûlés aux fours crématoires. Aprés juin 1944, des israélites hellènes de vieille Grèce, Athènes, Ioannina, Corfou, Rhodes, évalués à 6.000 personnes arrivèrent également à Auschwitz.

De ce nombre de 15.000 personnes entrées dans les camps depuis mars 1943 jusqu' en juillet 1944, il ne restait en décembre 1944 que 523 en vie; les autres moururent pendant ce laps de temps de typhus, Malaria, Tuberculose, Pneumonie, Phlegmons, et le plus grand nombre sous l' effet des conditions déplorables de vie dans le camp qui faisaient en peu de mois de ces hommes et femmes, des cadavres ambulants, et n' étant plus aptes au travail. Le médecin S.S. du camp les envoyaient à la chambre à gaz ou les tuaient par une injection de 5cc de phénol intracardiaque.

En janvier 1945 vu l' avance des russes en Pologne, l' ordre d' évacuation est arrivé le 18 et nous nous sommes mis en marche avec un froid de 12 degrés sous zéro légèrement habillés faisant passé 30 kilomètres par jour pendant 8-15 jours selon la distance du camp qui nous était destiné à l' intérieur de l' Allemagne. De par ces conditions nous avons laissé en route 1/5 de notre effectif du fait aussi que chaque fois que quelqu' un ne pouvant plus marcher s' arrêtait il était impitoyablement abattu par la garde qui nous convoyait. Le 11 avril, date de notre libération par les armées américaines, le nombre des survivants grecs du camp de Buchenwald s/Weimar était de 63.

Je ne crois pas exagérer en affirmant que du nombre de 55.000 israélites hellènes déportés à Auschwitz, il n' y a que 350 à 450 survivants.

⤜⥊⤛

117

K. Diamantopoulos, Ambassador in Washington, to the Greek Ministry of Foreign Affairs

dispatch   Washington, 28 August 1945

I have the honour to submit, attached hereto, a copy of a communication addressed to me, on the 8th inst., by the Central Conference of American Rabbis, conveying, in execution of a decision resolved unanimously at its last session, the "appreciation and profound gratitude" of the American Rabbis for the care and support received from the Greek people by the Jews in Greece during the course of the war.

I have replied in an appropriate manner to the said Organisation, informing them, in parallel, that I am forwarding a copy of their communication to the Hellenic Government.

⤜⥊⤛

ATTACHMENT TO 117*

F. Isserman, Chairman, Commission of Justice and Peace, Central Conference of American Rabbis, to K. Diamantopoulos, Greek Ambassador in Washington

letter   St Louis, 8 August 1945

Dear Mr Diamantopoulos

Since the liberation of Greece we have heard that thousands of Jews outlawed by Hitler who would have been murdered by his orders were saved and rescued because of the humanity and sympathy of many of the Christian citizens of Greece.

Frequently, they went to the aid of their Jewish fellow-citizens at the risk of their own lives and the lives of their dear ones. We American Rabbis are deeply appreciative for this magnificent service rendered by the Greek people at a time when their burdens were especially heavy.

At the annual meeting of the Central Conference of American Rabbis, the oldest rabbinical association in America and the largest in the world, it was unanimously voted to extend through you to the people of Greece our appreciation and our deep gratitude not only for the lives they saved but also for the inspiring evidence of moral and spiritual stamina, granite-like character and loyalty to the highest humanitarian values which they manifested.

118

J. Romanos, Counsellor, Embassy in London, to the Greek Ministry of Foreign Affairs

report   London, 3 September 1945

I have the honour to inform you that your telegram No. 20032 of 25 August of this year was received by us on 26 August, that is, it was sent two days, and received three days, after the conclusion of the World Jewish Congress.

It was thus impossible for the pro-Jewish Greek gesture in favour of the Jewish estates in abeyance in Greece to be praised in the addresses delivered during the Congress. However, since Mr Robert Raphael, representing the Jewish community of Greece at the Congress, had not yet left London, I hastened to inform him of the content of your telegram and to arrange with him, in person, for the greatest possible publicity to be given to the measure taken by the Government in favour of the Jews.

As a result, Mr Robert Raphael hastened to bring the measure to the attention of the Presidium of the World Jewish Congress and of the Palcor Jewish Press Agency, while our Press Service acted in a similar manner via the international Overseas News Agency.

Following this action, the Presidents of the Congress, Mr Wise of the United States and Mr Goldman of Britain, addressed to the Prime Minister the telegram of 30 August of which a copy is enclosed herewith (Attachment 1).

The Palcor Agency and the Jewish Telegraphic Agency had already published, on 29 August, the two news telegrams also enclosed herewith (Attachments 2 and 3). The Overseas News Agency acted likewise. Our Information Service will report to you, in due course, on the publicity which these news items have received in the British Press. Unfortunately, as far as I am aware, there is no evidence that these Agencies drew the stark contrast referred to in your telegram between the action taken by Greece and the conduct of Bulgaria towards the Jews. However, the Jewish Organisations of America have already sent telegrams to our Information Service here asking to be sent the text of our law concerning the Jewish estates in abeyance.

I should avail myself of this opportunity to inform you that, during the Congress, and despite the fact that the Government's measure in favour of the Jewish estates in abeyance had not yet been announced, the pro-Jewish attitude of Greece was praised in the speech delivered by Mr Raphael, as can be seen from the extract from the Proceedings of the Congress enclosed herewith (Attachment No. 4), while in the Press telegram enclosed herewith (Attachment No. 5) the Palcor Agency praised the government measure taken in favour of 380 young Jewish migrants. In the same connection, Mr Shertock, Political Secretary of the Jewish Agency, sent the Prime Minister the telegram enclosed herewith (Attachment No. 6).

———

ATTACHMENT a TO 118*

Dr S. Wise and Dr W. Goldman, Chairmen of the World Jewish Congress, to Admiral Voulgaris, Prime Minister

letter   30 August 1945

On behalf of the Executive Committee of the World Jewish Congress we consider it our pleasant duty to transmit to you our feelings of gratitude for the magnanimous attitude of the Greek Government on the question of heirless Jewish property which is to be used for the rehabilitation of Jewish displaced persons. We hope that the example set by the Greek Government will be followed by other Governments of Europe, thus enabling them to correct at least to a certain degree the tremendous wrong inflicted upon the Jewish population of former Nazi-occupied countries.

———

ATTACHMENT b TO I I 8*

Report from Palcor Agency

London, 29 August 1945

Title: Important Decision by Greek Government

Mr Robert Raphael, delegate from Greece to the World Zionist Conference in London, has been officially informed by the Greek Legation in London that on the 24th August the Cabinet in Athens gave approval to a law providing for the designation of the properties of Greek Jews exterminated during the war, which are not claimed by their legal heirs, to public purpose, priority to be given to the rehabilitation of surviving Jews.

It is pointed out in the Legation's letter that this new provision modifies in favour of Jewish survivors the existing law whereby all such properties should normally revert to the State.

The news of this new decree of the Greek Government was received with great satisfaction in Jewish Agency circles.

ATTACHMENT c TO I I 8*

Report from Jewish Telegraphic Agency

London, 29 August 1945

The Greek Legation here has officially informed Mr Robert Raphael, delegate of the Greek Zionists to the Zionist World Conference in London, that on August 24th the Cabinet in Athens has approved a law, assigning all property left by Greek Jews who were exterminated during the war and unclaimed by legal heirs to public purposes, priority being given to the rehabilitation of Jewish survivors in Greece.

A spokesman of the Jewish Agency for Palestine has expressed the Agency's satisfaction at this step by the Greek Government.

ATTACHMENT d TO **118***

*R. Raphael, Greek Delegate to the Special European Conference of
the World Jewish Congress*

report   London, 22 August 1945

Mr Robert Raphael presented the final report given by delegates, and reviewed
the history of the Jewish community in Greece since 1941.

The first steps taken by the Germans against the Jews came in July 1942, when
the first anti-Jewish law was issued in Greece. All Jews in Salonika between the
ages of 18 and 45 had to register and the 8,000 who did were sent for slave labour
for the Todt organisation. The treatment meted out to them was such that in one
month two hundred of them died. Strong steps were taken by the then archbishop
of Athens Damaskinos, supported by the Greek intellectuals headed by the Greek
poet Sikelanios [*sic*] to obtain better treatment for Jews. As a result of this protest,
Dr. Merten representative of the Rosenberg Commission in Salonika proposed
to conclude the agreement with the Jewish community of Salonika where–by
those workers who were not fit for work, would be released for one year on
payment of 6,000 gold sterling. This sum was paid but, after four months, Jews had
to reregister and a new Ghetto was established in Salonika. No food rations were
given to Jews, and deportations begun in February 1943. 48,000 Jews were
deported from Salonika under the most terrible conditions. Only Jews of Italian,
Spanish and Turkish nationality, about 600 in all, were exempted from the deportations.

As soon as Italy collapsed, in September 1943, the Germans took under
control all those parts of Greece which were occupied by the Italian military and
their first act was to deport the Jews. The Jews of Athens, numbering about 5,000
to 6,000, who already had the bitter experience of what happened in Salonika, had
already taken steps to provide shelter for them among Greek families who did
everything possible to help them. The youngest joined the partisans in the
mountains, and it is estimated that about 200 to 300 young Jews fought with the
partisans against the Germans until the liberation of Greece. The Archbishop of
Athens, Damaskinos, and the Greek population of Athens generally rendered
sterling service with the result that only 800 Jews of Athens, 15% of the Jewish
population, were deported by the Germans. It is a significant fact that Archbishop
Damaskinos himself was imprisoned by the Germans for helping the Jews.
Unfortunately, the communities of Ioannina and Corfu were completely

exterminated. The communities of Larissa, Volo and Trikala received great help from the Greek population and 80% of them escaped.

There are now about 8,000 Jews left in Greece. Their moral is very low and they are in desperate need of help. Although both the Jewish Brigade and the Joint had brought some assistance, the general distress of the Greek population made it very difficult for the extremely serious needs of the Jews to be catered in a special way by the Greek government, inspite of every good will on its part. Greece has been plundered on a large scale by the occupation of Italians, Germans and Bulgarians, and the Greek government is facing the very serious problem of sheltering the many refugees of Macedonia and Thrace whose homes and belongings have been destroyed by the Bulgarians. In these circumstances, the Greek government cannot devote itself especially to Jewish problems. UNRRA did not exercise any discrimination in favour of Jews.

With regard to the problem of the restitution of Jewish property, Mr Raphael stated that a law had been issued, giving the Jews the right to recover their properties providing that the owners themselves or the relatives to the fourth degree present their claims. The communities can recover their property, but can dispose of it only if 50% of their former members reconstitute themselves as a community, otherwise they can only receive the income from their property.

It is estimated that the pre-war assets of the Jewish population of Greece amounted to 20 billion pounds gold sterling. The Jewish community of Salonika still possesses about 10 million pounds worth of property, but it cannot yet dispose of it. The Jewish community is trying to get a special body established which will concentrate all Jewish heirless property. An example of the good will and the sincere effort of the Greek government to help is shown by the fact that last week a decree was issued permitting 380 Jews between the age of 18 and 40 to go to Palestine inspite of the fact that they would normally be liable to military service.

ATTACHMENT e TO 118*

Report from Palcor Agency

Athens, 16 August 1945

A special decree promulgated by the Greek Prime Minister, authorises the departure for Palestine of 380 Greek Jews, aged between 18 and 40, who were otherwise liable for military service, their claims to be submitted by the representative of the Jewish Agency in Athens. In the preamble to the decree it is stated that the measure is intended as an expression of the Greek Government's desire to come to the assistance of Greek Jews who had suffered so terribly from Nazi atrocities.

This decree removes the most serious obstacle to the establishment of a Halutz movement in Greece arising from the liability of men from the age of 18 upwards for military service. Negotiations for the exemption from military service of young Jews desiring to settle in Palestine and going into agricultural training in Greece prior to their immigration were initiated by Mr Moshe Shertock, head of the Political Department of the Jewish Agency, on his visit to Athens in April last when he visited the Greek Prime Minister, and were brought to a successful conclusion by the Jewish Agency's special emissary to Greece, Mr Jacob Czernowitz.

◆━◆

119

G. Christodoulou, Consul in charge for Palestine and Trans-Jordan, to the Ministry of Foreign Affairs

report   Jerusalem, 6 September 1945

I have the honour to inform you that the repatriation to Greece, arranged by UNRRA, of the Greek Jews who had taken refuge in Palestine during the War has created grave displeasure among Jewish circles here, and that this has manifested itself in a variety of ways.

A considerable number of articles have been published in the Jewish Press, regardless of political credo, opposing the repatriation being carried out. The Press which supports the official Jewish Agency has expressed its pity for those who have already departed or are about to depart, hinting that the situation in Greece is so dreadful that it is not impossible that the repatriated persons will themselves insist before long on being returned to Palestine. The newspapers opposed to the Agency emphasise that the Zionist organisations themselves bear grave responsibility for the repatriation, since they did not take steps to ensure that those who arrived here were provided with opportunities to live comfortably and make a living.

In general, however, all these articles have been critical of UNRRA, which, according to the columnists, has overstepped the framework of its duties and has encouraged the departure of the Greek Jews. It should be noted that the representatives of UNRRA in Palestine and, in general, in the Middle East, undoubtedly include a very large proportion of American Jews who are opposed to the Zionist idea and have followed in the question of the repatriation of the Greek Jews a policy of their own which is in contradiction with the wishes of the Jewish Agency and the friendly advice of our Consular Authority.

The view of the Jewish Agency on this matter is as follows: given that the Greek refugees/immigrants in question, like the refugees/immigrants of the other European countries, have received the protection of the Zionist organisations and were issued with immigration certificates, they came to occupy places in the quota of Jews whom the British Government has allowed to settle freely in Palestine. When some of these persons leave, and since the British authorities refuse to delete the names of those leaving from the lists of immigrants, a significant number of places for immigrants will be lost and it will thus not be in the interests of the Zionists to facilitate Jewish immigrants from Europe in leaving Palestine and returning to their former homes in Europe. Regardless of this, the principal argument for the formation of a Jewish state in Palestine put forward by the Zionists – that is, that the Jews are, so it is claimed, unable to continue living in Europe since life there has become intolerable for them everywhere – is *ipso facto* demolished when the persons concerned acknowledge in practice that they prefer to return to their homelands in Europe rather than continuing to reside here. In this way, for the extreme nationalist and terrorist Jewish organisations, any Jew who makes his way to Palestine and later leaves the country is a traitor to the Jewish ideals.

Apart from these newspaper articles, rumours circulated very widely in Palestine immediately after the departure, around 20 August, of a large shipment of Greek refugees being repatriated by UNRRA – including a small proportion of Jews – that the ship had sunk. For some days, those with relatives and friends on the French vessel *Eridan*, which was carrying the refugees, were in a state of anxiety. Fortunately, after about ten days a telegram was sent from Athens to the League of Greek Jews of Tel Aviv to the effect that all the passengers had arrived safely at their destination.

It is obvious that this rumour was spread by the same Jewish circles as were opposed to the departure of the Jewish refugees, especially in view of the fact that UNRRA is making preparations for the departure, within the next few days, of a fresh shipment of repatriated refugees including a large number of immigrants (in particular, the 240 persons on the list given to us by Mr Venardis in early August and dealt with at the end of my telegram No. 546 of 5 August 1945).

To conclude, it is my duty to report that I have received confidential information to the effect that nationalist Jews are now debating whether it might not be advisable for the Greek Government and its official representatives here to receive the appropriate warnings that reprisals will be taken if the flow of repatriated persons is not stopped.

In view of this, I thought it advisable that I channel to the Jewish Press the information – provided by the Royal Consulate General on other occasions in the past – that the Greek Government and its representatives in Palestine are exerting no pressure whatsoever towards repatriation of the Greek Jews who have taken refuge here, but that each of them is completely at liberty to remain in Palestine or, if he wishes to retain Greek citizenship, to return to Greece. Here, it should not be forgotten that some Greek Jews contend that they never had any intention of settling in Palestine and that the immigration certificates they received after their arrival here were supplied by sleight of hand.

I should also not omit to mention that approximately the same difficulties were experienced some months ago by the consular authorities of Czechoslovakia and Yugoslavia when they attempted to repatriate Czech and Yugoslav Jewish immigrants to those countries. The authorities in question, and some of the persons concerned, received threatening letters, after which the consulates were obliged to publish official announcements in the Press denying that any of their nationals had been subjected to direct or indirect coercion to return to their home countries.

It will be clear from the above that the Greek Government was quite right in expressing from the beginning the view (explained in communication No. 1274 of 24 February 1945 from the Embassy in Cairo) that the Greek Jewish immigrants would not be repatriated as refugees but, as Greek citizens located abroad, would simply be issued with regular Greek passports, after which they themselves would have to arrange their transport back to Greece, together with any visas they might require. Such a tactic, if implemented thoroughly, would have dispelled any objections on the part of the Jewish organisations and would have reduced the number of persons seeking repatriation as a result of the difficulty of obtaining private travel facilities and of the lack of funds to meet the cost involved. However, it would not now be possible to return to this approach after its abandonment in view of the more recent instructions received from the Welfare and Repatriation Service in Cairo and from yourselves (as mentioned in your telegram of 8 August 1945), and if I report these matters to you today, I do so in order simply to emphasise that even the more serious-minded Jewish circles who are opposed to the return to Greece of the Greek Jewish immigrants are aware of the difficult position in which the Greek Government finds itself in this instance and tend rather to cast the blame on UNRRA.

I attach hereto, in translation, certain of the comments of Jewish newspapers on this question:

"Among the thousands of Greek refugees in Palestine", reported *Davar*, the well-known Labour mouthpiece of the Jewish Agency, on the 9th of this month, "are several hundred Jews who have hardly had time to gain an acquaintance with Jewish Palestine and the achievements accomplished by the Jews in this land. Now these Greek Jews, despite the fact that they hold immigration permits, are returning to Greece. Those who are familiar with the situation in Greece, and in particular with the position of Jews in that country, will wonder why these Jews are returning. But people are free to do as they please, and the door out of Palestine is open. But who knows whether in the near future these same Jews will not wish to come back to Palestine, and whether the entrance will not be closed then."

And *Davar* continues: "On the other hand, rumours are circulating to the effect that UNRRA is influencing these refugees to return to Greece by promising them every possible facility. UNRRA provides the visas, arranges the journey, and even supplies visas for a return to Palestine. And we ask ourselves: is it UNRRA's duty to engage in experiments on the Greek Jews? Has UNRRA deteriorated into a mere travel agency? The employees of UNRRA will certainly be completely familiar with the situation in Greece today: consequently, what right, what moral right, does it have to influence the Jews into returning to a place where the situation is so bad? The whole matter needs to be looked into and investigations should be conducted both in the headquarters of UNRRA and in its offices in Palestine."

Another Jewish newspaper, *Ha'Aretz* of Tel Aviv, published a long report under the title "The people who return to Greece from Palestine". In it, the columnist attempts to analyse the reasons why the Greek Jews are being compelled to return to the land of their birth, adding that he had spoken with approximately one hundred Jews who were about to return to Greece and that he believes the main reasons for their decision were as follows:

1) The difficulties of the new life in Palestine, the lack of housing, the impossibility of finding work, etc.

2) The wish of the refugees to retrieve at least part of the property they left in Greece.

3) The indifference which the main Jewish organisations – that is, the Jewish Agency, the National Jewish Council and the Union of Greek Jews of Palestine – have displayed towards these refugees.

"There can be no doubt", continues the columnist, "that the refugees themselves are under a grave responsibility. These people ought to have learned a good lesson from their tragic past, and not attempt to return to Greece."

The article concludes with the statement that, in addition to the Greek Jews being repatriated in the next few days, who number some 200 persons, Jews from Yugoslavia, Romania, Czechoslovakia and elsewhere are also being repatriated, the principal purpose of their journey being to have their real estate restored to them. For that reason, the columnist proposes the establishment in Jerusalem of a central organisation to handle the question of the property of Jews residing in Palestine, thus preventing them from being obliged to return to their countries of origin and exposing themselves to unpleasant surprises.

On 5 September 1945, the newspaper *Hamboker* of Tel Aviv carried a leading article under the title "Our migration policy" devoted in particular to the departure from Palestine of the Greek Jews.

The newspaper accuses these Jews of ignoring all the efforts being made by the Jewish nation in Palestine, emphasising that at a time at which the Jewish Agency is calling for the free migration to Palestine of Jews from all parts of Europe, where, as it contends, there is no future for them any more, the departure from Palestine of the Greek Jews is endangering the entire policy of the Jewish Agency and of Zionism.

The columnist is harshly critical first of the national Jewish organisations, and primarily of the Jewish Agency, for failing to take sufficient interest in the immigrants from Europe and of having done nothing to provide them with good conditions in which to settle in Palestine.

Hatzofeh, another Jewish newspaper published in Tel Aviv, published a leading article in the same spirit on the 6th of this month, asking "Why were the Greek Jews left to their own devices here? Why were they left shut up in a refugee camp?" The newspaper concludes by stating that the refugees in question are returning to countries in which there is no hope for them.

Lastly, on the 6th of the month *Davar* returned to the question in an article published in a prominent position on its front page.

"In connection with the departure of the Greek Jewish refugees", it notes, "who will be abandoning Palestine in the next few days, we have been informed that the staff of UNRRA see it as their sacred duty to repatriate Jews from Palestine to their countries of origin, by all possible means. The staff of UNRRA have moved mountains and, indeed, quite heated diplomatic struggles took place between the representatives of the Greek Government and the staff of UNRRA before it became possible to persuade the Greek authorities to permit the return to Greece of the Greek Jewish refugees. The representatives of the Greek Government took the line that, regardless of their return or otherwise, the Jewish refugees who have immigration certificates for Palestine will not be deprived of any of the rights of Greek citizens under Greek law on condition that they retain their Greek citizenship. However, the staff of UNRRA influenced the refugees and Jewish immigrants into returning to Greece."

120

*G. Christodoulou, Consul in charge for Palestine and Trans-Jordan,
to the Ministry of Foreign Affairs*

report   Jerusalem, 12 September 1945

'Concerning Mr Czernowitz's statements on his return from Greece'

I have the honour to report that, on his return to Palestine after a three-month
stay in Greece as a representative of the Red Shield of David, Mr Czernowitz
made lengthy and interesting statements to the Press about the general situation
in Greece and, particularly, the living conditions of the Jews there.

The main points of Mr Czernowitz's statements are the following:

"The greatest devastations suffered by the Jews in Greece occurred in the
cities of Thessaloniki, Drama, Kavala and Serres. In Ioannina there remain only
46 Jews, in Corfu 100. The total number of those Greek Jews who have already
returned or are going to return from Poland shall not exceed 2,000."

Mr Czernowitz went on to say that, today, the only wish of the Jews of Greece
is to emigrate at once to Palestine. At least 1,000 children must depart without delay,
especially those dwelling in Larissa and Thessaloniki where living conditions are still
very difficult.

Mr Czernowitz reported that, in his peregrinations in a large part of the
country, he observed everywhere that the Greek authorities are exhibiting their
concern about the Jews and sincerely trying to satisfy their needs. As concerns
the Greek population, Mr Czernowitz said that everywhere he went, he encountered general sympathy towards the Jews with the exception of certain cities
such as Thessaloniki where the inimical attitude of the inhabitants is attributed to
material interests arising during the occupation (evidently he was hinting at those
inhabitants who are now holding Jewish buildings and are loath to accept their
restitution to their rightful owners).

With this opportunity I would also inform you that the Jewish Press did not
fail to mention the establishment of a Greek-Palestinian Association in Athens
as well as the celebration of the event at the Athens Chamber of Commerce. All
Jewish newspapers had only laudatory comments to make on this news and the
various speeches during the said session.

121

G. Christodoulou, Consul in charge for Palestine and Trans-Jordan,
to the Ministry of Foreign Affairs

Press report   Jerusalem, 12 September 1945

'Concerning the position of the Jews in Greece by comparison with their position in the
other Balkan countries'

I have the honour to inform you that the weekly Jewish periodical *Hed
Hamisrah* ('Voice of the East') recently published a lengthy article signed by S.
Ben-Yitsok concerning the position of the Jews in the various Balkan countries.

The columnist demonstrates that the only Balkan country in which absolute
freedom of thought prevails is Greece. There are a large number of foreign
journalists and observers in that country, who are able to write and report around
the world on everything that takes place there, which is impossible both in
Bulgaria and in Yugoslavia.

"Greece", continues the columnist, "is the only Balkan country in which a
certain minority is not in a position to crush the majority. This state of affairs has
been a matter of great importance for the Jews, among others. After liberation, a
specific small group of Jewish Communists did indeed attempt to oppress the large
majority of Jewish Zionists, but this proved impossible precisely because of the
liberty prevailing in Greece. By way of contrast, since that freedom does not exist
in Bulgaria and Yugoslavia, the Jewish Communist minorities there were able to
impose themselves on the large majority of Jewish Zionists.

"In addition, thanks to the freedom prevailing in Greece, the Jewish
community of Greece is the only one in the Balkans which is able to communicate
with the major Jewish organisations around the world and with the Jewish Agency
in Palestine. The Greek Government is the only administration in the Balkans
which is favourably inclined towards Zionism and which has assisted the Zionists
in an entirely exemplary manner, not hesitating even to exempt from military
service such young Jews of military age who wish to emigrate to Palestine. Greece
was also the only Balkan state which permitted a Jewish representative – Mr
Robert Raphael – to travel to London to be present at the World Jewish Congress."

After describing the wretched condition of the Jews of Bulgaria and
Yugoslavia today, the columnist concludes by stating that only truly democratic

regimes, and not totalitarian regimes, could improve the condition of the Jews in those countries and would permit them to express their beliefs freely.

━━◈━━

122

Newspaper article from Atlantis

[illegible] January 1946

An anti-Semitic proclamation and an announcement of the Diocese of Thessaloniki

Some time ago, a self-styled 'Organisation of Christian Youth' of Thessaloniki filled the main streets with anti-Semitic posters in which it stressed the dangers allegedly threatening Christianity from the foundation of the State of Israel, the 'State of Antichrist' as it called it. The Jewish community of Thessaloniki, disturbed by the inimical and anti-Semitic tenor of the proclamation protested both to the Holy Diocese of Thessaloniki and the General Governance of Macedonia.

A few days later, the Holy Diocese of Thessaloniki issued the following official statement, which was published by all the local papers. In publishing the above statement of the Holy Diocese ourselves, we take this opportunity of reminding our readers of and praising the laudable attitude inspired by a true Christian spirit of His Beatitude Gennadios, Metropolitan of Thessaloniki, when the Jews of Thessaloniki were suffering the deadly persecutions of the Germans. Of this attitude much could be written.

The statement issued by the Holy Diocese is as follows: "Some days ago, a committee of the Jewish Community of Thessaloniki came here and reported the proclamation of the 'Religious Union of Orthodox Youth', a copy of which they gave to us with the request that we proceed to the required measures.

"Although the Committee was advised beforehand that such a religious organisation did not exist, nonetheless, we proceeded to the necessary inquiries and ascertained its non-existence. The same conclusion was reached by the Police Director of Thessaloniki, who informed the Holy Diocese accordingly.

"Consequently, the proclamation which was circulated was not genuine and apparently aimed at defaming our Church and creating dissent between Christian and Jewish Greeks. Therefore, no importance should be attributed to it nor should

our Jewish fellow-citizens, with whom our relations have always been fraternal, let themselves be concerned. Indeed, it is a well-known fact how sad we felt at the inhuman persecutions of the Jewish community by the foreign occupation authorities, which, despite our early efforts and protests, we were unable to prevent. So much for the information of the public and our Jewish fellow citizens."
In reply to the above statement, the Jewish Community of Thessaloniki has sent to the Holy Diocese the following letter of thanks:

ATTACHMENT TO 122

The President, M. Molho, and the Secretary, I. Tiano, of the Jewish Community of Thessaloniki to the Holy Diocese of Thessaloniki

letter   Athens, 15 January 1946

Your Beatitude

It was with a sense of lively satisfaction that the Jewish Community of Thessaloniki learned from the daily Press of the communiqué of the Holy Diocese concerning the protest of our Community relating to the attempt at slander by the self-styled 'Religious Union of Orthodox Youth'.

Our Community, in addressing the Holy Diocese of Thessaloniki, was certain beforehand of your kind efforts to repudiate the wicked purpose of certain irresponsible persons who pursued the defamation of the Jews.

The statement of the Holy Diocese of Thessaloniki affirms once again, as has already been proved repeatedly in the past, that it will not allow the harmonious relationship between Greek Christians and Jews which has existed from time immemorial to be disrupted.

Moreover, we shall never forget the generous efforts and courageous protests made by the Holy Diocese through its worthy head, Metropolitan Gennadios, to the conqueror for the termination of the awful persecutions against the Greek Jews, which unfortunately had no effect not because of a lack of courage but of the unprecedented ferocity and cruelty of the Nazis.

Conveying to you our thanks and feelings of gratitude for Your attitude.

123

A. Kyrou, Director, Ministry of Foreign Affairs, to the Greek
Consulate in Boston

letter   Athens, 15 January 1946

We have the honour to convey to you the following information about the question of the Greek Jews, having been informed that it might be possible to make use of it in the American Press.

I. Before the War, approximately 72,500 Jews lived in Greece in conditions of complete equality before the law, given that our homeland was actually the only country in which no political wing or party ever thought of engaging in even the mildest anti-Semitic activities. The Jews, regarding themselves as Greeks and viewed as such by their Orthodox compatriots, gave brilliant demonstrations of their patriotic feelings during the military operations of 1940-1941. The memory of the heroic death in North Epirus (on 5 December 1940) of the Jewish Colonel Mordechai Frizis - for whom a fine civil memorial service was held on 23 December 1945 by the League of Invalid Officers – will long remain among us.

II. The horror of enemy occupation and the year 1943, with its terrible consequences for the Jews, then forged still stronger bonds between the Greeks and the Jews, doing so in blood and iron. The Bulgarians – those same Bulgarians who today have the impudence to present themselves as fervent pro-Semites and as allegedly having strongly defended the Jews of Bulgaria against the hostile intentions of their Teutonic allies – in fact preceded the Germans in taking measures against the Jews, since in early March 1943 they suddenly arrested all the Jews of the cities of Serres, Drama, Kavala, Alexandroupoli, Xanthi and Komotini, whom they shipped to Bulgaria and thence to Poland. These Jews were robbed of their valuables by Bulgarian civil servants and gendarmes, while the real property confiscated by them was sold to Bulgarian colonists for 20 million lev. Of the 6,000 prosperous Jews of Eastern Macedonia and Western Thrace, no more than 100 survived, in a pitiful physical and financial state.

In the German-occupied parts of northern Greece, the displacement and extermination of the Jews took place a little later, with Teutonic efficacy. Thus, in the period before the end of May 1943, all the Jews of Thessaloniki, Langadas, Verria and elsewhere (including those from the Didymoteicho-Soufli triangle), numbering more than 50,000, were abducted and despatched under conditions of unspeakable brutality to Poland, where – with very few exceptions – they met a terrible end in the notorious concentration camps of Auschwitz, Buchenwald, Belsen, and others. The number of Jews who succeeded in fleeing from Thessaloniki and surviving (some by joining guerrilla bands in the mountains, others by acquiring false identity papers and making their way to Athens, to which the anti-Jewish measures of the Germans had not yet been extended) numbered 3-4,000, to which figure one must add the few hundred who returned from Germany and Poland.

The same measures began to be applied to central, western and southern Greece and the islands in late September 1943. In the Athens area, the proportion of Jews who survived was very large (85-90%, including the venerable Mr Kanaris Konstantinis, President of the Community), thanks to the experience gained from the precedent of Thessaloniki but primarily to all the classes of the Greek people, headed by His Beatitude Archbishop Damaskinos, who supported and hid Jews to the point of self-sacrifice despite the fact that this was punishable by death. In the other Greek cities, the success of the German measures was almost complete wherever the Jews believed the deceitful assurances of the Germans that they would not be harmed (as, for example, in Ioannina). In contrast, in the Communities where the Jews did not believe the Germans - as in Patra, Chalkis, Volos, Larissa, Trikkala and Karditsa - more than 75% survived.

The total number of Jews who survived in Greece or escaped to the Middle East (the latter category consisting of not more than 1,000 individuals), together with the small number who returned from Poland and Germany, amounts to 10-11,000 on the basis of the figures assembled to date.

III. On its return to liberated Athens and after a government reshuffle, the Papandreou administration hastened by Law No. 2 of 26 October 1944 to rescind the legislative measures concerning the confiscation of Jewish property which the Germans had dictated to the Rallis Quisling government. The question which, as in all the Axis-occupied countries, occupied most attention was that of the fate of the property which had been abandoned by those who left no living relatives close enough to be regarded as heirs, the number of whom was quite obviously going to be very large.

It is common knowledge that, in accordance with the law on intestate succession, the estate reverts to the State. Nonetheless, at the meeting of the Cabinet on 24 August last the Government took the following decision:

"The Greek Government, not wishing to benefit in any way from the persecution undergone by the Jews at the hands of the enemy occupation authorities, has resolved that all assets which would have reverted to the Greek State by reason of intestate succession in the case of Jews who lost their lives in concentration camps,

Thessaloniki 1947. Inaugural ceremonies of the reopening of the 'Pichas' clinic. Rabbi and author Michael Molho is depicted in the centre. The 'Pichas' clinic was inaugurated in 1926. Its principal purpose was the support the homeless of the Jewish communities of Eastern Thessaloniki (Kalamaria, 151, Karagatch, 6). After the war the clinic was renovated with the support of the AMERICAN JOINT DISTRIBUTION COMMITTEE and functioned as a maternity hospital as well until 1954. From 1961 until 1979 it accommodated the child care shelter of the Jewish Community of Thessaloniki. It was demolished in 1980 to make way for the Egnatia Via. Archive of the Jewish Community of Thessaloniki, donated by Isaac Menache (Athens) and David Amir (Israel).

leaving no legitimate heirs, shall not revert to the State, but shall be used for special charitable purposes, provision being made for meeting the needs primarily of the Jewish community."

In taking this decision, the Greek Government made a literally pioneering move in the process of regulating an issue which is indeed of very great significance for Jews everywhere, given that the problem of the Jewish estates in abeyance is still awaiting settlement in all the liberated countries, while the generous solution provided in Greece cannot fail to serve as an example everywhere. For that reason, it was welcomed with enthusiasm not only by the Central Board of Jewish Communities of Greece, in Athens – which, it should be noted, was invited by the Minister of Finance to advise him on the best manner in which the intestate property in question could be disposed of – but also by the representatives here of the Jewish Agency in Palestine and by the head of the American Joint Distribution Committee, which operates within the framework of UNRRA.

124

C. Bitsidis, Minister of Finance, to the Prime Minister

telegram   Athens, 3 March 1946

Prime Minister

Reuters reported from Greece that, despite the existence in Greece of a law settling the fate of the property abandoned by Jews who were executed or abducted as hostages during the occupation, the persons now in possession of Jewish property are refusing to restore it to the rightful owners and heirs or to the Jewish Community foundations. The Agency added that the question has become one of political dealing among the various political groupings.

Information has already been received here to the effect that this news item has created a bad impression in America, in Egypt and in other countries where Jews live. As a result, you should react by a clear statement in order to dispel the impression created.

125

G. Kapsambelis, Consul General in Jerusalem, to the Greek Ministry of Foreign Affairs

letter   Jerusalem, 12 June 1946

I have the honour to inform you that, a few days ago, the following news item was published in the Cairo newspaper *'Phos'*:

"Jewish property. In reply to the congratulations conveyed by the Central Board of the Jewish Communities in Greece, on the occasion of the formation of the new Greek Government, the Prime Minister, Mr C. Tsaldaris, in his reply expressed his thanks and deep sorrow along with that of the Greek people for the terrible fate of the Jewish element as a result of the abominable German persecution. The Prime Minister stressed that the special interest Mr Moissis recollects in his letter and which was the basis of Mr Tsaldaris' action during the dark days of March 1943 for the purpose of reducing or averting that disaster constitutes a proof of the friendly feelings of his Government towards the Jewish element.

"Further, the Prime Minister outlined the community of perception of the Jewish rights reigning in the new Greek Cabinet and promised the application of Law Nos 2/1944, 337 and 808/1945 for the release and restitution of Jewish property."

Nevertheless, despite these continual proofs of the most favourable treatment of Jews and their property in Greece as well as the friendly feelings of the Greek people shown to them, the Jewish Press in Palestine, as a whole, with great diffidence and following my persistent almost daily efforts, has been led to somewhat change its attitude towards Greece and its problems.

I have repeatedly submitted to you as well as to the Press Ministry several communications, reports and telegrams on this subject and, more specifically, my telegrams Nos. 506 and 509 of 15 and 16 April respectively.

In consequence, considering that I have received no answer to these reports and telegrams of mine, especially on whether the above telegrams 506 and 509 sent to you during the last strike had ever reached you (see my telegram No. 598 of 30/4/46 and my communication No. 682 of 8/5/46 by which I asked you to have the kindness to acknowledge receipt of my above telegrams) I would ask you once again to acknowledge their receipt as well as let me know your views on this matter and what action you have taken, if any.

126*

C. Chervin, President, and Hirsch Triwaks, General Secretary, Central Committee for the Assistance of Jewish War Victims and Refugees, to the Greek Chargé d' Affaires in Buenos Aires

letter   Buenos Aires, 2 July 1946

Dear Sir

We have the honour to inform you that we have received your communication of 17 June, the content of which we have fully understood.

In reply, we would like to advise you that we were profoundly gratified to be informed of the measures taken by your loveable country in favour of the Jews resident in Greece, for which reason we would like to address to you our most sincere and deepest gratitude.

In conclusion, we would like to reiterate our thanks and are, Sir, your obedient servants.

127

I. Tomazos, Press Attaché, Greek Legation to the Union of South Africa, to the Greek Ministry of Press and Information

telegram   .   Pretoria, 3 September 1946

I have the honour to forward to you, enclosed herewith, newspaper cuttings publishing a summary of the lecture on Greece delivered by Dr Roth of the University of Oxford.

As you will be aware, Dr Cecil Roth recently visited Greece and is in South Africa in the hope of promoting the Jewish question.

Apart from the above lecture, Dr Roth also spoke on Greece on Johannesburg Radio.

In conversation, Dr Roth assured me that if he made any inaccurate statements, these were not the result of malicious intentions or bad faith, given that he is inspired with the most friendly sentiments towards Greece. He added that in his reports to the Union of South Africa and the Jewish Community here he has stressed the need for financial support of the Jewish population in Greece and for the migration to South Africa of orphans of Jewish descent.

⟶⟨⬧⟩⟵

ATTACHMENT TO 127*

Professor Roth, Oxford Univerity

letter   [without specific date] 1946

Observer in Athens

On my way to South Africa from England, I spent a few weeks in the Middle East, lecturing to the troops under the self effacing auspices of the Central Advisory Council for Education in His Majesty's Forces.

(I wish I had the opportunity of saying more about this remarkable organisation, the only possible criticism of which is that it should have come into existence long before it did.)

In connection with this work I went for a short while to Greece, which is now included in the Middle East Command. My position there was I think unusual. I am, it seems, one of the very few civilians who have gone there recently without having made up his mind already about the various local disputes and problems; and I want to give a single account of what I saw, without comment or embellishment.

Outwardly, everything in the country was at the time calm, except for a few explosive inscriptions on the walls according to the custom of Mediterranean lands; though disquieting reports on this subject have been published in the press during the past few days.

In the circles in which I moved, at least, the King is popular. But everywhere people said to me that, were the British troops to be withdrawn there would be an outbreak of bloody civil war before a week was over, far worse than the last. Salonika is ringed about by hills. Beyond them lies Bulgaria under Soviet control. No person to whom I spoke military or civilian seemed to have the least idea of what was going on there. On the other side of the hills beyond the outer ring of the Steel Curtain, Russian forces lie entrenched, but no one knows how many or of what type or what they are doing. The cheerful, lonely British soldier wants nothing more than to fraternise with this [sic] war time Allies, but does not even see them. Steel Curtains are never going to assist international understanding, whoever puts them up.

The Greek Army is being retrained and re-equipped along British lines, and under British supervision. When the process is complete, I am told, (it will not take much longer) our troops will be withdrawn. But I met no one, even of the most pronounced leftist opinions, who looked forward to this with anything but apprehension.

The outstanding impression that one takes away from the few large cities is, unfortunately, one of plenty. I say 'unfortunately' because Greece is the country that suffered more than any other during the period of occupation, and still suffers tragically from the outcome. There is more starvation, distress and under-nourishment there probably than in any other country in the world. But the visitor to Athens sees no trace of this. The shop windows are full, the streets busy, the cafés crowded. He can enjoy in the restaurants meals as no one has seen in England for years (I will not speak of S. Africa) and buy in the cake shops toothsome delights such as the West End of London was never able to provide – and all sold openly, without any taint of the black market which is the result of the opulent in other parts of the continent of Europe. Moreover, in the popular streets near the market, piled high on either side with local fruits and vegetables in wonderful profusion, it is possible to buy without any formality (such as the surrender of coins or coupons) all manner of imported tinned food; to take one example, seven pound cans of American cheese, each containing the ordinary Englishman's ration for the best part of the year.

Of course, this appearance of plenty is illusory. The black coated workers and those with fixed incomes, do not know how to make ends meet. I was told by a lady whom I took to a café that she and her husband who used to make it their nightly resort, had been unable to afford to set foot in it for months. Moreover, outside Athens – in the country districts, the remoter cities, the Epirus, the Peloponnese – the destitution is appalling. There are some towns where there are no children left. And I was told of one where all the males have been exterminated, so that the office of Mayor is of necessity filled by a woman – something hitherto unknown in Greece. In these districts, communications have not yet been restored and disease still stalks rife. I had an interview one evening with the Acting Prime Minister who explained to me some of the difficulties of the situation with which he had to cope – the destruction of communications, the intense individualism of the people, the triumph of the Black Market as a patriotic institution during the period of German occupation, the special conditions in the capital, and the tactical error of failing to introduce drastic rationing at the time of liberation. All this he indicated, was responsible for the gross unevenness of distribution which I witnessed the removal of which would not affect the ordinary starving citizen; and he spoke to me in the most moving terms of the utter misery and destitution in the country districts. I accepted implicitly every word he said, but I told him frankly that the overstocked shop windows and over flowing restaurants of the capital were the worst possible propaganda for his sorely afflicted country in the eyes of the 30,000 or so British Ambassadors in khaki then in Greece. He could imagine (I added) what reports they were sending home; and whether or not rationing would be effective, something should be done to make a show at least of tackling the problem and to remove the more glaring abuses. I fancy what I said impressed him and may bear fruit.

There are relics of the war period at every turn. I spent one sunny afternoon in a military camp at the Adolf Hitler Baths, constructed by British Prisoners of War in 1941-42, and was photographed in the shadow of a bombastic Nazi inscription. I could have been a millionaire a hundred times over had I been willing to stoop so low; for there were bank notes of incredibly high denominations blowing about the gutter - not of course valid currency, but the paper money with which the country was flooded by the Germans during the period of occupation. I picked up one or two specimens as souvenirs, but thought it as well to write the word SPOOF across them, in case I inadvertently tried to tender them for some payment. However, the official currency is itself in a pitiful state. Before the war, the normal rate of exchange was, I fancy, about five hundred drachmas to the pound; now, it is over 20,000. This means that one obtains upwards of 1,000 drs for a shilling; but the resultant purchasing power is far less as British soldiers realise to their cost. You can imagine what this means to persons with fixed incomes.

The harbour of Salonika is still filled with sunken ships – some blown up by the Germans before they left, some the victims of the relentlessly accurate allied bombing. In the suburbs of Athens there are many ruined houses, tragic relics of last year's civil war. The centre however is untouched, and the Parthenon still glows gloriously over the city from the height of Acropolis. I could not help contrasting this with the fate of Florence, the Medieval Athens, the centre of which was blown up by the Germans before they left, so that it know lies like a beautiful woman with her eyes gouged out.

Without a doubt, the most gruesome relic of the German occupation is the tragic state of the Jewish communities of the country – excepting only that of the capital two thirds of whose components were saved through the sympathy of their neighbours under the leadership and inspiration of the Patriarch of the city, the ecclesiastical head of the local Church. Elsewhere, they were all but exterminated.

Tens of thousands of helpless men, women and children were deported into Central Europe and murdered horribly in the death chambers of Dachau, Belsen and Auschwitz. Some of the communities lost 99% of their members. The Jews of Crete (where they were living before the Christian era) were loaded on a boat which was sunk before it reached the mainland. At Serres only three persons survived out of 600.

Salonika was until recently almost a Jewish city where a ship arriving on Saturday could not be discharged, as most of the stevedores and harbour workers were Jews. Five years ago, its community still numbered 56,000 souls. Now there are fewer than 2,000 left; the rest are dead. I saw women who had been sterilized by the Nazis in their sadistic experiments, eyewitnesses of the heroic revolt of the Greek Jews in the death chambers, where they have managed to seize control for a couple of hours, men who had escaped from the German camps and fought in the battle of Warsaw before returning to join the ranks of the partisans in Greece, lonely individuals who were the solitary survivors of families of as many as 40 souls. All the few survivors who had returned from Germany bore tattooed indelibly on their wrists, the prison-camp numbers; the women were sometimes branded in a similar way for the basest and most shameful of objects. All told only one tenth of the pre-war Jewish community of Greece now survives; the rest have perished miserably.

These conditions are reflected everywhere else in the Jewish world, wherever the shadow of the Nazis fell. Something will have to be done by the conscience of civilised humanity to prevent a repetition of this appalling tragedy and make it impossible even if, God forbid, another Hitler should some day arise.

⇥⬦⬦⬦⬧

128*

M. Gottschalk, American Jewish Committee, to the Greek Minister of Foreign Affairs

letter   New York, 10 December 1946

Excellency

At the eve of my departure from Greece, I learned about the very generous initiative taken by the Greek Government, in sending two destroyers to rescue eight hundred stranded Jews en route to Palestine.

I am sure to express the feeling of the members of my Organisation, in thanking very sincerely the Greek Government for this gesture of Human Solidarity which has become so unusual in our days.

—•◆•—

129

G. Kapsambelis, Consul General for Palestine and Trans-Jordan, to the Greek Ministry of Foreign Affairs

report   Jerusalem, 17 December 1946

Further to my telegram No. 2599 of 9th inst. concerning the Jewish stowaways rescued on the island of Seirina, I have the honour of informing you that Mr Ben-Zevie, President of the National Council of the Jews of Palestine, before visiting me yesterday in order to thank me for the assistance granted by the Greek Government and myself to the said refugees (see also the relevant telegram from the Jerusalem Office to the Press Ministry), sent me, in a letter dated 13 December 1946, a copy of his telegram on the matter to the Prime Minister, dated 13 inst.

The text of the said letter from Mr Ben-Zevie is as follows:

"I have the honour to enclose herewith a copy of telegram addressed to-day by the Vaad Leumi to your Government, expressing the widespread feelings of gratitude and admiration roused in the Yishuv by the chivalrous and spontaneous rescue work carried out by the Greek Government and your Navy and Red Cross personnel".

It should be noted that the bulletin dated 11th inst. of the secret Jewish organisation 'The Voice of Jewish Resistance' carried the following report:

"The Government of Greece, which is in no way responsible for the situation of the immigrants, did as much and also sent two destroyers of its meagre navy to their assistance".

—•◆•—

130[*]

Newspaper article from The Palestine Economic Review

[illegible] March 1947

Title: The Settlement of the Problem of Jewish Property in Greece

"Greece was the first liberated country in Europe to deal with the difficult problem of heirless Jewish property." These were the headlines which appeared in the world's press, especially, in the Jewish press in Palestine a year ago. The principle adopted by the Greek Government has been as humanitarian as just. "The Greek State will never accept the property of the Nazi victims to enlarge our wealth," the then Foreign Minister Mr Politis declared, thus laying down the basic principle of Greece's policy concerning this problem.

When the law known as "Law Number 808" was published by the Greek Government, satisfaction was expressed by the remnant of Greek Jewry as well as by representatives of world Jewry. Dr. Stephen Wise, Chairman of the Jewish World Congress and member of the Jewish Academy transmitted by cable the thanks of world Jewry to the Greek government for the liberal measures adopted by the latter. The "Law Number 808" unhesitatingly specified that the legal heirs of Jewish property, after submitting their legally approved claims, will become entitled to such property. In the case of Jewish property where the heirs have disappeared, the State, notwithstanding the existing laws, will not take over such properties, but will hand them over to the Union of Jewish Communities in Greece which will use them in order to rebuild Jewish institutions, schools and other centers of social activities in Greece.

Certain difficulties immediately arose, when the authorities endeavored to carry out this law. The tragedy of the Greek Jews is well known. There have been many cases where some Jews of their own accord handed over their property away, and so on. Therefore, a long list of so called emergency by-laws have been promulgated in order to enable Justice to be done to the Jewish citizens of Greece. These by-laws have been of great help especially in Athens where the majority of Greek Jews is living at present. There is now no question of un-returned Jewish property in the Hellenic capital.

The problem was somewhat more complicated in Salonica, the second capital of Greece, where the Nazi murderers barbarously deported and killed about 50,000 Jews. Six months ago, when Mr P. Tsaldaris became Prime Minister, the question of Jewish property in Salonica was dealt with by the Greek Minister of Justice Mr Hadjipanos. He convoked the leaders of Greek Jewry and informed them that the Government are decided to settle the problem once for all in accordance with the above mentioned principles.

A few weeks later, Mr Hadjipanos introduced the newly prepared law to the Greek Parliament by which it was unanimously adopted. Thus the era of practical action for the definite settlement of this problem was ushered in. For the last two months about 2,000 applications by lawful heirs have been submitted to the courts. During the same period many hundreds of buildings, shops and workshops have already been returned to the lawful heirs. The settlement of this question will last two years, because the number of applications is growing daily. Meanwhile, the majority of Jewish communal buildings, plots of land and institutions – such as schools, hospitals, old aged homes etc. – have already been handed over to the Jewish communities whose budget has recently been enlarged and helped by a special subsidy granted by the Greek Government.

This is, in a few words, the actual position regarding the problem of heirless Jewish property in Greece. The Greek government and the Hellenic nation are proud to be the first among liberated countries in Europe which started energetically, and is continuing to promote by all possible means the measures adopted for the return of Jewish property. This fact was only a short time ago emphasized also by the Foreign Section of the Jewish World Congress whose sincere appreciation of the efforts of the Greek Government in this connection has been published by the Hebrew press in Palestine, too.

⸺⊷⊶⸺

131[*]

*A. Easterman, Political Secretary, World Jewish Congress, to the
Greek Ambassador in London*

letter   London, 13 March 1947

Your Excellency

I would like to thank you for having had the kindness to receive me this morning and giving me an opportunity to discuss with you matters concerning the property of the Jewish victims of Nazi and Fascist persecution in Greece. I pointed out to Your Excellency that we are particularly concerned over the

April 1947. Survivors of the death camps are pictured outside the Monastiriotis synagogue of Thessaloniki following the memorial service to the victims of the Holocaust. Archive of the Jewish Community of Thessaloniki, donated by Isaac Menache (Athens), David Amir (Israel).

question of the property of Jewish families who were exterminated and left no heirs.

As I informed you, I had the pleasure of discussing this problem recently with Mr Tsaldaris in New York. The more particular problem in this case is the implementation of Law 846/1946, which provides for the foundation of a special organisation to assemble and administer the property of the intestate Jewish families. Unfortunately, there has been a significant delay in the entry of this decree into force, and the special organisation has not yet been set up.

Mr Tsaldaris had the kindness to say, after my talks with him in New York, that he would issue instructions by telegram to the competent authorities in Athens to proceed without further delay to set up the above special organisation. I regret to say, however, that my most recent information is to the effect that the decree has still not entered into force.

I have been informed that the Law providing for the founding of the organisation has now been signed by the Minister of National Education. It remains for it to be signed by the Minister of Finance and then submitted to the Council of State for final approval. I am informed that this last procedure is a formality before the Law can be published in the Government Gazette.

The Minister of Finance has so far failed to sign the decree. The reasons for this are not clear, but the outcome is that the founding of the above special organisation has been delayed and imperilled.

I reported to Your Excellency that the World Jewish Congress has greatly appreciated the policy and actions of the Greek Government, which was the first in Europe to settle the just demands of the Jews who survived the Nazi and Fascist terrorism that they should have restored to them the property confiscated and stolen from them and that the Government should accept the principle that this property should be used for the rehabilitation of Jews. It would be most regrettable if difficulties should be created in the practical application of the principles which the Greek Government showed such understanding in adopting towards the Jews.

I should therefore be grateful if Your Excellency would pass on to the Government in Athens our concern over this matter and our sincere hope that the decree to which I have referred will be signed and put into force as soon as possible.

—◈—

132*

Newspaper article from the Jewish Chronicle

London, 13 June 1947

Title: Greek Jews' Grievances Reviewed

The Greek Cabinet, at a forthcoming meeting, is to discuss all pending questions of Jewish concern. A statement to this effect was made to me by the Prime Minister, D. Maximos, following a visit to him by representatives of the Central Board of Jewish Communities, who described to him the plight of Greek Jewry occasioned by the unjustified delay in putting into effect relevant laws concerning their welfare.

These laws deal with the restitution of Jewish property confiscated by Nazi orders and handed over to Greeks, mainly collaborators, following the deportation of the Jews; and the establishment of a special body to administer heirless Jewish property for the benefit of the survivors as a whole. The Jewish delegation, in calling for the setting up of the administrative body, pointed to the bad physical conditions of Jews, and stated that to-day the number suffering from T.B. was ten times that before the Nazi persecutions. Of the 400 Athens Jewish children aged between 1 and 16, 260 had been given a medical examination, and it had been found that 40 per cent of them showed signs of T.B. or a disposition of T.B. In Salonika, where there were seven T.B. cases in March, the figure for May was 40. Two of these have since died. The Athens section of the "Joint" under the leadership of Miss Bele Mazur, has launched a campaign to save the infected children by means of medical supervision, extra food and holiday camps, but the "Joint" cannot indefinitely cope with all the needs of the 6,000 pauperised Jews (out of a total of 10,000) who have survived the deportations, yet the body envisaged in the law of January 1946, to administer heirless Jewish property could provide all the necessary resources for the relief institutions already in existence.

Meanwhile, the Ministry of Justice has submitted a proposal to Parliament calling for the abrogation of Article 13 of the law for a moratorium on rents which made a dangerous racial distinction against Jews classed as "not of Hellenic nationality", and gave to the occupants of their property scandalous privileges such as protection against expulsion following a decision by rent tribunals.

133

The Cabinet Office

act   28 June 1947

The Deputy Prime Minister and Minister of Foreign Affairs, Mr Tsaldaris, declared it to be absolutely essential that the Cabinet arrive at decisions in connection with the question of Jewish property, which has long been pending. The question, he observed, stands as follows today:

During the enemy occupation, the property of the Jews was placed in custody by virtue of laws issued by the occupation governments, and custodians were appointed for large numbers of properties. Immediately after liberation, these occupation laws were rescinded and it was ordered that the Jewish properties be restituted to their owners. As is common knowledge, however, many of the Jews abducted by the Germans have disappeared and, as a result, the question arose as to the disposal of the property belonging to Jews who are deceased or have been declared missing without leaving heirs by testate or intestate succession.

Under the law in force, if there are no heirs by testate or intestate succession, the State enters into the estate as heir. Under the Sophoulis Government, Law 846/1946 was issued, in accordance with which, in the instance of the estates of Jews who were Greek subjects who were lost during the course of the War as a consequence of the racial persecution applied by the enemy, on condition that the Jews in question had left no heirs by testate or intestate succession, the provisions in force by which the State enters into the estate as heir in such cases were not to be implemented, the estates in question passing to a legal entity to be set up by Royal Decree and having as its purpose the rehabilitation of the Greek Jews.

Prior to the introduction of that law, the Voulgaris Government had already taken the decision, in the year 1945, that the property of those Jews who had disappeared would revert to the State but would be used for special charitable purposes and, in particular, to meet the needs of the Jewish population.

Emergency Law 846/1946 makes provision for the issuing of a Royal Decree setting up the legal entity and determining the details of its functioning. To date, no such Decree has been issued. Repeated representations have been made by the Central Board of Jewish Communities and by the representatives of the European Division of the World Jewish Congress, urging that the above Decree be issued rapidly.

The question now arises of whether, first of all, such a Decree should be issued and whether the law issued by the Sophoulis Government should be implemented. If the law had not been issued and had not entered into force, the question might be raised, observed Mr Tsaldaris, of how expedient it is for the property of the Jews who have disappeared not to revert to the State in accordance with the provisions in force. However, bearing in mind that the law has been issued and is in force, he did not believe it to be expedient that the law should be rescinded today, in view primarily of the poor impression that such an act would make world-wide. In view of this, Mr Tsaldaris was of the opinion that the competent Ministers ought to take action as soon as possible for the rapid issuing of the executive decree implementing the law.

Furthermore, Mr Tsaldaris observed, particular care should be taken to protect the interests, on the one hand, of the State and, on the other, of those persons now established in property belonging to Jews, whether they are established as custodians or by virtue of lease agreements concluded with the custodians appointed during the occupation. To this end, he proposed the following measures:

1) The formation of a Board of Management of the Organisation, consisting

of civil servants and eminent Jews. The entire administration and management of the Organisation will be under the supervision of the State.

2)   Since, essentially, these estates constitute inherited property, they should be taxed according to the provisions of the relevant law.

3)   Protection of the persons now established in the immovable property of the missing Jews and establishment of the fact that these persons are tenants on the basis of the provisions in force concerning rent moratorium; whereupon the Cabinet

Decrees:

That it accepts the proposals of the Deputy Prime Minister and resolves:

1) That Emergency Law 846/1946 shall be implemented.

2) That a Ministerial Committee consisting of Messrs. Kanellopoulos, Hatzi-panou, Chelmis and Papathanassis shall be set up to carry out an investigation and submit proposals to the Cabinet in connection with the manner in which the proposals of the Deputy Prime Minister can be carried out, that is, matters connected with the operation of the Organisation, the taxation of the property and the protection of those persons established in property belonging to Jews, to prepare the Royal Decree which has to be issued in execution of the Law, and to propose all other measures necessary.

Having issued the present Act 525 for the above purpose.

——≺≡≻——

134

I. Koutsalexis, General Director, Ministry of Foreign Affairs, to the Permanent Greek Delegation, New York

report   Athens, 21 July 1947

To Mr Vice President

As you will know, by virtue of a recent decision of the Cabinet, the elaboration of a new Royal Decree in execution of Law 1946 abolishing the right of inheritance of the State of estates in abeyance of missing Jews, which will come into the possession of an organisation to be set up for the care and rehabilitation of Jews, has been entrusted to a committee of Ministers.

Mr Ekonomopoulos has been asked that the necessary instructions be given on the Prime Minister's behalf to the committee to expedite its task.

On this occasion, we consider advisable, taking into account the controversy created by Jewish organisations abroad and the Jewish Press on the above issue as well as on the question of the restitution of Jewish properties, that your delegations abroad inform international public opinion and organisations and eventually any governments interested in the matter of the beneficial measures taken by the Hellenic Governments in favour of the Jews since liberation.

Thus: (1) As early as November 1944, the first concern of the Greek State was to legislate (Law No. 2) the rescinding of the confiscation of Jewish properties in Old Greece and their restitution to their former owners. Later, Law No. 337 of 1945 extended this measure to Jewish properties in the region of the General Governance of Macedonia. Finally, a third law, No. 808 of 1945, supplemented the above two laws and regulated chiefly the issue of re-establishment of returning Jews in rented residences and payment by custodians or third-party occupants of these of the current value of missing items of movable property. By virtue of these laws, Jewish properties and rented accommodation have been returned and are being returned. In this connection, difficulties arising in practice are resolved by the judicial authorities.

(2) Another measure taken by the State in favour of Jews was the exemption, by a joint decision of the Ministers of Finance and of National Economy of 6 June 1945, of properties of Jewish subjects of hostile states from custody on condition that these reside in Greece and did not collaborate in any way with the enemy during the course of the occupation of the country. Thus, by extra-ordinary exemption, those who are Jews and enemy subjects are relieved of the consequences of their identity as such.

(3) Apart from the above measures of an economic nature, the Greek State took care by a new law of the year 1945 to reconstitute the Jewish Communities which were governed before the war by a law of the year 1921. Under the law in question, a Co-ordination and Consultative Council was set up for the co-ordination of the function of Jewish Communities and their single representation in dealing with the authorities, replacing the similar Council set up on liberation. A related measure is the grant, resolved upon by a decision of the Cabinet of 8.5.47, of eight million drachmas as aid of the Greek State during the current financial year for the educational and religious needs of the Jewish Communities.

Finally, (4) in the year 1946, a law was issued regulating the relations arising from the marriage of Jews, which the new civil code had made subject to common civil law. By a new law, these relations, which were formerly ruled by a law of 1914 recognising the competence of sacred Jewish law, were brought afresh under the latter.

The above measures of the Greek State are, we think, sufficiently illuminating as to the interest which it has shown and still shows in favour of those Jews residing within it, faithful as ever to the old Hellenic tradition of religious freedom and toleration towards the various religious and racial minorities which live under the shelter of the Greek State.

⟶⊰⊱⟵

<h1 style="text-align:center">135</h1>

P. Skeferis, Ambassador in Ankara, to the Greek Ministry of Foreign Affairs

Press report   Ankara, 25 July 1947

I have the honour of enclosing herewith for your information a copy of an interesting article published by the French Language Jewish newspaper of Constantinople *Journal d' Orient* of 10 July under the title 'What the Jews of Greece owe to their country' concerning the friendly attitude of the Greek people, shown both during the occupation and after the liberation, towards the Jews.

As you will observe, this article stresses the multiple assistance offered to the Jews by the Greek people, the new legislation ruling the fate of Jewish property in Greece after its liberation as well as the interest shown by the various post-War Greek Governments in the Greek Jews.

⟶⊰⊱⟵

<h1 style="text-align:center">136</h1>

M. Stassinopoulos, Political Counsellor, Military Command of the Dodecanese, to the Ministry of Foreign Affairs

letter   Rhodes, 18 October 1947

I have the honour to inform you that, before the War, there were about 2,000 Jews in the Dodecanese, of whom 1,800 lived in Rhodes and 200 in Cos. The Italians had granted these Jews minority status similar to that granted to the

Greeks and the Orthodox population (see attached Local Decree 53/1930). The Jewish Communities founded in Rhodes and Cos were never abolished despite the persecution of the Jews that took place during the War that ended recently, and thus were in existence, officially, during the period of British occupation of the islands. As can be seen from a letter dated 18 October 1945, a copy of which I attach hereto, it would appear that the British recognised the existence of this Community.

Today, there are about 60 Jews in Rhodes and one in Cos. However, they present both Communities as being in operation.

Please be so good as to inform me, as soon as possible, of the attitude which the Military Command should adopt towards these Communities.

⤛⊛⤜

137

*Rear-Admiral P. Ioannidis, Military Commander of the Dodecanese,
to the Ministry of Foreign Affairs*

report   Rhodes, 18 October 1947

In connection with your telegram No. 31321 of 1 July and further to my communication No. 39180 of today's date, I have the honour to report to you the following:

By two decisions of the former British Military Commander here, dated 15 March of this year, the management of the property belonging to missing Jews of Rhodes was assigned to Mr Soriano, President of the Jewish Community here (see attached copies). By a similar decision, the management of the properties of the missing Jews of Cos was assigned to Mr Menache, President of the Community there, which has only one member.

As can be seen from communication No. 55064/31 of 15 July from the British custodian of enemy property in the Dodecanese, most of these items of property were handed over to the Jews before I assumed the Military Command.

In view of this situation, I dispatched to you my telegram No. 18522 of 23 June, in reply to which I received your telegram No. 31321 informing me that these properties should be handed over to the Military Command. This was done for the remaining property which had not already been handed over to the Jews.

As I have been informed by the Jews themselves, the management of this property by the two Presidents referred to above is taking place in a manner tantamount to usurpation. A few days ago, indeed, a letter was received from Mr Soriano concerning the handing over of four safe deposit boxes containing valuables.

I would thus be grateful if you would have the kindness to provide me with instructions in this matter, in conjunction with the question of the legal position of the Jews in the Dodecanese.

More specifically, I would like to request you to be good enough to inform me, as soon as possible, if I should ask these persons to hand over the items of property which they have received and, if in the affirmative, please let me know whether I should apply the process of having the owners declared missing persons, in which case, in implementation of Law 2310/1920, there being no other heirs, the property will revert to the State, or whether Emergency Law 846 of 18/22 January 1946 concerning the abolition of the State's right of succession to the Jewish property should be extended to the Dodecanese.

I should like to take this opportunity of informing you that there are no destitute Jews in the Dodecanese.

Similarly, I would be grateful if you could inform me whether criminal proceedings are to be brought against the above managers in the event of it being ascertained that there have been financial irregularities in their management.

⇥⊛⊢

ATTACHMENT a TO 137*

J. Adam, British Custodian of Property, British Consul in Rhodes, to the Deputy Controller of Finance and Accounts of the Greek Military Command of the Dodecanese

letter   Rhodes, 15 July 1947

Thank you for your letter dated 9 July 1947 with reference to Property in custody belonging to unknown Jews.

The handover of Jewish Property has been in progress since March this year and although it is not yet complete most of the moveable property is already in the hands of the Jewish Community.

Actually the value of much of the moveable property is very small indeed and I do not think you would consider it worth your while to take the remaining items belonging to unknown Jews into your care. However, I will not hand over any more unknown property until we have discussed this matter further.

The method adopted with the handover of Jewish Property, much of which was in store houses, was to list the items in the stores, obtain a provisional receipt and hand the key of the stores to the Jewish Community. At the moment complete lists of Jewish property are under preparation and will be attached to hand over certificates and signatures obtained in due course.

Thus it will be appreciated that although the handover is not completed and the accounts still open, the majority of the moveable property is already out of my hands.

ATTACHMENT b TO 137

I. Stephanou, Director, Ministry of Foreign Affairs, to the Ministry of Finance

document   Athens, 6 December 1947

We have the honour to dispatch to you, attached hereto, a copy of communication No. 39289 dated 18 October 1947 from the Military Administration of the Dodecanese, together with the documents attached to it, in connection with the abandoned Jewish property of the Dodecanese, for your information.

We would like to inform you in this respect that we have already instructed by telegram the Military Administration in Rhodes that in the event of the complaints against the Presidents of the Jewish Communities of having usurped the said property being proved to be grounded in fact, they are to be deprived of the management of the property and provisionally replaced in their task. Otherwise, they are to be permitted to continue as managers of the property in their hands on a provisional basis, until the publication of the Decree of Law 846/18-22 January 1946.

ATTACHMENT c TO 137*

Proclamation of the British Brigadier Parker

Rhodes, 15 March 1947

We, Arthur Stanley Parker, OBE, Brigadier, hereby proclaim the following:
To Article 7 of Proclamation No. 5 concerning the custody of property, a power numbered (x) shall be added to the powers of the custodian listed as (i) to (ix): "Subsequent to such guarantee he may, as he sees fit, entrust the care and management of any property to any responsible person in a highly favourable position to manage the property to the benefit of the owner".

⟶⟡⟵

ATTACHMENT d TO 137

E. Soriano, President of the Jewish Community

authorisation   Rhodes, 15 March 1947

Jewish property

It is hereby announced that Mr Elias Soriano, President of the Jewish Community of Rhodes, has been authorised by the Custodian of Property of Article 7 (x) of Proclamation No. 5 concerning the custody of property, as modified by Proclamation No. 43 concerning the custody of property (amendment) to take under his supervision and manage henceforth any Jewish movable or immovable property abandoned in Rhodes by missing Jews and which, for their benefit, is in the custody of the Custodian of Enemy Property.

⟶⟡⟵

ATTACHMENT e TO 137

Elias Soriano, President of the Jewish Community of Rhodes, to the Directorate of the Tax Office of the Military Command of the Dodecanese

application   Rhodes, [illegible] March 1947

Subject: granting of permission for the return of four safe-deposit boxes

I, the undersigned, Elias Soriano, President of the Jewish Community of Rhodes, have the honour to request the above Directorate to be kind enough to permit me to take delivery of the four (4) safe deposit boxes located with it which were abandoned there by Jews deported by the Germans.

ATTACHMENT f TO 137*

A. Hasson to T. Chryssanthopoulos, Greek Military Command of the Dodecanese

letter   Rhodes,15 October 1947

Messieurs,

Avec la présente, je viens vous informer que bien qu' ayant été nommé par l' Administration Britannique, membre de la Communauté Israélite, je n' ai jamais participé à l' Administration de la susdite Communauté.

De plus je tiens à vous informer que un mois à peine c'était écoulé depuis le jour où j' avais été membre de la susdite Communauté, que par écrit j' ai notifié Président Mr Soriano que je me démettais de ma charge.

Veuillez bien en prendre note, et agréer, Messieurs, l' expression de ma considération distinguée.

138

Government Gazette

Athens, 15 October 1947

Ministerial Decision No. 265716/706 by D. Chelmis, concerning the appointment of the Central Board of Jewish Communities as Manager of abandoned Jewish property [*sic*]

Having taken into consideration: a) the provisions of Article 5 of Law 808/1945 'concerning the supplementation of Compulsory Laws 2/1944 and 367/1945', b) the provisions of Article 5 of Emergency Law 367/1945 'concerning the re-establishment of the Jewish Communities', c) the provision of the single article of Emergency Law 846/1946 'concerning the abolition of the State's right of inheritance on abandoned Jewish property', d) communication No. 1590/19.9.47 from the Central Jewish Council for Co-ordination and Consultation, and e) the expert opinion granting approval dated 1.10.47 of the Central Department for the Management of Jewish Property, we hereby decree:

That we appoint the Central Jewish Council for Co-ordination and Consultation as provisional manager of the abandoned Jewish property which, by virtue of the provision contained in the single article of Emergency Law 846/46, passed to the Foundation for the care and rehabilitation of the Jews of Greece provided for in that law, until the issuing of the executive Decree provided for in the said law setting up the Foundation in question.

In accordance with the above, the management of the abandoned Jewish property will be exercised in accord with the provisions of the legislation in force and of the relevant ministerial decisions and will be subject to the supervision of the Central Department for the Management of Jewish Property and of the Consultative Committee set up by virtue of Decision No. 788/1945, which will advise on all matters arising from the exercise of that management.

In connection with those persons established, for whatever reason, on 30 September 1946 in Jewish property, management is hereby assigned to the Central Jewish Council for Co-ordination and Consultation, which, however, shall not be entitled to evict or in any other manner eject those persons without a previous decision of the above Consultative Committee unless there is a delay in rent or where the protection of a moratorium has been lifted.

Thessaloniki 1947. Following his release from the Nazi concentration camps, Dr Albert Menache returned to Thessaloniki and was elected President of the Jewish Community. Around 1950, he migrated to the United States, where he died in 1991. Archive of the Jewish Community of Thessaloniki, donated by Isaac Menache (Athens) and David Amir (Israel).

139

I. Karmiris, General Director of Religious Affairs, Ministry of Education, to the Ministry of Foreign Affairs

report   Athens, 24 January 1948

In reply to your communication No. 49769/30.12.47 to the Ministries of the Interior and Finance, to which a copy was forwarded to us, we have the honour to inform you that, in accordance with Article 6, para. 2 of Law 367/1945 'concerning the restoration of the Jewish Communities', the Central Board of Jewish Communities is obliged, as soon as the elected Boards of Management of the Jewish Communities are formed, to convene a conference of their representatives in Athens and submit to them an account of its activities, after which the Council shall be deemed to have dissolved. The same council of representatives of the Jewish Communities may propose to the Ministry of Religious Affairs and Education the foundation of a Union of Jewish Communities of Greece to co-ordinate their common goals in accordance with the law and to ensure the united representation of the Communities.

The elected Boards of Management have now been formed and the above conference is expected to convene and submit to the Ministry a proposal for the amendment of Law 367. However, until the amendment of the above Law, we have no objection whatever to the extension of the Law in question to the Dodecanese.

It should be noted that, in accordance with Law 2456/1920, Article 1, Jewish Communities recognised as legal persons under public law may function in those towns and cities in the Kingdom which have permanent populations of at least twenty (20) Jewish families, by Royal Decree.

Furthermore, in accordance with Emergency Law 367/1945, Article 3, when at the time of publication of the Law the number of Jewish families remaining in a town or city has fallen below the figure of 20 required by Law 2456/1920, Article 1, for the recognition of a Jewish Community, such Communities shall be deemed to have become inactive. The Ministry of Religious Affairs and Education appoints a committee of three or five members, on the proposal of the competent Prefect or of the Central Board of Jewish Communities, to manage the affairs and interests of the Community.

I40

The Military Command of the Dodecanese to the Ministry of Foreign Affairs

telegram   Rhodes, 26 January 1948

With reference to your telegram No. 45344 of 7 January and your communication No. 49769 of 30 December last, and further to my communications Nos 39180, 39289, 49600 and 52053, I have the honour to inform you that during his stay here a few days ago, Mr Miner, Counsellor to the American Embassy in Athens, expressed his surprise over the fact that Greece had taken the decision to waive, in favour of the Jewish Communities, its rights on the property of Jewish hostages without heirs who have disappeared, particularly at a time of such economic difficulties for the country.

I4I[*]

Newspaper article from the New York Times

31 January 1948

Title: Unclaimed Property is Sought for Jews

Paris. January 30. Distribution of unclaimed and uninherited Jewish property among surviving European Jews was recommended here today by Milton Winn, New York lawyer, who has just completed a tour of Turkey, Greece and Czechoslovakia for the American Jewish Committee.

Mr Winn pointed to recent Greek legislation as a model to be used in every country once occupied by the Nazis. The Greek Government has agreed to turn over uninherited Jewish property to a special foundation that in turn will use any profits from the exploitation of such property to aid Greek Jews. He explained that the Greek law will go into effect as soon as a royal decree creates an administration foundation. Premier Themistocles Sophoulis, Mr Winn said, had given him his "personal assurance and guarantee" that the decree would be issued shortly.

The American Jewish Committee envoy pointed out that redistribution of unclaimed Jewish property to Europe's few remaining Jews would do no more than give them a start towards "again becoming a self-supporting group of people".

Mr Winn said that although there were some local problems, restitution of Jewish property was going along in all liberated countries except in the Soviet Zone because the "Russians don't believe in the principle of the restitution of private property".

⊷⊶

142*

Central Jewish Documentation in Paris

[illegible] March 1948

Le Colonel Vitale préside la séance.

Le Président - Mesdames, Messieurs,

J' ai l' honneur d' ouvrir la 3ème séance du Congrès.
La parole est au Représentant de la Grèce.

I. Schneersohn. - Je demande un moment pour vous dire que nous avons reçu un télégramme de l' YIVO qui nous salue et nous envoit ses meilleurs voeux.

Je vous propose de répondre à l' YIVO par un télégramme ainsi conçu:

"Conférence Européenne Adresse Yivo Salutations Cordiales Exemple Votre Illustre Institut Guidera Vos Travaux et Rendra Plus Etroits Liens Notre Amitié".

M. Moissis donne lecture de son rapport.

Le Président. - Nous remercions M. Asher Moissis pour son très intéressant rapport très douloureux mais qui nous donne une idée des possibilités de la vie juive en Grèce, de la reconstruction juive.

Nous prions M. Gottgarstein de donner une traduction en yiddish du rapport de M. Moissis.

Le Président. - Me Livian désire poser une question à M. Moissis.

Me Livian. - Avant de poser une question à M. Moissis, le Centre de Documentation me charge de saluer la présence parmi nous de Mr David Jeroham, Président du Consistoire Juif en Bulgarie, qui vient d' arriver et que nous n'espérions plus voir.

M. Jeroham. -De la part du Consistoire Juif de Bulgarie et de tous les Juifs de Bulgarie, c'est-à-dire de 50,000 personnes, je vous salue et j' espère faire un bon travail en France.

Me Livian.-Je voudrais demander de M. Moissis qui nous a fait un exposé si éloquent, si nourri de chiffres, si dans la politique de répression des Allemands si sanglante, il s'est trouvé beaucoup de collaborateurs grecs qui les ont aidés dans leur tâche.

M. Moissis.-Comme dans tous les pays, il y avait certainement en Grèce des grecs qui se sont mis à la disposition des autorités allemandes. Ces grecs n'ont pas seulement collaboré avec les Allemands contre les juifs, mais contre toute la population grecque. Ils étaient de vrais collaborateurs.

Malheureusement, parmi les collaborateurs, il y a eu aussi des juifs, des juifs traîtres, qui ont été condamnés à mort par la Cour Martiale hellénique. Le Conseil Central fait tous ses efforts pour faire exécuter ses traîtres car la population juive se montre très irritée.

On ne peut pas dire que la population hellénique a montré des dispositions défavorables à l' égard des Juifs, tout au contraire. S' il y a eu 10,500 Juifs sauvés en Grèce il faut l' attribuer à l' aide de la population hellénique, principalement à l' aide de l' église Orthodoxe. Je dois signaler d' une manière spéciale l' aide et le concours qui nous ont été offerts par l' Archevêque Damaskinos qui a été régent quelques mois après la Libération, d' une manière générale, on peut affirmer que la population hellène [sic] a beaucoup contribué à sauver des Juifs de Grèce.

M.Schneersohn.-Je voudrais demander s' il y a eu des camps de concentration et quelle en était l' origine.

M. Moissis.-Les Allemands ont employé des méthodes différentes de déportation et de persécution en Grèce qui ont été divisées en deux catégories; la première persécution a eu lieu à Salonique et dans la Grèce du Nord en mars 1943. A ce moment-lá, le reste du pays était occupé par les autorités italiennes et celles-ci ne permettaient pas aux Allemands de mettre en pratique leurs méthodes de persécution; au contraire, les autorités italiennes de la Grèce du sud, où je me trouvais moi-même, nous ont beaucoup aidé et les Allemands n' ont pas appliqué les mêmes méthodes.

A Salonique, les Juifs ont été rassemblés dans des camps de concentration et envoyés en Pologne en 18 convois successifs.

Ces méthodes n'ont pas été appliquées dans le reste du pays.

Après la capitulation de l' Italie, les Allemands ont pris possession de toute la Grèce et ont immédiatement mis en application le système des persécutions des Juifs. Dans diverses villes juives on a rammassé en une journée, celle du 24 mars 1944, un nombre considérable de Juifs qui ont été déportés immédiatement.

La méthode de l' étoile jaune n' a pas été appliquée en Grèce; au contraire, les Allemands ont permis aux Juifs de vivre tranquillement et c'est au dernier moment qu' ils nous ont déporté.

M. Jeroham.-Je vais poser une première question à M. Moissis.

Les Juifs de Grèce sont près des Juifs de Bulgarie et pour nous il est très important de savoir quelle est la situation des Juifs en Grèce. Ils sont revenus 10,000 et je voudrais savoir quelle est la situation de ces 10.000 personnes, car cela peut avoir une influence en Bulgarie.

2ème question.-En Bulgarie, il y a des diplomates Juifs, des fonctionnaires et je voudrais connaître l' attitude du Gouvernement hellénique envers les Juifs et je voudrais savoir s' il y a des diplomates, des employés dans les Ministères et de hauts fonctionnaires .....[*sic*].

M. Cheftel.- Pour faciliter la tâche de M. Moissis, je vais poser une question dans le même ordre que celle posée par M. Jeroham: l' attitude hellénique vis-à-vis des Juifs sous l' occupation qui est tout à fait dans les traditions glorieuses de la Grèce.

M. Moissis nous a dit également que le Gouvernement Hellénique était le premier gouvernement du monde qui s' est préoccupé du sort des biens en déshérance et qui a renoncé aux droits de l' état hellénique sur ces biens au profit des victimes des poliations et des massacres. Il nous a dit que cette loi devait être mise en application par un décret et comme en France nous sommes devant une situation semblable et qu' un Séquestre est à l' ordre du jour, je voudrais poser la question: comment fonctionne cette loi, ce qui a été réalisé et comment on a mis ce mécanisme en application.

Cette réponse sera également la réponse concernant la situation des 10.000 Juifs rescapés puisque ce Séquestre était précisément destiné à la reconstruction de l' économie des rescapés Juifs.

M. Gottfarstein traduit en français une intervention de M.Wulf, faite en yiddish.

M. Wulf.-Déclare qu' il serait préférable de ne pas toucher à ces questions puisqu' elles ne sont pas en rapport directe avec les préoccupations de notre Conférence et de se limiter à notre sujet principal.

M. Jeroham.-Je déclare ne pas faire de politique, ce qu' il nous intéresse, c'est ce qui se passe dans les Balkans, nous vivons ensemble et la vie des Juifs en Grèce nous intéresse. Nous voulons connaître la situations des Juifs en Grèce et ceci à titre de renseignement.

Nous voulons au cours de cette Conférence, profiter de la présence du Président du Consistoire de Grèce, pour savoir comment on vit à présent.

M. Moissis.-Je réponds avec empressement et avec enthousiasme à toutes les questions qui m' ont été posées et qui démontrent l' intérêt que le judaïsme européen a pour mon propre pays et pour le judaïsme de Grèce.

En Grèce, il n' y a jamais eu d' antisémitisme. Le peuple hellène [*sic*] est un peuple libéral; l' antisémitisme est un mot qui n' a pas cours en Grèce et nous n' avons jamais connu de pogromes ni discrimination. La législation hellénique a toujours été libérale et progressive, même pendant la période de l' occupation, alors que le pays était administré par les gouvernements Quisling. Aucune mesure de discrimination n' a été prise contre la population juive, alors qu' en Bulgarie les mêmes gouvernements fascistes ont pris des mesures catastrophiques contre les Juifs de Bulgarie.

Les institutions helléniques pendant l' occupation ont été ouvertes à l' élément juif. Malgré la pression exercée par les Allemands, le barreau n' a jamais voulu faire effacer de ses listes le nom des avocats juifs; l' Association des médecins, des pharmaciens, la Chambre de Commerce, malgré l' ordre des occupants, n' a jamais fait de discrimination de juifs et n' a pas obéi. Ceci pour montrer, en réalité, les sentiments et l' esprit libéral et philosémite qui prédominaient parmi les éléments chrétiens de la population hellénique.

En ce qui concerne la situation actuelle économique, morale et sociale, il est certain que la guerre et la persécution nous ont beaucoup affectées. Comme je viens de vous le dire, il ne reste presque plus rien de notre fortune immobilière; pourtant la première loi qui a été promulguée par le gouvernement hellénique dès la libération, a été la restitution des biens juifs. Mais vous devez savoir que même pendant l' occupation et la persécution, nous n' avons jamais été privés légalement de nos droits comme il en a été dans d' autres pays. Les biens juifs n' ont pas été confisqués au point de vue légal, et les Juifs en sont toujours restés propriétaires.

C'est seulement après la libération qu' une loi nous a permis de reprendre possession de nos biens qui étaient entre les mains de non-Juifs.

Que notre situation économique ait été affectée, ceci est tout naturel car de 75,000 Juifs que nous étions, nous sommes restés 10,000 et notre fortune est passée entre les mains des traîtres. Grâce à l' appui que nous recevons du Gouvernement et des organismes Juifs à l' étranger et principalement du JOINT, la vie économique juive commence à se reconstituer.

Le nombre des Juifs qui reçoivent des subsides du JOINT est de plus en plus restreint, ce qui démontre que la situation s' améliore peu à peu.

Au point de vue général et communal des Institutions, dans mon rapport, je vous ai déclaré que nous espérions, grâce à la création de l' Institution d' assistance et de restauration, que les organismes philanthropiques pourront fonctionner sans avoir besoin de l' aide de l' étranger.

Quant aux possibilités de l' accès aux fonctions publiques il n' y a jamais eu d' obstacles. Il y a maintenant en Grèce un Conseiller Juif à la Cour d' Appel, très estimé par toute la population, des avocats juifs, je suis moi-même avocat à la Cour de Cassation. Nous avions de professeurs juifs, malheureusement ils ont été exterminés et nous avions des députés juifs mais le nombre de la population juive ne nous permet pas d' être représentés au parlement hellénique de facto au sein des éléments prédominants.

Je vous ai déjà dit que la Grèce a été le premier pays qui a reconnu le principe des biens juifs abandonnés, c' est-à-dire en déshérance par suite à la persécution raciale, que ces biens devaient servir en faveur de la reconstruction de la vie juive.

Je me rappelle de la déclaration qui m' a été faite par le Général Plastiras, en mars 1945, quelques mois après la libération quand j'ai sollicité des mesures en faveur des fortunes juives. Il m' a déclaré textuellement: L' Etat grec est un état pauvre, mais un état honnête et il ne voudra jamais profiter de l' extermination de ses citoyens juifs pour enrichir le Trésor public.

Comme le gouvernement de cette époque a hésité à promulguer une loi pour transférer tous ces biens, qui appartenaient à l' état d' après la législation commune, aux juifs, nous nous sommes adressés à tous les partis politiques parce qu' il n' y avait pas de parlement en Grèce et que le pouvoir législatif était exercé par le gouvernement qui était le seul à pouvoir décider, nous nous sommes adressés à tous les chefs des partis politiques pour obtenir leur consentement.

Tous, sans exception, depuis l' extrême gauche jusqu'à l' extrême droite ont donné au Conseil Central une déclaration écrite donnant leur accord pour la promulgation d' une telle loi.

En réalité, cette loi a été promulguée par le gouvernement Sophoulis en janvier 1946, loi 846 par laquelle l' état hellénique se désistait de ses droits d' héritage sur les fortunes juives en déshérance en faveur de l' Institution juive appropriée.

Je vous ai dit que jusqu' à ces derniers mois le décret exécutoire de cette loi n' a pas été promulgué, ce n' est pas parce que le Gouvernement l' avait réprouvé, mais parce qu' il craignait que l' Institution juive, dès qu' elle serait créée, exigerait l' expulsion des immeubles juifs de tous les Grecs qui y étaient installés, soit arbitrairement, soit par suite de réquisitions ordonnées par les autorités allemandes ou helléniques.

Une situation anormale au point de vue social aurait été créée pour le Gouvernement.

Le Conseil Central a fait une déclaration au Gouvernement disant que l' Institution Juive reconnaitrait comme locataires légaux tous ces occupants à condition qu' ils paient un loyer. A la suite de cette déclaration, le Gouvernement a consenti à passer immédiatement la jouissance de tous ces biens au Conseil Central et maintenant ce dernier est l' administrateur légal de tous ces biens.

Je crois qu' après l' Italie, c' est le seul pays où le Conseil Central Juif administre les fortunes juives abandonnées.

J' espère que d' ici quelques semaines toutes les formalités techniques seront terminées et que le décret exécutoire de la loi 846 sera promulgué. Nous serons alors propriétaires et aurons la disposition des biens juifs abandonnés.

M. Hosiassion.-Vous avez dit que l' Eglise Orthodoxe avait beaucoup aidé les Juifs sous l' occupation. Est-ce que cette dernière agissant en tant qu' Institution ou le faisait-elle à titre individuel.

M. Moissis.- Quelques jours avant la persécution décretée par les Allemands, l' Archevêque Damaskinos avait lancé une circulaire à toutes les églises et à tous les monastères chrétiens orthodoxes du pays, les exhortait à donner leur aide et leur concours aux Juifs pour pouvoir les sauver des persécutions allemandes. C'est-à-dire qu' il ne s' agissait pas d' un acte à caractère individuel, mais d' un geste organisé de la part du chef de l' Eglise Orthodoxe.

143

Information bulletin

Athens, 9 April 1948

Yesterday, 9 April 1948, the Jews of the community here held a day of mourning to mark the anniversary of the arrest by the Germans and elimination of the Jews of Athens. All the Jewish shops and offices were closed all day.

In the morning, many Jews who were related to those in Germany made their way to the cemetery. At 16.15, a memorial service was conducted in the Synagogue at 5 Melidoni St. The service was attended by Athens Chief Rabbi Schreiber, Athens Rabbi Barzilai, Mr Kanaris Konstantinis, President of the Central Board of Jewish Communities, the Community Council (with the exception of its President, Mr Vital, who was indisposed), the Director of the Palestine Migration Bureau, Mr Salomon Bitti, and approximately 600 people.

After the memorial service, the congregation was addressed by Kanaris Konstantinis, President of the Central Board of Jewish Communities, who referred to the details of the capture and elimination of his co-religionists during the Occupation.

He then thanked the Greek Christians who, at the risk of their own lives, gave all possible help to the Jews. Such Jews as survived have the Greeks to thank for it.

The congregation was then addressed by Samouil Cohen, member of the Central Board of Jewish Communities, who listed the losses sustained by the Jewish people as a result of the German persecution. He said that of the Jews in Greece, 65,000 had been exterminated, while 6,000,000 Jews had been put to death in Europe as a whole. He then stated that after mourning their dead, the thoughts of all Jews turned towards Palestine, where the Jews, as true descendants of the Maccabees, were fighting not to make conquests but to win back the land of their fathers.

Many Jews from Greece are fighting in the front line of the battle in Palestine and all the Jews of Europe are fighting for the same purpose and under the same banner. Mr Cohen ended by stating that we must all be ready to do our duty when the voice of our homeland calls, as we have fought for Greece, our adopted land, in various wars.

Similarly, we have received information to the effect that a collection was taken up among a small circle of members of the Jewish community here for the erection of a monument to the missing Jews of Greece. The collection realised a sum of over 10,000,000 drachmas.

⇥⊷⇤

144

V. Dendramis, Ambassador in Washington, to the Greek Ministry of Foreign Affairs

report   Washington, 12 April 1948

I have the honour to inform you that Mrs Raie Canetti, former President of the Jewish Organisation Béne Bérith Women's Chapter in Greece, when addressing the Supreme Council of the Béne Bérith Women's Chapter in Washington on 6 April stated that she had visited Athens in 1946. The Jews were starving and dressed in rags. Some of them had lost as many as 25 or 30 family members in the Nazi death chambers. Systematic care for the survivors was now beginning to produce results. However, the conditions of the market in Greece are most irregular. Without foreign aid, the Greek people would not be alive today. The Greeks are aware of the American contribution and appreciate it, said Mrs Canetti, but it would be useful if the Americans could help with distributing the supplies.

Mrs Canetti was responsible for organising the Women's Chapter of Béne Bérith in Athens in 1925. She prepared the school curriculum for Jewish children, set up summer camps which evolved into a permanent children's home, established a vocational school, etc. In her speech Mrs Canetti noted that all these works had been destroyed by the Germans during the occupation.

145

K. Konstantinis, President, Central Board of Jewish Communities, to the Prime Minister and Deputy Prime Minister

letter   Athens, 17 April 1948

We have the honour to return to the question of the publication of the Executive Decree of Law 846 'concerning the establishment of an organisation to care for and rehabilitate the Greek Jews who have survived the persecution'.

A considerable time ago, we were informed that the delay in publishing the Decree in question was the result of the wish of the Government to secure the property in Palestine of a Greek citizen.

Although we believe that no connection should be made between that instance and the question of the abandoned Jewish properties being handed over for the purpose of caring for and rehabilitating the Greeks of the Jewish religion who fell victims to the most extensive and most brutal persecution in history, our Council undertook to settle the matter, so as not to create difficulties for the Government, and did what it could to resolve the question.

Unfortunately, and much to our regret, all the efforts made by us proved to be in vain as a result of the chaotic situation prevailing in Palestine today.

In view of this, and in order to bring about the publication of the said Decree – which the surviving Jews of Greece await with real anguish, in the hope that they will be able to recover from the moral and economic degradation to which the terrible persecution has doomed them – our Council would like to offer to secure the immovable property in Palestine of the said Greek citizen with abandoned Jewish property in Greece of an equal value from the property being handed over to the Organisation of Law 846. This property will be transferred to the person in question on his application if, within a period of time determined by him or by the Government, the affair concerning him in Palestine has not been settled.

In the hope that this proposal will be accepted in the spirit of paternal care towards the Jews of Greece in their sufferings that has distinguished you, and that you will subsequently be good enough to issue the appropriate instructions for the publication of the Royal Decree of Law 846, which has already been approved.

◆

146

K. Konstantinis, President, Central Board of Jewish Communities, to the Ministry of Foreign Affairs

list   Athens, 26 April 1948

Subsequent to our verbal agreement with you and in execution of the relevant verbal instructions, we have the honour to submit by the present a detailed list of the Jewish gold looted by the Germans (in coin and bullion only), as stated in 174 solemn statements, copies of which have already been passed to you.

The attached list, in duplicate and with translations into French and English, contains the total sums claimed by the victims of the looting themselves or by their lawful heirs or representatives.

Gold sovereigns	55,683 pieces
Gold five-pound pieces	44
Gold half-sovereigns	4
Gold Turkish pounds	9,749
Double Turkish pounds	370
Turkish five-pound pieces	244
French gold twenty-franc pieces	8,320
French gold ten-franc pieces	157
Gold dollars	2,271
Gold five-dollar pieces	1
Gold florins	443
Austrian florins	42
Italian and Belgian gold twenty-franc pieces	32
Miscellaneous gold coins	1,143
Gold bullion	6,943 drams

The above amounts do not include those covered by a further 55 affidavits from Jews; these sums have been declared and claimed (in coin and bullion), but copies have not yet been delivered to us to allow the compilation of a complete list.

Please be so good as to take action for the return to us of the remaining 55 copies of statements, so as to allow the relevant work to be carried out rapidly.

We would like to draw your attention also to our communication No. 504/13.4.48, which states precisely the amount of gold claimed by our Council and by the various Jews from whom it was stolen.

We return to you the copies of 174 affidavits delivered to us.

⋙⋘

ATTACHMENT TO 146

K. Konstantinis, President, Central Board of Jewish Communities, to the Ministry of Foreign Affairs

letter   1 [partly illegible] April 1948

With reference to our communications Nos. 940 and 941 of 3 May 1946 and further to our communication Nos. 119/26.1.48, 190/5.2.48, 233/13.2.48 and 317/25.2.48, by which we submitted to you, in translation, affidavits by Jews laying claim to gold looted by the Germans, we have the honour to inform you of the following.

In our communication No. 941/3.5.46, we informed you that, according to the calculations of our Council, the Germans seized from the Jews gold in coin and bullion of a total value of approximately 1,700,000 (one million seven hundred thousand) gold sovereigns. Against this value, affidavits claiming 133,906 sovereigns had been submitted to you.

Now, the statements returned to you in translation contain claims for an amount slightly smaller than the above 133,096 sovereigns, as a result of the fact that the statements returned do not include those of certain Jews who are resident abroad and of others who were unable to provide the relevant translation.

Regardless of this, however, the sum claimed remains as it was, that is, 133,096 sovereigns.

Consequently, the balance of the 1,700,000 sovereigns, amounting to 1,566,904 (one million five hundred and sixty six thousand nine hundred and four) sovereigns, is claimed by our Council since it belonged to intestate Jews who were robbed and exterminated, leaving no heirs. This is by virtue, on the one hand, of Emergency Law 846/46, since these estates passed to the special legal person to be set up to care for and rehabilitate the Jews, and, on the other hand, of Emergency

Law 367/45 and Decision No. 265716/706/15.10.47 of the Minister of Finance, by which the management of abandoned Jewish property was assigned to us until the publication of the Royal Decree putting into effect Emergency Law 846, as above.

Lastly, we would like to inform you that statements laying claim to the stolen gold could not be submitted by the Jews who disappeared in this manner, since they died without leaving any heirs.

147

K. Konstantinis, President, Central Board of Jewish Communities, to the Ministry of Foreign Affairs

list   Athens, 10 May 1948

Further to our communication No. 701 of 26 April, we have the honour to submit to you supplementary lists showing the gold belonging to Jews (in coin and bullion) looted by the Germans in accordance with a further 49 affidavits from these Jews.

Consequently, the grand total of the sums claimed by these Jews is as follows:

Gold sovereigns	74,467 pieces
Gold five-pound pieces	44
Gold half-sovereigns	4
Gold Turkish pounds	11,048
Double Turkish pounds	383
Turkish five-pound pieces	249
French gold twenty-franc pieces	11,650
French gold ten-franc pieces	57
Gold dollars	2,321
Gold five-dollar pieces	1
Gold florins	643
Austrian florins	48
Italian and Belgian gold twenty-franc pieces	32
Miscellaneous gold coins	2,743
Gold bullion	15,613 drams

We return to you the above 49 affidavits.

148*

K. Konstantinis, President, Central Board of the Jewish
Communities of Greece, to the Ministry of Foreign Affairs

solemn statement   Athens, 12 May 1948

The Central Board of the Jewish Communities of Greece, established in Athens lawfully representing the entirety of the Jews established in Greece, hereby responsibly confirms to the Hellenic Ministry of Foreign Affairs that the total gold (in different gold coins and gold in bars) which was seized and taken away by the Germans from co-religionists, who were abducted in large numbers from Greece and who were killed and massacred in Germany and Poland, and this while Greece was under German occupation, was calculated by us on well-founded data and according to our most moderate calculations as amounting to the sum of gold pounds (sterling) 1,700,000 approximately.

Unfortunately, on account of the disappearance of the total number of our co-religionists abducted and the entirely arbitrary and violent way in which the gold possessed by them was taken, it has been impossible, as this can be readily understood, to gather precise and detailed data for the compilation on the basis of same of detailed and analytical statements of the gold taken away from each particular person abducted and massacred, as we have been able to do for our very few co-religionists who survived, for whom we have submitted, as far as possible, detailed statements and testimonials.

In view of the fact that the Greek Government, by Compulsory Law No. 846 of 22 January 1946, waived the hereditary rights of the Hellenic State to the estates of the victims of the race persecution launched by the Germans, who died without leaving heirs by testament or next of kin in intestacy as their heirs, in favour of a Legal Body to be formed by virtue of a Royal Decree for the purpose of relieving and assisting the Jews of Greece to settle down again, whereas, furthermore, our Council was entrusted, by virtue of Article 5, para. 2, of Compulsory Law 367/45 and by Decision No. 265716/706/15.10.47 of the Minister of Finance, with the task of gathering and preserving the estates abandoned by the Jews, and were, likewise, entrusted with the temporary administration of such estates until such time as the Executive Decree establishing the above Institution, foreseen by Compulsory Law 846/46, is promulgated, we claim, in our aforesaid capacity, the amount in Drachmas representing the balance of pounds gold (sterling) 1,566,904 (which remains from the total sum of gold pounds (sterling) 1,700,000 after deduction of the sum of pounds gold (sterling) 133.096, for which sum we have already submitted the aforesaid detailed statements) and we recognize, without reserve, that the whole of the said gold belongs, of right, to the Greek Government, according to the Greek legislation existing on the matter many years ago.

In any case, on the basis of the information we have been able to gather in this connection, from the total gold possessed by our co-religionists, calculated as above at pounds gold (sterling) 1,700,000, part was deposited in the year 1936 in safes with Banks, and had been declared at the time by the owners and had been enlisted out by the State Committee, instituted for this purpose by Compulsory Laws 33, 257 and 309 of the year 1936, as can be ascertained from the official data in the possession of the competent Service of the State General Accounts Office.

149*

Rabbi Abraham Schreiber, Chief Rabbi of Greece, to V. Dendramis, Greek Ambassador in Washington.

letter   May 28, 1948

I am happy to send you a copy of the article (and its translation) about me which appeared in the important Jewish newspaper, *Morning Journal.*

The editor requested of me a report on the Jewish comunity of Greece, and the enclosed article is the interview which I granted them.

"Chief Rabbi of Greece Reports on Greek Jewish Community"

A report on the present Jewish community of Greece, as well as of the unusually fine treatment of Greek Jews by the government and the people, was rendered yesterday to the *Morning Journal* by a very distinguished guest from that country, who arrived here a few days ago for a short visit.

The visitor is Rabbi Abraham Sofer-Schreiber, Chief Rabbi of Greece. He is a scion of a distinguished family and is himself one of the great scholars of this generation. He is the son of the renowned Rabbi Simeon Sofer, and in direct line of descent from Rabbi Abraham Sofer and Rabbi Moses Sofer.

Rabbi Abraham Sofer-Schreiber, who served as the spiritual leader of the

Jewish community of Gorizia, Italy, published with his annotations seven volumes of Rabbi Menachem Meiri's "Beth Ha Bhirah" and was one of the editors of the "Otzar Ha-Poskin". He is also author of a book of important compilations on the Prophets and the Hagiographa.

Rabbi Sofer-Schreiber settled in Palestine eight years ago. When the request came for help to reorganize the Jewish community of Greece, which consisted of 12,000 souls, he was persuaded by Rabbi Herzog, Chief Rabbi of Palestine, to assume this holy obligation. Rabbi Sofer-Schreiber has been living in Athens, Greece, for the last six months and has already done much to reorganize the religious life of Greek Jewry and to reestablish the institutions necessary for that purpose.

He has during that time visited fifteen communities and has devoted himself to the organization of synagogues and schools, the establishment of a system of ritual slaughter, and the organization of youth study groups.

To establish the education system upon a solid foundation, Rabbi Sofer-Schreiber is now arranging for ten Israeli teachers to come to Greece.

Rabbi Sofer-Schreiber also reported that he is negotiating with the Greek Government concerning the return to the Jewish Community of property of Jews who lost their lives during the Nazi occupation of Greece. The Greek Government is ready to return these properties to the Jewish community, and the transfer is awaiting only a final decree, which he feels sure will be forthcoming in the very near future.

Rabbi Sofer-Schreiber spoke in highest terms of the fine and friendly treatment of the Jewish community by the Greek Government and the Greek People.

He particularly stressed the heroism and selflessness of the Greek people in saving Jews from the hands of the Nazis. The remnant of Israel which is now left in Greece largely owes its existence to the Greek People, which hid and cared for large numbers of Jews during the Nazi occupation. The Church too, protected many Jews, and was responsible for the saving of many Jewish lives.

Before the war the Jewish community of Greece consisted of over 65,000 souls, about 50,000 of them living in Salonika. All that remains of this community is 12,000. Rabbi Sofer-Schreiber's spiritual leadership served to bring hope and faith into the lives of this remnant.

During his brief visit in America, Rabbi Sofer-Schreiber will confer with the Joint Distribution Committee and other Jewish agencies with a view towards strengthening the new Jewish community of Greece.

150

K. Korozos, Minister of Northern Greece, to the Sub-Ministry of the Press and Information

report   Thessaloniki, 24 December 1948

The settlement of Jews in Thessaloniki dates back to pre-Christian times, since St Paul preached in the synagogue there on three Sabbaths. During the seventh and eighth centuries, the Jews began to spread throughout the Balkans. In the eleventh century, there was a Jewish community in Thessaloniki, as witnessed by a letter discovered in Cairo stating that the Jewish colony had been relieved of the payment of tax by the Emperor Alexios Comnenos and the Patriarch of Constantinople. In 1173, the Jewish traveller Benjamin of Toledo found in Thessaloniki a community of some 500 Jews (though not clarifying whether this was the number of individuals or of families), all speakers of Greek and enjoying internal autonomy of administration under the leadership of a state representative and their own religious leader. The Jews of Thessaloniki were known as 'Greeks' or 'Romans' by the other Jews. Traces of the Greek language of that period have survived in the modern-day Ladino dialect, as well as their own form of public worship, published by Elia Levi. During the thirteenth and fourteenth centuries, quite a number of Jews migrated to Thessaloniki from Sicily, France, Germany and Poland, while in the sixteenth century a large number of exiles arrived from Spain and Portugal. They were particularly successful in developing trade and fostered the spiritual and intellectual progress of the community. The spiritual and intellectual zenith of the Jews of Thessaloniki came to an end in the mid-seventeenth century, when the false Messiah Sabbethai Sebi visited the city to preach the word of redemption. When he converted to Islam, he took with him many of his supporters, who formed the community known as the *dönmes* (i.e. Islamicised Jews). After the First World War, the *dönmes* moved to Turkey as Turks by religion.

Since the liberation of Thessaloniki (1912) and thereafter, the Jews of Thessaloniki have lived in freedom under the Greek administration, residing throughout the city without any restriction and engaging in trade in general and especially in manufacturing. In terms of civil and political rights, the Jews of Thessaloniki enjoy complete equality and are represented in Parliament. They are organised as a legal person under public law – that is, the Community – which functions by virtue of Law 2456/1920 'concerning Jewish Communities', which grants them wide-ranging autonomy in the management of the Community property and in fulfilling their religious, educational and charitable purposes. In religious matters, they are led by a Chief Rabbi who has in his jurisdiction a Religious Council and religious court called the Beth Din. The religious court deals with disputes among the Jews over matters of family law, applying the rules of Jewish Law; its decisions are ratified by the ordinary courts and are enforceable. The Chief Rabbi supervises the synagogues and chairs a Board of Management consisting of laymen which is entitled to impose personal taxes (such as the *petcha* and the *gabella*) on the members of the Community. Jewish primary education is provided free of charge and there are separate Community schools which receive grants from the Greek State. The Jews also have a hospital, a lunatic asylum, a poor people's clinic, orphanages for girls and boys, an old people's home (all these charitable institutions receive grants from the Municipality of Thessaloniki), and associations and societies, while they also publish four newspapers in Ladino and two in French. It should be noted that Jews freely practise the professions of medicine and the law, and they serve in the army, where they hold non-commissioned and officer rank. After the First World War, quite a number of the Jews of Thessaloniki – young men and women, in particular – settled voluntarily in Palestine (Tel Aviv), following the general trend at that time of moving to Palestine.

Outside the solid block of the Jewish Community of Thessaloniki, much smaller numbers of Jews (between 100 and 500 individuals, in each case) lived elsewhere in Greece: in Kavala, Verria, Kastoria, Ioannina, Larissa, Volos and Corfu.

As described above, the Jewish Community of Thessaloniki enjoyed complete freedom and prosperity and all the civil and political rights of Greek citizens until the time, during the German occupation of the Second World War, when the members of the community were deported by the Germans, in large numbers, to Germany and Poland, whence, unfortunately, very few of them returned. However, the Christian Greeks, at the risk of their lives, hid and rescued as many Jews as they could both in Thessaloniki and in Athens. As a result, about 5,000 Jews live in prosperity in Athens and some 2,000 in Thessaloniki, enjoying the freedom already referred to and the other privileges and protection granted by the State.

151

The Ministry of Foreign Affairs to the Greek Embassy in Berne

Athens, 24 February 1949

Jewish estates in abeyance

With reference to our communication No. 267/36.1.49, we have the honour to acquaint you with the following information so that you may kindly bear it in mind.

By Emergency Law 846/1946, the Greek State waived its right of inheritance on the existing estates belonging to Jews with Greek nationality who disappeared during the War in favour of a legal entity to be founded by Royal Decree for the relief and rehabilitation of those Greek Jews who have survived.

However, the issue of the said Royal Decree has been postponed up to now in order to protect Greek possessions in Palestine which suffered damage. Among other cases we refer to the real property belonging to the former Ambassador and Minister Mr I. Politis, the restitution of which, in spite of court decisions in his favour, is withheld by the Jews holding it.

As concerns the tax rate, please note that the Greek State, with the intention of imposing a tax on all inheritances which were not taxed during the occupation, that is, from 1 September 1941 up to and including 10 November 1944, proceeded in 1947 to the preparation of a draft law concerning 'the amendment and suplementation of the inheritance tax laws' which is better adapted to the existing situation than the previous legislation. According to Article 25 of the said draft law, which applies a progressive tax rate, as was the case with Law 1614/1919 'concerning the taxation of inheritances, donations and dowries', in the case of large estates, the rate reaches 40% of their true value.

Following a memorandum of the Athens Jewish Council stressing the high tax rate as well as how adverse as to Jewish inheritances certain other provisions of the said draft law are, by its letter No. 42358/2.10.47, addressed to the Under-Secretariat to the Prime Minister, communicated also to the Minister of Finance, the Ministry asked that the relevant instructions be given to the competent authorities, so that special care be taken in favour of Jewish property in abeyance in order not to have Law 846 deprived of its essential content and the gesture in favour of the Jews become meaningless. It should be noted that, according to the clause of Article 11, paragraph 1, instance 2 of Law 1614/1919, Greek charitable institutions are exempted from inheritance tax.

The matter stood at this point when about the middle of the year 1948 there rose the problem of indemnifying the Greek citizens in Palestine who, owing to the local hostilities suffered damage to their real property and movables estimated at several thousands pounds. Consequently, we proposed to the Ministry of Finance that it should find out whether it would be possible to assign a percentage of the taxation on Jewish inheritances in a state of abeyance to indemnifying our fellow citizens. By the time of writing, no answer as to the substance of the question has been received from the Ministry of Finance. It should be noted that the question of indemnification of Greek citizens in Palestine is going to be included on the agenda of the negotiations with the Israeli Government in conjunction with its recognition.

152

*M. Pessach, Chief Rabbi of Volos, to His Beatitude Spyridon,
Archbishop of Athens and All Greece*

letter   Volos, 10 June 1949

Your Beatitude

On the election and enthronement of Your Beatitude, by God's grace, as Archbishop of Athens and All Greece, we consider as our duty in our capacity of senior Chief Rabbi in Greece and interpreting the feelings of our entire flock to express our most cordial congratulations on your election by the Holy Synod as the religious head of the Eastern Orthodox Church of Greece in appreciation of the multiple national and religious services you have rendered to the Kingdom of Greece. We take this opportunity of stressing to Your Beatitude that the Jews of Greece do not forget the beneficent efforts on the part of the local ecclesiastical authorities, dictated to them by the religious spirit of love towards their suffering fellow human beings, for their salvation, as far as it was possible during their implacable persecution by the Bulgarians and the Germans. We do not forget either the strenuous efforts for the same purpose of the late Archbishop Damaskinos, nor the daring action taken by Your Beatitude for the protection of the Jews of Ioannina, who, together with their co-religionists all over Greece, were exterminated by the above enemy forces. We shall always remember that Your Beatitude took under your safekeeping at the Holy Metropolis of Ioannina the scrolls of our Sacred Bible and other articles of the Holy Synagogue there, which after liberation, Your Beatitude returned to the few Jews who had survived. For all these deeds we thank you with all our heart.

We should consider it an unjustified omission on our part if we did not mention also the courageous stance during those dark days of his Beatitude the Bishop of Volos, who in co-operation with you, facilitated by deeds and other charitable help and with the existence of certain other favourable circumstances the escape of the greatest number of our flock from the clutches of German terrorism, for which event, the Jewish community of Volos feel the deepest gratitude to him, by the grace of God.

Also, on the part of the Jewish race there is no lack of examples of love and sincere friendship towards the Greeks. From time immemorial we can discover feelings of partnership in the history of our two chosen peoples owing to which the knowledge and the majesty of divine power and its world-saving teachings were revealed to our forefathers, together with our incomparable civilisations. Through the same co-operation was transmitted the sacred light of godly justice in the application of the Holy Commandments of equality and love for each other which have become the cornerstone of our civilisation and the entire human edifice.

The same proofs of heartfelt devotion and deep respect of the Jewish Greeks towards their Greek Orthodox brethren exist also in our own time, as shown by their participation in the recent heroic and victorious war for the defence of the Greek homeland against the barbarian invaders, in the cruel trials undergone by both, especially the former, during the black occupation, in the sacred struggles of the national resistance, in today's mobilisation of the Greek nation against internal and external enemies and, finally, by their collaboration for its rehabilitation, progress and well-being, in which neither of whom were found lacking.

It is only natural that this same collaboration will continue between pious Greece and the peace-loving state of Israel which, with God's help, we are certain will bear the same beneficial fruit as in the past, to the glory of God and for the welfare and accord of the world.

Blessing Your Beatitude from the bottom of our heart, we pray God for your longevity in health and your good works to the benefit of the pious Greek people and the triumph of peace and concord in our dear Greece. Amen.

153

Spyridon, Archbishop of Athens and All Greece, to His Reverence the Chief Rabbi of Volos, M. Pessach

letter   Athens, 7 July 1949

It is with great joy and love that we perused letter No. 1226 of this year through which Your Reverence had the kindness to convey to us his congratulations and regards on the occasion of our election, by the Grace of the Almighty, to the Archbishopric of Athens and All Greece, thus greatly supporting our efforts to continue our pastoral duty also from this new post to which the Grace of God has led us.

Your letter reminded us of our common struggles and perils during the dark years of the enemy occupation and made us recall with deep sadness the terrible martyrdom undergone by our brother Greek Jewish element when the conquerors started with unwavering determination to turn against it and our Greek homeland. Whatever we did in defiance during those tragic times, either ourselves or the Reverend Bishops everywhere and the Greek Church in general, was simply a duty imposed not only by a sense of the need to help our suffering fellow human beings but mainly inspired by sincere love towards our imperilled brethren, dear children of the same Mother Greece, forming an inseparable part of its people, who have always willingly and actively made their precious contribution to the glory and well-being of our dear homeland. They have never lagged behind, and with selflessness have participated in all its struggles and sacrifices.

With our warm thanks to your dear Reverence for the good feelings and generous sentiments towards us, we pray with all our heart that the Almighty direct your steps in accordance with His sacred will, keeping in health and all good both you and your brethren and the beloved Jewish people of Greece.

We remain, with deep love,

154

Newspaper article from Ethnikos Kiryx

16 July 1949

Title: "The Rehabilitation of the Greek Jews"

The Minister of Finance by his circular to the authority managing the Jewish property of Thessaloniki informs them that the fiscal authorities must hand over into the hands of the administration of the local councils of the organisation which has been established for the relief and rehabilitation of Greek Jews the abandoned Jewish movable and immovable property under their management. A separate order will follow for the delivery of all deposits with the Bank of Greece and elsewhere collected from the management of Jewish property.

155

Newspaper article from Atlantis

6 September 1949

Title: "Congratulations of Greek Jews to His Beatitude the Archbishop of Athens".

The bonds of sincere friendship between the Greek and the Jewish Peoples are emphasised.

The Chief Rabbinate of Volos has communicated to us a copy of its letter of congratulations sent to his Beatitude Spyridon, Archbishop of Athens and All Greece, together with His Beatitude's answer. Both letters give emphasis to the bonds of sincere friendship and mutual support between the Greek and Jewish people.

156

The Ministry of Finance to the Ministry of Foreign Affairs

communiqué   Athens 12 October 1949

In reply to your communication No. 48437 of this year concerning the news from Athens published in the London *Jewish Chronicle* with regard to the question of the restitution of Jewish properties, we have the honour to inform you that the properties of all Jewish refugees and their relatives have been restored to them if they submitted the data required by law.

Certain cases in Thessaloniki are an exception, considering that the City authorities have stopped issuing certificates of kinship, which are an indispensable item for the continuation of the restitution of Jewish property. However, even in such cases, restitution of property to the owners has been completed on the basis of provisional or final customisation.

It would be noted that, at the insistent urgings of the Jewish organisations here, the said matter will be settled satisfactorily by a special law.

157

Ministry of Foreign Affairs

aide- mémoire   [without specific date] 1950

Matters of interest to the Jews dealt with by the Directorate of Economic
Affairs

1. During the occupation, the Germans removed the archives and the library of the Jewish Community of Thessaloniki.

An application from the Community concerning the 'restoration' of the archives and books removed was forwarded to the Military Mission in Berlin with the request that it should undertake to find the items and seek their 'restoration'.

The action taken by the Mission has had a positive outcome. The items in question were located in the American Zone and handed over to the Greek Military Mission, thanks to whose action they were transported to Greece free of charge and handed over to the Central Jewish Council for Co-ordination and Consultation. The Jewish Community of Thessaloniki has addressed its thanks to the Ministry for the interest it demonstrated.

2. In execution of the terms of the ceasefire, the Bulgarian Government has handed over to the Greek Military Mission in Sofia a variety of items abstracted from Greece, including valuables taken from Jews. All the items restored in this way were handed over to a committee set up by the Ministry of the Interior. The Directorate of Economic Affairs forwarded copies of the relevant protocols to the Central Jewish Council for Co-ordination and Consultation in Athens so that it can take action, under the competence assigned to it by the laws in force, to safeguard the items belonging to Jews.

3. The Chief Rabbinate of Volos has reported to the Ministry that during the occupation the Germans removed the entire library of the Chief Rabbinate and transported it to Germany. The application from the Chief Rabbinate, with the necessary supplementary particulars, was passed on to the Greek Military Mission in Berlin with the request that it take action to locate and restore the library or, possibly, to replace the items removed, in view of their nature. To date, the Ministry has not been informed of the outcome of the Mission's action. We return to the issue by way of reminder.

4. The Germans abstracted from the Jews of Greece, *inter alia*, a quantity of gold coin. As is common knowledge, under the agreement of January 1946 concerning German reparations, the gold coin located in Germany will be distributed among the countries receiving German reparations in proportion to the quantities of gold coin removed from them. On the invitation of the Directorate of Economic Affairs, the Central Jewish Council for Co-ordination and Consultation has submitted lists and documentation concerning the gold coin stolen from the Jews in Greece. These particulars have been passed on to our delegation to the Inter-Allied Reparations Organisation in Brussels, for the appropriate action. In view of the definition issued by the tripartite commission set up to distribute the gold found in Germany, according to which gold coin is only that held by central banks, instructions were given to our delegation to submit a claim to the effect that the gold removed from private citizens in Greece, and in particular from the Jews, be taken into consideration when determining our share of the German gold for distribution. To date, no decision of the commission in this respect has been communicated to us.

5. Individual applications submitted by Jews for special personal cases have been forwarded for action to the appropriate missions abroad.

158

*V. Dendramis, Ambassador in Washington, to the Information
Service of the Embassy*

note   Washington, 20 February 1950

I have the honour of informing that you should bear in mind, in case of a mention in the local Press, that, according to the information contained in a telegram from the Ministry of Foreign Affairs, the report that in the elections of 5 March 1950 the Jews are going to vote in separate polling stations is false.

Actually Jewish Greek citizens are going to vote together with the rest of the Thessaloniki residents exercising their voting rights in two or three polling stations in the city.

For the election of members of parliament in Thessaloniki their votes are to be counted together with the votes of all other voters of the Prefecture.

159

*G. Papadakis, Director, Ministry of Foreign Affairs, to the Union for
the Care and Rehabilitation of Jews of Thessaloniki*

letter   23 September 1957

With reference to your report No. 80 of 20 July to the Hellenic Parliament, forwarded to us by communication No ...../2479/1957 [*sic*] of the Directorate of Legislation and Draft Legislation of the Hellenic Parliament, we have the honour to inform you that we cannot become involved in the agreement on reparations between the State of Israel and the Federal Republic of Germany or in the manner in which the State of Israel makes use of the sums it has collected or will collect. Furthermore, we have no knowledge of the dispatch to Greece by the Conference on Jewish Material Claims against Germany of any amounts of money for distribution among the Jewish victims of National Socialism.

As for the letter dated 8 April 1957 from the Federal Ministry of Foreign Affairs attached to your report, it refers to a completely different issue. It is a joint demarche on the part of eight European countries, including Greece, seeking compensation for the citizens of those countries forcibly removed to Germany and confined in concentration camps. On this question, negotiations are being conducted between the Federal Republic of Germany and the eight European countries, but the talks have so far failed to end in agreement.

———

ATTACHMENT a TO 159

The President and the General Secretary of the Board of Management of the Union for the Care and Rehabilitation of the Jews of Thessaloniki

letter   Thessaloniki, 20 July 1957

To:
The Prime Minister of Greece
The Speaker of the Hellenic Parliament
The Minister of Finance
The Minister of Justice
The Leader of the ERE Party
The Leaders of the Liberal Party
The President of EDA
The Leader of DKEL
The Leader of EPEK
The Leader of the Agrarian Party
The Leader of the Popular Party
The Leader of the Progressive Party
The Members of the Hellenic Parliament
The Greek Press of Athens and Thessaloniki

Dear Sirs,
    It is with great emotion that the victims of the Second World War, including ourselves, followed the debate in Parliament.
    We were moved to note the interest taken by Parliament in the compensation of the victims. We are now submitting our case to you, in the hope that Parliament will take an interest in it and bestow on us our right. The facts of the matter are as follows.
    By virtue of a special international agreement between the German Government in Bonn, the Government of Israel and the Jewish Communities of the

Diaspora, it was decided that a sum of $100,000,000 should be made available as indemnity for the Jews resident outside Israel who suffered during the War for the loss and damage suffered by them as a result of their identity as Jews.

These Jews include the Greek Jews who continue to reside in Greece. This indemnity is independent of any other compensation to which Greece and the Greeks are entitled as a result of loss suffered during the War.

As we have been informed, the management of this compensation has been undertaken by the American-based organisation Conference on Jewish Material Claims against Germany; it has already received several million dollars, part of which, it has been said, has been sent to Greece. However, not even a drachma has so far reached the hands of the beneficiaries.

Our Union, which consists of people entitled to such indemnity and has as its purpose to lay claim to it, has addressed itself to the German Government, from which it has received a reply. As you will be aware, this affair involves a sizeable part of the Greek people and calls for particular attention and study.

In submitting the above to you, we shall be grateful if you will turn your attention to the case in question in order to put an end to the injustice and irregularity to which we have been subjected and which exposes our country to unfavourable criticism but, above all, which is to the detriment of Greek beneficiaries of compensation, thus restoring justice with the recognition of our rights. We attach hereto, in translation, a relevant communication from the German Government in Bonn.

In the hope that our request will attract your interest,

⊸⊷⊷⊶

ATTACHMENT b TO 159

The Greek Ministry of Foreign Affairs to the Union for the Care and Rehabilitation of Jews of Thessaloniki

letter   Bonn, 8 April 1957

Subject: Claim for reparations on the part of the League of Jewish Hostages (Deported Persons) of Thessaloniki

Dear Sir

The Ministry of Foreign Affairs hereby acknowledges receipt of your application to the President of the Federal Republic.

This affair took a fresh turn as soon as the Federal German Government made it clear to eight Governments, including the Royal Greek Government, that it will grant charitable aid to certain foreign citizens who suffered grave damage at the hands of National Socialism.

The Ministry of Foreign Affairs is aware that you have taken cognisance of this issue. Your previous reports are the subject of discussions which have not yet reached a conclusion. The Ministry of Foreign Affairs reserves the right to return to this matter at the appropriate time.

Thessaloniki, April 1962. Unveiling of the memorial to the 50,000 Jews of Thessaloniki who died in the Holocaust. The monument is located at the new Jewish cemetery in Stavroupoli, Thessaloniki. Archive of the Jewish Community of Thessaloniki.

The Burning Menorah, the Thessaloniki Holocaust Memorial. The monument was unveiled in November 1997 by the President of the Hellenic Republic, His Excellency Constantinos Stephanopoulos. The monument is the work of the Serb sculptor Nador Glind and is located at the intersection of Egnatia, Papanastassiou and Kleanthous Sts where housing development 151 was located. It was at this location that the Jews were gathered before being transported to the death camps.

ANNEX

TIME-CHART OF GREEK HISTORY 1908-1950[*]

1908	Young Turk revolution in Thessaloniki.
1909	Founding of the Labour *Fédération* by Abraham Benaroya.
July 1909	Formation of the *Military League*, led by Colonel Nikolaos Zorbas: the *Goudi coup d' état* takes place.
16 December 1909	The Committee in charge of the *Military League* invites Eleftherios Venizelos, President of the Cretan State, to form a government in Greece.
20 March 1910	The *Military League* dissolves itself.
8 August 1910	Elections are held for a national assembly empowered to revise the Constitution of 1864.
March 1912	Elections.
4 October 1912	Greece, Serbia, Bulgaria and Montenegro declare war on the Ottoman Empire: the Balkan Wars (1912-1913).
26 October 1912	The Greek Army liberates Thessaloniki. Among the city's inhabitants is a large Jewish community with a long history and tradition. King George I and Prime Minister Venizelos are from the start favourably disposed towards the petitions of the Jews.
December 1912	Congress of London: peace negotiations.
23 January 1913	Coup d'état in Constantinople: Enver Pasha and the Young Turks take power.
February 1913	Hostilities recommence; the First Balkan War resumes.
22 February 1913	The Greek Army liberates Ioannina.
5 March 1913	Assassination of King George I. He is succeeded by his son Constantine.
17 May 1913	Treaty of London. The Turks capitulate and recognise the territorial gains made by the Balkan Allies. Greece has liberated Epirus, Macedonia, the Aegean Islands and Crete.
19 May 1913	Greece and Serbia sign a pact agreeing on the distribution of the territory they have gained in Macedonia.
17 June 1913	Bulgaria, unhappy with the outcome of the First Balkan War, initiates the Second.
28 June 1913	Treaty of Bucharest. Greece occupies the cities of Drama, Serres and Kavala.

---

[*] This time-chart has been compiled using the Julian Calender (Old Style) down to 1 March 1923, on which date the Gregorian Calendar (New Style) was adopted in Greece, with the addition of 13 days.

1 November 1913	Treaty of Athens, by which Greece undertakes to respect the religions and customs of the inhabitants of the New Lands (including the Jews).
1914	Ichach Ben Tovi visits Thessaloniki in order to persuade the Jewish dockers of the city to emigrate to Palestine. The First World War cancels the plan.
August 1914	Hostilities break out between the Entente (Britain, France, Russia) and the Central Powers (Germany, Austro-Hungary).
21 February 1915	Venizelos resigns after the King changes his position over the question of making troops available for an operation to take the Straits. Beginning of the period known as the 'National Rift'.
31 May 1915	Elections, resulting in victory for Venizelos. Five Jewish deputies are returned, all representing the United Opposition (anti-Venizelos camp): M. Kofinas, C. Cohen, Joseph (Pepo) Mallah, D. Matalon and A. Kuriel. Four more Jews stand as Venizelist candidates but are not elected because of the 'first past the post' electoral system.
July 1915	Italy enters the War on the Entente side, after agreeing with Great Britain that she will receive territories in Asia Minor.
22 September 1915	Tsar Ferdinand of Bulgaria and the Central Powers make a secret pact. Bulgaria mobilises.
5 October 1915	Venizelos resigns for a second time after disagreeing with Constantine over Greek participation in the First World War.
6 December 1915	Elections. The Venizelists abstain. Four Jewish deputies are returned: L. Gattegno, M. Kofinas, S. Meir and J. Mallah.
January 1916	Entente forces occupy Corfu.
22 May 1916	Greece surrenders the Roupel bastion to the Germans and Bulgarians.
August 1916	Venizelist officers supported by the *'National Defence'* group (consisting of eminent citizens) carry out a coup d'état in Thessaloniki.
13 September 1916	*National Defence* disassociates itself from the Athens government.
October 1916	Venizelos arrives in Thessaloniki and forms a provisional administration: the National Defence government (1916-1917).
December 1916	British and French troops land in Athens in order to exert pressure on King Constantine to bring Greece into the War on the Allied side, to ensure control of weapons and *matériel,* and to protect the railway line north. The landing detachments suffer heavy losses at the hands of supporters of the King. The clashes lead to extensive reprisals against Venizelists in areas controlled by the royalist government. Outraged by the casualties, the Entente allies demand compensation and blockade Greece.

April 1917	Treaty of St Jean de Maurienne: the Entente cedes Smyrna to Italy in order to bring the country into the War.
29 May 1917	The Entente submits an ultimatum demanding the removal of Constantine. Constantine leaves the country. The Zaimis administration resigns, and on 14 June 1917 Venizelos takes over, reconvening the 'Lazarist Parliament': that formed at the first elections of 1915.
1 July 1917	Nikolaos Politis, Minister of Foreign Affairs and a close associate of Prime Minister Venizelos, makes a statement published in the periodical *Pro Israel* to the effect that Greece supports and looks favourably on the claim for the establishment of a Jewish state in Palestine.
5-6 August 1917	The greater part of Thessaloniki is destroyed by fire, leaving thousands of people - most of them Jews - homeless.
2 November 1917	The Balfour Declaration promising the formation of a Jewish National Home in Palestine.
16 September 1918	Allied forces under the command of French General Franchet d'Espéry - with the participation of nine Greek divisions - attack on the Macedonian Front. Bulgaria capitulates.
29 October 1918	Germany capitulates.
30 October 1918	Turkey signs the armistice of Mudros (hostilities had ceased on 25 September).
November 1918	A general armistice is signed by the belligerents of the First World War.
January 1919	The Allies conduct a campaign in south Russia, with the participation of Greek forces.
March 1919	The first Panhellenic Zionist Conference is held in Thessaloniki, on the initiative of the local Community and with the participation of 80 delegates from 15 out of the 24 Jewish Communities in Greece.
2 May 1919	Greek troops, supported by Allied warships, land in Smyrna.
1920	Chief Rabbi of Thesssaloniki Jacob Meir resigns and is replaced by Benzien Ouziel, formerly Chief Rabbi of Jaffa (Tel Aviv).
February 1920	The 'National Pact': a declaration of independence by the Turkish nationalists led by Kemal Atatürk.
28 July 1920	The Treaty of Sèvres is signed, bringing peace between Greece and Turkey. Greek sovereignty over the Aegean islands liberated during the Balkan Wars is confirmed, and it is decided that Greece will administer Smyrna for five years, after which a plebiscite will determine the future of the area.
12 October 1920	Death of King Alexander, who had succeeded Constantine in 1917. His brothers refuse to ascend the throne.

1 November 1920	Elections. The Liberals are defeated. The Jewish MPs D. Alhanati, I. Sciaky and I. Mallah are elected with the Popular Party. Prime Minister Gounaris is said to have offered the Ministry of Finance to Mallah, who declined it. The Jewish candidates standing with the Liberal Party also receive many votes. The Allies warn Greece not to restore King Constantine.
5 December 1920	A referendum on the return of the King produces an overwhelming majority in favour of his restoration.
February 1921	The interested parties hold a conference on the 'Eastern Question' in London: Italy and France make secret pacts with Kemal involving their withdrawal from Asia Minor.
June 1921	The Greeks unleash a major offensive in Asia Minor, believing they will strike at the centre of Kemal's guerrilla forces. They reach the river Sakarya, not far from their principal objective of Ankara, Kemal's chief strongpoint. After 22 days and nights of fighting in atrocious conditions, the Greek Army is compelled to regroup.
16 August 1922	Kemal counter-attacks in the Afyon Karahisar area. The front collapses and the Greek Army retreats in disorder.
9 September 1922	The Turkish Army takes Smyrna.
14 September 1922	A revolution takes place, headed by Venizelist infantry colonel Nikolaos Plastiras. Constantine is obliged to abdicate and is succeeded by the Crown Prince as George II.
15 November 1922	Trial of the six persons deemed responsible for the failure of the Greek Army's campaign in Asia Minor.
27 December 1922	Constantine dies in Palermo, where he had been living since his departure from Greece.
14 November 1922	Gonatas becomes Prime Minister.
1923	Benzien Ouziel resigns as Chief Rabbi of Thessaloniki. During the period that follows, the post is vacant and the duties of Chief Rabbi are performed by various *locum tenentes*.
30 January 1923	Venizelos and Ismet Inönü sign an agreement on an exchange of populations. The agreement provides for the compulsory exchange of Turkish citizens of the Orthodox religion established on Turkish soil and Greek citizens of the Muslim religion established on Greek soil. The Greeks of Constantinople, Imbros and Tenedos who could prove that they were established there prior to 30 October 1918 (the 'établis') are exempted from the exchange, as is the Muslim population of Western Thrace.
24 July 1923	The Treaty of Lausanne. Greece loses to Turkey the gains made by the Treaty of Sèvres in 1920, with the exception of Mytilene, Chios and Samos, over which Greek sovereignty is recognised, though with restrictions on the militarisation of the islands. Italy

	seizes the opportunity to go back on its obligation to cede the Dodecanese to Greece.
31 August 1923	Corfu is bombarded and occupied by Italy on the pretext of the murder of the Italian members of the committee set up by the Ambassadorial Conference to draw the Greek-Albanian border line. Greece is compelled by the League of Nations to compensate Italy, which withdraws its forces from the island.
22 October 1923	An attempted coup d'état whose leaders call for the resignation of the Gonatas-Plastiras government and fair elections. The coup fails; elections are held.
16 December 1923	Elections, with the anti-Venizelist wing abstaining. The Jewish deputies also abstain (with the exception of I. Alhanati, I. Samouilidis and I. Saias, who are elected with a mere 50 votes) in protest at the measure of separate electoral rolls for the minorities. The Muslims accept the measure, but the Jews are opposed to it out of a fear that it will create 'electoral ghettos'. The Greek authorities claim that the separate rolls ensure the minorities better representation, but in reality the Venizelists wish to use the measure to concentrate the anti-Venizelist vote.
18 December 1923	On the recommendation of Prime Minister Gonatas, King George II leaves Greece 'temporarily' so as to facilitate the resolution of the problem of the system of governance.
2 January 1924	Gonatas announces the resignation of his government.
11 January 1924	Venizelos, on the insistence of his supporters, returns to Greece.
4 February 1924	Eleftherios Venizelos forms a new administration. After a month, he realises he is no longer in control of the military. He hands over to Kafantaris and retires from public life, invoking reasons of health. Kafantaris is soon replaced by Papanastassiou.
13 April 1924	A referendum abolishes the monarchy and resolves that the country will be governed by a system of parliamentary democracy.
1925	An incident on the Greek-Bulgarian border worsens relations between the two countries.
20 June 1925	Parliament gives a vote of confidence to the administration of General Theodoros Pangalos, which has taken power by coup d'état. A few months later (4/26 January 1926), Pangalos dissolves Parliament and imposes a dictatorship.
7 August 1926	Pangalos is overthrown by a putsch led by General Georgios Kondylis and Colonel Napoleon Zervas.
7 November 1926	Elections: formation of an all-party Government of National Unity. The Jews take part in the election, and the separate electoral rolls are not used. Simple proportional representation is applied. The Jewish Political Union gains 70% of the Jewish vote, returning M.

Bessantchi and I. Sciaky, while the United Front (Communists) elects Sulam and Ventouras to Parliament. Venizelos observes that although the Jews are opposed to a separate electoral roll, they have in effect created one by their vote.

1926	Haim Habib takes over as *locum tenens* of the Chief Rabbinate of Thessaloniki, and serves until 1933.
2 June 1927	A new and democratic Constitution is passed.
February 1928	The all-party government resigns. Venizelos returns to political life as leader of the Liberals.
July 1928	Admiral Kountouriotis, President of the Republic, gives the mandate to form a government to Venizelos.
August 1928	Venizelos calls elections, held on the 19th of the month, and wins a large majority. The 'first past the post' system and separate electoral rolls are used, and M. Bessantchi and D. Matalon are elected as Independent Liberals. Venizelos had advised representatives of the Jewish community to accept the separate electoral rolls because otherwise, given the electoral system, the Jews were in danger of not being represented in Parliament.
25 September 1928	Greece and Italy sign a pact of friendship.
1929	The Depression begins. In Greece, a special law is introduced proscribing Communism.
11 October 1929	Greece and Yugoslavia sign a pact of friendship.
1929	Elections to the Senate. Kountouriotis is re-elected President of the Republic, and the Jewish candidate Ascher Mallah is elected with the support of the Liberal Party.
10 June 1930	The Treaty of Ankara is signed, settling the question of compensation for the refugees.
30 October 1930	Venizelos pays a state visit to Turkey and signs a pact of friendship between Greece and Turkey.
1931	An arsonist attack on the Campbell quarter of Thessaloniki. Some of the city's Jews emigrate, as a number of their co-religionists had done after the Fire of 1917. The most common destination is Palestine.
26 May 1932	On the resignation of Venizelos, Alexandros Papanastassiou takes over as Prime Minister.
5 June 1932	Papanastassiou resigns, and Venizelos becomes Prime Minister once more.
25 September 1932	Elections. Panayis Tsaldaris' Popular Party wins a small majority and forms an administration. Proportional representation is applied; D. Allalouf is elected by the Popular Party, M. Bessantchi as an independent, and M. Cazes with the United Front (Communists). I. Sciaky is elected to the Senate.

4 November 1932	Tsaldaris forms a minority government.
1933	After a visit to Thessaloniki by Amba Husi, mayor of the port of Haifa, 300 Jewish seamen and dockers emigrate to Palestine. The ship carrying them is the first to succeed in entering Haifa harbour.
1933	Dr Cevi Koretz, holder of a Ph.D. from the University of Berlin, takes up the post of Chief Rabbi of Thessaloniki.
15 January 1933	Venizelos forces the resignation of the Tsaldaris administration and elections are announced for 5 March. Venizelos is defeated. All 18 seats in Thessaloniki are won by the Venizelists, thanks mainly to the votes of the refugees from Asia Minor. The Jews elect D. Alallouf and I. Molho, both anti-Venizelists.
6 March 1933	The defeat of Venizelos prompts General Nikolaos Plastiras, leader of the putsch in 1922, to attempt a fresh coup d'état, which, however, is unsuccessful. The rift in the Greek nation widens, since there is a suspicion that Plastiras had Venizelos' consent for his action.
6 March 1933	A government is formed by Othonaios, but resigns within a few days.
10 March 1933	Tsaldaris forms an administration.
6 June 1933	Venizelos is the victim of an assassination attempt.
2 July 1933	Second round of parliamentary elections in Thessaloniki.
14 September 1933	Greece and Turkey sign a Pact of Friendship and Understanding.
9 February 1934	Greece, Yugoslavia, Romania and Turkey sign the Balkan Pact, containing mutual guarantees of the existing borders. Bulgaria and Albania do not sign, in view of Bulgaria's refusal to accept as final the borders established by the Treaty of Neuilly (1919) and of the persistence of both countries in stirring up questions of minorities.
1 March 1935	Attempted military coup to prevent the restoration of the monarchy. It fails; the three ring-leaders are executed on 22 April and 1,000 officers are cashiered. April: Venizelist civil servants are dismissed. Venizelos, who had agreed to lead the coup, steps down on 11 March and is forced into exile in Paris, where Plastiras has also taken refuge. Both are condemned to death, *in absentia*, in May of the same year.
1 April 1935	The Senate, controlled by the democratic wing, is abolished.
9 June 1935	Elections for a National Assembly. The Venizelists abstain in protest over the continued imposition of martial law and the Press censorship introduced after the coup in March. The Popular Party wins the elections. G. Kondylis forms a government. D. Alallouf and Pepo Mallah are elected with the governing party.

10 October 1935	The system of governance of parliamentary presidential democracy is abolished.
28 October 1935	The Constitution of 1911 is restored.
3 November 1935	Referendum on the restoration of the monarchy. The obviously rigged poll results in a royalist victory. The leadership of the Jewish Community is in favour of restoration.
25 November 1935	King George II returns from London, where he has spent the years of his exile. He grants an amnesty to the army officers and civilians who had taken part in the failed coup of March. The Kondylis government resigns.
30 November 1935	The King appoints Constantinos Demertzis, a moderate royalist professor of civil law at Athens University, as caretaker Prime Minister and elections are called.
17 December 1935	The Fifth National Assembly is dissolved.
26 January 1936	Elections, on the proportional representation system. The royalists are the largest party in the new Parliament, though with only two seats more than the Venizelists. The Communist Party, with 15 seats, holds the balance of power. Only one Jewish MP is elected.
6 March 1936	A Parliament for the revision of the Constitution is convened.
16 March 1936	Themistoclis Sophoulis becomes Speaker of Parliament. Ioannis Metaxas is Deputy Prime Minister. Negotiations between the royalists and the Venizelists on the formation of a coalition government, and leaks of secret talks between both sides and the Communists. General Papagos, Army Commander-in-Chief, warns that the Army may intervene, and is replaced, on the instructions of the King, by Metaxas. Successive deaths of eminent Greek politicians lead the King to appoint Metaxas as Prime Minister.
19 March 1936	Death of Venizelos, in Paris.
9-10 May 1936	A massive demonstration of tobacco workers in Thessaloniki and clashes with the police. Twelve demonstrators (two of them Jews) are killed. Increasing labour unrest, culminating in a general strike on 5 August, leads the King to approve the suspension of certain articles of the Constitution. Workers are mobilised.
4 August 1936	Effective beginning of the Metaxas dictatorship. Metaxas dreams of a Third Hellenic Civilisation; Fascist-type organisations are set up.
27 April 1938	A new Pact of Friendship with Turkey is signed, in Ankara.
28 July 1938	An attempted anti-dictatorship coup takes place in Crete.
31 July 1938	The Balkan Understanding ('Balkan Pact') countries sign a pact with Bulgaria.

September 1939	Outbreak of the Second World War.
15 August 1940	An Italian submarine torpedoes the Greek cruiser *Elli* in Tinos harbour, where the warship was taking part in the celebrations to mark the Dormition of the Virgin.
28 October 1940	Italy issues an ultimatum to Greece and declares war just a few hours later. Metaxas rejects the Italian ultimatum, and one of the most brilliant chapters in Greek history begins. The Jews of Greece send 12,898 men and 343 officers to join the ranks of the Greek Army.
1 November 1940	Death of Alexandros Diakos from Chalki in the Dodecanese, the first Greek officer to be killed in the war against Italy on the Albanian front.
5 December 1940	Death in the vicinity of Premeti, Albania, of the first high-ranking Greek officer to be killed, Colonel Mordechai Frizis, a Jew.
22-23 February 1940	Anthony Eden, British Foreign Minister, and senior officers visit Athens for talks with the Greek political leadership. It is decided that the Greeks will continue to resist the Axis forces, with the assistance of British troops. The operation is code-named 'Lustre'.
6 April 1941	Operation Marita, the German plan for attacking and occupying Greece, is put into effect.
9 April 1941	The Germans take Thessaloniki: the beginning of the end for the most populous and prosperous Jewish community in Greece. The Germans forbid Jews to enter cafés, cinemas, etc; charitable institutions such as the Baron Hirsch Hospital and houses belonging to Jews are confiscated; the offices, libraries and archives of the Jewish Community are raided.
15 April 1941	The members of the Community Council are imprisoned, and released a few days later.
18 April 1941	Suicide of Koryzis, the Greek Prime Minister. He is replaced by Emmanouil Tsouderos (on 21 April).
20 April 1941	Without authorisation from the Greek Government, General Tsolakoglou, Commander of the Army of Western Macedonia, negotiates an armistice with the Germans. The front collapses and the German forces advance very rapidly.
22 April 1941	The King, the Greek Government, the Greek Army and the British take refuge in Crete, where they carry on the fight.
27 April 1941	Fall of Athens.
May 1941	Cevi Koretz, Chief Rabbi of Thessaloniki, is arrested on a charge of having publicly criticised the Axis, and taken to Vienna. The Germans appoint Sabi Saltiel President of the Community. EEE

(the Hellenic Patriotic Union), a Fascist anti-Semitic organisation which Metaxas had dissolved, is re-formed. The Rosenberg special commandos confiscate Jewish cultural treasures and books.

20 May 1941   The Battle of Crete begins; it ends with the German conquest of the island despite heroic resistance by the Allied Greek and British forces.

27 May 1941   The Greek Government withdraws to Egypt.

31 May 1941   Manolis Glezos hauls down the German flag flying over the Acropolis of Athens. The first Greek Resistance groups are formed.

6 July 1941   Damaskinos (secular name Dimitrios Papandreou) becomes Archbishop of Athens. He initiates a number of courageous petitions calling for the Jews of Greece to be exempted from Nazi displacement measures.

Early September 1941   Founding of the National Democratic Greek League (EDES).

27 September 1941   Founding of the National Liberation Front (EAM), which developed into the largest resistance organisation. Later, EAM acquired a number of parallel organisations, such as the United Panhellenic Organisation of Young People (EPON), ERGAS (which operated in the field of national financial solidarity), ELAS (the National Popular Liberation Army), ETA (the Guerrilla's quartermaster organisation) and OPLA (militia). EDES and EAM-ELAS did much to rescue the Jews of Greece.

4 June 1942   The first executions of Greeks in Athens.

11 July 1942   The Germans order all the male members of the Jewish community of Thessaloniki aged between 18 and 45 years to assemble in Eleftherias Square. There, they are subjected to humiliation and torture and 3,500 of them are dispatched on forced labour assignments. The lootings and confiscations of property continue, and Chief Rabbi Koretz is re-arrested.

22 September 1942   Under the nose of the Italians, a Greek resistance group blows up the offices of the National Socialist and Patriotic Movement (ESPO), an organisation devoted to harassing the Jews and spreading anti-Semitic propaganda. The fire following the explosion burns out the German Officers' Club, located next door. Thanos Skouras, Costas Perrikos, Yannis Katevatis and Ioulia Biba are arrested and executed.

17 October 1942   The dreadful working conditions of the Jews of Thessaloniki on the forced labour assignments cause much death and disease. The Jewish community, with the collusion of the contractor Müller and the legal adviser to the occupation forces, Max Merten, buys out the freedom of its members for 8,000 sovereigns.

11 November 1942	Formation of the ELAS Thessaly Headquarters: the fact that National Resistance forces control the Thessaly region facilitates the escape of Jews.
25 November 1942	The Gorgopotamos railway bridge is blown up by guerrillas led by Aris Velouchiotis and Zervas together with British saboteurs under Brigadier Myers.
2 December 1942	Professor of medicine Logothetopoulos is appointed by the Germans as Prime Minister of occupied Greece; in effect, he had been serving in the post since the resignation of Tsolakoglou and the other ministers. Logothetopoulos was later the recipient of petitions from prominent members of Greek society pleading with him to exert all his influence on the Germans, as indeed he did, to have the Jews of Greece exempted from displacement.
6 December 1942	The Jewish cemetery of Thessaloniki, more than two thousand years old, is destroyed by the Germans.
Late December 1942	All Jewish businesses and shops are confiscated.
February 1943	The 'special treatment' of the Jews of Thessaloniki begins. Dieter Wisliceny and Aloys Brunner arrive in the city: the former commands the operation, with the latter as his deputy. Displacement is in the hands of the overseas bureau of the SS, and a special SD detachment is also used.
6 February 1943	Max Merten, military management consultant, announces the racial measures to be implemented against the Jews of Thessaloniki: a 5 p.m. curfew is imposed on access to some of the main city streets, and all the Jews of Thessaloniki are compelled by the occupation forces to wear the Star of David for the purposes of recognition. The Jews are also to move into ghettos. A deadline of 25 February is set for the latter two measures. Jews with Italian, Spanish and Swiss citizenship are exempt from the measures. Two areas are selected as ghettos: the fire zone in Sector 5 (the Syngrou ghetto) and the area from the White Tower to the Depot (the Miaouli ghetto). The Germans order the fencing in of the Baron Hirsch Jewish fire victims zone, close to Thessaloniki railway station.
12 February 1943	Wisliceny confirms that the racial measures are in force, and determines which Jews are to be prosecuted under the Nuremberg Laws. A 'Jewish Militia' of 250 men is formed.
17 February 1943	New regulations are introduced for the classification of houses, offices, shops and city plots as Jewish. Jews are prohibited from joining associations and other organisations.
22 February 1943	The Bulgarian commissioner for Jewish affairs, Alexandr Belev, and an SS officer sign a secret agreement on the displacement of

20,000 Jews from the parts of Macedonia and Thrace which the Bulgarian Army has occupied in exchange for its collaboration with the Axis forces and has annexed to Bulgaria (the communities of Alexandroupoli, Komotini, Xanthi, Kavala, Drama and Serres).

25 February 1943	The Jews of Thessaloniki are prohibited from engaging in any occupation and from joining any organisations.
1 March 1943	The Jews of Thessaloniki are ordered to make statements of all their assets. Apart from valuables and furniture, even pet dogs have to be declared.
3-4 March 1943	All the Greek Jews in Bulgarian-occupied areas are arrested: approximately 12,000 persons. The figure of 20,000 (see above) is made up with arrests of other 'undesirables' in Bulgaria. The displaced persons are taken under guard to the port of Lom on the Danube, where they are loaded on to old barges and handed over to the Germans. According to rumours, one of the barges sinks, while other sources state that all the detainees were taken to Treblinka, in seven trains, and put to death. Only a few of the Jews of Macedonia and Thrace survived: those who had been imprisoned before the mass displacements of 3-4 March and sent for forced labour.
6 March 1943	The Jews of Thessaloniki are forbidden to leave the ghetto.
7 March 1943	The shops of the Jews are turned over to custodians.
8 March 1943	The Greek collaborationist administration sets up a Department for the Management of Jewish Property (DMJP).
10 March 1943	Jews are banned from engaging in commercial transactions.
13 March 1943	The Germans compel the Thessaloniki Community to sell off the assets of the Jews and deposit the sum produced in a special bank account.
15 March 1943	The first shipment of Greek Jews from Thessaloniki to the death camp of Auschwitz. The first train carries 2,800 Jews who were imprisoned in the Baron Hirsch ghetto. More shipments follow (on the 17th, 19th, 23rd and 27th of the month); the Baron Hirsch ghetto now becomes a holding camp for Jews being moved from other ghettos in the city before they are loaded on to the trains for the extermination camps.
18 March 1943	The collaborationist Prime Minister Logothetopoulos sends a letter to von Altenburg, the Third Reich's representative in Greece, calling for suspension of the measures against the Greek Jews. A second petition follows on 22 March.
20 March 1943	The first shipment of Greek Jews arrives at Auschwitz. After the first stage in selection, only 417 men and 192 women are admitted to the camp.

24 March 1943 Archbishop Damaskinos makes representations to Ambassador von Altenburg in favour of "suspension of the persecution" of the Greek Jews. The petition is signed by 21 eminent members of Athenian society, including the presidents of learned societies and commercial associations and the rectors of the universities. In Thessaloniki, the displacements continue and male Jews from district 151 are arrested in a sweep and sent for forced labour to Lianokladi.

3 April 1943 The sixth train leaves Thessaloniki; others follow on the 5th, 7th, 10th, 13th, 16th, 20th, 22nd and 28th of the month.

7 April 1943 Ioannis Rallis takes over as Prime Minister of the last Quisling government.

9 April 1943 Dr Koretz, Chief Rabbi and President of the Jewish Community, meets Prime Minister Rallis at the offices of the Metropolitan Bishopric of Thessaloniki. The meeting is held subsequent to the mediation of Metropolitan Bishop Gennadios of Thessaloniki, in the hope of persuading Rallis to intervene with the German occupation authorities so as to suspend the orders for the displacement of the Jews of Thessaloniki.

10 April 1943 Dr Koretz is arrested and stripped of his offices of Chief Rabbi and President of the Jewish Community.

3 May 1943 Departure of the fifteenth shipment from Thessaloniki; another follows on the 9th of the month.

Late May 1943 The last two shipments of Jews include 2,034 persons from the smaller communities under the control of the Commander of Thessaloniki and the Aegean and from the German-occupied border zone along the Evros river (Didymoteicho, Soufli, Nea Orestiada).

1 June 1943 Departure of shipment 17, consisting of 820 persons. Among them are many of the so-called 'privileged Jews', who had helped the Germans to assemble and deport the other members of the communities. However, the 'privileged treatment' reserved for them consists of shipment to Auschwitz-Birkenau, where 512 of them are immediately sent to the gas chambers.

2 August 1943 A small shipment, of only 74 persons, leaves Thessaloniki; it includes Chief Rabbi Koretz, other Community officials, and some collaborators with the German SD. The shipment is joined by 367 Jews with Spanish citizenship.

1 August 1943 The last shipment of Jews from Thessaloniki, consisting of approximately 1,800 persons: all the survivors of the group of men who had been sent for forced labour at the start of the displacements.

8 September 1943	Italy capitulates. The way is now open for the displacement of the remaining Greek Jews, who had been under Italian administration.
21 September 1943	The Chief Rabbi of Athens, Eliau Barzilai, is ordered to present himself at Gestapo headquarters, where he is told to submit, within two days, complete lists of the names and addresses of his flock and of the assets they possess. He returns in two days' time, empty-handed. The Resistance organises his escape.
October 1943	Introduction of anti-Jewish measures in Athens, but after the escape of the Chief Rabbi only 200 Jews present themselves. The remainder go into hiding, with the assistance of the Greek authorities and the population. By mid-March 1944, 1,500 Jews have been recorded by the Germans.
13 December 1943	The Germans execute approximately 1,000 persons at Kalavryta in the Peloponnese, as a reprisal for Resistance activities.
Last quarter of 1943	Start of the 'first round' of the Civil War, with the forces of ELAS turning on those of Zervas.
29 February 1944	Signing of the 'Plaka Agreement' bringing to an end the four months of civil war between EDES and ELAS and determining the areas of operational control of each organisation. EDES is restricted to its base in Epirus.
24 March 1944	Almost 1,000 Jews from Kastoria are arrested and taken to Auschwitz.
25 March 1944	1,860 Jews are arrested in Ioannina.
31 March 1944	The Greek forces in the Middle East mutiny, demanding the inclusion of left-wingers in the government-in-exile. The Cairo government, headed by Emmanouil Tsouderos, resigns.
2 April 1944	A large shipment – 80 box-cars – leaves Athens for Auschwitz. It consists of the Jews arrested in Athens, and as the train travels north 90 Jews from Chalkis and 2,400 from the cities of Thessaly and Ioannina join it.
14 April 1944	A new government-in-exile is formed, under Sophoklis Venizelos.
20 May 1944	Arrest of approximately 300 Jews at Chania in Crete; with some 250 Christian members of the Resistance, they are loaded on to the ship *Tanais*, with Athens as their destination. The vessel sinks and all are drowned – or according to some sources, it is sunk by the Germans after their own men have been taken off.
24 May 1944	George Papandreou takes over as Prime Minister of the government-in-exile.
9 June 1944	1,795 Jews from Corfu are arrested and displaced; they are taken first to the Haidari army camp in Athens and then shipped to Auschwitz. The plan to displace 275 Jews from Zakynthos

	(Zante), on the other hand, fails, thanks to the action taken by the local Greek authorities, the Metropolitan Bishop and the Christian population.
July 1944	Approximately 1,700 Jews – Italian citizens – are arrested on Rhodes and Cos and displaced; they are shipped, initially, to Haidari in Athens.
August 1944	The last shipment of Jews from the Dodecanese leaves Athens; it also includes 90 more Jews arrested in Athens.
7 October 1944	An uprising takes place in the Auschwitz camp, with the active participation of Greek inmates.
12 October 1944	The Germans begin to retreat and Athens is liberated. The Jews who had taken refuge with Christian families or who had joined guerrilla bands in the Greek mountains can now breathe freely. Quisling Prime Minister Rallis issues a proclamation announcing the end of the occupation. The Department for the Management of Jewish Property (DMJP) takes over the task of settling and restoring Jewish property from the Central Department for the Management of Jewish Property (CMJP).
18 October 1944	The Government of National Unity, under George Papandreou and including five members of EAM, arrives in Greece.
30 October 1944	The Germans evacuate Thessaloniki.
26 December 1944	Churchill visits Athens.
31 December 1944	Archbishop Damaskinos assumes the post of Regent.
3 January 1945	Nikolaos Plastiras forms an administration.
12 February 1945	The Varkiza Agreement is signed.
8 April 1945	Plastiras resigns. Petros Voulgaris is appointed Prime Minister.
8 May 1945	Germany collapses. The few Greek Jews who succeeded in surviving the Holocaust begin to return home. Of the Jewish population of Greece in 1941 – approximately 71,000 – some 59,000 have been exterminated.
7 June 1945	Entry into force of Law 367 concerning the re-establishment of the Jewish Communities of Greece. Article 5 concerns the temporary foundation of a Central Board of Jewish Communities to represent the Jewish Communities of Greece.
11 August 1945	Reshuffle of the Voulgaris administration.
August/September 1945	The leaders of all the Greek political parties state their agreement with, and support for, the laws and measures of the Greek Government in favour of the Greek Jews, in recognition of the misery and hardships they have undergone.
17 October 1945	The Voulgaris government resigns; Archbishop Damaskinos takes over as Prime Minister.
1 November 1945	Panayotis Kanellopoulos forms a government.

22 November 1945	Themistoclis Sophoulis forms a government.
22 January 1946	Law 846 concerning the abolition of the State's right of inheritance in the case of abandoned Jewish property (Government Gazette No. 17, Vol. 1).
31 March 1946	Elections: the Sophoulis administration resigns.
2 July 1946	Trial of those who collaborated with the Nazis, including Jews: three Jews are found guilty and executed, one is sentenced to life imprisonment, and two more receive long prison terms.
1 November 1946	Caretaker government under Panayotis Poulitsas.
17 April 1946	Constantinos Tsaldaris forms an administration.
1 September 1946	Referendum on the restoration of the monarchy. The King returns to Greece on 27 September.
24 January 1947	Dimitrios Maximos forms an administration after the resignation of Tsaldaris.
10 February 1947	Greece and Italy sign a peace treaty in Paris. The Dodecanese are ceded to Greece.
12 March 1947	Announcement of the Truman Doctrine, granting economic aid to Greece.
1 April 1947	Death of George II; he is succeeded by Paul I.
26 June 1947	Trials of Jews who collaborated with the Germans; they are sentenced to long terms of imprisonment.
29 August 1947	Maximos resigns; Tsaldaris forms an administration.
7 September 1947	An administration under Themistoclis Sophoulis (Popular Party and Liberal coalition).
15 October 1947	Parliament passes Law 228694/6069 concerning the appointment of the Central Board of Jewish Communities as the manager of abandoned Jewish property.
2 March 1948	The Central Board of Jewish Communities issues a circular establishing a Day of Mourning in the Jewish Communities for the victims of the Holocaust.
7 March 1948	Incorporation of the Dodecanese into Greece.
18 November 1948	Sophoulis forms another administration.
21 January 1949	Sophoulis forms a Government of National Unity.
29 March 1949	The Organisation for the Care and Rehabilitation of the Jews of Greece is established by a decree published in the Government Gazette.
February 1950	Elections.
15 January 1951	Law 1657 amending and supplementing the provisions concerning Jewish Communities comes into force.

BIOGRAPHICAL NOTES

ADOSSIDIS, ANASTASIOS (1873-1942). Expert in public affairs, publisher for many years of the periodical *L'Hellénisme* (Paris). Son of Costis Pasha Adossidis, an official of the Ottoman Empire. Prefect of the Cyclades (1913), General Governor of Samos (1914), and Prefect of Thessaloniki (1916). A close associate of Eleftherios Venizelos, he was appointed General Secretary of the Committee for the Rehabilitation of Refugees.

AGNIDIS, ATHANASSIOS (1889-1984). Diplomat; born at Nigde, Asia Minor, graduate of the Great School of the Nation (Constantinople). Studied law and sociology at the Sorbonne. Served in various foreign postings. Permanent Under-Secretary of State for Foreign Affairs in the Tsouderos government-in-exile; Greek Ambassador in London (1942-1947); Greek delegate to the San Francisco Conference (1947); President of two UN committees (1946-1964). A member of the staff of the Academy of International Law at The Hague (1947-1967).

AMANTOS, CONSTANTINOS (1874-1960). Professor of Byzantine History and Culture (1925) and member of the Academy of Athens (1926). Compiler and Director of the *Historical Lexicon of the Greek Language*. As Minister of Education in the government of Nikolaos Plastiras (1945), tabled a bill introducing the use of the vernacular language in primary education. Published numerous academic papers and edited periodicals in the fields of folklore and history.

ARGYROPOULOS, PERICLIS. Prefect of Larissa (1910) and later of Thessaloniki after liberation (1912). Resigned in 1915 and stood for Parliament as a Liberal candidate. Member of the Provisional Government in 1916. Served as General Governor of Macedonia (1918), Ambassador, General Director of the Ministry of Foreign Affairs, and Minister of Foreign Affairs (1926).

ASCHER, MOISIS. Lawyer. President of the Hellenic Zionist Federation and President of the Jewish Community of Thessaloniki (1934-1938). Post-War, served as President of the Central Board of Jewish Communities and was Israel's first diplomatic representative in Greece. His published works include an *Introduction to the Family Law of the Jews in Greece* (1934), *The Friendship between Greeks and Jews over the Centuries* (1953), *Helleno-Judaic Studies* (1959), and *The Nomenclature of the Jews in Greece* (1971). His article on 'The Zionist Movement in Thessaloniki and other Greek Cities' is an important source for our knowledge of the Greek-language Jewish Press.

BENAROYA, Abraham (1887-1979). Born at Vidin, Bulgaria, died at Jaffa [Tel Aviv]. A prominent member of the Greek socialist movement and one of the founders of the Socialist Party (SEKE) which evolved into the Communist Party of Greece (KKE). Abraham Benaroya, a teacher and printer, settled in Thessaloniki in 1908 and worked in the Jewish Community. An anti-Zionist, he was the most important founder-member of the anti-Ottoman trans-Balkan Socialist Workers' Federation, usually known just as the *Fédération*. The Federation was overwhelmingly Jewish, and Benaroya – with Kuriel – succeeded in being elected to the Greek Parliament in 1915. The first workers' club in Greece was also a Jewish initiative – and Benaroya, head of the printers, was among its founders (who also included Samuel Saad, Abraham Hasson, and others). The Workers' Club made its first appearance at the celebration of Workers' May Day in 1909, when the streets of Thessaloniki filled with crowds of people wishing to parade and provide an answer to the Young Turks, who had hoped that all the workers would march together to commemorate the first anniversary of the Young Turk Revolution. At various times, Benaroya edited publications such as *El Jornal del Lavrador* ('The Worker's Newspaper', official organ of the Workers' Club, published in four languages), *La Solidoritad Obradera* ('Workers' Solidarity', organ of the Federation), and *Nea Epochi* ('New Age', organ of the right-wing faction of SEKE). Benaroya was a member of the General Confederation of Greek Workers and an active unionist for many decades; despite sentences of internal exile and imprisonment, he strove constantly to unite the workers of Greece. In 1941, during the persecution of the Jews of Thessaloniki, Benaroya and his comrades were taken to German concentration camps, from which only he returned; all the others were exterminated. After his return to Greece in 1945, he joined the *Socialist Party - Greek Popular Democracy (SK-ELD)* of Alexandros Svolos and Ilias Tsirimokos. In 1953, he moved to the new state of Israel, where he continued to write newspaper articles and books in support of his socialist ideals. His *The Early History of the Greek Proletariat*, reprinted in 1976, is an important work. Benaroya also wrote his memoirs. He died in Israel, at an advanced age.

BENUZIGLIO, Elie. President and great benefactor of the Jewish Community of Thessaloniki between the Wars. Died in Auschwitz.

BESSANTCHI, Mentech. Bessantchi began his education at the Talmud Torah school and continued it in the *Alliance*. He spoke at least 10 languages, and was particularly proficient in French. He began his career in journalism at an early age and worked on many newspapers published in Ladino or French. He was also a member of the Board of Management of the Jewish Community of Thessaloniki, and for some years served as President of the *Hellenic Zionist Federation*. Bessantchi contributed to the French-language *Journal de Salonique*, the Ladino *Libertad* and *La Epoqua*, and the evening paper *L' Indépendant*, of which he became joint publisher shortly after its first appearance in 1909. On *La Epoqua*, he worked side-by-side with a number of eminent columnists who later occupied important positions in the leadership of the Community and the local Zionist movement, including David Florentin and Joseph Nehama. Bessantchi also contributed to the newspaper *El Imparcial*, published in 1910. Although himself politically committed, he tried to ensure that his newspaper confined itself purely to conveying information, with an attitude of benevolent neutrality towards religion and the Zionist movement. In 1915, Bessantchi was on the editorial board of the weekly *La Esperanza*, the first Zionist periodical, launched on the initiative of the Ben Zion, Nordau, Maccabee and Kantima associations. Shortly after the great fire of 1917, Bessantchi and Elie Veissi brought out the newspaper *El Pueblo* ('The People'). Bessantchi was a passionate Zionist who distinguished himself for his trenchancy and combativeness as a journalist. In his efforts to escape the Nazis, who launched a search for him as soon as the German forces entered Thessaloniki, he sailed to Crete, where he immediately made contact with resistance groups and started work. However, when Crete, too, fell to the Germans (May 1941), Bessantchi was arrested and deported to Poland, where he died in an extermination camp for Jews in 1943.

CAZES, JACOB (1846-1935). President for a long period of the Jewish Community of Thessaloniki before the War.

DAMASKINOS, ARCHBISHOP OF ATHENS AND ALL GREECE (1890-1949). As Metropolitan Bishop of Corinthia (1922-1938), Damaskinos distinguished himself for his ecclesiastical and social work, especially after the devastating Corinth earthquake of 1928: it was thanks to his efforts, particularly in raising funds in the United States, that the reconstruction of the city was made possible. He was appointed Archbishop of Athens on 2 June 1941, as successor to Chrysanthos, the protégé of the Metaxas government. On 31 December 1944 – thanks to his universal acceptance among the people of Greece – he was appointed Regent; later (October 1945) he became Prime Minister. Damaskinos was responsible for great achievements in the field of social and humanitarian work, caring not only for his own flock but for all the people of Greece as they suffered under the yoke of the Nazi occupation forces. His appeals to the German command to spare the Greek Jews strike us even today as literary and humanitarian monuments. Apart from his secular and patriotic action, Damaskinos also left an important body of religious and ecclesiastical work, including Emergency Law 540/1946, which re-organised ecclesiastical education, founded new church schools and reinforced the Apostolic Diaconate, and Emergency Law 536/1945, introducing the payment of a state salary to the parish clergy.

DENDRAMIS, VASSILEIOS (1883-1956). Diplomat. Entered the Ministry of Foreign Affairs in 1910 and was placed in the Consulate General of Smyrna a year later. Served in various overseas posts. In 1920, took over as Director of the Greek secretariat at the League of Nations. After serving as Ambassador in Sofia (1928), returned to Athens in 1932 and was next posted to Cairo (1933). Headed the Greek delegation to the

United Nations (1946). In 1947, was appointed Ambassador in Washington, where he served until 1950.

DIAMANTOPOULOS, Kimon (1886-1946). Diplomat. Entered the Foreign Ministry in 1910. Served in various overseas posts. Promoted to the rank of Minister-Counsellor in 1931 and appointed to his first ambassadorial post, in Tirana, a year later. Transferred from there to Budapest, Sofia (1935), and Washington, where he died in service in 1946.

DRAGOUMIS, Philippos (1890-1980). Diplomat and politician, younger son of Prime Minister Stephanos Dragoumis. Studied law at Athens University. After the Balkan Wars (1912-1913), in which he took part, entered the Diplomatic Corps and served in various positions (the Consulate in Alexandria, etc.) until 1917, when he was dismissed as an anti-Venizelist. Was sentenced to internal exile in the Cyclades and Crete. After the assassination of his brother Ion Dragoumis, entered politics and between 1920 and 1946 was repeatedly elected as MP for Florina and Kastoria with the Popular Party and as an independent anti-Venizelist. Served as General Governor of Macedonia with the rank of Deputy Minister (1932-1933) and Minister (1933-1934), and was a member of administrations under Panayis Tsaldaris, George Papandrou and Constantinos Tsaldaris. Also served as Minister of Foreign Affairs (1952) in the government of Dimitrios Kioussopoulos and as Minister of National Defence under Panayotis Pipinelis (1963). Published various studies and collections of articles on diplomatic and national affairs.

FLORENTIN, David (1874-1941). Born in Thessaloniki. Studied at the Talmud Torah school and the *Alliance*. In 1897, took over as editor of the newspaper *El Avenir* with Moshe Mallah as editor-in-chief. Founded the Zionist association *Kantima* while Thessaloniki was still under Ottoman rule. For many years, led the Zionist movement in Thessaloniki and Greece as a whole. Visited Erets-Israel three times, and took part in eleven Zionist conferences representing Greece. Was an elected member of the Supreme Executive Committee of the World Zionist Organisation. Spent three years in London as Director of the Council of the Eastern Countries. A prolific journalist and writer, Florentin contributed to *L' Epoqua* (with Mentech Bessantchi and the historian Joseph Nehama) and to *La Verdad* (owned by the MP Isaac Sciaky, serving for many years as a member of its editorial board, along with Abraham Levi and Joseph Angel). He was an associate of David Matalon, the Member of Parliament and editor of *La Tribuna Libera*. In 1933 he emigrated to Israel and settled in Tel Aviv. Florentin was instrumental in the founding of the village of Mosav Chur Mosse, established in memory of the great Greek Zionist Moshe Kofina. In Tel-Aviv, he was among the founder-members of the Kantima Club. He died there in 1941.

FRANCES, Elie. Leading member of the Zionist movement in Thessaloniki. In 1917, after the Russian Revolution, he was a member of a group of Zionists who decided to publish a newspaper to oppose *Esperanza*, which they found too moderate, and to take a more combative line towards the Socialists and Communists – and especially towards Abraham Benaroya, their leader. The new paper was *La Renacencia Giudia*, published in Ladino and French. Frances' associates in the enterprise included Isaac Angel, Joseph Angel, Salomon Agarguir, Isaac Alvo, Isaac Florentin, Jacques Beza and Haim Levy. Later, Frances and Joseph Angel collaborated with Elie Veissi, editor of *L'Action*, first published on 9 August 1929. After they joined its management, the newspaper, which had originally advocated Socialism, turned openly towards Zionism. Frances was also the owner of the daily paper *Le Flambeau*.

FRIZIS, Mordechai (1893-1940). Colonel in the Greek Army. Born at Chalkis, where he completed his secondary education. Studied law at Athens University, obtaining a licence to practise as a lawyer which he never used. Joined the Greek Army in 1917 as a reservist and made it his career, meeting a hero's death on the Albanian front during the Greek-Italian war of 1940. When war broke out on 28 October, Frizis was in command of the Delvinaki sub-sector, close to the Albanian border. He took the first Italian prisoners in the war, after fighting at Vrysochori. Killed in battle on 5 December after days of brilliant command in the front line for which he had received congratulations, by telegram, from Prime Minister Ioannis Metaxas.

GATTEGNO, Leon. Teacher. President of the Jewish Community of Thessaloniki, 1938-1941. Elected to Parliament in the elections of December 1915.

GENNADIOS (Georgios Alexiadis) (1868-1951). Metropolitan Bishop of Thessaloniki, 1912-1951. Born at Moschopolis near Proussa, in Asia Minor. Studied at the Chalki Theological School. After serving as Metropolitan Bishop of Lemnos (1905), was transferred to the Metropolitan Bishopric of Thessaloniki just at the time when the Greek forces were liberating the city. A cleric of outstanding pastoral skills who achieved much in the social and administrative realm, Gennadios contributed to the religious and cultural renaissance of Thessaloniki during this interim period. Later, it was he who intervened to arrange a meeting between Chief Rabbi Koretz and Prime Minister Ioannis Rallis (in Thessaloniki) in the hope that Rallis might be talked into using his influence with the German occupation authorities to prevent the deportation of the rest of the Jewish community of the city (one third had already gone). Gennadios issued his priests with advice on how they and their flocks should treat the Jews during this difficult period, and had no hesitation in visiting, in person, the notorious German commander Max Merten to protest over the persecution of the Jews. He did much praiseworthy charitable work (serving as President of the Central Refugee Commission in 1922) and the construction of the YMCA building in Thessaloniki was his idea. He published a theological periodical entitled *Gregory Palamas* and, by his personal attitude, contributed to cementing the bonds between the Jewish and Christian communities of Thessaloniki. His work was honoured with numerous awards from the Greek State and the Ecumenical and Serbian Patriarchates.

GENNADIOS, Ioannis (1844-1932). Founder of the Gennadios Library and diplomat. Took part in the Greek delegation to the Congress of Berlin (1878) and the negotiations leading up to the Treaty of London which ended the First Balkan War. In 1916, took the Venizelist side. A scholar with a knowledge of many languages and a wide education, Gennadios left a considerable body of writing.

GONATAS, Stylianos (1876-1966). Soldier and politician. Member, with infantry colonel Plastiras and navy commander Phokas, of the 'troika' behind the Revolution of 1922. Prime Minister in the revolutionary government of 1922, Minister of Transport (1929), Minister and General Governor of Macedonia (1929-1932), and Speaker of the Senate from 1932 to the abolition of the body. Founded the *National Liberal Party*, which collaborated with the *Popular Party* in the elections of March 1946; Gonatas served as a minister in the administrations of C. Tsaldaris and D. Maximos.

GOUNARIS, Dimitrios (1867-1922). Politician from Patra, with an excellent training in law and a wide knowledge of foreign languages. Entered Parliament as an independent, later joined the Theotokis party, and became leader of the Nationalist (later Popular) Party; returned to Parliament from 1902 to 1920. Opponent of Eleftherios Venizelos. Minister of the Army and Prime Minister during the Asia Minor Disaster, Gounaris was found guilty on a charge of high treason at the notorious 'trial of the Six' and was executed, at Goudi, at 11.20 a.m. on 15 November 1922.

HABIB, Haim Raphael (1882-1943). *Locum tenens* Chief Rabbi of Thessaloniki from 1926 to 1933. Died in Auschwitz.

IOANNIDIS, Periklis (1881-1965). Rear Admiral. Took part in the Asia Minor operations. Cashiered when the 1922 Revolution was successful, he returned to the Navy in 1935 and retired immediately afterwards with the rank of Vice Admiral. Served as the first Military Commander of the Dodecanese (1947-1948).

JABOTINSKY, Vladimir. One of the most eminent leaders of the Zionist movement. He visited Thessaloniki in 1927 and delivered a lecture from the balcony of the Hotel Majestic.

KAKLAMANOS, Dimitrios (1872-1949). Diplomat. His first post was at the Consulate General in Beirut in 1909. Often served as a special envoy, and was Greek Ambassador in London until his retirement in 1934.

KALAPOTHAKIS, Dimitrios. Journalist, studied in the United States (Harvard) and Berlin. Senior Lecturer in History at the University of Athens; Athens correspondent of the

London *Times* and the *Morning Post*. Archivist of the American Embassy in Athens; appointed Director of the Press Department of the Ministry of Foreign Affairs in 1920. Left a considerable body of writings (articles and treatises).

KAPSAMBELIS, Georgios. Diplomat. Entered the Corps in 1923 and received his first foreign posting in 1925 (to the Belgrade Embassy). Various other posts in Greece and abroad followed. When recalled to service,* he was promoted to Director Class B and posted to the Consulate General of Greece in Jerusalem in 1946. In 1950, he served as Alternate Permanent Representative of Greece to the United Nations.

KOFINAS, Maurice (Moshe) (1871-1937). Born in Ioannina, grew up in Volos. Studied medicine in France. Served as a Municipal Councillor in Volos, setting up a first aid station at his own expense and being instrumental in the opening of a maternity hospital and a foundling home. Conducted studies for the draining of marshes and the settlement of refugees in Thessaly. First elected to Parliament in 1915 with the United Opposition (anti-Venizelist) wing. Crossed the floor to join the Liberals, and was a member of the 'Lazarist Parliament' (that which resulted from the first elections of 1915, reconvened by Venizelos after Constantine had been deposed by the Entente). Managed to hold his seat in the 1920 elections. A Zionist, he dreamed of founding a village of Greek Jews in Palestine – and succeeded in doing so just before his death. The village was named Chur Mosse in his honour. The population of the village still includes many families of Greek descent, together with Jews from other Balkan countries.

KONSTANTINIS, Kanaris, (1897-1976). General Inspector of the Greek Post and Telephone Organisation. Awarded a large number of distinctions, including the King George I Gold Cross. In the pre-War period, served as President and Deputy President of the

---

* See the *Yearbook for the Ministry of Foreign Affairs, Year 1951*, ed. D. Petrou, National Printing House, Athens 1951. With very few exceptions, the diplomats who happened to be serving in Athens in 1941 were dismissed by the Quisling Tsolakoglou government because they refused to serve under it and the occupation forces. Those on foreign postings continued, however, to serve in a self-sacrificing way, without means at their disposal and without pay. These diplomats made an important contribution by collecting information about the progress of the war and by making representations to promote the Greek national issues and obtain supplies of food for starving Greece. There were rudimentary MFAs in exile both in Cairo and in London. It is characteristic of the efficiency and recognition of the London MFA that ambassadors of other governments-in-exile representing countries under Nazi occupation were accredited to it (see A. Vlachos, *Once Upon a Time There was a Diplomat ...*, 6 vols., Estia, Athens; in Greek). The diplomats who had been dismissed were recalled to service by Constitutional Act 22/1945 of 1 March 1945. The period of their dismissal was counted, retroactively, towards their seniority under the same Act. (Our thanks to Ambassador C. Karabarbounis for the extremely useful information on this subject provided by his comments and unpublished records.) The biographical information about Greek diplomats is confined to the chronological framework relevant to the text (i.e., their communications to and from the MFA in Athens).

Jewish Community of Athens. Immediately after the Second World War, contributed to the re-establishment of the Jewish communities in Greece and was the first President of the Central Board of Jewish Communities in Greece (on its foundation, in 1945).

KORETZ, CEVI HIRSCH (1888-1943). Chief Rabbi of Thessaloniki after 1933; still in office at the time of the Holocaust. For a biographical account, see Errika Counio-Amarillo and Albertos Nar, *The Oral Testimony to the Holocaust of Jews of Thessaloniki* (in Greek), Thessaloniki 1998, pp. 438-440.

KOROMILAS, LAMBROS (1856-1923). Diplomat. A leading figure in the 'Struggle for Macedonia'. Studied physics and mathematics in Germany and politics and economics in Britain and France. Entered journalism and served as General Secretary of the Ministry of Finance in the A. Zaimis administration. As Greek Consul in Plovdiv (1904) and Director of the Consulate General of Thessaloniki, he favoured the use of arms to combat Bulgarian designs on Macedonia and organised the struggle himself. Recalled in 1907 as a result of a démarche from the Russian Government and behind-the-scenes action on the part of Bulgaria, he was appointed Ambassador to Washington. Elected to Parliament in 1910 with the Liberal Party, served as Minister of Finance (1910-1912) and Minister of Foreign Affairs (1912-1913) in the government of Eleftherios Venizelos. Resigned after disagreeing with Venizelos and took over the Greek Embassy in Rome, where he remained until 1920. Died in the United States three years later.

LOGOTHETOPOULOS, CONSTANTINOS (1878-1961). Physician; professor of gynaecology and obstetrics at Athens University. Sentenced to death as a collaborator for serving as Minister of Education and Prime Minister (1941-1943) in the occupation administrations. Escaped to Germany, but was arrested by the Allied forces and sent back to Greece, where he was imprisoned. Pardoned in 1951 and released. Despite his political record, Logothetopoulos contributed to the progress of medical training and hospital care in Greece. He also tried to help save the Jews of Greece by appealing to the German authorities.

MALLAH, ASCHER. Trained as a lawyer and began his political career while Thessaloniki was still in Turkish hands. Put on trial by the Young Turks, facing a charge of treason and the possibility of a death sentence. Was acquitted and continued his work, making a major contribution to the founding of the technical university (Technion) of Haifa; its central library contains a plaque commemorating his name. After the liberation of Thessaloniki, his good relations with Venizelos gained him a seat on the City Council. Stood in the 1920 elections but was unsuccessful despite attracting a large number of votes. Returned to the Senate at the elections of 1929, with the support of the Liberal Party. After losing his seat in the senatorial elections of 1932, emigrated to Palestine in 1934 and then to France. Returned to Greece for a short period in 1947 to help with the rehabilitation of the few survivors of the Holocaust. Died in France a few years ago.

MATALON, Dᴀᴠɪᴅ. President and founder of the *New Jewish Club* of Thessaloniki and of the local branch of the large American organisation Béne Bérith. Studied in Paris. Organised many of the Jewish associations of Thessaloniki (such as the *Alliance*) and was active in the fields of education and charity.

MODIANO, Sᴀᴍ. Worked for many years as Reuters correspondent in Greece. Also contributed to *Le Progrès*.

NAHMIA, Jᴀᴄᴏʙ (1913-1980). Studied at a Greek secondary school and continued his education in French institutions. Managed his father's commercial firm, *Chaim Nahmia & Sons*. In the Second World War, fought in the Greek Air Force – shortly before the voluntary enlistment of his brother Harry Nahmia, to whom he wrote the enthusiastic letter published in this volume. Deputy President of the Central Board of Jewish Communities (1963).

NEHAMA, Jᴏsᴇᴘʜ (1881-1971). Historian, inspector of the *Alliance Israélite Universelle*. Contributor to the newspaper *Avanti*. It was his intervention – thanks to the confidence of the French which he enjoyed as inspector of the *Alliance* – that led to permission being granted for the re-appearance of *Avanti* when it was closed down on the order of General Sarrail, commander-in-chief of the French and British forces in Thessaloniki. (*Avanti* had from the outset been opposed to Greek entry into the First World War.) Nehama was President of the Alliance Bank and wrote a history of the Jewish community of Thessaloniki. After his return from Bergen-Belsen, he and Michael Molho wrote the volume *In Memoriam* telling the tragic story of the Greek Jews in their exile to the Nazi concentration camps.

OUZIEL, Bᴇɴᴢɪᴇɴ Mᴇɪʀ Hᴀʏ. Born in Jerusalem. Chief Rabbi of Thessaloniki from 1920 to 1923 and Sephardic Chief Rabbi of Israel from 1931 to 1953. Died in 1954.

OUZIEL, Jᴏsᴇᴘʜ (1888-1968). Zionist from an early age. Began his education in the Talmud Torah school, continuing at the *Alliance* school and the Italian school in Thessaloniki. Contributor to *El Avenir*, *Tribuna Libera* and *Revista Populara;* later a member of the editorial committee of *La Esperanza*. Ouziel also wrote numerous novels on subjects taken from the life, customs and practices of the Jews of Thessaloniki. Translated Theodore Herzl's *Altneuland* into Ladino. In 1920, he was in Erets-Israel. In 1929, Joseph Ouziel took over as secretary to the Chief Rabbinate of Tel Aviv. In 1929, he published his most important work: *Amigdal Alavan* ('The White Tower'), which describes scenes from the city of his birth, its Jews, its harbour – where Saturday was the day of rest – and, in general, the social and private lives of the Jewish community of Thessaloniki. For many years, Joseph Ouziel was President of the Union of Greek Jews in Israel. He died in Tel Aviv.

PAPANASTASSIOU, ALEXANDROS (1876-1936). Jurist, sociologist and founder (in 1908) of the *Sociology Club*, the founding-members included some of his friends from his Berlin days, including Alexandros Delmouzos and Alexandros Mylonas. Papanastassiou was one of the most eminent political personalities of modern Greece. Sometimes referred to as 'the father of democracy', he sided with the Military League revolution of Goudi in 1909 and was elected to Parliament with the Liberal Party in 1910. Ultimately, he and other democrats resigned from the Liberal Party in order to reconstitute the old *Popular Party*, which, under the name of the *Democratic Union* was given the charter and organisational form of a modern party of principle in 1928 with the final title of the *Agrarian and Labour Party*. Papanastassiou was twice Prime Minister and also served as Minister of Transport, Minister of the Economy, and Minister of Agriculture. He sat in the Greek Senate, and has gone down in history as an idealist of unimpeachable probity who fought faithfully and conscientiously for his principles – which brought him prosecution, imprisonment and internal exile as well as recognition. Indeed, when he was first put on trial – before the Criminal Court of Lamia in 1922, charged with insulting the King and high treason – the services of George Papandreou as his self-appointed defence counsel did not save him from a sentence of three years' imprisonment. Died suddenly of a heart attack, leaving a huge volume of ideological work and a major contribution to Greek society, including the reconstruction of Thessaloniki after the fire of 1917, the founding of the Aristotle University of Thessaloniki, the re-organisation of the National Technical University, the founding of the Agricultural Bank, and many other measures which fostered the modernisation of Greek society.

PAPANDREOU, GEORGE (1888-1968). Son of a priest from Kaletzi in Achaia, one of the most important figures in modern Greek political life. His career spanned some fifty years. Papandreou first became Prime Minister – at the head of governments of National Unity and Liberation – in the dramatic period of 1944/1945, and held the post once again in the Sixties (1963-1965) with the *Centre Union* party. He studied law and economics, and held a postgraduate degree from the University of Berlin. He fought in the First Balkan War, and entered politics as a member of the Liberal Party. He served as General Governor of Lesvos, Chios and the Aegean Islands (1916-1920), Minister of the Interior (1923), and Minister of Education (1930) – in the administration of Eleftherios Venizelos, of which he was Deputy Prime Minister. His name became associated with the construction of new schools and the reform of the educational system. Papandreou founded the *Democratic Socialist Party*, and under the regime of Ioannis Metaxas was sentenced to internal exile on Cythera and Andros. In 1942, he took part in the national resistance movement and was imprisoned by the

Italians. In 1944, he succeeded in escaping to the Middle East, where he was placed at the head of the Government of National Unity. He returned to Greece as Prime Minister of the liberation government, later serving as a minister in various administrations. In 1961, Papandreou became leader of the *Centre Union*, winning a 52.8% share of the vote in the elections of 16 February 1964 and forming an administration. On 15 July 1965, after disagreeing with the King, he resigned. The leaders of the coup d'état of 21 April 1967 arrested him and incarcerated him in the Goudi army camp. His health damaged by an operation for a perforated stomach, he died on 3 November 1968. His funeral attracted an enormous crowd and gave the people of Greece an opportunity to express their opposition to the dictatorship. George Papandreou was a quick-thinking politician and, above all, an orator of the greatest skill who knew precisely how to captivate an audience. He was well-known for his caustic and epigrammatic - not to say humorous - ability to crush his opponents in a few words. His unshakeable belief in democratic institutions brought him the nickname of 'the Old Man of Democracy'. George Papandreou left an important body of writings. The formation – by his grand-daughter Sophia, daughter of Andreas Papandreou – of a *George Papandreou Foundation* was announced in June 1991.

PAPPAS, DIMITRIOS. Diplomat, first appointed attaché on 26 September 1917. First posted abroad two years later, to the Consulate in Boston. After various postings abroad and in Athens, took over as Consul General in Jerusalem in 1940 and in 1942 as Ambassador in Cairo; the Greek-Jewish community in Palestine was opposed to the latter posting, wishing him to stay on in Jerusalem in token of their appreciation of his work there. Deputy Minister of Foreign Affairs, 1963-1967.

PARASKEVOPOULOS, LEONIDAS (1860-1936). Soldier. Distinguished himself in the Greek-Turkish war of 1897, and fought in the Balkan Wars. At the time of the 'National Rift', joined the Venizelist side. Appointed Commander of the First Army Corps in 1916. As Commander-in-Chief of the Greek forces in 1918-1920, successfully completed the operation of occupying Thrace and Western Asia Minor. Resigned after the defeat of the Liberal Party, and moved to Paris. In 1929, elected *honoris causa* to the Senate and became its Speaker.

PESSACH, MOISSIS SYMEON (1869-1955). Chief Rabbi of Volos. Born in Volos, son of Symeon Pessach, Chief Rabbi of 'Old Greece'. Very active in the social, religious and patriotic fields. Made an important contribution during the wars of 1897 and 1914-1918, as well as during the Asia Minor Disaster. Founded many charitable associations in the community, and was awarded the Gold Cross of the Phoenix by King George II. Also bore the title of Grand Chief Rabbi. M.S. Pessach was responsible for saving the lives of many Greeks and Allied officers, whom he helped to escape from Volos to the Middle East, for which he was awarded a scroll of honour by Allied Headquarters in 1945. During the occupation, he hid – by arrangement with the Mayor of Volos and the Metropolitan Bishop of Demetrias – on Mt Pelion, succeeding in saving the lives of the greater part of his flock. The Greek State awarded him the order of the George I Gold Cross. Chief Rabbi Pessach died on 13 November 1955, and in 1977 his remains were taken to Israel and buried on the Hill of the Wise. He was succeeded as Chief Rabbi by Joseph Vital, of Corfu.

POLITIS, IOANNIS (1890-1959). Diplomat. Entered the Diplomatic Corps in 1911, serving in the Embassies of Berlin (1930), Vienna (1936), Stockholm (1938) and Rome (1940). Was a member of the Greek delegations to the Paris Peace Conference in 1919-1920, the Lausanne Conference (1922), the United Nations Conference in San Francisco (1945), and the Paris Conference (1945). Elected to Parliament with the *Liberal Party* (1946-1950), he was Minister without Portfolio (1947), Minister of the National Economy (1948), Permanent Under-Secretary of State for Foreign Affairs (1950-1951), and Minister of Foreign Affairs (1945 and 1951).

POLITIS, NIKOLAOS (1872-1942). Diplomat and expert in international affairs. Taught international law at various universities in France; on the invitation of Eleftherios Venizelos, came to Greece and entered the Ministry of Foreign Affairs (1914), rising in only ten years to the highest ambassadorial rank. Director of the Ministry of Foreign Affairs (1914-1916), Minister of Foreign Affairs in the National Defence government (1916-1917) and then in the Venizelos administration of 1917-1920. First representative of Greece at the League of Nations and later Ambassador in Paris (1924-1925, 1927, 1930-1931). Among the founding members of the Academy of Athens, taught at the International Academy at The Hague and represented Greece at the *International Court of Justice.* Published numerous papers and books on international law in French.

RAPHAEL, RAPHAEL. Diplomat. Entered the Diplomatic Corps in 1912. Served in various posts abroad. Permanent representative of Greece at the *League of Nations* in 1930, Ambassador in Ankara (1936), and promoted to Minister Plenipotentiary in 1946, the year he was also posted as Ambassador to Paris, where he remained until his retirement in 1957.

RALLIS, IOANNIS (1878-1946). Politician, Prime Minister in the third and last occupation government (1943-1944). Son of Dimitrios Rallis, who also served as Prime Minister, studied law at Athens University and in France and Germany. In 1906, elected to Parliament for the first time (for the Megarid constituency); Rallis held his seat for almost 30 consecutive years down to the time of the Metaxas dictatorship, being unseated only at the elections of 1935. Served as Minister of the Navy in his father's last administration (1920) and the Kaloyeropoulos government (1920), Minister of the National Economy in the government of Dimitrios Gounaris, Minister of Foreign Affairs in the first administration of Panayis Tsaldaris (1932-1933), and Minister of Transport (1933), Minister of Aviation (1933-1934) and Minister of the Interior (1933) in his second. A bitter opponent of the Venizelist putsch of 1 March 1935 and one of the main advocates of the 'purges' of the machinery of state that followed. As a monarchist, stood for Parliament in 1935 with the *Royalist Party* (Metaxas, Rallis, G. Stratos). Returned to Parliament for the last time at the last pre-War elections (January 1936) with the *General Popular Radical Union*. Opposed the Metaxas dictatorship. On 7 April 1943 took over as Prime Minister (succeeding the Quisling administrations of Tsolakoglou and Logothetopoulos). While he was in office, the notorious *Security Battalions*, which operated in favour of the Axis interests and fought chiefly against the National Resistance movement, were founded with the full support of the occupation authorities. The Rallis government collapsed on liberation (October 1944) and Rallis himself was tried as a collaborator. Sentenced to life imprisonment, he died in prison.

RECANATI, ABRAHAM. President of the Misrachi organisation and of the revisionist Zionists of Thessaloniki. Contributed to *Pro Israel*, a Zionist newspaper originally published in Ladino and French. Senior member of the Community and leader of the revisionist Zionists (Misrachi and Beitar) in the pre-War period. Also served as Deputy Mayor of Thessaloniki. Emigrated to Israel in 1934, and was elected to Parliament there.

REPOULIS, EMMANOUIL (1863-1924). Politician with a background in law and close collaborator of Eleftherios Venizelos; a Member of Parliament for many years, he also served in ministerial posts. An outstanding public speaker, Repoulis devoted himself principally to journalism, contributing political articles to various Athenian newspapers. In 1903, appointed General Secretary of the Ministry of Finance, but soon resigned. In 1906, was among the leaders of the progressive political movement called The *Japanese Group* (with Stephanos Dragoumis, Dimitrios Gounaris, and others). In 1909, supported the Goudi coup. As Minister of the Interior (1910-1915 and 1917-1918) and Minister of Finance (1915) in the governments of Eleftherios Venizelos, brought about numerous radical administrative changes (such as Law 4057/1912 concerning local government, for which he was *rapporteur*). Also played a decisive part in the historically crucial period after the First World War: as Deputy Prime Minister from 1918 to 1920, he stood in for Eleftherios Venizelos on his frequent long absences abroad. After the defeat of Venizelos in the elections of November 1920, Repoulis moved to France. He was re-elected for Parliament in 1923 (for the Argolid and Corinthia), and returned – in poor health – to Greece the following year, dying shortly afterwards. Was awarded the *Grand Cross of the Order of the Saviour*.

ROUBEN, SALOMON (1908-1985). Journalist, poet and dramatist. Contributed to *La Nation*, organ of the Jewish youth movement, published by B'rit Trubeldor, youth wing of the B'ene Misrachi organisation. Also contributed to *La Vara* ('The Ruler'), a left-wing paper owned by Leon Carasso, and *El Rizon* ('The Jester'), published by the printer Moysis Assael. General Secretary of the revisionist Zionists (*Beitar*). Emigrated to Israel around 1930. Served as President of the Israeli-Greek League.

SEFIHA, Lazaros (1900-1994). Wealthy merchant of Thessaloniki, founder of the *Hephaestus* commercial firm now run by his grandson (also Lazaros), son of Andreas Sefiha, President of the Jewish Community of Thessaloniki. Lazaros Sefiha was well-known in Thessaloniki society for his probity and personal integrity.

SCIAKY, Isaac(1880-1944). Born in Larissa; later moved to Thessaloniki, where he worked as a tailor. The various trade organisations existing in the city at that time had no single agency to express them, leading Sciaky to found the *Federation of Jewish Unions*, which little by little acquired considerable influence in local society. With the assistance of David Florentin, Joseph Angel and Abraham Benaroya, Isaac Sciaky published *La Verdad*, organ of his Federation. In parallel with these activities, Sciaky – a supporter of the Popular Royalist Party – was elected to Parliament in 1920 and 1927 and to the Senate in 1932. At the 1926 elections, held with simple proportional representation and separate electoral rolls, he stood successfully with the *Jewish Political Union (EPE)*. Also stood at the 1928 elections (run on the first-past-the-post system, though with separate electoral rolls, and won by Venizelos with a large majority), but was not elected. Sent by the Nazis to the concentration camps of Poland, from which he did not return.

SORIANO, Elias (1870-1964). Father of the current President of the Jewish Community of Rhodes, who held the same post between the years 1946 and 1960. Although his work was the money exchange business, he was also involved in the trading of petroleum-based products. For a period he represented the oil companies of Shell and BP in the Dodecanese. Along with his family, Elias was arrested and imprisoned in a German detention camp in Rhodes before being transported to the death camps. Fortunately he escaped shortly before being transported.

STASSINOPOULOS, Michael. Born in Kalamata, lawyer and writer. President of the Republic (1974-1975). Deputy President of the Council of State. Professor of Administrative Law at the Panteion School of Political Sciences (1943). Chaired the committee which drew up the Civil Servants' Code (1948-1951). Served as Minister to the Prime Minister and Minister of Labour in caretaker governments (1952 and 1958). Political adviser to the Military Command of the Dodecanese (1948).

TSALDARIS, Constantinos (1884-1970). Born in Alexandria, a nephew of Panayis Tsaldaris. Studied law in Greece and other countries, served as Prefect of Achaia, Ilida and Corfu and as General Governor of Crete, was frequently elected to Parliament, and was Minister of Transport, Minister of Foreign Affairs and (on a temporary basis) Education, Minister of Social Welfare and Minister of Justice. As the leader of the Popular Party, was twice Prime Minister, travelling to the USA in December 1946 to secure economic aid for Greece under the Truman Doctrine. Also took part in the Paris Peace Conference and the UN General Assembly. On 7 September 1947, although he held a majority in Parliament, resigned from the office of Prime Minister so as to facilitate the formation of a Popular-Liberal coalition government under Themistoclis Sophoulis in the hope of ending the Civil War. In 1956, was elected to Parliament with the *Democratic Union*, but lost his seat at the elections of 1958, in which he headed the *Popular Party Union* ballot-sheet. Retired from politics, making his last appearance in public life during the crisis of July 1965, when he took part in meetings of the Crown Council.

TZWI, ISAAC BEN. Leader of the Zionists; second President of Israel, with the *Labour Party (Mapai)*, after the death of Chaim Weizmann (1952).

VEISSI, ELIE. Journalist and publisher of Jewish newspapers in Thessaloniki, including *El Pueblo* and *El Messagero*. On 2 October 1917, two months after the great fire which destroyed a considerable part of Thessaloniki, Veissi and Mentech Bessantchi launched the daily newspaper *El Pueblo* ('The People'). On 9 September 1929, having ceased to be a partner in *El Pueblo*, Veissi joined the editorial staff of the new paper *L'Action*. At first, Veissi's paper reflected Socialist principles and ideals, but before long its owner took Elie Frances and Joseph Angel – two of the leading members of the Zionist movement in Thessaloniki - into the partnership and the paper changed its line, coming out openly in favour of Zionism. However, Veissi continued to serve also on the editorial board of the first Zionist periodical, the weekly *La Esperanza*, first published in 1915 (July-August) on the initiative of the Zionist associations of Béne Zion, Nordau, the Maccabees and Kantima. On 24 November 1935, Veissi founded a newspaper called *El Messagero*. Despite the anti-Zionist views of its publisher, the paper ultimately took the Zionist line. *El Messagero* closed on 9 April 1941, shortly before the fall of Thessaloniki to the Germans, and it was the last paper to be published in *Ladino*, using *rashi* characters. Elie Veissi ended his life as a prisoner in a Nazi concentration camp.

VENIZELOS, ELEFTHERIOS (1864-1936). Eminent Greek statesman who dominated the political life of the country for a quarter of a century. A fighter for the freedom of Crete, made his way to Athens after the declaration of the island's independence and its union with Greece, gaining more votes than any other candidate in the elections of 1910. He also won the elections of 1911 and 1912, and served as Prime Minister on a total of seven occasions. Venizelos did much to reform Greek society, revising the Constitution and introducing new and particularly progressive laws. He was the moving force behind the Balkan Alliance, modernised the Greek Army, took the side of the Entente in the First World War, and led Greece to the signing of the Treaty of Sèvres in 1920. The clash between Venizelos and the King, who wished Greece to enter the war on the side of the Central Powers, and the King's return from self-imposed exile, caused the 'National Rift'. The errors committed at that time lay behind the Greek defeat in the Asia Minor war, when her allies forsook her. This disaster was followed by the Treaty of Lausanne (July 1923), Venizelos' brief absence in Paris, and his return to active political life for a short period during which he concentrated on improving Greek-Turkish relations, signing - with Kemal Atatürk – the Ankara Treaty of 1930.

Venizelos was a brilliant diplomat and a politician of vision. He became a legend, seen by some as an example to be followed and by others as a danger to the entire country. Venizelos possessed great personal magnetism and as a public speaker could electrify his audience. He had, however, no sense of moderation, and these factors combined to win him fanatical supporters and equally fanatical foes. Venizelos came to a sad end. After surviving two assassination attempts - one in Paris in 1920 and another in Athens in 1933 – he died in self-imposed exile in Paris on 18 March 1936. He had been sentenced to death, *in absentia*, for his part in the failed putsch of 1 March 1935.

VOULGARIS, Petros (1883-1957). Admiral, Commander of the Fleet (1944-1945), and Prime Minister (1945), forming a government after the resignation of the Plastiras administration. As Prime Minister, he also held the portfolios of the Army, Navy and Air Force and, on a temporary basis, of Foreign Affairs. Voulgaris and his administration were forced to resign within six months, having shown themselves incapable of responding to the demands and the atmosphere of a turbulent time. Voulgaris was succeeded as Prime Minister by the Regent, Archbishop Damaskinos, who was the most popular figure of the day.

ZAIMIS, Alexandros (1855-1936). Politician, son of Thrasyvoulos Zaimis. Studied law. Served as President of the Hellenic Republic (1929-1935), Speaker of Parliament (1895-1897), and Prime Minister, Minister of Foreign Affairs and Minister of the Interior at various times from 1897 to 1928. Succeeded Prince George as High Commissioner for Crete (1906). Senator, Speaker of the Senate in 1929, and elected as President of the Republic in the same year. Zaimis was re-elected President in 1934 and served until the restoration of the monarchy in October 1935.

NOTES

ACTION ('Action'). This newspaper first appeared on 9 August 1929. Its editor was Elie Veissi (see biographical note). To begin with, *Action* promoted socialism and served as an organ of the Popular bloc. Subsequently, however, two leading members of the Zionist movement in Thessaloniki, Elie Frances and Joseph Angel, entered into partnership with Veissi; this resulted in a complete change in the newspaper's line and it came out fully in support of Zionism. *Action* achieved a perceptible improvement in the Ladino Press in the field of the provision of information, and soon became a point of reference in Jewish community life. Under its new management, *Action* began to appear in a new, large format. Amongst the innovations which it introduced was a hitherto unexplored range of subject-matter, such as folklore, which no one had dealt with before. On 1 August 1938, the editorship passed into the hands of Albert Molho. Nevertheless, in spite of the leftist position of the latter, the Zionist line of the newspaper remained unaltered. In February 1940, *Action* ceased to be published, in accordance with the terms of an agreement concluded between Molho and Elie Veissi some time previously.

ALLATINI (ORPHANAGE) Founded in 1910, on the initiative of the jurist El Salem, by the Union of Former Students of the Alliance School, in collaboration with Matanoth Laevionim (*q.v.*). The 300 or so orphans who were cared for in the orphanage were able to gain a university-level education and some rose to important positions in commerce and in major enterprises in Greece and abroad.

ALLIANCE ISRAELITE (Jewish Alliance). Founded in 1873, the Alliance ran a high school, a girls' school, a kindergarten, a vocational school for girls, a night school for boys and two for girls, in the Kalamaria and Hirsch suburbs. It had a noteworthy library and for more than 40 years of systematic social and educational work was a centre of positive cultural influence in the city of Thessaloniki.

AMERICAN JEWISH COMMITTEE. Central administrative authority of the Jews of the United States; still functioning today.

AMERICAN JOINT DISTRIBUTION COMMITTEE. A US Jewish organisation. It made a major contribution to the recovery of the Jewish communities of Greece after the Holocaust. The aid which it gave by the provision of food and clothing to the rest of the Greek population was also of importance.

AVANTI ('Forward'). *Avanti* was brought out by the journalists of *La Solidoritad Obradera* (see biographical note: Abraham Benaroya). In 1915, the newspaper opposed Greece's entry into the First World War. When French and British troops entered Thessaloniki on the orders of General Sarrail, its publication was suspended. However, it soon appeared again, thanks to the intervention and efforts of Joseph Nehama, inspector of the World Jewish Alliance school, who enjoyed the trust of the French military authorities. Isaac Epstein, who was the head of the Talmud Torah school, also worked on the *Avanti* newspaper.
In 1923, *Avanti* was transformed into a mouthpiece of the Communist Party, and the journalist and MP Jacques Ventoura was entrusted with the editorship.

AVENIR, El ('The Future'). A newspaper founded on 16 December 1897 and edited by Rabbi Mosse Mallah. It advocated the need for Jewish education and the teaching of the Hebrew language in community and Jewish schools.

BÉNE BÉRITH. Centrist Zionist organisation. It rallied the moderate Jews, the majority of whom were Venizelists. Its members were drawn from the bourgeois class. The organisation held lectures and supported scholarship programmes for promising university students and a host of high-school children.

BETH DIN. Religious court.

BIKOUR HOLIM (CLINIC). A foundation providing free medical treatment and pharmaceuticals for the needy. Before the fire of 1917 it was in the Kaddi district (Ermou and Aristotelous Sts). Afterwards, it was housed in a building between Spartis and Paraskevopoulou Sts, still standing today; earlier it also served as a school. The clinic operated under the protection of the Former Students of the Alliance (*q.v.*), whose president was the historian Nehama. Those who attended were trained during their stay in crafts and occupations of their choice.

EPOQUA, La ('The Age'). This newspaper made its first appearance on 1 November 1875. Its editor-in-chief was Sam Levi, a well-known and inspired journalist, who had worked on many other newspapers. The content of *La Epoqua* was rich and kept its readers up to date on world politics and the life of the Jewish world, as well as printing news items from the Ottoman Empire. A watch on authority, criticism and social issues formed the staple subject-matter of its issues. The newspaper showed a constant improvement in quality, but never ceased to combat Zionism. Its position on the revision of strict formalities in the religious ritual of the community led to the 'excommunication' of its founder, Saadi Alevy. The major names in the world of Jewish journalism and of writers who served the community in various capacities were to be found from time to time in its columns. Among them were David Florentin, Mentech Bessantchi, and the historian Joseph Nehama. *El Avenir*, which first appeared in 1897, followed a diametrically opposed line.

ESPERANZA, LA ('Hope'). The first Zionist periodical to be published on a weekly basis. It made its first appearance in July (or August) of 1915, on the initiative of the Ben Sion, Nordau, Maccabee and Kantima associations. The managers of these associations, Joseph Ouziel, Isaac Alvo, Abraham Recanati, Elie Veissi, David Florentin, Mentech Bessantchi, and Aaron Pardo, formed the periodical's editorial board. After the fire of 1917, *La Esperanza* ceased publication. It started to come out again in a revised form in November 1918. When the Zionist Federation was set up, it became its official mouthpiece. It closed down on the departure of Joseph Ouziel for the Land of Israel.

'FEDERATION'. Socialist Workers' Federation, founded and led by Abraham Benaroya. Set up in 1909.

GABELLA. Special taxes on kosher food and beverages collected by the Communities.

GENERAL FEDERATION OF JEWISH LABOUR IN PALESTINE. Jewish labour union.

HIRSCH (Hospital, now the 'Hippocrateio'). Founded in 1908 by the wealthy Austrian Jewish businessman Baron Hirsch, who was the first to set up a company for the construction of railways in Turkey. He was also the founder (1873) of the Alliance Israélite Universelle in Thessaloniki. The hospital, with 97 beds, had first-class technical equipment and was very well run. It functioned in an exemplary manner until it was requisitioned by the German Red Cross. After liberation, it passed into the hands of the Greek Red Cross.

INDÉPENDANT, L' ('The Independent'). An evening newspaper which first appeared in 1909. It was printed in French and its proprietors were Abraham Matarasso and Lazar Nefousi. A little later, they were joined by Mentech Bessantchi and Eli Attas. Bessantchi's articles in *L'Indépendant* had a considerable influence on Greek society, an influence which transcended the bounds of the Jewish community. The newspaper's stand over the dangers of Nazism and its attacks on Hitler's Germany meant that Bessantchi was high on the wanted list as soon as the German occupation forces entered the city.

KANTIMA ('Forward'). The name of a Zionist organisation.

MACCABEES. A sports association with a Zionist ideology, it was founded in 1908. It had a name chiefly for football and boxing. Maccabee boxers such as Jacques Razo, Marco Azous (who appears in the pages of the writer Yorgos Ioannou), and Solomon Aruch (hero of Robert Young's film *Triumph of the Will*) fought at Auschwitz, where they too had been sent, to help their imprisoned co-religionists. The association was revived in 1968. Today it specialises in boxing and basketball.

MATANOTH LAEVIONIM ('Contributions to the Needy'). Jewish charitable organisation. The city's largest such association, it was founded at the feast of Purim in 1901 by a group of bold pioneers led by Abraham Revach, a benefactor who stood by it from the time of its foundation to the very end. One of Revach's most vigorous associates was Samuel Asseo. The mission of Matanoth was the provision of a midday meal for impoverished schoolchildren from the community schools, for preference orphans. The first such 'soup kitchen' began to operate in 1902 at the community school in the Hirsch suburb. Another started to function a little later in the Kalamaria suburb. The Talmud Torah Haggadol school had, in 1905, its own separate canteen, for 80 children. The zeal of the founders of the organisation called forth many donations. The Alliance Israélite, for example, subsidised the organisation's work with 1,500 gold francs a year. The field of action of Matanoth expanded rapidly. In 1925, when it celebrated its 25th anniversary, it cared for 650 children; in 1940, their number had risen to 2,580, of whom 800 lived in the centre of the city (Matarasso), 400 at the Cazes school, 300 in district No. 6, 350 in the Hirsch district, 550 in the Rezi-Vardar district, and 180 in the district of Aghia Paraskevi.

In April 1941, Matanoth was forced to suspend its operations. Nevertheless, in December of the same year, seeing the hunger which was decimating the children of the poor, it resumed its social work, distributing some 300 rations of food daily. The Greek Red Cross, prompted by Revach, decided to give generous financial support to Matanoth Laevionim. It was followed by the International Red Cross. Donations flowed in ceaselessly, and the rations distributed daily reached 500. Respectable families who had been entirely deprived of means by the war and inflation received daily aid and were thus saved from death by starvation.

MEIR ABOAV (ORPHANAGE). Its foundation in 1925 was made possible by a gift of 1,000 pounds sterling from the heirs of Meir Aboav. From its very first year it housed some 40 orphans, who, after their elementary education, were trained as seamstresses, nurses, social workers, etc.

MISRACHI. A Thessaloniki Zionist association, founded in 1918. It represented those whose Zionism was of a predominantly religious inspiration. Its leader in Thessaloniki was Abraham Recanati. (Misrach = East, in the direction of the Land of Israel).

PETCHA. Levy imposed by each Community on its members.

PUEBLO, El ('The People'). The first issue of *El Pueblo* was brought out on 2 October 1917, two months after the catastrophic fire of Thessaloniki, by two distinguished journalists, Mentech Bessantchi and Elie Veissi. The paper fought for the equal participation of rich and poor in community elections. In its columns a fierce controversy between the views of Bessantchi and those of David Matalon, President of Béne Bérith, over the electoral system in force and more general political issues was carried on. The newspaper ceased publication in 1933.

PROGRÈS, LE ('Progress'). A newspaper with a long tradition, its purpose being primarily to inform. Its proprietor was the lawyer Abraham Levi, and its journalists included Sam Modiano (see biographical note). It addressed itself chiefly to the world of commerce, and in general terms followed a neutral line over the Zionist movement.

PRO ISRAEL. Zionist newspaper. It was original bilingual, in Ladino and French, but later came out only in French. Its editor was Abraham Recanati, President of the Misrachi organisation and of the Revisionist Zionists of Thessaloniki.

RASHI. A simplified Hebrew script (with vowels) for the rendering of the form of Castilian (Ladino) used by the Sephardic Jews. The word is derived from the initials of its inventor: Rabbi Salomon Itzhaki.

RED SHIELD OF DAVID. The Hebrew *Magen David Adom*. The Israeli equivalent of the Red Cross.

RENACENCIA GIUDIA, LA ('Jewish Rebirth'). Brought out for the first time in 1917, after the Russian Revolution, by a group of Zionists consisting of Elie Frances, Isaac Florentin, Isaac Angel, Joseph Angel, Salomon Agarguir, Isaac Alvo, Jacques Beza, and Chaim Levi. This group decided to bring out *La Renacencia Giudia* in order to oppose the Socialist-Communists and their leader Abraham Benaroya. It was published in two versions, Ladino and French. Its tendencies were generally Zionist. It ceased publication in 1921, but came out again, refurbished, in 1926, serving as the mouthpiece of the Zionist Federation. As of 18 March 1932, it included a section in Greek. In 1936, because of the restrictions imposed by the Metaxas dictatorship, it was forced to cease publication.

SERVICE FOR THE MANAGEMENT OF JEWISH PROPERTY (SMJP). Set up in 1943 as a public law legal person in order to manage the Jewish property of Thessaloniki and, subsequently, of the rest of Greece. In 1946, it ceded the management of these properties to the Organisation for Restitution and Relief of the Greek Jews.

TIEMPO, EL ('Time'). Daily anti-Zionist newspaper, founded by Isaac Florentin. Compared with other Jewish newspapers, its influence and range of subject-matter were limited.

TORAH. The Book of the Law of the Jewish religion. More exactly, *Sepher Torah*.

UNION OF FORMER STUDENTS OF THE WORLD JEWISH ALLIANCE (ALLIANCE ISRAÉLITE). Founded in 1897, the 'Alliance' played an active role in the life of the Jewish community of Thessaloniki. In 1917 it had established itself in a building of its own and was able to pursue its aims with the help of a considerable income from property. Its library was one of the best-stocked in the city; it had a lending library with hundreds of readers and a reference section with a large collection of encyclopaedias and other works in a variety of languages. For more than 40 years, the Alliance – with its lectures, night schools, social events, museum, sporting events, vocational school and the Allatini orphanage – was a true adornment to the history of the Jewish community of Thessaloniki – and to the city itself.

VERDAD, La ('Truth'). *La Verdad* was one of the newspapers which made the education of the Jews of Thessaloniki its mission. It was founded by Isaac Sciaky (see biographical note), and David Florentin, Abraham Levi, and Joseph Angel were on its editorial board. *La Verdad* consistently promoted the aspirations and rights of the Jews of Thessaloniki, firmly upholding the principle of equality between them and the rest of the country's citizens. Almost at the end of its life, Albert Molho and Salomon Rouben joined the journalists working on the newspaper.

BIBLIOGRAPHY

Selective Bibliography

BENJAMIN SCHWARZ AND APOSTOLOS N. ATHANASSAKIS. 'The Greek-Jewish songs of Yannina: a unique collection of Jewish religious poetry', *Modern Greek Studies Yearbook*, Vol. 3, (1987), pp. 177-240.

Historical evidence shows that the Jews settled early in Ioannina, the major city in Epirus founded sometime in the ninth century. By the end of the 15th century, the ranks of the completely Hellenised Epirot Jewry had swollen with those fleeing the persecutions in Spain. In complete contrast to what happened in Thessaloniki, Constantinople and Smyrna, the newcomers, instead of imposing their culture and language on their local brethren, soon adopted the Greek language themselves. The Jews of Ioannina therefore wrote their *piyyutim* (hymns) in Greek using, however, the pointed square Hebrew script. These *piyyutim*, reproduced here in the original and in translation, show the Epirot Jews having lost nothing of their vibrant faith but also celebrating nature and the female form under thinly veiled biblical allusions. Some of these hymns, however, are deeply melancholy, even poignant. There are at present practically no Jews left in Ioannina after the Holocaust.

HAGEN FLEISCHER.*Greek Jewry and Nazi Germany. The Holocaust and its Antecedents*, Athens, Gavrielides, 1995. 24pp.

The Jewish presence in Greece, the author believes, has been longer and more varied than in any other European country. Greek-speaking Jews, or 'Romaniots', settled there from ancient times. Ashkenazim and Hispanophone Sephardim came later to Greece, reflecting different degrees of social and cultural integration into the mainstream. The degree of integration of such communities was directly proportional to their ability to escape the Holocaust. Although in the inter-War period the Populist party was on the whole more sympathetic towards the Jews than the Venizelist Liberals, during the Axis occupation practically all Greeks are shown to have co-operated to save the Jews of Athens. The casualties of the Holocaust, numbering over 60,000 people, were mainly among the – mostly unassimilated – Thessaloniki Jewry, which was exterminated.

ADINA WEISS LIBERLES. The Jewish Community of Greece in: *The Balkan Jewish Communities*, New York, University Press of America, 1984, pp. 102-126

This brief but informative survey of the Jewish community in Greece is part of a world-wide study conducted under the auspices of the Center for Jewish Community Studies. According to the author, the Greek Jews number today some 5,400 souls living mainly in Athens (2,800), Thessaloniki (1,060), Larissa (400) and Volos (190). *The Central Board of Jewish Communities*, with its headquarters in Athens, is the umbrella organisation for all Greek-Jewish communities.

Other countrywide organisations based in Athens are the *Heirless Property and Jewish Rehabilitation Fund* (OPAIE), the *Zionist Federation* and the *Béne Bérith.* The Jewish Museum, also in Athens, day schools in Athens, Thessaloniki and Larissa, youth centres and summer camps help maintain the cultural cohesion of the Greek Jews. The *Jewish Review, Chronicles* and *New Generation* are the periodic publications of the community.

NICHOLAS STAVROULAKIS. *The Jews of Greece,* Athens, Talos Press, 1990. 127 pp.

The two-thousand year old Jewish presence in Greece, from the immigration that followed the fall of the second Temple, to the Holocaust and after is the subject of this interesting study. Stavroulakis, one-time director of the Jewish museum in Athens, elaborates on the relationship between Jewish and Greek culture. "If Hellenism was infiltrating into Judaea", he notes, "a reciprocal process was taking place in which Jews began to settle in great numbers in the cities of the Greek Diaspora." It was Paul, a Jew of that Diaspora, with access to both civilisations, who made the form of Judaism implicit in the teachings of the Nazarene accessible to the Gentiles of the Greek and Roman world. The author presents with erudition the Byzantine, Ottoman and Modern Greek developments in the life of the Jewish communities. His handbook will be very useful to all those interested in the Jewish presence in Greece.

RENA MOLHO. Venizelos and the Jewish Community of Salonika 1912-1919, *Journal of the Hellenic Diaspora,* vol. XIII, Nos 3 & 4 (Fall-Winter 1986), pp. 113-123.

A graduate of the Hebrew University of Jerusalem and the Aristotle University of Thessaloniki presents, in this paper, the policies regarding the Jews pursued by the Greek Liberal statesman Eleftherios Venizelos. The author describes Venizelos' decisive measures to quell anti-Semitic incidents in newly liberated Thessaloniki reflecting primarily a general expression of anger because of the pro-Turkish stand by Salonika Jews. She mentions the visits to Jewish quarters by members of the Greek royal family, quotes at some length from Press reports and praises Venizelos for his consistent liberal policies based on principle, since his electoral support among the Jews was always minimal. The Venizelists, however, were not always without blemish in the way they treated the Jews of Thessaloniki.

ALEXANDER KITROEFF .*Wartime Jews. The Case of Athens,* Athens, ELIAMEP, 1995. 120pp.

The author deals with the silent approval of many Athenians towards efforts to protect the Greek Jews against Nazi persecution. After the Italian armistice in September 1943, the German occupation forces tried to round up Athens' Jewish population. The EAM-ELAS left-wing resistance movement, the Archbishop of Athens, Damaskinos, and the Chief of Police, Angelos Evert, all conspired successfully to conceal the Jews from Nazi arrest. The account is supplemented with documents and eyewitness testimonies.

GEORGE C. PAPADEMETRIOU. *Essays on Orthodox Christian - Jewish Relations,* Bristol, England, Wyndham Hall, 1990. 130 pp.

The volume includes the reprint of the 1567 encyclical of the Ecumenical Patriarch Metrophanes III (1520-80) condemning the oppression of Jews in Crete. The text is contemporaneous with Martin Luther's attack on the Jews, but Papademetriou does not attempt a comparison of the two attitudes. Metrophanes argues that the unjust person is never relieved of responsibility for foul acts under the pretext that the injustice is done against a heterodox and not a believer.

Suggested Bibliography

1. ALLATINI, MOISE, *A Sketch of the State of Primary Education among the Jews of Salonica*, London, Wertheimer, Lea and Co., Printers, 1875.
2. ALLGEMEINE ZEITUNG DES JUDENTHUMS, 'Die Juden in Griechenland', 54/1 (1980), pp. 3-4.
3. AMERICAN JEWISH COMMITTEE, *The Jews in Greece*, June 1944.
4. ANGEL, RABBI MARC D., *The Jews of Rhodes. The History of a Sephardic Community*, New York, Sepher-Hermon Press, Inc., 1978, 1980. A comprehensive historical and cultural account of the Sephardic community of Rhodes, including several passages on its destruction during the Holocaust. Post-war Rhodes, under Italian occupation since 1912, reverted to Greece in 1947. ,
5. ARDITI, BENJAMIN, *Yehudei Bulgariah bishnot ha-mishpat ha-nazi: 1940-1944* [The Jews of Bulgaria during the years of Nazi occupation: 1940-1944], Tel Aviv 1962. The author provides evidence from Bulgaria in connection with the Jews of Thrace and Macedonia.
6. ARGENTI, PHILIP P., *The Occupation of Chios by the Germans 1941-1944*, Cambridge, Cambridge University Press, 1966. Rare book on the occupation of Chios and the destruction of its small Jewish community.
7. ASCHER, ARIELLA, *La communauté juive de Salonique – une communauté de survivants. Identité collective ou sentiment d'appartenance.* [DEA en Sociologie, dir. Dominique Schnapper], Paris, EHESS, 1984.
8. ATTAL, ROBERT, *Les Juifs de Grèce. Bibliographie.* Jerusalem, Institut Ben-Zvi, 1984.
9. AVNI, HAIM, 'Spanish Nationals in Greece and their Fate during the Holocaust', *Yad Vashem Studies*, VIII (1970), 31-68. A revised version was published in a lengthier study by the author (in Hebrew) entitled 'Sepharad ve-ha-Yehudim biyeme ha-Shoah ve-ha-Emancipaziah' *Modern Spain and the Jewish People*, Jerusalem 1975, based on an analysis of Spanish documents and interviews.
10. BARZILAI, ELIAS, 'Report on the Tragedy of the Jews in Greece', Greek American Council, New York 1945.
11. BEN, JOSEPH, 'Jewish leadership in Greece during the Holocaust', *Patterns of Jewish Leadership in Nazi Europe 1933-1945*, Proceedings of the Third Yad Vashem International Historical Conference, Jerusalem, 1979. Pp. 335-352. Recent article on Koretz and the 'immense naiveté' he showed as leader of the Jewish Community of Thessaloniki.
12. BEN, MARGUOLITH, 'Une colonie de Juifs de Grèce en Palestine', *Pro-Israel*, Thessaloniki, 2/51 (1919), p. 7.

13. BENN, YOSEPH, *Sho'ath Yehudei Yavan*, 1941-1944 [The Holocaust of the Jews in Greece], MA thesis at the University of Tel Aviv, 1977 (unpublished). The writer has used the Yad Vashem and Zionist archives. Based chiefly on Jewish sources available in Israel.

14. BENVENISTE, ANNIE, 'Identité et intégration: parcours d' immigration des Juifs de Grèce', Pardès 12 (1990) pp. 211-218.

15. BENVENISTE, DAVID, *Yehudei Saloniki be-doroth ha-aharonim* [The Jews of Thessaloniki in recent generations], Jerusalem 1973. A large part of the book is devoted to the War years and the Holocaust.

16. BICKERMAN, ELIAS J., *The Jews in the Greek Age*, Cambridge, Ma, Harvard University Press, 1988.

17. BOWMAN, STEVEN, 'Jews in Wartime Greece', *Jewish Social Studies*, Volume XLVII, Number 1, Winter 1986, pp 45-62. Detailed article containing a general overview of the Jews of Greece and their destruction during the Holocaust.

18. BOWMAN, STEVEN, 'Remnants and Memories in Greece', *Forum on the Jewish People, Zionism and Israel 2* (1976), pp. 63-71.

19. BOWMAN, STEVEN, 'The Great Powers and the Jews: British and French Consuls on Interwar Greek Jewry'. *Proceedings of the World Congress of Jewish Studies*, 10, 1992, B2, pp. 379-86.

20. BOWMAN, STEVEN, *Towards a Bibliography of Greek Jewry*, Athens 1973.

21. BUENO, HENRY J., 'L'anniversaire de l'indépendance grecque et les juifs', *Israel* 20/31 (1936), p.2.

22. BUENO, HENRY J., 'Les élections législatives et les Juifs de Grèce', *Israel* 17/2 (1936), pp.1,4.6 (1936), p.4.8 (1936), p.4.11 (1936), p.4.

23. BUENO, HENRY J., 'Lettre de Grèce; les cérémonies de la restauration et les Israélites', *Israel* 16/20, (1935), p.4.38 (1935), p.2.46 (1935), p.4.49 (1935), p.5.

24. CAPRI, DANIEL, 'Notes on the history of the Jews in Greece during the Holocaust period; the attitude of the Italians (1941-1943)', *Festschrift in Honor of Dr George S. Wise*, Tel Aviv 1981, pp. 25-62.

25. CENTRAL COMMITTEE OF EAM, *The Jews and the Greek Resistance: A Report of the Central Committee of EAM on the Jews of Greece and the Liberation Struggle*, New York 1945.

26. CENTRE DE DOCUMENTATION JUIVE CONTEMPORAINE. Musée du mémorial du Martyr juif inconnu. Exposition des Juifs dans la lutte contre le hitlérisme (Paris 1965). Pages 50-54 contain material on Greece and give the names of five Greeks who saved Jews.

27. CENTRE DE RECHERCHES SUR LE JUDAÏSME DE SALONIQUE - UNION DES JUIFS DE GRECE (olé Yavan), *Salonique: Ville Mère en Israel. Jérusalem, Tel-Aviv: - Fonds d' oeuvres culturelles Alcheh-Fonds pour étudiants, Leon Recanati*, Jérusalem 1967.

28. CHARY, FREDERICK B., *The Bulgarian Jews and the Final Solution 1940-1944*, Pittsburg 1972. Includes a chapter on deportations from Thrace and Macedonia.

29. CHOURAQUI, ANDRÉ, *Cent ans d' histoire; l' Alliance Israélite Universelle et la renaissance juive contemporaine (1860-1960)*, Paris 1965 [on Greece: see Index].

30. COHEN, ISRAEL, 'The Jews of Greece', *Congress Weekly*, 25 January 1951, pp.11-12.

31. CORNESCU, ALEXANDER, 'Sephard and Ashkenazim Jews in the Balkans', pp. 781-783, in *Actes du 1er Congrès International des Etudes du Sud-Est Européen*, Athens 1972, vol. 3.

32. CZECH, DANUTA, 'Deportation und Vernichtung der Griechischen Juden Im KL Auschwitz' *Hefte von Auschwitz II*, Auschwitz State Museum, Oswiecim 1970. Pp 5-37. In German. Authoritative report regarding the liquidation of the Greek Jews, in the light of surviving documents and records at the Auschwitz State Museum. Includes details and statistics on transport, admittance to camp, and the notorious 'selections'.

33. DALVEN, RAE, *The Jews of Ioannina*, Cadmus Press, Philadelphia 1990. Social and cultural history of the Romaniot (Greek-speaking) Jewish community in Ioannina. Includes an account of the near-destruction of the community during the Holocaust, and its rehabilitation in the post-War years.

34. DUMONT, PAUL, 'The Social Structure of the Jewish Community of Salonica at the End of the Nineteenth Century', *Southeastern Europe* 5, Pt.2 (1979), pp. 33-72.

35. ECK, NATHAN, 'New Light on the Charges Against the Last Chief Rabbi of Salonika'. *Yad Vashem Bulletin*, Volume 19, December 1965. Complete version of Eck's article, the first to place emphasis on the innocence and naiveté of Rabbi Koretz.

36. ELAZAR, DANIEL J., 'The Sunset of Balkan Jewry', *Forum* 2/27 (1977), pp. 135-141.

37. ELAZAR, DANIEL, ET AL. *The Balkan Jewish Communities.Yugoslavia, Bulgaria, Greece and Turkey*, University Press of America, Lanham 1984. Survey of surviving Jewish communities in the Balkans and their existence since the Holocaust, prepared from a comprehensive world-wide study by the Center for Jewish Community Studies. Includes studies by various writers on the communities in Yugoslavia, Bulgaria, Greece and Turkey.

38. EMMANUEL, I., 'Los Judios de Salonique', *Zikhron Saloniki*, Tel-Aviv 1972, p.26

39. EMMANUEL, I., *L' histoire de l' industrie des Israélites de Salonique*, Paris 1939.

40. EMMANUEL, ISAAC S., *Mazeboth Saloniki* [Precious stones of the Jews of Thessaloniki], two volumes, Jerusalem 1963-68. A collection of some 1,900 epitaphs dating from between 1502 and 1937. The appendices include lists of rabbis and teachers killed by the Nazis, synagogues and other foundations destroyed, and of religious academies, and various educational, Zionist, and religious organisations in pre-War Thessaloniki. It also includes a number of photographs which document the destruction of the cemetery and the use of its stones for municipal repairs and private buildings.

41. EMMANUEL, J.S., *Histoire des Israélites de Salonique. Histoire sociale, économique et littéraire*, Thonon-les-Bains, 1936 [de 140 a.v. J-C à 1640].

42. EMMANUEL, J.S., *Zikharon Saloniki, Gedulateh ve-Horbanah shel Yerushalayim de-Balkan*, [In memoriam of Thessaloniki, the greatness and destruction of the

Jerusalem of the Balkans], edited by David Recanati, Vol. I, Tel Aviv 1972 (in Hebrew). A memorial volume containing a history of the Jews of Thessaloniki.

43. ESKENAZI, LYDIA, 'Greek Jews Survive', *Canadian Jewish Chronicle Review* 12 (1973), pp.12, 128-129, 132-139.

44. Felstiner, Mary, 'Alois Brunner: 'Eichmann's best tool', *Simon Wiesenthal Center Annual*, Simon Wiesenthal Center, Los Angeles, Volume 3, 1986, pp. 1-46. Only comprehensive article to date on SS Captain Alois Brunner, who, along with Wisliceny, was one of the key individuals responsible for the deportation of the Thessaloniki Jews. Having escaped Allied capture at the end of the War, Brunner is currently the No1 wanted war criminal. Despite extradition attempts by the German and French governments, Brunner is living in Damascus under the protection of the Syrian Government.

45. FISCHER, A.J., 'The Rise and Fall of Greek Jewry', *Jewish Affairs*, Vol. 8, 8 Aug. 1953, pp. 23-29.

46. FLEISCHER, HAGEN, 'Greece under Axis Occupation, 1941-44: A Bibliographical Survey', *Modern Greek Society: A Social Science Newsletter*, Vol. V:1 (December 1977), 4-47.

47. FLORENTIN, DAVID, 'Les possibilités d' installation des Juifs de Grèce en Palestine', *Études Sionistes* 1 (1933), pp. 17-21.

48. FOX, ROBERT, *The Inner Sea. The Mediterranean and its People*, Alfred A. Knopf, New York 1993. Observations on the various Mediterranean countries and their histories. Chapter on Greece includes Thessaloniki, and the destruction of the Jewish community.

49. FRANCO, HIZKIA M., *The Jewish Martyrs of Rhodes and Cos*, Harper Collins Publishers, Harare, 1994. Account of the destruction of the communities of Rhodes and Cos, by the former President of the Jewish Community of Rhodes. Includes a list of deportees.

50. FRIEDMAN, PHILIP, 'The Jews of Greece during the Second World War. A Bibliographical Survey', *Joshua Starr Memorial Volume*, New York 1953, pp. 241-248. Good early bibliography of many international books, articles and sources on the Holocaust in Greece.

51. GAON, SOLOMON, AND SERELS, M. MITHEL, (editors), *Sephardim and the Holocaust*, Jacob E. Safra Institute of Sephardic Studies, Yeshiva University, New York 1987. This publication incorporates a variety of brief articles on Sephardic communities during the Holocaust. Includes: 'The Holocaust in Ioannina', by the late E. Rachel Dalven; 'The Holocaust in Salonica', by Professor David F. Altabe; and 'Destruction of the Jews of Rhodes', by Rabbi Dr Marc D. Angel. Also features articles on communities in France, Holland, Bulgaria, Yugoslavia, Morocco, Tunisia and Iraq.

52. GELBER, N.M., 'An Attempt to Internationalise Salonica, 1912-1913', *Jewish Social Studies*, Vol. XVII, 2, April 1955, pp.105-114.

53. GILBERT, MARTIN, Le drame des Juifs Hellènes; *Département hellénique d' information*, Cairo [1944].

54. GILBERT, MARTIN, *The Holocaust. A History of the Jews of Europe During the Second World War*, New York 1986.

55. GRUNWALD KURT, TORKEN HIRSCH, *A Study of Baron Maurice de Hirsch, Entrepreneur and Philanthropist*. Jerusalem, Israel Programs and Scientific Translation, 1966.

56. HADALI, YACOV, *A Greek Jew from Salonica Remembers*, Herzl Press, N.Y.

57. HASSAN JACOB M., 'In Memoriam: Joseph Nehama (1881-1971)', *Sefarad* 31 (1971), pp. 470-474.

58. HERZSTEIN, ROBERT EDWIN, *Waldheim. The Missing Years*, Arbor House, William Morrow, New York, 1988. Kurt Waldheim, former Secretary General of the United Nations and President of Austria, is examined in this detailed account of his War years. Includes documents on Waldheim in Greece and Yugoslavia recently discovered by the author. Waldheim, whose 'material amnesia' generated world-wide criticism a few years ago, was attached to German Army Group E during the War, and stationed near Thessaloniki towards the end of the deportations. While he has not been specifically branded a 'war criminal', in 1987 the Reagan Administration placed Waldheim on the 'Watch List', thereby prohibiting him from entering the United States.

59. HILBERG, RAUL, *Document of destruction: Germany and Jewry 1933-1945*, Chicago 1971 [on the Jews of Thessaloniki: pp. 160-165; on Rhodes, pp. 165-171].

60. HILBERG, RAUL, *The Destruction of the European Jews*, Chicago 1962 [on Greece: pp. 442-453 and *passim*].

61. IATRIDES, JOHN O. (editor), *Greece in the 1940s: A Bibliographic Companion*, Modern Greek Studies Association, University Press of New England, 1981. A comprehensive survey of published and unpublished, primary and secondary sources on the War in Greece and the occupation. Incorporates the detailed 'Greece under the Axis occupation', by Hagen Fleischer; and selected preliminary bibliography, 'Jews in wartime Greece', by Steven Bowman.

62. INSTITUTE OF JEWISH AFFAIRS, *The Jewish Communities of the World; Demography, Political and Organizational Status, Religious Institutions, Education, Press*, London 1959 [on Cyprus: p.43; on Greece: p.64], Vol.2: 1963 [on Cyprus: p.40, on Greece : pp. 62-63].

63. IZTHAKI, SOLOMON, 'Lights and Shadows in the Balkans', *Congress Weekly*, 12 January 1944, 9-10. Lays emphasis on the role of the Greeks in helping the Jews of Thessaloniki.

64. JEWISH COMMUNITY OF THESSALONIKI, *The Jewish Community of Thessaloniki*, Thessaloniki 1992. In English and Greek. Small pamphlet by the Jewish Community with photographs. Includes information on the history of the community through the Holocaust, their re-organisation after the War, and the community today. Published in commemoration of the 500th anniversary of the expulsion of the Jews from Spain and their settlement in Thessaloniki.

community today. Published in commemoration of the 500th anniversary of teh expulsion of the Jews from Spain and their settlement in Thessaloniki.

66. Jewish Resistance During the Holocaust (minutes of the conference on forms of Jewish resistance, Jerusalem, 7-11 April 1968), Jerusalem 1971.

67. JOINT FOREIGN COMMITTEE FOR THE JEWISH BOARD OF DEPUTIES AND THE ANGLO-JEWISH ASSOCIATION, Minorities in Greece, London 1924.

68. KABELI, ISAAC, 'Les Juifs dans la résistance grecque', Dispersion et Unité 4 (1963-1964), p. 85-90, republished in Amif 16 (1967), pp. 1978-1989.

69. KABELI, ISAAC, 'The resistance of the Greek Jews', Yino Annual of Jewish Social Science 8 (1953), pp. 281-288.

70. KALINOV, RINAH, Kehilath Saloniki. [The Community of Thessaloniki], Tel Aviv 1970.

71. KAPLAN, ROBERT, Balkan Ghosts, St Martin Press, New York 1993. Survey of communities in the Balkans. Includes sections on the Jewish communities of Thessaloniki and Greece. Several references to the Holocaust and WWII.

72. KECHALES, HAIM, Koroth Yehudei Bulgaria, [History of Bulgarian Jewry], Vol. 3: Bi-tkufath ha-Shoah 1939-1944, Tel Aviv 1969. Pp. 89-149 deal with the tragedy in Thrace and Macedonia and contain much German and Bulgarian documentation. A brief summary of the material by the author in the Encyclopedia of the Jewish Diaspora, vol. X: Bulgaria. Edited by Dr A. Romano, Joseph Ben et al. Jerusalem-Tel Aviv 1969 (in Hebrew).

73. KITROEFF, ALEXANDROS, 'Documents: The Jews in Greece, 1941-1944. Eyewitness Accounts', Journal of the Hellenic Diaspora, Pella Publishing Co., New York, Vol. XII, No. 3., Fall 1985, pp. 5-34. Reprints documents pertaining to the Holocaust in Greece. Includes: Military Intelligence Division W.D.G.S. reports by the Minlitary attaché in Istanbul, American Consulate General in Istanbul, Burton Y. Berry. Office of Strategic Services, Reports on Greece.

74. KLARSFELD, SERGE, Memorial to the Jews deported from France 1942-1944. Documentation of the Deportation of the Victims of the Final Solution in France, Published by the Beate Klarsfeld Foundation, New York 1983. Detailed tribute to the Jews of France incorporating the transport lists of over 75,000 French Jews. Includes two chapters of eyewitness accounts and documentation on the arrest and deportation of the mainly Greek Sephardic population in Paris.

75. KOCH, EDWARD I., 'A Modern Greek Tragedy', New York Post, 17 September 1986.

76. Koretz, Mrs Gita Koretz and Koretz, Aryeh. 'The testimony of (the Rabbi's wife) Mrs Gita Koretz and of her son, Aryeh Koretz, lawyer. Interviewed by Joseph Ben and Miriam Peleg. January 11 1979. English translation by David & Chana Golinkin, Yad Vashem Archives, 0-3/3875. Unique interview with wife and son of the Chief Rabbi Zvi Koretz. Provides first-hand insight into the personal life and experiences of Koretz as well as his first appointment by the Germans as President of the Jewish Community.

77. KREINDLER, RABBI JOSHUA, 'Greece and the Jews', Journal of Modern Hellenism 2 (1985), pp. 113-117.

78. LAGOUDAKIS, CHARILAOS, 'Jews of Greece', Congress Weekly 10/22 (1943), pp. 9-11.

79. Le Cinquantenaire de la fondation de l' Alliance Israélite Universelle à Salonique. Salonique: Imprimerie Progrès, Mai 1910.

80. LEVY, SAM, 'Appel aux Séfaradims de Grèce', Annuaire de l' Orient, le Guide Sam 1929, pp. 35-37 [Grèce].

81. LIBERLESS, ADINA WEISS, 'The Jewish Community in Greece', in J. Elazar (ed.) Balkan Jewries Today: Bulgaria, Greece, Turkey and Yugoslavia, Jerusalem - Philadelphia, Center for Jewish Community Studies, 1974.

82. LORD, J.O. - GOLDBERG J.B., 'Greece', Jewish Intelligence 15 (1849), pp. 76-84, 105-109.

83. MACCAS, LEON, 'La Grèce et les Israélites', Athens 1913, 55 p. (a reprint from the Messager d' Athènes).

84. MAGNES, LUCIEN, 'Le Congrès Juif de Grèce', Pro Israel 2/42 (1919), pp.1-8.

85. MAGNES, LUCIEN, 'Le Sionisme et la diplomatie Hellénique', Pro Israel 1/16 (1918) p.3.

86. MATALON, MARCEL , 'The Greek Jews under the Nazis', The Alliance Review 12/31 (1957), pp. 24-26.

87. MATALON, MARCEL, 'Ce que nous avons fait pour lutter contre les Nazis', Journal des Hellènes, Paris, 27 September 1947.

88. MATSAS, JOSEPH. 'The participation of the Greek Jews in the national resistance, 1940-1944' Journal of the Hellenic Diaspora, Pella Publishing Co. New York, Volume 17.1., 1991. Pp. 55-68. Complete translation of Joseph Matsas' account of the Jews of Greece and the role they played in the Greek resistance. Includes an introduction: 'Joseph Matsas and the Greek resistance', by Steven Bowman.

89. MATSAS, MICHAEL N., 'How the West Helped the Destruction of the Greek Jewry', The Jewish Week, April 13-19, 1978, pp. 48, 70. [Correction on 20-26 April and reply of Sidney Koretz on 11-17 May].

90. MAVROGORDATOS, GEORGE T., Stilborn Republic, Social Coalitions and Party Strategies in Greece, 1922 - 1936, University of California Press, Berkeley 1983.

91. MAZOWER, MARK, Inside Hitler's Greece. The Experience of Occupation 1941-44, New Haven, Yale University Press, 1993.

92. MAZUR, BELLE, Studies on Jewry in Greece, Athens, Hestia Printing Office, 1935.

93. MESSINAS, V. ELIAS, The Synagogues of Salonika and Veroia, Gavrielides Editions, Athens 1997.

94. MISRAHI, I., 'Lettre de Grèce', Israel 17/10 (1936), p. 4, 12 (1936), p. 4.

95. MODIANO, LEON, 'Greek Jewry's sunset?', Jewish Chronicle, 26 November 1971, pp. 79-82.

96. MODIANO, LEON, Le judaïsme et l' Alliance Israélite. Conférence faite le 30 Octobre 1909 à l' Association des Anciens Elèves de l' A.I.U. Salonique: sans éd., Novembre 1910.

97. MOISSIS, ACHER, 'La situation de communautés juives en Grèce', in Les Juifs en Europe (1939-1945), Paris 1945, pp. 47-54.

98. MOISSIS, ASCHER, 'Jews in the Army of Greece', in J. Slotsky and M. Kaplan (ed.) Jewish Soldiers in the Armies of Europe, Tel Aviv 1967, pp. 182-185.

99. MOLHO, MICHAEL AND NEHAMA, JOSEPH, *In Memoriam - Hommage aux victimes Juives des Nazis en Grèce*. Communauté Israélite de Thessalonique, Thessaloniki 1988. In French. Volume I, 1948, Volume II, 1949, Volume III, 1953. Probably the single most important contribution to the history of the Greek Jews during World War II and the incorporated ducuments and articles by surviving Sephardic scholars. Three-volume reprint by the Jewish Community of Thessaloniki, 1988.

100. MOLHO, MICHAEL, 'In Memoriam, hommage aux victimes juives des Nazis en Grèce', Vol. 1, Thessaloniki. [on Volume 2, see J. Nehama].

101. MOLHO, MICHAEL, 'La nouvelle communauté juive d' Athènes', *The Joshua Starr Memorial Volume* (New York 1953), pp. 231-239.

102. MOLHO, MICHAEL, 'Le judaïsme grec en général et la communauté juive de Salonique en particulier entre les deux guerres mondiales', *Homenaje a Millas-Vallicrosa* 2 (1956), pp. 73-107.

103. MOLHO, RENA, 'Education in the Jewish Community of Thessaloniki in the Beginning of the Twentieth Century', *Balkan Studies* 34 (1993) pp. 259-269 [Also published in *Proceedings,World Conference of Jewish Studies* 11 (1994) B3, pp.179-186].

104. MOLHO, RENA, 'Popular Antisemitism and State Policy in Salonica during the City's Annexation to Greece', *Journal of Jewish Studies* 50, pp.3-4, Summer-Fall (1988-1993), pp. 253-264.

105. MOLHO, RENA, 'Salonique après 1912. Les propagandes étrangères et la communauté juive', *Revue Historique* 287 (1992) pp.127-140.

106. MOLHO, RENA, 'The Jewish Community of Salonika and its Incorporation into the Greek State', 1912-19, *Middle Eastern Studies*, Vol. 24,4 (1988) pp. 391-403.

107. MOLHO, RENA, *Les Juifs de Salonique, 1856-1919. Une Communauté hors norme*, Thèse de Doctorat de l' Université de Strasburg, 1996, 662 p.

108. MOUTSOPOULOS, NIKOS, *Thessaloniki 1900-1917*, Thessaloniki, Molho Publications, 1981.

109. NEHAMA, JOSEF, 'La situation juive de Grèce', *Les Cahiers de l' Alliance Israélite Universelle* 26 (1948), p. 9.27 (1948), p. 13, 28-29 (1948-1949), p.15.

110. NEHAMA, JOSEF, 'Rev. Michael Molho (1964)', *Les Cahiers de l' Alliance Israélite Universelle supplément en langue française du Macbeth* 21 (1965), pp. 558-561.

111. NEHAMA, JOSEF, 'Situation actuelle du judaïsme en Grèce', *Bulletin intérieur de l' Alliance Israélite Universelle* 8 (1946), pp. 5-9 republished in *Les Cahiers Séphardis* 1-2 (1946), pp. 12-15.

112. NEHAMA, JOSEPH, (*op. cit.*, Vol. 1, pp.107-110 and Vol.1, Paris-Thessaloniki) and E. Emmanuel, *Histoire des Israélites de Salonique*, Lausanne 1936, p.46. Nehama expresses the view (Vol.3) that the Ashkenazi synagogue of Thessaloniki was probably founded between 1470 and 1475, on the new arrivals of Ashkenazim. Their first arrival in Thessaloniki is dated to 1378, immediately after the city fell to the Turks for the first time.

113. NEHAMA, JOSEPH, 'Le cimetière juif de Salonique', *Les Cahiers Séphardis*, I (1947), pp.134-136.

114. NEHAMA, JOSEPH, 'Les bibliothèques juives de Salonique détruites par les Nazis', *Les Cahiers Sephardis*, I (1947), pp.224-226.

115. NEHAMA, JOSEPH, *Histoire des Israélites de Salonique*,Vol. 1, Paris - Thessaloniki 1935, pp.40-51

116. NEHAMA, JOSEPH, *Histoire des Israélites de Thessalonique*, Thessaloniki: Communauté Israélite de Thessalonique, 1935-78 [7 vols].

117. NOVITCH, MIRIAM, 'The end of the Macedonia and Thrace Jewish Communities', *Ozar Yehudei Sepharad*, IV (1961), LIV-LVI. Novitch, Miriam, 'Gerush Yehudei Saloniki' [Expulsion of the Jews from Thessaloniki], in *Dapim te-heker ha-Shoah ve-ha-Mered*.

118. NOVITCH, MIRIAM, 'L' enfant Juif grec pendant la deuxième guerre mondiale', *Amif* 296 (1981), pp. 478-491.

119. Novitch, Miriam. *Le passage des barbares. Contribution à l' histoire de la déportation et de la résistance des Juifs Grecs*. Paris, 1967. Second edition: Ghetto Fighters House Publishers, Ltd, 1982. In French. Unique and important collection of documents and accounts of the Holocaust in Greece, with emphasis on individuals and the Jewish leaders of the Greek resistance.

120. OFFICE OF UNITED STATES CHIEF OF COUNSEL FOR PROSECUTION OF AXIS CRIMINALITY, *Nazi Conspiracy and Aggression*, US Government Printing Office, Washington, D.C., 1946-1948. Red Series, 8 volumes & 2 supplements. Testimony of Dieter Wisliceny, given before the International Military Tribunal at Nuremberg, 3 January 1946. Affidavit C, volume 8, pp. 606-621. As witness for the Allied Prosecution at Nuremberg, Wisliceny produced several documents and personal testimonies, many of which were used at the Eichmann trial in 1961 in Jerusalem.

121. PATAI, RAPHAEL, *The Vanished World of Jewry*, London 1981 [on Greece: pp. 86-97].

122. PETROPOULOS, ELIAS, *A Macabre Song. Testimony of the Goy [Christian] Elias Petropoulos concerning anti-Jewish Sentiments in Greece*, with a postscript by Pierre Vidal-Naquet, Paris 1985.

123. PETROPOULOS, ELIAS, *Les Juifs de Salonique: In Memoriam*, Paris, 1983.

124. POHL, JOHANN, 'Die ehemalige griechische Regierung in Ihren Freundschaft beteuerungen gegenuber der Juden', *Die Judenfrage* 6 (1942), pp. 177-78.

125. POHL, JOHANN, 'Die Zahl der Juden in Griechenland', Weltkampf 1942, pp. 221-22.

126. RABINOWITZ, L.I., 'The Greek Islands and their Jewish associations', *Jewish Affairs* 18/9 (1963), pp. 14-18, 31.

127. RECANATI, ABRAHAM S., 'Greek Jewry after the Nazi disaster', *The Sephardi* 9/3 (1954), pp. 3-4.

128. ROCHLITZ, JOSEPH, (editor). 'Excerpts from the Salonika diary of Lucillo Merci (February-August 1943)'. Compiled by Joseph Rochlitz, with an introduction by Menachem Shelach, *Yad Vashem Studies* XVIII, Jerusalem, 1987, pp. 293-323. Diary extracts of Lucillo Mercy, who served with the Italian Consulate in Thessaloniki as liaison officer with the German authorities. Contains personal reminiscences of the men involved in the deportation of Salonica Jews.

129. ROSENBAUM, ELIE, *Betrayal: The Untold Story of the Kurt Waldheim Investigation and Cover-up*, St Martin's Press, New York 1993. Recent controversial documentation on Kurt Waldheim and his complicity in Nazi war-crimes.Waldheim's service in Greece and Yugoslavia is covered in-depth, and Rosenbaum uncovers such documents as a Waldheim order which precipitated a German raid on the Jewish community of Ioannina in 1943. The book is a result of a six-year effort by the author, who is currently a war crimes investigator with the U.S. Justice Department.

130. ROTH, CECIL, 'Last days of Jewish Salonica. What happened to a 450-year-old civilization', *Commentaire*, July 1950, pp. 49-55. Early concise account of the extermination of Sephardim in Thessaloniki, by noted Jewish scholar Cecil Roth.

131. SABILLE, JACQUES, 'Attitude of the Italians to the Jews in Occupied Greece', L. Poliakov - J. Sabille (ed.), *Jews under the Italian Occupation*, Paris 1955, pp. 151-160.

132. SAIAS J., *La Grèce et les Israélites de Salonique*, Paris 1920.

133. SAIAS J., MOLHO R., 'Venizelos and the Jewish Community of Thessaloniki 1912-1919', *Journal of the Hellenic Diaspora*, 1986, p.114.

134. SAIAS J., *Salonique en reconstruction*, Athens 1920.

135. SAPORTA Y BEJA E., *Saloniki sus Djudios*, Paris 1979.

136. SCHREUTMAN, B., 'Communautés juives en Grèce', *Dispersion et Unité* (1970), pp. 217-227.

137. SCIAKY L., *Farewell to Salonika*, New York 1946.

138. SEMAH, VICTOR, 'Greece', *American Jewish Year Book* 61 (1960), pp. 217-222. 66 (1965), pp. 399-405.

139. SORGEN, CAROL, 'Greek Jewry in peril, local man asserts', *Jewish Times*, Baltimore, 15 October 1982, pp. 24,26.

140. STARR, JOSHUA, 'The Socialist Federation of Saloniki', *Jewish Social Studies*, VII (1945), pp. 323-336.

141. STAVRIANOS, L.S., 'The Jews of Greece', *Journal of Central European Affairs*, Volume 8, No. 3, October 1948, pp. 256-269. Early account of the Jewish communities in Greece and their destruction. Draws upon early sources and documents.

142. STAVROULAKIS, NICHOLAS AND DEVINNEY, TIMOTHY, *Jewish Sites and Synagogues of Greece*,Talos Press, Athens 1992. Recent historical and cultural guide to the various synagogues and locations of past and present Jewish communities throughout Greece. Includes a general overview of each community and each fate during the Holocaust, with detailed maps and photographs.

143. STEINBERG, LUCIEN, 'Greek Jews in the battle against Nazism', in the volume edited by M. Mushkat, *Jews in the Allied Forces in the Struggle against Nazism*, Merhaviah 1971, pp. 327-331 (in Hebrew).

144. STROM, YALE, *The Expulsion of the Jews. 500 Years of Exile*, Shapolsky Publishers Inc. Books, New York 1992. A photo documentary history of 'Sephardim in the Mediterranean Today'. Covers surviving post-Holocaust Sephardic communities in Spain, Portugal, Greece, Turkey, Bulgaria and Yugoslavia.

145. *The Jewish Museum of Greece Newsletter.* Published several times a year by the Jewish Museum of Greece in Athens. Often contains recently discovered information and articles on the Holocaust in Greece. Jewish Museum of Greece, Athens.

146. TSATSOU, IOANNA, *The Sword's Fierce Edge. A Journal of the Occupation of Greece 1941-1944.* Trans. Jean Demos (Nashville Vanderbilt University Press, 1969). Records the efforts of Archbishop Damaskinos to save Jews.

147. VEINSTEIN, GILLES, (ed.) *Salonique, 1850-1918. La 'ville de Juifs' et le réveil des Balkans,* Paris, Autrement, 1993.

148. VOGEL, GEORGE, *Diplomat unter Hitler und Adenauer,* Düsseldorf, Econ, 1969. Describes, pp. 94 *et seq.,* the deportation of the Jews of Athens.

149. WIDOGER, GEOFFREY, 'Greek Jews lead prosperous lives... Without Content: The Community seems destined for eventual oblivion', *Jerusalem Post* 44/14154 (1974), p. 7.

150. WISLICENY, DIETER, 'Trial of the Major War Criminals before the International Military Tribunal', Blue Series, 1946-1951, Washington D.C., 42 volumes. Testimony of Dieter Wisliceny at the Nuremberg Tribunal, 3 January 1946. Volume 4, pp. 355-366.

151. WOOD, NATALIE, 'Greek Jewry is a modern tragedy', *Jewish Telegraph,* 20 April 1979.

152. WORLD JEWISH CONGRESS ADVISORY COUNCIL ON EUROPEAN JEWISH AFFAIRS, *Reports on the Jewish Situation,* 'The Situation of the Jews in Greece', New York 1944.

153. YAACONI, YOHANAN, *The Road to Captivity. A Short History of the Palestinian Units which served in the campaigns of Greece and Crete in the Spring of 1941,* MA thesis at the University of Tel Aviv, 1976 (unpublished, the text in Hebrew, with a summary in English).

154. ZUCOTTI, DR SUSAN, *Italians and the Holocaust: Persecution, Rescue, Survival.* Basic Books, New York 1987. Examination of the Italian Holocaust, and the reason behind the very low percentage of Jews (15%) deported from Italy during the War. In Greece, Italian authorities likewise resisted German demands to deport Jews from the Italian-occupied zones, and provided a safe, if temporary, haven for Jewish refugees.

Miscellaneous

1. 'Nuova statistica della Grecia Israelitica', *Mose* 5 (1882), p.29.

2. 'Greece', *Annual Report of the Anglo-Jewish Association,* 1891, p. 28-30.

3. 'Grecia', *Vessilo Israelitico* 55 (1907), p. 315. 56 (1908) p. 98. 59 (1911), p. 215-216,407. 61 (1913), p. 718. 62 (1914), p. 288. 64 (1916), p. 56. 65 (1917) pp. 150-151. 66 (1918), p. 82. 67 (1919), p. 41. 68 (1920), p. 374.

4. 'Griechishe Umtriebe', *Ost und West* 10 (1910), p. 49-60.

5. 'Les Congrès juifs de Grèce', *Pro-Israel 2/42 (1919), p. 1-7.*

6. 'La Conférence des Sociétés Sionistes de Grèce à Salonique', *Pro-Israel* 2/48.

7. 'Les droits de minorité des Juifs de Grèce; texte complet du memorandum présenté au Gouvernement par la Communauté Israélite de Salonique', *Pro-Israel* 3/70 (1920), p. 2-3.

8. 'L' antisémitisme en Grèce', *Pro-Israel* 2 (1922), p.3.

9. 'L' antisémitisme en Grèce', *Chalom* 3/11 (1924), pp. 57-58. 4/14 (1925), pp. 130-131.

10. 'Les obligations militaires des Juifs [en Grèce]', *Paix et Droit* 7/4 (1927), p.11.

11. 'Grèce; le Ministre des Affaires Etrangères et les Israélites', *Paix et Droit* /1 (1928), p. 10-11.

12. 'E. Venizelos et les juifs Helléniques', *Israel* 9/31 (1928), p.2

13. 'Les élections communales Israélites', *La Volonté* 28 May 1934, p.1

14. 'E. Venizelos et les juifs [en Grèce]', *Paix et Droit* 14/8 (1934), p. 11-12.

15. 'Grèce; les événements de Mars et les juifs', *Paix et Droit* 15/3 (1935), p.12.

16. 'The situation of the Jews in Greece', *The Congress Bulletin* 4/26 (1938), p. 3.

17. 'Greece', *American Jewish Yearbook*, 45 (1943-44), p. 316. 49 (1947-48), pp. 434-436. 50 (1948-1949), pp. 370-373. 51 (1950), pp. 312-313. 54 (1953), 294-300. 57 (1956), 359-365. 61 (1960), 217-222.

18. 'Jews in Greece under Nazi Occupation', *The Ghetto Speaks*, 22 (1944), p. 3-6. 25 (1944), pp. 3-4.

19. *Département Hellénique d' Information; Le drame des Juifs Hellènes, Cairo 1944.*

20. 'The massacre of a People', *Jewish Frontier Association*, New York 1944 [on Greece: p. 93].

21. 'Tableau comparatif de la population israélite de la Grèce avant 1940 et après l' invasion des Barbares', *Les Cahiers Sefardis* 1-2 (1946), p.6.

22. 'Greek Jewry's Treatment; disillusionment in Greece, Jewish property still withheld', *Jewish Chronicle* 4074 (1947), pp. 12-13.

23. 'The situation of Greek Jewry', *The Alliance Review* 3/16-17 (1949), p.10.

24. *'La persécution des Juifs dans les pays de l' Est; présentée à Nuremberg',* Paris 1949 [on Greece: pp. 244-247].

25. 'A story with a happy beginning [about Greek Jewish displaced persons]', *The Sephardi* 7/1 (1951), p.7.

26. 'The Jewish Remnant in Greece', *Congress Weekly*, 17 September 1948, 14.

27. *European Jewry, ten years after the war,* New York 1956 [on Greece: pp. 162-179].

28. 'Une mission en Orient du Grand Rabbin Israel Levi 1908-1909)'. *Les Cahiers de l' Alliance Israélite Universelle* 106 (1957) [on Thessaloniki: pp. 23-24].

29. 'Un criminel nazi: Max Merten', *Les Cahiers de l' Alliance Israélite Universelle*, 118, 1958, pp. 6-8.

30. 'How Greek provinces became 'judenrein'', *Jewish Chronicle* 5238 (1969), p.18.

31. 'Greek Jewry's status Normalised', *Jewish Chronicle* 5244 (1969), p.14.

32. 'Griechenland; Untern Durchsnitt', *Der Spiegel* 25/32 (1971), pp. 67-68.

33. 'The 5000 Jews in Greece', *Israeli Horizons* 21/5 (1973), pp. 18, 29.
34. 'Héritiers de deux millénaires de judaïsme sépharade: six mille Juifs Grecs', *Israelitisches Wochenblatt* 74/30(1974), p.34.

Bibliography in Greek

1. *Από το Λευκό Πύργο στις πύλες του Άουσβιτς*, Ίδρυμα ΕΤΣ ΑΧΑΙΜ, Ισραηλιτική Κοινότητα Θεσσαλονίκης.
2. *Εβραϊκές Γιορτές και Παραδόσεις*, Ισραηλιτική Κοινότητα Βόλου.
3. *Θεσσαλονίκη 1850 - 1918*, εκδ. Εκάτη.
4. *Οι διωγμοί των Εβραίων εν Ελλάδι 1941-1944*, Εκδόσεις Παπαζήση. Αθήνα 1969.
5. *Οι Εβραίοι στον Ελληνικό χώρο: Ζητήματα ιστορίας....* Εταιρεία Μελέτης Ελληνικού Εβραϊσμού, (Πρακτικά συνεδρίου), εκδ. Γαβριηλίδη.
6. ΑΓΟΥΡΙΔΗΣ, ΣΑΒΒΑΣ, *Ιστορία της Θρησκείας του Ισραήλ*, εκδ. Ελληνικά Γράμματα.
7. ΑΛΕΞΙΟΥ, ΖΟΥΜΠΟΥΛΑΚΗ, ΚΑΡΑΠΟΣΤΟΛΗ, ΛΙΠΟΒΑΤΣ, *Ρατσιστές δεν είναι μόνο οι άλλοι*, εκδ.Εκπαιδευτηρίων Κωστέα-Γείτονα.
8. ΕΡΙΚΑ ΚΟΥΝΙΟ-ΑΜΑΡΙΛΙΟ & ΑΛΜΠΕΡΤΟΣ ΝΑΡ., *Προφορικές Μαρτυρίες Εβραίων της Θεσσαλονίκης για το Ολοκαύτωμα*, Ίδρυμα Ετς Αχάιμ, εκδ. Παρατηρητής, Θεσσαλονίκη 1998.
9. ΑΜΠΑΤΖΟΠΟΥΛΟΥ, ΦΡΑΓΚΙΣΚΗ, *'Λογοτεχνία ως Μαρτυρία'*, εκδ. Παρατηρητής.
10. ΑΜΠΑΤΖΟΠΟΥΛΟΥ, ΦΡΑΓΚΙΣΚΗ, *Το Ολοκαύτωμα στις Μαρτυρίες των Ελλήνων Εβραίων*, εκδ. Παρατηρητής.
11. ΑΝΘΕΜΙΔΗ, ΑΧΙΛ., *Ελλάς και Εβραίοι'*. 1973. (Μονογραφία για τις σχέσεις Ελλήνων και Εβραίων). Εκδ. Εθνικού Εβραϊκού Κεφαλαίου.
12. ΒΑΚΑΛΟΠΟΥΛΟΣ, Απ. , *Ιστορία της Θεσσαλονίκης*, Θεσσαλονίκη 1983, σ.217.
13. ΒΑΚΑΛΟΠΟΥΛΟΣ, ΑΠΟΣΤΟΛΟΣ, *Ιστορία της Μακεδονίας 1354-1833*, Θεσσαλονίκη, Εκδόσεις Βάνιας, 1992.
14. ΒΑΚΑΛΟΠΟΥΛΟΣ, ΚΩΝΣΤΑΝΤΙΝΟΣ Α., *Οικονομική λειτουργία του μακεδονικού και θρακικού χώρου στα μέσα του 19ου αιώνα στα πλαίσια του διεθνούς εμπορίου*, Θεσσαλονίκη, Μακεδονική Βιβλιοθήκη, 1980.
15. BALMARY, MARIE, *Η απαγορευμένη θυσία*, εκδ.Γαβριηλίδης.
16. BARTHOLDY, JAMES, *Ταξιδιωτικές εντυπώσεις*.
17. ΒΑΣΔΡΑΒΕΛΛΗ, Ι., *Ιστορικά αρχεία Μακεδονίας. Α' Αρχείο Θεσσαλονίκης 1695 - 1912*. Θεσσαλονίκη 1952. (Περιέχει και αρκετά σημαντικά στοιχεία για τους Εβραίους της Θεσσαλονίκης από οθωμανικές πηγές και αρχεία).
18. ΒΑΦΕΙΔΗ, ΝΙΚ., *Η Ισραηλιτική Κοινότητα Διδυμοτείχου*. (Από τον 2ο - 3ο αιώνα μ.Χ. μέχρι το 1940). Αθήνα 1954.
19. ΒΕΛΛΑ, ΒΑΣ., *Χρονολογικοί πίνακες της ισραηλιτικής ιστορίας*. Αθήναι 1956.
20. ΒΕΛΛΑ, Μ. Β., *Εβραϊκή Αρχαιολογία: Αι συναγωγαί*. Καθηγητού Πανεπιστημίου Αθηνών. Έκδοση Αποστολικής Διακονίας. Αθήναι 1980.
21. ΓΑΒΡΙΗΛΙΔΗΣ, ΑΛΜΠΕΡΤΟΣ, *Θεός - Ζωή - Άνθρωπος (ποιήματα)*, εκδ. Γαβριηλίδη.

22. ΓΙΑΝΝΟΠΟΥΛΟΥ, Ν., *Συμβολή εις την ιστορίαν των ιουδαϊκών παροικιών εν τη Ανατολική Ηπειρωτική Ελλάδι*. Αθήναι 1930.

23. ΓΙΟΕΛ, Μ., *Η δεκαετηρίς του Ισραήλ εις την Ελλάδα*. Αθήνα 1959, σ.48.

24. ΓΙΟΜΤΩΒ, ΓΙΑΚΟΕΛ, *Απομνημονεύματα 1941-1943*, εκδ. Ίδρυμα Ετς Αχάϊμ, Θεσσαλονίκη, Παρατηρητής, 1993.

25. ΓΚΡΕΙΒΣ, ΡΟΜΠΕΡΤ - ΠΑΤΑΙ, ΡΑΦΑΕΛ, *Εβραϊκοί Μύθοι*, (μετάφραση Στ. Ροζάνη) εκδ. Ύψιλον.

26. ΓΡΗΓΟΡΟΠΟΥΛΟΥ, ΑΛΕΞ., *Η Ελλάς και οι Εβραίοι*. Θεσσαλονίκη 1937.

27. CHONIKA-ZIKRONOT. *Jewish Community of Thessaloniki*. 1984. In Greek. Special magazine edition commemorating the Jewish presence in Thessaloniki, on the 2,300 anniversary of the founding of the city. Several sections of the Holocaust. English supplement with history of the Jewish Community (reprinted from the Jewish Encyclopedia) and chronology.

28. ΔΕ ΒΙΑΛΗΣ, ΣΠΥΡΙΔΩΝ, *Η Εβραϊκή Κοινότητα Ζακύνθου επί Ενετοκρατίας*. 1892

29. ΔΗΜΗΤΡΙΑΔΗ, Β., *Τοπογραφία της Θεσσαλονίκης κατά την περίοδο της τουρκοκρατίας 1430 - 1912*. Θεσσαλονίκη 1983. (Περιέχει ενδιαφέρουσες αναφορές για την Ισραηλιτική Κοινότητα).

30. ΕΘΝΙΚΟ ΕΒΡΑΙΚΟ ΚΕΦΑΛΑΙΟ, *Ελλάς και Εβραίοι*, 1973.

31. ΕΝΕΠΕΚΙΔΗ, Π. *Οι διωγμοί των Εβραίων εν Ελλάδι 1941 - 1944* (επί τη βάσει των μυστικών αρχείων των ΕΣ-ΕΣ). Αθήνα 1969, σ.199.

32. ΕΝΕΠΕΚΙΔΗ, Π., *Το Ολοκαύτωμα των Εβραίων της Ελλάδος*, εκδ. Εστία.

33. ΕΝΕΠΕΚΙΔΗΣ, ΠΟΛΥΧΡΟΝΗΣ, *Η Θεσσαλονίκη στα χρόνια 1875-1912*, Θεσσαλονίκη 1981.

34. ΕΝΕΠΕΚΙΔΗΣ, ΠΟΛΥΧΡΟΝΗΣ, *Οι διωγμοί των Εβραίων*, 1941-44.

35. ΕΡΡΙΚΟΣ, ΣΕΒΙΛΙΑ, *Αθήνα - Άουσβιτς*, εκδ. Εστία.

36. ΕΥΘΥΜΙΟΥ, ΜΑΡΙΑ, *Εβραίοι Χριστιανοί στα τουρκοκρατούμενα νησιά του Νοτιοανατολικού Αιγαίου: Οι δύσκολες πλευρές μιας γόνιμης συνύπαρξης*. (Αθήνα: «Τροχαλία», 1992). *(Χρονικά)* 11ος, 12ος 1992. Σελ.34-35.

37. ΖΩΓΡΑΦΑΚΗ, ΓΕΩΡΓΙΑ, *In Memoriam. Αφιέρωμα εις την μνήμην των Ισραηλιτών θυμάτων του ναζισμού εν Ελλάδι*. Θεσσαλονίκη 1974, σ.504.

38. ΖΩΓΡΑΦΑΚΗ, ΓΕΩΡΓΙΑ, *Μαρδοχαίος Ι. Φριζής, ο πρώτος ανώτερος αξιωματικός που έπεσε μαχόμενος στον ελληνοϊταλικό πόλεμο*. Αθήνα 1977, σ.63. Εκδ. Κεντρικού Ισραηλιτικού Συμβουλίου.

39. ΘΕΜΕΛΗ, ΜΗΤΡΟΠΟΛΙΤΟΥ ΧΡΥΣΟΣΤΟΜΟΥ, *Η εν Μεσσήνη και εν έτει 1843 εκχριστιάνισις Εβραίων*. Ανάτυπο από τα πρακτικά του Α' Συνεδρίου Μεσσηνιακών Σπουδών. Καλαμάτα 2 4 Δεκεμβρίου 1977, σ. 17-36.

40. ΘΩΜΟΠΟΥΛΟΣ, ΣΩΖΩΝ, *Ελληνική Εβραϊκή Βιβλιογραφία. Αυτοτελείς εκδόσεις, 1716-1985*, Αθήνα. Κεντρικό Ισραηλιτικό Συμβούλιο, 1987.

41. ΙΑΤΡΙΔΗ, ΓΙΑΝΝΗ, (Μετ. Αμαλία Λικιαρδοπούλου). *Η Ελλάδα στη δεκαετία 1940 - 1950. Ένα έθνος σε κρίση*. (Στο δεύτερο μέρος του βιβλίου αυτού υπάρχει έρευνα με τίτλο 'Οι Εβραίοι στην Ελλάδα την εποχή του πολέμου' από σ. 184 έως 197 όπου και κριτική βιβλιογραφία - επιλογή του Steven Bowman), Αθήνα 1984.

42. ΙΝΟ, ΦΑΙΣ, *Τσεδακά*, εκδ. Λιβάνη.

43. ΙΣΡΑΗΛΙΤΙΚΗ ΚΟΙΝΟΤΗΤΑ ΘΕΣΣΑΛΟΝΙΚΗΣ, *Θεσσαλονίκη,* Ισραηλιτική Κοινότητα Θεσσαλονίκης, 1992.

44. ΚΑΙΡΟΦΥΛΑ - ΦΙΛΙΠΠΟΤΗ, *Αθηναϊκό Ημερολόγιο 1995,* εκδ. Φιλιππότη.

45. ΚΑΛΑΜΑΝΤΗΣ, ΓΙΩΡΓΟΣ, *Θεσσαλονίκη 1950-1918, Η πόλη των Εβραίων και η αφύπνιση των Βαλκανίων,* Αθήνα, Εκάτη, 1994.

46. ΚΑΛΟΓΙΑΝΝΗ, ΒΑΣΩ, *Λάρισα. Μάντρε ντ' Ισραέλ.* Λάρισα 1959. (Η ιστορία του Εβραϊσμού της Λαρίσης).

47. ΚΑΜΠΕΛΗΣ, Ι., *Οι Εβραίοι της Θεσσαλονίκης,* Λεύκωμα Βόρειας Ελλάδας, Αθήναι, 1934, τ.1.

48. ΚΑΡΑΔΗΜΟΥ - ΓΕΡΟΛΥΜΠΟΥ, ΑΛΕΚΑ, ΚΟΛΩΝΑΣ ΒΑΣΙΛΗΣ, *Η ανοικοδόμηση της Θεσσαλονίκης μετά το 1917,* Πρακτικά του Α' Συμποσίου Ιστορίας, Οι Εβραίοι στον ελληνικό χώρο, ζητήματα ιστορίας στη μακρά διάρκεια, σελ. 231-254, Αθήνα, Γαβριηλίδης, 1995.

49. ΚΕΝΤΡΙΚΟ ΙΣΡΑΗΛΙΤΙΚΟ ΣΥΜΒΟΥΛΙΟ, *Βιβλίο μνήμης,* Αθήνα, Κ.Ι.Σ., 1979.

50. ΚΟΝΤΟΣΤΑΝΟΥ, ΜΕΘΟΔΙΟΥ, *Αρχείον και καθημερινά περιστατικά γεγονότα επί ιταλικής και γερμανικής κατοχής.* Κέρκυρα 1949. (Εξιστορεί και τα των διωγμών των Εβραίων Κερκύρας).

51. ΚΟΡΝΑΡΟΣ, ΘΕΜΟΣ, *Στρατόπεδο του Χαϊδαρίου.* Αθήνα 1975. (Αναφέρεται σε βασανισμούς και Εβραίων κρατουμένων ομήρων).

52. ΚΟΥΝΙΟ, ΧΑΙΝΤΣ, *Έζησα τον Θάνατο,* Ισραηλιτική Κοινότητα Θεσσαλονίκης.

53. ΚΟΨΙΔΑΣ, ΚΩΣΤΗΣ, *Οι Εβραίοι της Θεσσαλονίκης,* εκδ. Κοψιδά.

54. ΚΥΡΙΑΖΟΠΟΥΛΟΥ, Β., *Τα πενήντα χρόνια του Πανεπιστημίου Θεσσαλονίκης (1926 - 1976).* Θεσσαλονίκη 1976. (Περιέχει και στοιχεία για το ρόλο της Ισραηλιτικής Κοινότητος στην πνευματική ζωή της πόλεως καθώς και για την ανέγερση του Πανεπιστημίου στο χώρο των εβραϊκών νεκροταφείων).

55. ΚΩΝΣΤΑΝΤΙΝΗΣ, ΜΩΥΣΗΣ, *Η συμβολή των Εβραίων εις τον απελευθερωτικό αγώνα των Ελλήνων.* Μελέτη. Αθήναι 1971, σ.14. (Αναφέρεται στην Ελληνική Επανάσταση του 1821).

56. ΛΕΒΙ, ΠΡΙΜΟ, *Αν όχι τώρα, ποτέ,* εκδ. Θεμέλιο.

57. ΛΕΒΙ, ΠΡΙΜΟ, *Λίλιθ,* εκδ. Ροδαμός.

58. ΛΕΒΙΝΑΣ, ΕΜΜΑΝΟΥΕΛ, *Τέσσερις Ταλμουδικές Μελέτες,* εκδ. Πόλις.

59. ΛΕΤΣΑ, ΑΛΕΞ., *Ιστορία της Θεσσαλονίκης.* Θεσσαλονίκη 1961. (Περιλαμβάνει και στοιχεία για την Ισραηλιτική Κοινότητα).

60. ΛΙΑΚΟΥ, ΑΝΤΩΝΗ, *Η Σοσιαλιστική Εργατική Ομοσπονδία Θεσσαλονίκης (φεντερασιόν) και η σοσιαλιστική νεολαία. Τα καταστατικά τους.* Θεσσαλονίκη 1985.

61. ΜΑΖΑΟΥΕΡ, ΜΑΡΚ, *Στην Ελλάδα του Χίτλερ,* εκδ. Αλεξάνδρα.

62. ΜΑΤΑΡΑΣΣΟ, Ι., *Κι όμως όλοι τους δεν πέθαναν.* Αθήνα 1948. (Η καταστροφή των Ελληνοεβραίων της Θεσσαλονίκης κατά τη γερμανική κατοχή).

63. ΜΕΓΑΣ, ΓΙΑΝΝΗΣ, *Souvenir,* εκδ. Καπον.

64. ΜΕΝΑΝΕ ΦΙΝΤ, ΕΣΘΗΡ, *Οι Εβραίοι στη Ρόδο. Ιστορία μιας αρχαίας κοινότητας που εξοντώθηκε από τους Χιτλερικούς.*

65. ΜΕΝΑΣΣΕ, ΑΛΒΕΡΤΟΣ, *Birkenau Auschwitz II.* Θεσσαλονίκη 1974. (Αναμνήσεις αιχ-

μαλωσίας και αφήγηση για το πώς χάθηκαν 72.000 Έλληνες Εβραίοι). Εκδ. Ισραηλιτικής Κοινότητος Θεσσαλονίκης.

66. ΜΕΡΤΖΟΣ, ΚΩΝ., *Μνημεία μακεδονικής ιστορίας*. Θεσσαλονίκη 1947. Εκδ. Εταιρείας Μακεδονικών Σπουδών. (Περιέχει και εκτεταμένες αναφορές στην Ισραηλιτική Κοινότητα).

67. ΜΕΤΑΛΛΙΝΟΥ, ΑΓΓΕΛΙΚΗ, *Εικονογραφημένο Λεύκωμα των παλαιών Θεσσαλονικέων μετά βιογραφίας αυτών*. Θεσσαλονίκη 1941 (περιέχει και στοιχεία για εβραϊκές οικογένειες).

68. ΜΙΖΡΑΧΗ, ΧΑΓΙΜ, *Ιστορικαί σημειώσεις της Ισραηλιτικής Κοινότητας Κερκύρας*. Κέρκυρα 1948, (Οι Χεβρότ 'Γκεμιλούτ Χασαδήμ').

69. ΜΟΣΚΩΦ, ΚΩΣΤΗΣ, *Η Θεσσαλονίκη. Τομή της μεταπρατικής πόλης*, Αθήνα 1978, σ.73-78.

70. ΜΟΣΚΩΦ, ΚΩΣΤΗΣ, *Εισαγωγή στην ιστορία του κινήματος της εργατικής τάξης*. Θεσσαλονίκη 1979. (Περιλαμβάνει στοιχεία και για τη Σοσιαλιστική Εργατική Ομοσπονδία 'Φεντερασιόν' των Εβραίων της Θεσσαλονίκης).

71. ΜΠΕΝΑΡΟΓΙΑ, ΑΒΡΑΑΜ, 'Η αρχή της σοσιαλιστικής κίνησης' (στα εβραϊκά), *Zikhron Saloniki*, σελ. 309-320 και περίληψη στα ισπανοεβραϊκά, 41-42, Κωστή Μοσκώφ, ό.π., Λιάκου Αντώνη, *Η σοσιαλιστική εργατική ομοσπονδία Θεσσαλονίκης (Φεντερασιόν) και η σοσιαλιστική νεολαία - Τα καταστατικά τους*, Θεσσαλονίκη 1985, Αβραάμ Μπεναρόγια, *Η πρώτη σταδιοδρομία του ελληνικού προλεταριάτου*, Αθήνα 1978.

72. ΜΠΕΝΑΡΟΓΙΑ, ΑΒΡΑΑΜ, *Η πρώτη ιστορία του ελληνικού προλεταριάτου*. Αθήνα 1975. (Περιέχει στοιχεία και περί της συμβολής των Εβραίων στο ελληνικό συνδικαλιστικό κίνημα).

73. ΜΩΥΣΗ, ΑΣΕΡ, *Ελληνο-ιουδαϊκαί μελέται*. Αθήναι 1958.

74. ΜΩΥΣΗ, ΑΣΕΡ, *Η φιλία Ελλήνων και Ισραηλιτών διά μέσου των αιώνων*. Αθήναι 1938, σ.29.

75. ΜΩΥΣΗ, ΑΣΕΡ, '*Ισραήλ*'. Ταξιδιωτικές εντυπώσεις. Αθήνα 1963, σ.270.

76. ΜΩΥΣΗ, ΑΣΕΡ, 'Η Μακαμπή και τα γεγονότα του Κάμπελ' (στα εβραϊκά), *Zikhron Saloniki*, Tel Aviv 1972, 361-365 και Χαϊμ Τολεδάνο, '28-29 Ιουνίου 1931' (στα εβραϊκά), *Zikhron Saloniki*, Tel Aviv 1972, σ. 357-360.

77. ΜΩΥΣΗ, ΑΣΕΡ, 'Οι Εβραίοι στον ελληνικό στρατό' (στα εβραϊκά), *Zikhron Saloniki*, Tel Aviv 1972, σ.331-333.

78. ΜΩΥΣΗ, ΑΣΕΡ, *Ιστορία της εν Ελλάδι Σιωνιστικής Κινήσεως*, Τελ Αβίβ, 1969.

79. ΜΩΥΣΗ, ΑΣΕΡ, ό.π. ΚΑΙ ΜΟΛΧΟ Ρ., 'Η εβραϊκή κοινότητα της Θεσσαλονίκης και η ενσωμάτωσή της στο ελληνικό κράτος 1912-1919', *Η Θεσσαλονίκη μετά το 1912*, Θεσσαλονίκη 1986, σελ. 216-302.

80. ΝΑΡ, ΑΛΜΠΕΡΤΟΣ, *ΤΟΙΣ ΑΓΑΘΟΙΣ ΒΑΣΙΛΕΥΟΥΣΑ, Θεσσαλονίκη Ιστορία & Πολιτισμός*, Κοινοτική οργάνωση και δραστηριότητα της εβραϊκής κοινότητας Θεσσαλονίκης.

81. ΝΑΤΖΑΡΗ, ΜΑΡΣΕΛ, *Χρονικό 41-45*, εκδ. Ίδρυμα Ετς Αχαμ, Ισραηλιτική Κοινότητα Θεσσαλονίκης.

82. ΝΑΧΜΑΝ, ΕΥΤΥΧΙΑ, *Γιάννενα: Ταξίδι στο Παρελθόν*, εκδ. Τάλως.

83. ΝΑΧΜΙΑ, ΝΙΝΑ, *Ρέϊνα Ζιλμπέρτα, ένα παιδί στο γκέτο της Θεσσαλονίκης*, εκδ. Ωκεανίδα.

84. ΝΑΧΟΝ, Μ., *Μπιρκενάου - Το στρατόπεδο του Θανάτου*, εκδ. Ίδρυμα ΕΤΣ Αχαιμ, Ισραηλιτική Κοινότητα Θεσσαλονίκης.

85. ΝΕΧΑΜΑ, ΙΩΣΗΦ, *Οι Ισραηλίτες της Κερκύρας.* (Χρονικό επτά αιώνων), Κέρκυρα 1978. Εκδ. Ισραηλιτικής Κοινότητας Κερκύρας.

86. ΝΕΧΑΜΑ, ΙΩΣΗΦ, *In Memoriam.* Θεσσαλονίκη 1976. (Χρονικό της εξοντώσεως των Εβραίων της Θεσσαλονίκης).

87. ΝΕΧΑΜΑ, ΙΩΣΗΦ, *Ιστορία των Ισραηλιτών της Θεσσαλονίκης.* Θεσσαλονίκη 1978.

88. ΝΤΗΝ, ΚΑΡΟΛΟΣ, (Μετ. Κ. Χαραλαμπίδη). *Η Θεσσαλονίκη.* Θεσσαλονίκη 1980 (επισημαίνεται ο ρόλος της Ισραηλιτικής Κοινότητας στην ανάπτυξη της πόλεως).

89. ΠΑΠΑΔΟΠΟΥΛΟΣ, Λ., *Άσμα Ασμάτων*, εκδ. Καστανιώτη.

90. ΠΑΠΑΔΟΠΟΥΛΟΣ, Ν., *Στοιχεία ιστορίας της Κοινότητος.* Θεσσαλονίκη 1978. Εκδ. Ισραηλιτικής Κοινότητος Θεσσαλονίκης.

91. ΠΑΠΑΙΩΑΝΝΟΥ, Κ., *Οι Ισραηλίται και οι Έλληνες.* Αθήναι 1953, σ.16.

92. ΠΕΡΕΣ, ΣΙΜΟΝ, *Μαχόμενος για την Ειρήνη*, εκδ. Λιβάνη.

93. ΠΕΤΡΟΠΟΥΛΟΣ, ΗΛΙΑΣ, *Η πυρκαγιά του 1917.* Θεσσαλονίκη 1980. (Στοιχεία και φωτογραφίες για την πυρκαγιά που κατέστρεψε εβραϊκές περιουσίες).

94. PIERRAN, BERNARD, *Ιστορία των σχέσεων μεταξύ Ελλήνων και Εβραίων* (1994). Ινστιτούτο Ανατολικών Γλωσσών και πολιτισμών. Διδακτορική διατριβή.

95. ΡΕΓΚΟΥΚΟΣ, ΚΩΝ., *Σχέσεις Ελλήνων και Ιουδαίων εις παλαιότερους χρόνους.* Θεσσαλονίκη 1958. Εκδ. Μορφωτικής Λέσχης Ισραηλιτών 'Η Αδελφότης'.

96. ΡΕΚΑΝΑΤΗ, Σ. ΑΒΡΑΑΜ, 'Οι Εβραίοι στην πολιτική και διπλωματική ζωή της Ελλάδος', (στα εβραϊκά), *Zikhron Saloniki*, Tel-Aviv 1972, 328-330, *Η Ελλάς μεταξύ δύο πολέμων*, 1923-1940, τόμ. 2, β' έκδοση, Αθήνα 1974, σ.227-230.

97. ΡΟΖΑΝΗΣ, ΣΤΕΦΑΝΟΣ, *Ο Σύγχρονος Ιουδαϊσμός*, εκδ. Ελληνικά Γράμματα.

98. ΡΟΥΜΠΕΝ, ΜΟΡΔΕΧΑΙ ΣΟΛΟΜΩΝ, 'Ο εβραϊκός τύπος στη Θεσσαλονίκη και γενικότερα στην Ελλάδα', *Χρονικά* 10, (1978), 3-19.

99. Σειρά *Se Funot.* Ινστιτούτο Ερευνών Μπεν-Τσζή (Ιερουσαλήμ). 11ος τόμος. Ελληνικός Εβραϊσμός.

100. ΣΙΜΠΗ, ΙΑΚΩΒ, *Συμβολή στην ιστορία των πρώτων Εβραίων στην Ελλάδα..*

101. ΣΙΜΠΗ, ΜΠΑΡΟΥΧ, *Αγκαντά σελ Πέσσαχ*, Θεσσαλονίκη, Ισραηλιτική κοινότητα Θεσσαλονίκης, 1987.

102. ΣΙΜΠΗ, ΜΠΑΡΟΥΧ, *Οι Εβραίοι της Θεσσαλονίκης.* Θεσσαλονίκη 1976.

103. ΣΙΜΧΑ, ΠΑΥΛΟΣ, *Οικογένεια Δημητρίου*, εκδ. Σιμχά.

104. ΣΤΡΟΥΜΣΑ, ΙΑΚΩΒΟΣ, *Διάλεξα την ζωή*, Ίδρυμα ΕΤΣ Αχάϊμ.

105. ΣΧΙΝΑ, Ν., *Οδοιπορικά Μακεδονίας.* Εν Αθήναις 1886. (ταξιδιωτικές εντυπώσεις με στοιχεία για την Ισραηλιτική Κοινότητα της Θεσσαλονίκης στο τέλος του 19ου αιώνα).

106. ΤΖΟΥΛΙΟ, ΚΑΙΜΗ, *Συναντήσεις*, εκδ. Γαβριηλίδη.

107. ΤΣΕΛΕΜΠΙ, ΕΒΛΙΑ, *Ταξίδι στην Ελλάδα*, εκδ. Εκάτη.

108. ΤΣΕΛΕΜΠΙ, ΕΒΛΙΑ, 'Οι Εβραίοι στην Ελλάδα του 17ου αιώνα'. Από το *Ταξίδι στην Ελλάδα*, 1991. Εκδόσεις Εκάτη.

109. ΤΣΟΛΑΚΗΣ, ΠΑΝΟΣ, *Η Εβραϊκή συνοικία της Καστοριάς*, εκδ. Ελληνικά Γράμματα.

110. ΦΑΙΣ, ΜΙΣΕΛ (επιμέλεια), *Στην άλλη ακτή, στην άλλη όχθη*, εκδ. Πατάκης.

111. ΦΑΙΣ, ΜΙΣΕΛ, *Τζούλιο Καΐμη: Ένας αποσιωπημένος*, εκδ. Γαβριηλίδη.

112. ΦΑΡΜΑΚΙΔΗ, Ε., *Η Λάρισα από των μυθολογικών χρόνων μέχρι της προσάρτησης αυτής εις την Ελλάδα 1881*. (Με κείμενα και φωτογραφίες αναφορικά με την Ε-βραϊκή παρουσία στη Λάρισα). Βόλος 1926.

113. ΦΛΑΙΣΕΡ, ΧΑΓΚΕΝ, *Στέμμα και Σβάστικα: Η Ελλάδα της Κατοχής και της Αντίστα-σης*, Α' και Β' τόμοι, εκδ. Παπαζήση.

114. ΦΟΥΓΙΑ, ΜΕΘΟΔΙΟΣ, *Ελληνισμός και Ιουδαϊσμός*, εκδ. Λιβάνη.

115. ΦΟΥΓΙΑ, ΜΕΘΟΔΙΟΣ, *Η Ελληνική Ιουδαϊκή Παράδοση*, εκδ. Λιβάνη.

116. ΦΡΕΖΗΣ, ΡΑΦΑΗΛ, *Η Ισραηλιτική Κοινότητα Βόλου*, Ισραηλιτική Κοινότητα Βό-λου.

117. ΦΩΤΟΠΟΥΛΟΣ, ΑΘΑΝΑΣΙΟΣ, *Σύμμεικτα ιστορικά και λαογραφικά Καλαβρύτων*, τεύ-χος 1ο. Άρθρα περί εγκαταστάσεως Εβραίων . Ανατύπωση εκ του Δ' τόμου (1972) της επετηρίδος των Καλαβρύτων. Αθήνα 1972.

118. ΧΑΓΙΜ, ΜΠΕΗ - ΣΕΜΟΥΕΛ ΜΙΖΡΑΧΗ, *Ιστορικαί σημειώσεις της Ισραηλιτικής Κοινό-τητας Κερκύρας*.

119. ΧΑΙΡΕΤΗ, ΜΑΡΙΑ, 'Ανέκδοτα βενετικά έγγραφα περί των Εβραίων εν Κρήτη'. Ανά-τυπον εκ του ΛΓ' τόμου της *Επετηρίδος της Εταιρείας Βυζαντινών Σπουδών*. Αθήνα 1964, σ.163- 184.

120. ΧΑΜΟΥΔΟΠΟΥΛΟΣ, Χ.Α., *Οι Ισραηλίται της Θεσσαλονίκης*, Αθήνα, Τυπογραφείο Κύκλου, 1935.

121. ΧΑΜΟΥΔΟΠΟΥΛΟΣ, Ν., *Οι Ισραηλίται της Θεσσαλονίκης*. Θεσσαλονίκη 1935. (Σύ-ντομη ιστορία της Ισραηλιτικής Κοινότητος).

122. ΧΑΣΤΟΥΠΗΣ, Αθ., *Βιβλίο μνήμης*. Αθήνα 1979. (Περιέχονται ονοματεπώνυμα Ελλή-νων μελών των ισραηλιτικών κοινοτήτων που χάθηκαν στα χιτλερικά στρατόπε-δα). Εκδ. Κεντρικού Ισραηλιτικού Συμβουλίου.

123. ΧΑΤΖΗΙΩΑΝΝΟΥ, ΜΙΧΑΗΛ, *Αστυγραφία της Θεσσαλονίκης*. Θεσσαλονίκη 1880, και β' εκδ. Φωτοτυπημένη το 1976. (Μικρή ιστορία της Θεσσαλονίκης με αναφορές στην Ισραηλιτική Κοινότητα της πόλεως).

124. ΧΑΤΖΗΚΥΡΙΑΚΟΣ, Γ., *Οδηγός Μακεδονίας 1909 - 1910*. Θεσσαλονίκη 1910. (Με πλή-ρη στοιχεία για την Ισραηλιτική Κοινότητα της πόλεως κατά την εποχή εκείνη).

125. ΧΙΟΝΙΔΗΣ, ΓΕΩΡΓΙΟΣ *Ιστορία της Βεροίας, της πόλης και της περιοχής*, Τόμος 1ος, Βέ-ροια 1960 (Αρχαίος Χρόνος) και Τόμος 2ος, Θεσσαλονίκη 1970 (Βυζαντινός Χρό-νος).

126. ΧΡΙΣΤΟΠΟΥΛΟΣ, ΠΑΝ., '*Βιβλιοκρισίαι: Εβραίοι και Εβραϊκή Κοινότης εις την ιστο-ρίαν της μεσαιωνικής Κρήτης*'. Ανάτυπο από τα *Κρητικά Χρονικά* αριθ. 21/1969, σ.527-531. (Η συμβολή εις την έρευναν της ιστορίας της Κρήτης του καθηγητού του Πανεπιστημίου Ιερουσαλήμ και Οχάιο Zvi Ankori).

127. *Καταστατικόν του εν Αθήναις συλλόγου Κέρεν Αγιέσοδ*, Αθήνα 1937. [Greek Union for the Rebuilding of Palestine].

128. *Ο ηρωισμός των Ελλήνων Εβραίων*, Αθήνα, 1953.

129. 'Η υπό των Γερμανών καταστροφή των Εβραίων της Ελλάδος', *Ελλάς-Ισραήλ*, Β/13 (1960), σσ. 12-13, 32.

Greek Periodicals

1. ΑΒΔΕΛΑ, ΕΦΗ, 'Αφιέρωμα: Εβραίοι στην Ελλάδα. Προσεγγίσεις σε μια Ιστορία των Νεοελληνικών Μειονοτήτων', *Σύγχρονα Θέματα* σελ. 52-53 (1994).
2. ΑΝΤΩΝΑΚΟΣ, ΣΑΡ., 'Η Αστυνομία Πόλεων αρωγός στο δράμα των Εβραίων', *Χρονικά* 33 (1980), σ. 8-10.
3. ΑΣΤΕΡΙΑΔΗΣ, ΑΓΙΣ, 'Οι Βούλγαροι συναγωνίζονται τους Γερμανούς σε αντιεβραϊκό μένος', *Χρονικά* 48 (1982), σ. 8-9.
4. ΒΑΚΟΠΟΥΛΟΣ (ΣΤΡΑΤΗΓΟΣ), *Η εντύπωσίς μου από τους Εβραίους στρατιώτας*, Αθήνα 1943.
5. BARZILAI, ELIAS, 'Διάσωση των Εβραίων της Αθήνας κατά την περίοδο της Ναζιστικής καταστροφής', *Guinzach Saloniki*, (Archives Saloniciennes), τεύχος Α', επιμ. Barouh Ouziel (Τελ Αβίβ 1961), 90-92 (στα εβραϊκά). Αγγλική μετάφραση από τον Steven Bowman υπάρχει στη Γεννάδειο Βιβλιοθήκη στην Αθήνα.
6. ΒΑΡΩΝ, ΟΝΤΕΤ, 'Οι Εβραίοι στον ελληνικό χώρο: ένα συμπόσιο', *Ιστορικά* 14-15, σελ. 236-237, 1991.
7. ΒΑΦΟΠΟΥΛΟΣ, Γ.Θ., 'Η τραγωδία των Εβραίων', *Χρονικά* 38 (1981), σ. 3-6.
8. CHRONIKA (ΧΡΟΝΙΚΑ). In Greek. Bi-monthly magazine published by the Central Board of Jewish communities in Greece. With occasional sections and summary in English. Regularly features articles on the Holocaust in Greece. ΧΡΟΝΙΚΑ. Sourmeli 2, 10439 Athens, Greece. Tel: (30) (1) 88-39-951.
9. ΕΘΝΙΚΟ ΕΒΡΑΙΚΟ ΚΕΦΑΛΑΙΟ, *Ελλάς και Εβραίοι*, 1973.
10. ΕΝΕΠΕΚΙΔΗΣ, Κ. ΠΟΛΥΧΡΟΝΗΣ, *Οι διωγμοί των Εβραίων εν Ελλάδι 1941-1944 επί τη βάσει των Μυστικών Αρχείων των Es-Es*, Αθήνα 1969, σ.199.
11. ΖΑΛΟΚΩΣΤΑΣ, ΓΕΩΡΓΙΟΣ, *Οι Εβραίοι και η Αντίστασις*, Αθήνα 1942.
12. ΖΕΥΓΑΔΑΚΗΣ, ΝΙΚ. Ε, 'Οι Εβραίοι της Κρήτης κατά την Γερμανικήν κατοχήν', *Μεσόγειος*, 4 Σεπτεμβρίου 1963.
13. ΖΩΗ, ΛΕΩΝΙΔΑ, 'Ισραηλίται εν Ελλάδι', *Ημερολ. Παρνασσός*, 1912 σ. 77-79.
14. ΙΩΑΝΝΙΔΗΣ, ΙΩΑΝΝΗΣ, *Οι Εβραίοι εις την αντίστασιν*, Ιωάννινα - Αθήνα 1948.
15. ΚΕΝΤΡΙΚΟΝ ΙΣΡΑΗΛΙΤΙΚΟΝ ΣΥΜΒΟΥΛΙΟΝ (ΚΙΣ), *Ο Εβραϊσμός της Ελλάδος*, Αθήνα 1945.
16. ΚΟΡΟΜΗΛΑΣ, ΓΕΩΡΓΙΟΣ, 'Οι Εβραίοι στας αρχαίας Αθήνας'. Ανάτυπα από τα τεύχη 15 και 16 του περιοδικού *Τα Αθηναϊκά*. Αθήναι 1960, σ. 10-16 και 19-26.
17. ΚΩΝΣΤΑΝΤΙΝΗΣ, ΜΩΥΣΗΣ, *Η συμβολή των Εβραίων εις τον απελευθερωτικό αγώνα των Ελλήνων*, Αθήνα 1971.
18. ΜΑΖΜΟΡΙΔΗΣ, ΛΑΖΑΡΟΣ, 'Περί Ελλήνων και Εβραίων της Θεσσαλονίκης', *Μακεδονικόν Ημερολόγιον*, σελ. 93-96, 1940.
19. ΜΑΤΣΑΣ, ΜΙΧΑΕΛ Ν., 'Η συμμετοχή των Ελλήνων Εβραίων στην Αντίσταση', *Χρονικά* 89 (1986), σ. 16-21.

20. Μοσκωφ, Κ., 'Η Ισραηλιτική Κοινότητα', *Χρονικά* 70 (1984), σ. 21-23.

21. Μπεναρογια, Αβρααμ, *Η πρώτη σταδιοδρομία του ελληνικού προλεταριάτου*, Αθήνα 1975, 1986.

22. Μπεν-Γιοσεφ [Ι. Καμπελη], *Οι Εβραίοι της Ελλάδος και η Ελευθερία*, Αθήνα 1944.

23. Μωυσης, Ρ. Ασερ, *Ελληνο-Ιουδαϊκαί μελέται*, Αθήνα 1958.

24. Μωυσης, Ρ. Ασερ, *Η φιλία των Ελλήνων και Ισραηλιτών δια μέσου των αιώνων*, Θεσσαλονίκη 1953.

25. Μωυσης, Ρ. Ασερ, *Ιστορία της εν Ελλάδι Σιωνιστικής κινήσεως*, Τελ Αβίβ 1969.

26. Ναχον, Μαρκος, *Μπίρκεναου. Το στρατόπεδο του θανάτου*, Ίδρυμα Ετς Αχάϊμ, Θεσσαλονίκη 1991, επιμ. Φρ. Αμπατζοπούλου.

27. Νεχαμα, Ζοζεφ, *Η συμμετοχή των Εβραίων στους πολέμους της Ελλάδας (1821-1949)*, Χρονικά 12 (1978), σ. 5-9, 17.

28. Παπαδοπουλος, Ιωσηφ, *Ελληνο-Ισραηλιτικόν πνεύμα*, Θεσσαλονίκη 1956.

29. Παπακυριακος, Κωστας, *Οι Αντισημίται*, Αθήνα 1960.

30. Σακκης, Μωυσης, 'Σαράντα περίπου χρόνια από τότε', *Χρονικά* 86 (1986).

31. Σαραντιδης, Αντωνης, 'Η καταλήστευση των Εβραϊκών περιουσιών από τους Γερμανούς', *Χρονικά*, 18 (1979), σ.6-9.

32. Σιμπη, Μπαρουχ, 'Ιστορικαί σημειώσεις [για τους Εβραίους της Ελλάδας]'. Αγκαδά Πέσσαχ, Θεσσαλονίκη 1970, σ. 5-20.

33. Σιμπη, Μπαρουχ, 'Τα 35 χρόνια του αφανισμού του ελληνικού εβραϊσμού', *Χρονικά* 7 (1978), σ. 7-8.

34. Σκουρτης, Ιωαννης, 'Μετανάστευση των Εβραίων της Θεσσαλονίκης στη Γαλλία κατά το μεσοπόλεμο', *Θεσσαλονίκη* 3, σελ. 235-254, 1992.

35. Σποριασης, Γ., 'Ο μεγάλος διωγμός. Το ξεκλήρισμα των Ελλήνων Εβραίων', *Έθνος* 17, 1-2 Μαρτίου 1955.

36. 'Εβραίοι στην Ελλάδα: Προσεγγίσεις σε μια ιστορία των νεοελληνικών μειονοτήτων' *Σύχρονα Θέματα* σελ. 52-53, 1994.

37. Τσαλαχουρης, Κωνσταντινος, 'Διάφορα στοιχεία για την Ισραηλιτική Κοινότητα Ρόδου', *Χρονικά* Ιούλιος-Αύγουστος 1998, σελ. 3-5.

INDEX

Abenyez, Joseph 234

Aboav, Meir (Orphanage) 115, 153, 438

Abu Simbel 27

Action 139, 168, 170, 177, 183, 184, 186, 187, 188, 189, 140, 141, 191, 206, 223, 423, 433, 435

Adam, J. 364

Adossidis, A. 94, 96, 98, 99, 101, 417,

Aegean 19, 263, 264, 428

Agnidis, A. 419

Agarguir Salomon 423, 439

Agudas Israel World Organisation 235

Albala 260, 274

Albania 34, 260, 316

Aleppo 22, 293, 294, 295

Alexander (King of the Hellenes) 103, 11

Alexander the Great 27, 254

Alexandria 27, 28, 422, 432

Alexandroupolis 271, 343

Allalouf, Jean 34

Allatini, Carlo (Orphanage) 153, 435, 440

Alliance Israélite Universelle 21, 91, 127, 130, 238, 420, 427, 435, 436, 437, 438, 439, 440

Alsace 145, 204

Altcheh, A. 261

Altcheh, Isaac 129, 148, 194

Altcheh (schools) 129

Altenburg, G. 254

Amantos, C. 317, 419

Amaratzi, Leon 210

Amarillo, Isaac 207, 21

Amarillo, Samuel 210

American Jewish Council 36

American Joint Distribution Committee 333, 346, 375, 385, 435

American Red Cross 83, 95

Andartes 285

Andoniades 148

Angel, Isaac 204, 206, 209, 210, 423, 439

Angel, Joseph 422, 423, 431, 433, 435, 439, 440

Anglo-Jewish Association 75, 77, 79, 80, 83,

Ankara 22, 239, 240, 241, 242, 243, 284, 430, 433

Apararea Nacional 244

Apostolatos E. 293, 294, 295

Apoyevmatini 263, 264

Aramaic 27

Arditti, A. 183, 208, 210

Argentina 21

Argyropoulos, P. 82, 419

Argyros 133

Aristobulus 28

Aristotle 27

Armenians 111

Arrow Cross 36

Artsenou (Zionist association) 201, 206, 209,

Ashkenazim 29, 219

Asia Minor 31, 37, 240, 419, 423, 424, 429, 433

Aşkale 22

Atikva 210

Atlantis 341, 392

Attica 16, 19, 282

Auschwitz 19, 34, 327, 328, 344, 352, 420, 424, 437

Austria 30, 35, 145

Avanti 142, 143, 157, 159, 160, 161, 162, 427, 436

Avenir, El 436

Aghia Paraskevi 95

Azaria, Atoun 29

SECOND EDITION APRIL 1999
3.000 COPIES